POLITICS AND THE PUBLIC INTEREST
IN THE SEVENTEENTH CENTURY

STUDIES IN POLITICAL HISTORY

Editor: Michael Hurst
Fellow of St. John's College, Oxford

CHIEF WHIP: The Political Life and Times of Aretas Akers-Douglas 1st Viscount Chilston by Eric Alexander 3rd Viscount Chilston.

GUIZOT: Aspects of French History 1787–1874 by Douglas Johnson.

MARGINAL PRYNNE: 1660–9 by William M. Lamont.

LAND AND POWER: British and Allied Policy on Germany's Frontiers 1916–19 by H. I. Nelson.

THE LANGUAGE OF POLITICS in the Age of Wilkes and Burke by James T. Boulton.

THE ENGLISH FACE OF MACHIAVELLI: A Changing Interpretation 1500–1700 by Felix Raab.

BEFORE THE SOCIALISTS: Studies in Labour and Politics 1861–81 by Royden Harrison.

THE LAWS OF WAR IN THE LATE MIDDLE AGES by M. H. Keen.

GOVERNMENT AND THE RAILWAYS IN NINETEENTH CENTURY BRITAIN by Henry Parris.

THE ENGLISH MILITIA IN THE EIGHTEENTH CENTURY: The Story of a Political Issue, 1660–1802 by J. R. Western.

SALISBURY AND THE MEDITERRANEAN, 1886–96 by C. J. Lowe.

VISCOUNT BOLINGBROKE, Tory Humanist by Jeffrey Hart.

W. H. SMITH by Viscount Chilston.

THE McMAHON LINE: A Study in the Relations between India, China and Tibet, 1904–14; in two volumes by Alastair Lamb.

THE THIRD REICH AND THE ARAB EAST by Lukasz Hirszowicz.

THE ELIZABETHAN MILITIA 1558–1638 by Lindsay Boynton.

JOSEPH CHAMBERLAIN AND LIBERAL REUNION: The Round Table Conference of 1887, by Michael Hurst.

SOCIALISTS, LIBERALS AND LABOUR 1885–1914 by Paul Thompson.

POLAND AND THE WESTERN POWERS, 1938–1939 by Anna M. Cienciala.

DISRAELIAN CONSERVATISM AND SOCIAL REFORM by Paul Smith.

WOMEN'S SUFFRAGE AND PARTY POLITICS 1866–1914 by Constance Rover.

POLITICS
AND THE
PUBLIC INTEREST

in the

Seventeenth Century

by
J. A. W. GUNN

'*Our Trimmer thinketh it no advantage to a government to endeavour the suppressing all kind of Right which may remain in the body of the People, or to employ small authors in it . . . they forget that in their too high strained arguments for the Rights of Princes, they very often plead against humane nature . . . and therefore no maxims should be laid down for the Right of Government to which there can be any Reasonable Objection; for the World hath an Interest, and for that Reason is more than ordinary discerning to find out the weak sides of such arguments as are intended to do them hurt. . . .*'

Halifax, *The Character of a Trimmer*

LONDON: Routledge & Kegan Paul
TORONTO: University of Toronto Press
1969

First published in 1969
by Routledge & Kegan Paul Ltd.
Broadway House, 68–74 Carter Lane
London, E.C.4

Printed in Great Britain
by Richard Clay (The Chaucer Press) Ltd.
Bungay, Suffolk

SBN 7100 6174 9
UTP SBN 8020 1575 1

CONTENTS

PREFACE

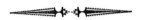

THIS BOOK IS a political scientist's attempt at historical explanation. Although the problem treated here was suggested by current thinking in political science, much the greater part of the text treats political literature of the seventeenth and early eighteenth century from the standpoint of intellectual history. References to contemporary scholarly writing intrude only in order to demonstrate problems of interpretation and thus to justify this study.

While a political philosopher might find the treatment distressingly specific and detailed, historians are certain to lament the absence of background material. Because of the variety of perspectives from which the central idea has been approached, a single chapter on background seemed impractical. Instead, traditional and novel ideas about the public interest are contrasted in a number of different contexts. The first half of the book deals with the period of the Civil War and the Commonwealth; the later chapters cover the problem of the public interest as it appeared in three aspects of life in post-Restoration England—in the struggle for religious freedom, in economic argument and in some of the more formal treatises on political philosophy written during those years. Detailed description of the particular facts of these controversies has been curtailed except where it serves to display a new understanding of the public interest. The choice of the period has been dictated by a desire to examine a tradition of discourse in its early development. At this stage it is more apt to be questioned and discussed than when it becomes generally accepted. This explains the absence here of familiar individualists of the late eighteenth century, some of whom are noted in the appendices.

It follows that a good many of the writers cited here are obscure figures, some justifiably so. The theme of this study places great weight upon the exact language of a number of these unknown texts, since the difference between a significant comment and a banality often turns on the nuances of a few phrases. For this reason quotations are rather frequent, although writing an anthology was no part of the author's purpose. In quotations from early sources spelling and punctuation has been modernized when the original form seemed likely to hinder comprehension. Archaic forms have been retained in titles to facilitate tracing references. In the case of anonymous works not generally attributed to any author there is additional guidance. Here the relevant footnote contains a shelf-mark either for the Bodleian copy or for that of the British Museum. These sources are identified by the abbreviations B and BM respectively, preceding the shelf-mark. The place of publication of primary sources has been given only if it was other than London.

In writing this book I have benefited greatly from the assistance of a number of individuals and organizations. I am especially grateful to Dr. J. W. Gough of Oriel College and Professor J. P. Plamenatz of All Souls who supervised the first version of the study when it was written as a D.Phil. Thesis at Oxford. Mention must also be made of Mr. G. C. Morris of King's College, Cambridge, and Mr. K. V. Thomas of St. John's College, Oxford, who were both kind and helpful in their role as examiners. Two years' research in England was made possible through the generosity of the Commonwealth Scholarship Commission in the United Kingdom. My election to a studentship at Nuffield College did much to make the stay an enjoyable one, and for this I thank the Warden and Fellows. This work has been published with the help of a grant from the Social Science Research Council of Canada, using funds provided by the Canada Council.

Kingston, Ontario
August, 1967

INTRODUCTION

THE IDEA OF a 'public interest' is fundamental to systematic
political thought and argument, and both its importance
and its ambiguity have been amply discussed in the scholarly
literature of the last decade. The intent of this study is to clarify
certain aspects of one tradition of argument relating to the
public interest. Examining this one tradition involves saying a
good deal about the concept in general, since most academic
treatments of the subject fail to mention the fact that historically there have been well-defined patterns in the use of the expression. Some authors who do mention the history of arguments from public interest harbour very strange ideas about it.[1]
Furthermore, an assumption of modernity colours twentieth-
century writings on the subject, extending particularly to vocabulary. It is too little appreciated that the very expression 'public
interest' was familiar by the middle of the seventeenth century,
gradually replacing the 'common good' of scholastic philosophy
and the 'salus populi' favoured by Roman law.[2] There is then no

[1] Thus Professor Oakeshott has claimed that the notion of a public good
independent of particular interests arose in the early modern period. See
'The Masses in Representative Democracy', in A. Hunold (ed.), *Freedom and
Serfdom* (Dordrecht, 1961), pp. 151–70, at p. 162. Despite the vogue of state
necessity, the opposite is closer to the truth. Opposition to the common
good as an entity independent of individual goods dates from this time.

[2] Several of the attempts to trace the origins of utilitarianism suffer from the
assumption that any work using the expression 'public interest' or some
equivalent must have contained the seeds of Benthamism. See E. L. Kayser,
*The Grand Social Enterprise A Study of Jeremy Bentham in Relation to Liberal
Nationalism* (New York, 1932), p. 17, and David Baumgardt, *Bentham and
the Ethics of Today* (Princeton, 1942), p. 49.

need to seek exotic parallels in the language of the royal prerogative or a general will.[1]

The most famous set of ideas about the public interest is surely that of English individualism, the strand in the liberal–radical tradition that viewed the welfare of the community in terms of the interests of private persons. The fame of this doctrine may easily be explained. Individualists of this sort were unusually forthright in describing the public interest in general terms, instead of limiting themselves to substantive descriptions of concrete policies. The misleadingly simple slogan about the common good being an aggregate of particular goods has given comfort to numerous students of social theory, who have agreed that whatever the public interest might be, it was not that. Thus the best-known comments about the public interest are often rejected as a necessary preliminary to saying anything about the concept.

The idea has been condemned as incoherent and as illustrative of the worst sort of *incivisme*. Here political scientists of the consciously tough-minded school have joined hands with moralists believing in an ethically conceived common good.[2] The former group would, of course, go beyond the observation that particular interests are irreconcilable to insist that no common good existed. They agree, however, in identifying the analytical deficiencies of individualism. The main difficulty has been seen either as that of advocating unlikely coincidence among all the different interests of individuals or an unreal harmony between the individual and the community.[3] In either event classical individualism stands condemned as the champion of an impossible harmony of interests, sometimes even seen as, in a sense,

[1] This sort of comparison is not unusual. See Glendon Schubert, *The Public Interest* (Glencoe, Ill., 1959), p. 8, and J. Hauptmann, 'The Concept of the Public Interest', in R. M. Miwa *et al.*, *Problems in Political Theory* (Columbia, Missouri, 1961), p. 30.
[2] Early representatives of these two trends in scholarship include A. F. Bentley, *The Process of Government* (Bloomington, Indiana, 1949) (1st edn. 1908), pp. 220, 422, and W. Cunningham, *The Common Weal, Six Lectures in Political Philosophy* (Cambridge, 1917), p. 44. Many others have followed the same paths.
[3] Both criticisms may simultaneously be made. See R. B. Perry, *Puritanism and Democracy* (New York, 1944), p. 500. For other examples see Nathan D. Grundstein, 'Bentham's Introduction to the Principles of Morals and Legislation', *Journal of Public Law*, Vol. 2 (1953), pp. 344–69, at p. 352.

'natural' or spontaneous. The inevitable conclusion has been that such thinkers were prepared to tolerate anarchy or expected an impossible uniformity of interest on the part of enlightened humans.

Here it will be argued that an individualistic rendering of the public interest was not as muddled an idea as has usually been claimed. It first occurred as an ingenious weapon for combating alternative conceptions that ignored the perennial needs of human nature and the specific needs of seventeenth-century citizens. Traditionally the idea of the public good had been the measure of all private interests and the ideal to which private ambition was forced to bow. Beginning in the seventeenth century, the established antithesis between private and public interest came to be weakened through the convergence of several factors. One of these factors was the political situation where the crown had prejudiced private rights claiming necessity of state. This precipitated a reassessment of the meaning of the public interest by opponents of Stuart absolutism. The ancient maxim '*salus populi suprema lex esto*' was expounded so as to minimize emphasis on traditional *arcana imperii*, elevating instead private rights as the substance of the public good. Fortified by the new respectability of proclaiming one's 'interest', people argued that each man's legitimate concern for his own safety and property was the proper starting-point for any search for the public good. This sort of interest provided both the means of knowing how to preserve the public good and the essence of that good.

While pamphleteers attacked the old notions of a public good consisting of national power, others probed the relationship between private and public interests from different perspectives. Most spokesmen for official opinion defended traditional morality and were thus hostile to claims for rights and active self-interest on the part of subjects. A few political thinkers, chief of whom was Hobbes, condemned both Parliamentmen and the received wisdom regarding the public good.

This position served further to accentuate the problem of how the public good might be made to accommodate private goods. A tradition of discourse extending back to Hooker was discarded as irrelevant, for increasingly men saw that there was no point in inferring preference for the public good from the pattern of the universe if no attempt were made to give a plausible explanation of how certain private interests were to be preserved. Interregnum thought about the public good may be seen as culminating in Harrington. His thought on the subject was complicated by an attachment to the language of Hooker's treatment. However, his concrete analysis dealt with private interests as the foundation of the public good, and not altruism on the part of private men. From the Restoration to the Hanoverian succession and beyond, the pattern of discourse unfolded. The differences between traditional and individualist assumptions about the public good became more explicit until the Revolution signalled a major triumph for the new ideas.

In choosing to examine individualism in its heroic age, I do not wish to obscure the sinister aspects of this ideology. Many writers discussed here were involved in special pleading, but rarely did they justify an egoism that excluded all responsibility to the community. They expected nothing but chaos if all particular interests were to be pursued without restraint, and their doctrine made no such assumption.

All this becomes clear only by placing ideas in their social and political context. Thus this study finds its antecedents in those scholars who have said that the public interest is best understood by looking at its use in argument[1] or that early texts employing the concept were conditioned by immediate circumstances.[2] Perpetuating confusion about the public interest has no obvious advantages; removing it may serve the purposes both of history and political science.

[1] See B. M. Barry, 'The Use and Abuse of the Public Interest', in C. J. Friedrich (ed.), *The Public Interest* (New York, 1962), pp. 191–204, at p. 196.
[2] See H. R. Smith, *Democracy and the Public Interest* (Athens, Ga., 1960), p. 28.

I

PRIVATE MEN AND PUBLIC INTEREST 1640–60

SALUS POPULI SUPREMA LEX

SIGNIFICANT DISCUSSION ABOUT the public interest begins with the Civil War. Earlier literature was unanimous in giving a favourable connotation to the public weal or the common good; generally it neglected to say what the concept meant except to indicate the subordination of particular interests to it. *Pars pro toto* was the rule, and it admitted of few exceptions. In an age when political decisions were presumably still infused with religious significance, seeking the public good often meant no more than doing the will of God and, in general, being virtuous.[1] Economic life had certain dicta that were more concrete, but not inconsistent with this position. If the subject needed any more specific directive he found it in the voluminous Elizabethan literature on the necessity of loyalty to rulers, supported with accounts of the terrible vengeance that awaited traitors. Purely secular discussions of social duties seemed to equate love of the public good with patriotic service against foreign enemies.[2]

Instructions and advice to rulers were not much more explicit.

[1] It must be emphasized here that the concept had long existed in England; indeed it seems to have been indispensable for sophisticated political thought. For early examples of its use see S. B. Chrimes, *English Constitutional Ideas in the Fifteenth Century* (Cambridge, 1936), p. 305 n.

[2] On the failure of sixteenth-century thinkers to consider the national interest in terms other than dynastic aggrandizement see Garrett Mattingly, *Renaissance Diplomacy* (London, 1955), pp. 162–3. He notes the inadequacy of early ideas in comparison to nineteenth-century practice which measured military successes against the costs to private interests. In fact, a much more subtle form of accounting became widespread as early as the seventeenth century, as this study will demonstrate.

Primary emphasis seems to have been placed upon their function of protecting the people. This was not an unusual attitude considering that most manuals of advice for princes and ministers dwelt largely upon military tactics, the skills requisite for physical protection. Only a few English writers, who had practical experience in state affairs, spelled out the public interest in terms of concrete policies and conditions that contributed to national power.[1] Probably the great mass of writers also were referring to such matters, for terms such as common weal or public weal not only served to describe the good of the community but were also a common way of referring to the state.[2] The virtual identity of common good and the welfare of the state had more concrete and less ambiguous associations than those appearing later.

There are several reasons why the Civil War proved so fruitful in material about the public interest. At this time the English political vocabulary underwent radical changes induced by the unprecedented political conditions and by the enormous increase in the number of political writings. For the first time there was the opportunity for effective political argument conducted on a large scale. Previous crises had seen official doctrine aimed at Catholics, domestic or foreign, or at rebels; but there had been almost no opportunity for any dialogue.

As the struggle became more intense, all parties identified their cause with that of the public. Not only did their proposals about the organization of government and its policies differ, but, as a consequence, they came to understand the concept of a public interest in different ways. While men had always felt the need of justifying their own designs by reference to some common benefit, most such references offered little scope for analysis. This was because vague and unchallenged allusions to the acknowledged worth of a public good suggested no content for that good, and failed to identify the public. Now, however, writers had to defend their own understanding of the concept

---

[1] See, for instance, Francis Bacon, 'Observations on a Libel' and 'Of the True Greatness of the Kingdom of Britain', in *Works* (London, 1819), Vol. III, pp. 44–8 and 424–5.
[2] Tudor writers themselves noted this dual meaning. See Thomas Elyot, *The Boke Named the Governour*, ed. H. H. S. Croft (London, 1880), Vol. I, p. 1, and J. Barston, *The Safeguard of Societie* (1576), p. 25.

against competing definitions, for the ship-money case and the influence of Strafford had brought the opposed claims of national power and private right into the centre of debate.

Another aspect of the times was somewhat less favourable to attempts to trace the history of ideas. The same conditions that made the cry of public interest so common produced versions of it that were carefully tailored to the extreme situation that prevailed. Public interest, in many tracts, took the form of *'salus populi'*,[1] an expression best suited to justifying self-preservation in times of crisis. Only after repeated use as a revolutionary slogan were new perspectives on the public interest applied to government activity in normal times. Still, the period provided a showcase for almost all of the ideas about the public interest that were to appear until the present century.

The problems arising from 1640–60 were novel. So was the vocabulary in which discussion was carried on. These factors impose a dual function upon this survey of the period, for one must dwell both upon the substance of political argument and upon the very language of discussion. The survey of political argument is intended to show the prevalence of certain individualistic formulations of public interest. This outlook could be conveyed by various means, but in all cases the end product was a claim that the public interest involved more than what was conventionally understood as the preservation of the nation and its inhabitants.

The analysis of vocabulary looks principally at the remarkable vogue of the term 'interest' used in a political sense. The term became so very popular as a cachet of sophistication that, at times, it surely had no precise meaning at all. Applied to the affairs of the state as one unit in the international order, it produced the genre of 'interest of England' works. At the same time it supplied the guide and rule of individual political decisions. Finally, it designated the parties concerned in political disputes. Not all uses of 'interest' were equally significant for present

[1] This expression and others certainly looked to the vocabulary of the past, but if the controversialists of the Civil War were familiar with any early analyses of the public good, they were generally silent about it. Occasionally they quoted Aristotle on the subject, but only in the most general way. See R. Holdsworth, *The People's Happiness* . . . (Cambridge, 1642), p. 21, and Anon., *Some Observations* . . . *Upon the Apologeticall Narration* (1643), p. 35 (BM: E 34).

3

purposes, just as some valuable discussions of the public interest completely avoided the term. Nevertheless, the two inquiries illuminate each other at every turn. Both found their highest development in Harrington, whose importance warrants devoting a whole chapter to him.

The Parliament's case took many forms, but one of its most frequently used arguments centred on the ancient maxim '*salus populi suprema lex esto*'. To the great distress of the learned,[1] the maxim was distorted to fit contemporary needs. It became so much a part of every-day vocabulary that projectors borrowed it to serve non-political ends.[2] A distraught royalist complained that

'. . . every man who hath but arrived at one sentence in Latin, is ready to beat me down with the irresistible power of axiom . . . *salus populi lex summa*.'[3]

The year 1642 saw more new political tracts than in any previous year in English history, more indeed than in any other year of the crisis. Some of the most important of these publications were from the pen of Henry Parker. As the authoritative voice of Parliament, Parker had important things to say about *salus populi*, which he deemed the 'transcendent àkuǹ of all politics'. In a proclamation Charles had assured the people of his concern to protect them. This smacked too much of reason of state in a form unrelated to the most pressing private concerns. In his rejoinder, Parker hoped that

'. . . under this word protect, he intends not only to shield us from all kind of evil, but to promote us also to all kind of political happiness.'[4]

He did not specifically try to relate private interests to happiness, but on the same page he seemed to equate 'all single persons' with the 'whole state'. Of course, in one sense, the state was nothing else but all single persons. But the royalists, as Digges

[1] See John Selden, *Table Talk*, ed. R. Milward (1689), p. 40; from conversations held between 1634 and 1654.
[2] See P. Chamberlin, *A Vindication of Publique Artificial Baths* (1648), p. 1.
[3] 'Theophilus Craterus', *A Calm Consolatory Discourse of the Sad Tempestuous Affairs in England* (1647), p. 5 (BM: E 384).
[4] [Parker], *Observations Upon Some of His Majestie's Late Answers and Expresses* (1642), p. 3.

4

and Maxwell were to show so vigorously, chose to look at matters from a different point of view.[1]

Parker had insisted that all communities had a right of self-preservation, and also that communities were unlikely to use this power unwisely, since a community could have no private ends. At the same time he had suggested that *salus populi* was not a mere negative avoidance of evil but consisted in a positive good. He never said what he intended by 'all kind of political happiness', but it seems likely that his distinction between protection from evil and the active promotion of happiness corresponded rather closely to that between defence against external enemies and the promotion of domestic prosperity. The chief subject of debate at this time concerned control over the militia, with the king arguing that he could best provide for the safety of his people if he were able to use their money to keep up the militia. Parker took up this question of the militia in another tract where he asked rhetorically which of the Parliament or the king would better provide for the public safety. Charles had promised effective military defence of the community. Parker gave a different kind of assurance, saying that Parliament would not be likely to seize the estates of subjects. This was because its members were 'more knowing than other privadoes in regard of their public interest'.[2] He then went on to show the identity of interest between members of Parliament and the public.

It would be misleading to exaggerate the importance that Parker attached to these comments on the public interest. His work was not nearly so analytical as the answers it provoked from the royalists. He provided no careful defence of his views, though in a later work, published after Maxwell's attack, he referred, rather obliquely, to the subject of the dispute. He especially insisted that promoting the people's good involved maintaining prosperity, and he attacked foreign military adventures.[3] He came closest to a direct confrontation when he noted how some divines made the people's profit either secondary to the king's good or inconsistent with it. He added that

---

[1] Royalists of this sort are discussed below in Chapter II.
[2] [Parker], *Some Few Observations Upon His Majestie's Late Answer to the Declaration . . . of the Lords and Commons* (1642), p. 2.
[3] [Parker], *Jus Populi . . .* (1644), pp. 30 and 52.

'. . . if the major part be not condemned to slavery and poverty, they conceive the weal of the whole is exposed to great hazard.'[1]

This did not quite meet Maxwell's objections, but it shows that Parker had not retreated from his exposed position. Despite his great concern for private rights, Parker has also been hailed as one of the frankest early exponents of reason of state.[2] He clearly appreciated the nature of that extra-legal power which, in his own words, 'looks rather to the being, than well-being of states'. Nevertheless, he never associated it with the public interest in the same way as he had property, and insisted that reason of state was something to which the other side was much more addicted.[3]

Others on the parliamentary side strove to be more careful in defining the content of *salus populi*. In discussing the 'publike interest', Philip Hunton gave oblique support to Parker by insisting that a state was, after all, only all 'particulars' united.[4] Samuel Rutherford felt obliged to render Parker less vulnerable by taking issue with his royalist critics. He showed how Maxwell had taken an extreme interpretation of Parker's comments about promoting people to all happiness. Obviously, as he pointed out, the monarch was bound to promote some of his citizens, not to all happiness, but to the gallows.[5] This in no way constituted a repudiation of Parker, just a clarification.

In suggesting why Parliament was a better guardian of the public interest than the king, Parker had also a restricted view of what the public interest was. Many others took up the theme that the interests of Parliament and people were identical. In most cases the writers then implied that understanding of the public interest which best displayed Parliament's advantage over the king. Sometimes the argument went no further than the statement that such an identity of interest existed, without specifying its exact basis. Thus someone claimed that decisions by Parliament would serve the good of the community, for

[1] *Ibid.*, p. 24.
[2] See M. A. Judson, 'Henry Parker and the Theory of Parliamentary Sovereignty', in C. Wittke (ed.), *Essays in History and Political Theory in Honour of C. H. McIlwain* (Cambridge, Mass., 1936), pp. 155–6.
[3] [Parker], *The Contra-Replicant, his Complaint to his Majestie* (1643), p. 29.
[4] [Hunton], *A Treatise of Monarchy . . .* (1643), p. 43.
[5] [Rutherford], *Lex Rex; The Law and the Prince . . .* (1644), p. 224.

'. . . though every man in Parliament aim at his greatest particular interest, yet except it be agreeable to the interest of the major part, it will never pass into an act, and if it be advantageous for the most, it is to be esteemed public.'[1]

The author really meant that these men were to seek their personal interests, despite a claim that Parliament contained public-spirited men. He praised them only on the limited grounds that they would have no greater bent towards their 'private interest' than the population as a whole, which surely entailed no exaggerated estimate of the general level of altruism. Having assured himself that venality would be no problem in an assembly of prosperous gentlemen, he was quite prepared to have them vote in their own best interests.

A more developed version of the same idea appeared in a work by Charles Herle, one that has been singled out as indicative of the growing power of 'interest' in political writing.[2] Herle saw the variety of selfish interests in Parliament as a great advantage. His statement displays several dimensions of the basic idea, warranting more extensive quotation:

'. . . experience shows that most men's actions are swayed . . . by their ends and interests, those of kings . . . are altogether incompatible and crosscentred to those of subjects . . . with which the Parliament's either ends or interests cannot thus dash and interfere, the members are all subjects themselves, not only entrusted with, but self-interested in these very privileges and properties; besides they are many, and so they not only see more, but are less swayable; as not easily reducible to one head of private interest.'[3]

One further example should suffice. This time it is taken from a fairly obscure work by a well-known man, John Cook, Solicitor-General and the prosecutor of Charles I. Cook combined two seemingly antithetical points of view. He believed in the conventional social ethic that every Englishman, as a member of the nation, should conclude that what was good for it was good for him. At the same time, he had no illusions about human nature and was convinced that men would simply refuse

[1] J. M., *A Reply to the Answer to a Printed Book Intituled Observations Upon Some of His Majestie's Late Answers and Expresses* (1642), pp. 32–3 (B: 4 X 44 Jur.).
[2] See J. E. C. Hill, *Society and Puritanism in Pre-Revolutionary England* (London, 1964), p. 412.
[3] [Herle], *A Fuller Answer to a Treatise Written by Dr. Ferne . . .* (1642), p. 12.

to prejudice themselves for the public good.[1] Hence the old ethic was not very effective. He was frankly unclear about what course of action to recommend, and examined the possibility of binding members of Parliament by oaths. But Herle had already given a crushing answer to this position, and Cook quoted it without acknowledgment:

'I know there is a strong reason to be given why it is needless; because in true policy interests are better state security than oaths. The Lords and Commons vote for themselves, for their own goods as well as the kingdoms. If the kingdom suffer, they suffer in their private estates, and therefore the highest point of policy that humane prudence can reach unto is this, when a man cannot hurt me but he must hurt himself.'[2]

Clearly he saw it as the privilege of an M.P. to pursue his own interests in the process of finding the public good. Cook could imagine cases where the identity of interest might be imperfect, and representatives who were 'exceedingly concerned in point of profit' might be tempted to vote against the public good. In such an event, he did not ask them to vote contrary to their interests but entreated them to abstain.[3]

Herle and Cook shared the same general assumptions, one of which was that a justified concern for their own estates might well lead members of Parliament to the public good. Others were more explicit in treating property and its rights as the basis for a common interest. Thus the whole question of the property qualification of representatives becomes relevant to the problem. No doubt there had always been ideas on this subject, implicit in the practice of the ages.[4] However, only when the

---

[1] Cook, *Redintegratio Amoris, or a Union of Hearts* . . . (1647), p. 44.
[2] Ibid., p. 173.   [3] *Ibid.*, p. 45.
[4] The historically minded strove to uncover ancient precedents for the stake-in-the-country theory, but they were not very successful. Early statutes, such as 1 Henry V, c. 1, and 23 Henry VI, c. 15, said only that knights of the shire should literally be knights or be of comparable standing; yeomen would not do. A more promising precedent was a royal proclamation of 6 November 1620 barring indigent persons from Parliament. While this made bankrupts unwelcome, it said nothing about the positive qualities demanded of representatives. See Robert Steele, *A Bibliography of Royal Proclamations of the Tudor and Stuart Sovereigns . . . 1485–1714* (Oxford, 1910), Vol. I, No. 1290. Bulstrode Whitlock cited the qualifications of sheriffs as a demand for a substantial 'interest' in the commonwealth. See 'Treatise of Government' (1658) (BM: Add. MSS. 4993, fols. 127–8).

House of Commons was elevated as the focus of politics did the matter claim a great deal of attention.

The testimony of Parliament itself is the best evidence of the prevalence of this idea. A parliamentary declaration of 1642 claimed that it was most unlikely that its substantial members

'. . . should conspire to take away the law, by which they enjoy their estates, are protected from acts of violence . . . and differentiated from the meaner sort of people.'[1]

Parliament continually boasted of the personal fortunes commanded by its members. In some way the 'great interest of honour and estate' in their hands made them reliable custodians of the public good.[2] Some such statements strike the modern reader as rather curious. Thus the official parliamentary birth-certificate of the Commonwealth contained assurances about those members, who

'. . . besides their particular interests (which are not inconsiderable) . . . more intend the common interest of those whom they serve and clearly understand the same.'[3]

The property interests of the individual members were to lead them towards the public interest, though the search for it might be facilitated by goodwill towards the people.

Now there were a number of reasons why rich men should be deemed good members of Parliament. Some advocated it on no other grounds than that such men might be more immune against bribes or would have property that might be forfeited in the event of malfeasance.[4] The opinion that rich men were less likely to flee the country in time of danger was occasionally heard in these years. However, this theme does not appear to have become common until used by the landed interest against merchants later in the century. The earlier emphasis was on linking the interests of representatives with those of the public

---

[1] *An Exact Collection of all Remonstrances, Declarations, Votes, Orders, Proclamations, Petitions, Messages, Answers . . . Between the King's Most Excellent Majesty and his High Court of Parliament December 1641–March 21, 1643* (1643), p. 494. This was known as the *Book of Declarations*.

[2] *Ibid.*, p. 264.

[3] *Declaration of the Parliament of England Expressing the Grounds of their Late Proceedings and of Setting the Government in the Way of a Free State* (March 1649).

[4] William Ashhurst, *Reasons Against Agreement . . .* (1648), p. 11.

at large, through a common interest in property and shared burdens, such as taxation.[1]

There seems to have been a widespread assumption that there was a direct and immediate connection between men's estates and the public interest. Men of substance would feel it in their purses if the nation's affairs were ill managed, while presumably poor men had no interest one way or the other. An even more interesting assumption was the one that poor men had an interest that was positively detrimental to the public interest. This was well illustrated by a discussion of representation and majority rule by one L.S. He vindicated majority rule by the fact that no one man always knew what was best for the public. Nor would all agree on these issues. Thus the light of nature prescribed taking a majority vote in Parliament for the will of the whole. The aim of this work was certainly that of showing how government might best be organized for the public good.[2] In this connection he introduced one criterion for excluding legislators. The poor were not to have equal authority with the rich 'in making laws that concern men's estates', because their interests were clearly opposed to the preservation of private property. Or again,

'. . . seeing men are by innate and hereditary distemper biased towards wicked practices, indigent people who are not restrained from injustice by any self-interest, but on the contrary, tempted to rapine and perfidiousness, are altogether unfit to manage the public affairs of a nation.'[3]

[1] For tracts referring to this theme with varying degrees of clarity see J. Robinson, *The People's Plea* (1646), pp. 7 and 15 (BM: E 328); Anon., *The Standard of Equality in Subsidiary Taxes and Payments* (1647), para. 26 (BM: E 1167); Anon., *England's Remembrancers* (1656), p. 7 (BM: E 884); Anon., *A Letter from a Person in the Country . . . Giving his Judgement Upon a Book Entituled A Healing Question* (1656), p. 18 (B: G.P. 1363); and Anon., *An Alarum to the Counties of England and Wales* (1660), p. 9 (B: Wood 610). One of the few writers who favoured keeping rich men out of Parliament only serves to support the connection between the possession of property and concern for the public, since he assumed that the main criterion in choosing representatives was the size of their estates. This factor would determine how they allocated the burden of taxation. See W.W., *Proposals to the Officers of the Army . . . for Taking off all Excise, Taxes and Custom . . .* (1660), p. 6 (B: Wood 526).
[2] L. S., *Nature's Dowrie: Or, the People's Native Liberty Asserted* (1652), pp. 6 and 14 (BM: E 668).
[3] *Ibid.*, p. 13.

The objection to poor men was not, then, that they might be bribed or might misuse public money but that they might use their political power to attack property.

The writer's concern with private rights was made even more evident in the closing passages of the work. Any law beneficial to a subject gave him an 'interest', for which he might contend as lawfully as for anything else that was his own.[1] This was the justification for opposing all tyrants (presumably both kings and the rabble) who abridged private rights. The one right that he concretely specified was that of men's 'livelyhoods'. Private rights were the essence of the people's liberty. He ended with perhaps a side glance at a more famous text:

'. . . every man is an island, or a little world; and hath somewhat which he may call his own, and which he not only lawfully may, but also out of duty to God ought to defend from acts of violence . . . against all other men in the universe.'[2]

This was a far cry from the organic social scheme so common only a few years before, different too from earlier comments about a corporate right of self-defence resident in the people.

The chief problem encountered in making some connection between private-property rights and the public interest is that most tracts left the relationship an implied one. They did not say in so many words that they chose to view the public interest as consisting largely in the preservation of property; but they certainly did imply it, both positively, by juxtaposing references to property (in the narrow meaning of estates) and the public good, and negatively, by a failure to offer any other content for the concept.

All of the sources cited here struck the same note. The good of the nation was a much closer concern to men with large estates, thus suggesting, at least, that the protection of estates was a large element in the public interest. Of course, saying that it was in the interest of private men to procure the public interest was not the same thing as saying that the public interest consisted of private interests, variously combined. It would be quite plausible to imagine men finding it worth their while to protect national sovereignty. But the Protestant cause, national independence or even national prosperity, would have been of great

[1] *Nature's Dowrie*, p. 20.   [2] *Ibid.*, p. 22.

concern to all men, the last especially so in an age when writers affirmed endlessly that finding work for the poor was the end and the measure of a buoyant economy. What Parliament and its supporters needed was some version of the public interest that could best be provided for by its members. Despite the internationalism of Levellers or Anabaptists or the king's foreign intrigues, all of them were equally interested in most aspects of a national good. Not even the Levellers, despite some of their rhetoric, can have thought that Charles wished to destroy the nation in the sense of ending its existence as a national unit. But in the area of private rights there was bitter opposition to arbitrary taxation and other uses of prerogative. Here was an aspect of the common good worth emphasizing, since it demonstrated an identity of interest between Parliament and the public. No doubt the writers in question would have allowed that other things, besides the preservation of property and other rights, were also in the public interest. The point is simply that their arguments suggested the formulation of the public good best suited to their circumstances. When looking at the royalists and their thoughts on this subject it will be obvious that many of them found it convenient to stress how the king's personal interest was identical with the national interest conceived in terms of national power. There was no necessary inconsistency between these different perspectives; what from one view point was national survival was the preservation of men's estates from another.

A number of the tracts quoted here point to the above interpretation and make more sense when viewed in terms of it. One other well-known source may further contribute to the picture. In the Putney Debates, Commissary-General Henry Ireton gave a classical exposition of what was involved in having a stake in the kingdom. One modern study on the property qualifications of members of Parliament cites this as an early instance of an idea that was not of primary importance until the overt clash between landed and monied interests after the Restoration.[1] Actually the theme would seem to have attracted considerable attention during the Interregnum, though special emphasis upon property in land may have been rare before Har-

---

[1] Helen E. Witmer, *The Property Qualifications of Members of Parliament* (New York, 1943), p. 16. Ireton did not concern himself with property in land as much as did later writers, or as much as this study suggests.

rington. Some earlier writers were plainly more interested in the size of estates than in their degree of liquidity; others may just have assumed that property meant land.

Ireton's contribution was the insistence that members of Parliament with a 'permanent fixed interest' in the kingdom '. . . taken together do comprehend whatever is of real or permanent interest in the kingdom.'[1]

Discussing what he called 'local interest' or a minimum substance and standing in one's district, he said:

'It doth not relate to the interest of the kingdom if it do not lay the foundation of the power that's given to the representers, in those who have a permanent and a local interest in the kingdom, and who all taken together do comprehend the whole interest of the kingdom.'[2]

Now 'comprehend' in this context was ambiguous, and Clarke's report of proceedings does nothing to clarify matters. He used the same expression about comprehending the whole interest of the kingdom some five times, but provided no alternative way of making the same point. The context certainly suggests very strongly that 'comprehend' was used in the sense of 'constitute' and not with any reference to cerebral processes. This ambiguity is not very serious, since here the word could simultaneously bear both meanings.

The important characteristic of members of Parliament was that they had substantial personal concerns that had a locus. They could be located in space in so far as anything as insubstantial as a concern could be. Their interests also had a temporal dimension, having the relative permanence associated with a fixed location. The sort of personal concern that best fitted requirements was a freehold, but Ireton only used this as an example and made it quite clear that other interests would do.[3]

[1] A. S. P. Woodhouse (ed.), *Puritanism and Liberty* (London, 1951), p. 54. Ireton displayed a different outlook in a document attributed, in part, to him. See *A Remonstrance of his Excellency Thomas Lord Fairfax . . . and of the General Councell of Officers held at St. Albans the 16th of November, 1648*, p. 14 (B: Ashm. 1006). Here, for purposes of checking the Levellers, he distinguished rigorously between particular men's interests and those of the nation. For Ireton's role in drafting the document see R. W. Ramsey, *Henry Ireton* (London, 1949), pp. 115–16.

[2] Woodhouse, p. 55.

[3] Woodhouse, pp. 57–8. He specifically put the trading interest in the boroughs on the same level as the landed interest.

Interest could, of course, mean a right, though it seems unlikely that Ireton meant it to, for he spoke of having 'a right to
an interest'. Having a right to exercise a right does not seem
sensible, especially for one who was involved in repudiating the
Leveller doctrine of native rights. Again, Ireton's statement is
curiously ambivalent, for the sort of interests he was talking
about were also rights that had legal recognition. The substantial men who gathered together in Parliament could thus be
viewed as an animate collection of interests that could be
depended upon to produce the essential elements of the national
interest. They might well 'comprehend' the whole interest of
the kingdom in the sense of understanding it, though since the
electorate also comprehended that interest,[1] he was certainly
not just speaking about the wisdom of their counsels.

Here, then, is a perfect example of the public interest of the
kingdom being derived from, and, in the literal sense of the text,
consisting in, the maintenance of private interests; not all private interests were involved, just those that contributed to the
'peace' and the 'better settlement' of the kingdom.[2] Permanent
fixed interests cohered perfectly with this national interest; they
were that interest in another form, in a sense in which interests
that men could 'carry about' with them were not. Here was a
sum of interests in virtually the only form that made sense.
Ireton's thoughts on this occasion were not uniquely his; others
had already expressed them in slightly different terms. Eight
years later Cromwell was to use substantially the same vocabulary to make the same point.[3] The various writers who thought
in terms of an interest, or reason of state, diffused among the
populace, were also in this tradition.[4]

Ireton, and writers like him, were saying that the fulfilment
of certain private interests provided the necessary, and probably sufficient, conditions for realizing the public interest. This
was in no way incompatible with a public interest that consisted in peace and order. The private, local interests taken together ensured such peace and order. A concept such as the

[1] *Ibid.*, p. 54.   [2] Woodhouse, p. 58.
[3] 'a nobleman, a gentleman, a yeoman (that is a good interest and a great
one)', in *The Writings and Speeches of Oliver Cromwell*, ed. W. C. Abbott
(Cambridge, Mass., 1945), Vol. III, p. 435.
[4] See pp. 35 and 128 below.

public interest is so general and so abstract that no one set of predicates can exhaust its meaning. Ireton was not saying anything new when he spoke of peace and the 'better settlement' of the nation as the interest of the kingdom. However, he was suggesting the essence of a new tradition in minimizing the amount of tension between particular interests and the general interest. In different ways and for different reasons others were making the same departure.

Those who were concerned with the property qualifications of members of Parliament had little to say about the people not actually present at Westminster. Ireton said more clearly than most that the interest of the representatives was that of all men with an interest in property. The need of showing a harmony of interests between Parliament and the people made this a premise of most such works. At the same time there were numerous claims for private interests arising in other contexts. John Durie, for instance, took it as beyond dispute that

'. . . a public interest is nothing else but the universal private good of everyone.'[1]

However, his insistence that any truly public good must accommodate the 'near interest' of individuals was blunted by a refusal to see the public good in other than spiritual terms. Plainly it was difficult to formulate a version of *salus populi* that looked to the good of the community, while taking men's 'near' interests into account. The fact that some people had begun to discuss a public good in terms of private ones was already causing disquiet among royalists, who had their alternative definitions ready. One royalist approached the point rather obliquely by observing that there was an ambiguity in the slogan of *salus populi*. To some people '*populi*' meant the community, while to others it referred to 'every man's particular self'.[2] Awkward though it was, Symmons' distinction was fair comment on the tendency for members of the popular party to appeal to the good of particular men rather than the strength of the state.

In the early stages of debate the grounds of argument had yet

---

[1] John Durie, *A Motion Tending to the Public Good of this Age and of Posteritie* (1642), p. 6.
[2] Edward Symmons, *A Loyal Subject's Belief, Expressed in a Letter to Master Stephen Marshall* (1643), p. 39.

to be clarified and so many allusions to the problem of the public good tended to be obscure. Gradually there was a shift in emphasis from recounting a king's duties to his people to defending the people's right to look to their own interests. This need not take the form of insisting upon specific private benefits as a part of *salus populi*. Some Roundhead supporters stressed the necessity of private involvement in preserving the public weal. One such writer followed Symmons in emphasizing the ambiguity of the word 'public', saying:

'. . . there is a strange misprision of the word public, when it is taken for the essential independency of the kingdom; for it doth, or ought to receive influence from every member, and so by participation they are both compleated.'[1]

He obviously had an antipathy to any view of the public safety that relied upon conventional reason-of-state precepts, although he would have made himself clearer had he analysed instead the other term in *salus populi*. He combined an insistence on self-fulfilment through participation in affairs of state with an undiminished concern for the public interest.[2] Apparently his intention was to pierce the veil of the *arcana imperii* and at the same time call ordinary citizens to their duty. He complained that the vulgar believed that a kingdom possessed some invisible power to preserve itself; but in this they were wrong. He suggested that the error stemmed, in part, from a failure to appreciate how all 'interests' were interrelated.[3] The message differed very little from Algernon Sydney's comment three decades later, that

'. . . men can no otherwise be engaged to take care of the public, than by having such a part in it as absolute monarchy does not allow.'[4]

It is well established that there was a certain progression in political argument from grounds of law and historical precedent

---

[1] J. S., *Some New Observations and Considerations Upon the Present State of Things in England* (1642), p. 8 (BM: E 93). It was reprinted the next year under the title *Malignancy Unmasked*.
[2] This is the only possible interpretation of the meaning of 'both' in the above quotation. Involving citizens in preserving the public 'compleated' or served both the kingdom and the citizens.
[3] *Ibid.*, p. 9.
[4] *Life, Memoirs Etc. of Algernon Sydney* (1794), p. 561. This sentence does not appear in some editions of Sydney's writings.

to grounds of reason and natural right.[1] Some of the earliest Parliamentmen had chosen to plead from the laws of necessity and nature, and especially that of self-preservation. Officially authorized parliamentary tracts suggested that the common people might redress their own grievances in default of help from Parliament. Royalists were quick to proclaim Parliament's inadequacy as spokesman for the community, thus giving an opening to new forces from the left. Thus both of the original parties provided forms of argument that could be turned to good account when the struggle unleashed more popular forces.

Without worrying about the various institutional schemes for expressing the will of the people, it is still useful to ask how private men thought the public good might be attained; for in examining the problem of how it might be discovered one may learn much about what the concept meant to early democrats. Suggesting discovery of the public interest by the common people themselves invited difficulties, for some of the most respected maxims in political life barred the way. Generations of sermons and works on social morality had proclaimed the incapacity of ordinary citizens to deal with public policy. Traditional morality prescribed that citizens be loyal and obedient. They were to prefer the public good to their own, but otherwise there had been no directives about how they might preserve the public good. Moralists had assumed that if private men kept to their own callings they were contributing to the public good. Apart from this tenuous connection, the common good was seen as somehow qualitatively different from private profit.

The common suspicion of private interest had its legal embodiment in the dictum of the law that no man should be judge in his own case, or as earlier documents put it, in his own 'cause'.[2] Writers of all persuasions were prepared to quote Coke or Hobart against any tendency on the part of their opponents to act for their own interests, even when such interests might be

---

[1] The Levellers' attempt to escape from history as a basis for rights is discussed in S. Kliger, *The Goths in England* (Cambridge, Mass., 1952), Appendix B, and J. A. Pocock, *The Ancient Constitution and the Feudal Law* (Cambridge, 1957), p. 126.

[2] This may have been based upon the distinction between a case decided by the ordinary courts using the letter of the law and a 'cause', brought into Chancery. In the latter event self-evident principles of natural law governed the decision. See G. de Malynes, *Lex Mercatoria* (1622), p. 467.

of a broad, 'public' nature concerned with the general protection of private rights, rather than selfish and private advantages. The dictum proved useful to royalists, Levellers or to the minions of the Protector writing against the would-be tyrannicide Sexby. Everyone seemed to recognize its relevance to political discussion. Indeed, when argument had largely passed out of the realm of purely legal precedent, this maxim kept pace and came to be phrased in terms of a law of nature.[1]

Faced with this verbal wall, what were men to do? The most fruitful course was to affirm the principle and to deny its relevance to the current situation. Thus Parliament had chosen to see itself not as acting as judge in its own case but as functioning as an impartial arbiter between king and people, or, if it could not claim impartiality, it might claim to be deciding the case in the interests of the people and not of itself.[2] At the same time Parker and others had tried to show that, in the nature of things, a community could have no private ends. This referred originally to Parliament, the 'artificial' or legal embodiment of the people, but soon the 'rude bulk of the universality' claimed to speak for itself.[3]

Popular initiative for the securing of *salus populi* took various forms. Some writers claimed only a right of the people to revolt against intolerable oppression. This constituted no advance over the Monarchomachs of the previous century and had little to do with coherent ideas about the public good. It was in this tradition that someone called William Cokayne complained of the depredations on private men's estates and asked:

'. . . if we may not declare our pressures, as also propound ways to redress to our trustees, what are we but perfect slaves?'[4]

Other sources said much more clearly that the grievances which Parliament had failed to remedy, or had even exacerbated, were common to the people as a whole. Numerous tracts noted that the chief grievances centred on a failure to protect men's estates and that protection of estates was the true public interest. A number of the people who held such opinions may be

[1] See Amon Wilbee, *Comparatis Comparandis* (1647), p. 28.
[2] *Book of Declarations*, p. 697.
[3] The expression is Parker's. See *Jus Populi*, pp. 18–19.
[4] Cokayne, *The Foundations of Freedom Vindicated* (1649), p. 3.

called Levellers, though Lilburne himself, with his many legal precedents and massive self-quotation, is not the most rewarding source.

Lilburne certainly made some of the important points. Despite his frequent assertions that the public had been misled and its understanding clouded by evil plots, he still felt that the public good could be grasped and implemented by ordinary men. The public good was so obvious to him that he persistently attributed to malice any refusal to accept his views. This propensity to discover conspiracies against the public was one of the most characteristic aspects of Leveller thought and it provoked sneers from their more sophisticated opponents.[1] Since Levellers based their thoughts on the public interest upon the naturalness of self-preservation, they claimed that the nature of this interest was self-evident. This was what led Lilburne to state so confidently that it should be

'. . . evident and apparent unto all rational . . . people in the world, that the real and hearty good and welfare of the people of this nation, hath . . . been that, that their souls have hunted for . . . in all the late, bloody wars.'[2]

This neglected the fact that people had fought for different things.

In all his works Lilburne managed to avoid the vocabulary of individualism by railing at self-lovers and praising the 'well-affected' whose every thought was of the public weal. He gave the impression that should men fail to provide for their vital interests, they would be wicked and rebellious to the natural order. Thus self-preservation became a self-enforcing law that left individuals no discretion in applying it, since it furthered divine as much as human purposes.[3] There was nothing strange in this fusion of right and duty, especially in a period when

---

[1] See S. Sheppard, *The False Alarum* . . . (1646), p. 10, and J. Canne, *The Discoverer* . . ., Part I (1649), p. 28.

[2] J. Lilburne, *An Impeachment of High Treason Against Oliver Cromwell* (1649), p. 5. This same certainty about the content of the public good is the most striking aspect of Ludlow's attitude in his interviews with Cromwell. See *The Memoirs of Edmund Ludlow*, ed. C. H. Firth (Oxford, 1894), Vol. I, p. 435, and Vol. II, p. 28.

[3] See Lilburne, *Innocency and Truth Justified* (1645), p. 59, and *The Free Man's Freedom Vindicated* (1646), p. 11.

nations measured their happiness by numbers of people and theologians all condemned self-destruction as a failure in social duty as well as a mortal sin. Even when Lilburne went farthest in explaining his private needs, he retained his concern for the good of the community. Extreme seventeenth-century individualists sometimes said that only by preserving particular interests was the common interest preserved. His approach was to say:

'. . . as I am an individual, I am part of the whole, and if it perish in the eye of reason, I and mine must perish with it.'[1]

This, he continued, meant that he was bound 'in duty to self and universal preservation' to save the community, whether it wanted to be saved or not. Interestingly enough, in discussing the same question, his colleague Overton reversed the order of priorities, saying that

'. . . no more may be communicated to the general, than is included in the particulars, whereof the general is compounded.'[2]

Unfortunately the Levellers were not always specific about what was included in the public interest, since self-preservation took in a great deal of ground. Clearly Lilburne contemplated forms of destruction other than in the literal, physical sense. Like Parliament, when it justified its opposition to the king by the right of any man attacked with a lethal weapon, the Levellers were given to misleading analogies.[3] In one of his earliest tracts Lilburne attacked the High Commission Oath as detrimental to self-preservation.[4] More importantly, he claimed that taking away a man's property was the effective equivalent of taking away his life. Thus the right to life might be extended to encompass other rights, though Lilburne did not make a great deal of the point.

Despite his emotive language and his penchant for extreme examples, Lilburne by no means limited popular initiative in procuring *salus populi* to dire emergencies when physical sur-

---

[1] [Lilburne], *To His Honoured Friend, Mr. Cornelius Holland* (1649), p. 24.
[2] R. Overton, *An Appeale from the Degenerate Representative Body . . .* (1647), p. 8.
[3] Thus Overton insisted that saving the public was as obvious an undertaking as getting one's neighbour's oxen out of a ditch. See *The Baiting of the Great Bull of Bashan . . .* (1649), p. 6.
[4] [Lilburne], *The Christian Man's Triall* (1641), p. 25.

vival was at stake. Obviously if representatives were honest and diligent no spontaneous action by the unorganized public would be necessary. Still, a capacity to know when one's own interests and those of the public were in jeopardy implied a capacity to know when all was right with the public. On one occasion he put popular action to secure the common good on no higher basis than mere convenience. In the event rulers or their policies proved 'useless, hurtful or unprofitable', he who had put them in office might

'. . . modifie, restrain, remove or nullify even as seemed good unto him and may most conduce to his good and safety.'[1]

This general right of action still did not explain why the public interest should appear so obvious to Lilburne. The best answer was contained in Lilburne's answer to charges of wishing to establish a community of property. In exoneration he insisted upon his devotion to the welfare of the commonwealth, adding that it was

'. . . the utmost of our aim that the commonwealth may be reduced to such a pass that every man may with as much security as may be enjoy his propriety.'[2]

In taking this view, Lilburne largely ignored those aspects of *salus populi* that were concerned with external relations and national defence. In the course of encouraging people to seek their 'common interest', he did once refer to the danger posed by the French.[3] But he said much more emphatically that the danger from such a 'public adversary' was its being used as a pretext by Parliament to infringe upon the safety and welfare of the people.[4]

[1] [Lilburne], *Plain Truth Without Feare or Flattery* (1647), p. 17.
[2] *A Manifestation from Lieut.-Col. John Lilburne, Mr. William Walwyn, Mr. Thomas Prince and Mr. Richard Overton* (1649), p. 5 (B: Firth e. 59). 'Propriety' no doubt included rights other than the free enjoyment of one's estate. But here, as elsewhere, the right of property, narrowly defined, served to symbolize personal rights in general.
[3] Lilburne, *London's Liberty in Chains Discovered* . . . (1646), pp. 56–7.
[4] *Plain Truth*, p. 9. Exactly the same complaint had often been raised in Parliament in the ship-money debate. See, for instance, *The Speech or Declaration of Mr. St. John Delivered at a Conference of Both Houses of Parliament . . . Concerning Ship-Money* (1641), pp. 26–7 (BM: E 196). Those writers on the popular side who were aware of the international implications of events

This indicates that for at least one major representative of radical opinion the public interest was a condition where private rights and interests were preserved. If this were Lilburne's view, and he is not the best subject for close analysis, two questions arise. How common was it? Why was this a useful and significant perspective? These questions are best answered by broadening the field of inquiry.

The relationship between the 'people' and the public interest was more amply discussed in several other tracts that were faithful to Leveller thought and vocabulary. One such anonymous publication placed the common man's apprehension of the common good firmly on the basis of natural law. This law had various dictates, but for present purposes the writer saw the same message in all of them. Thus the case for direct, preventive action to sustain the public good rested on

'. . . that law of nature and common prudence which enjoins every man to preserve himself, and to seek his own good . . .'[1]

A further ethical justification was

'. . . that law that obliges every commoner according to his ability, and opportunity to seek the good of that politic body of which he is a member . . .'[2]

The writer never suggested that there might be any conflict between these principles; one complemented the other.[3]

Proceeding by a formal process of indicating objections and then refuting them, the writer reached the most important objection. The rulers obviously had erred in attaining the public good, might not the people also err? As far as he was con-

did not stress dangers from abroad so much as the joy with which Protestant Europe would greet their success. See J. E. C. Hill, 'The English Revolution and the Brotherhood of Man', *Science and Society*, Vol. XVIII, No. 4 (1954), pp. 289–309, at p. 297. Of course there were also Independents, such as the irrepressible Hugh Peter, who contemplated turning the Civil War into a crusade to free Europe. See R. P. Stearns, *The Strenuous Puritan* (Urbana, 1954), pp. 288–90.

[1] *The Grand Informer, or the Prerogative of Princes, Privileges and Powers of the Magistrate Asserted* (1647), p. 8 (BM: E 398).

[2] *Ibid.*, p. 9.

[3] Earlier references to this twofold law of nature tended to include the observation that the good of the individual might have to be sacrificed to that of the whole. This tradition is discussed below in relation to Harrington. See Chapter III.

cerned, they would not. The people were rational, both in conceiving their ends and in choosing the means most proper to them.[1] Stated differently, the answer was that

'. . . things of common equity, and which are of public concernment for good, do not lie at any such great distance from the apprehensions of most men, but that they may be felt and handled, as it were, by them: For who knows not, that for every man to enjoy and securely possess his own right, is good?'[2]

Such things were not matters for dispute; one might as well deny that the sun was shining, when indeed it was, or claim that two and two were not four.[3]

Like the other Leveller works, this one showed a strong sense of community. Men ought to seek the public good, and by their nature were bound to do so. They were rational, in a manner both substantial and instrumental, and so were competent to discern a common good that consisted in maintaining their legitimate private interests. The voice of the people could be relied upon to indicate a genuine common good, because criticizing magistrates was a dangerous business and they could not hope to gain from unrighteous complaints.[4]

Two other works may be cited to illustrate the same basic pattern. Both may have been by Richard Overton.[5] The problem was the old one; the people's good was the supreme law, but it had not been implemented. How was it to be discovered? Rulers had been wicked and negligent, forgetting that it was no man's particular good, but that of all, that made a kingdom great. This public good was no mystery, it required only the will to obtain it. The author was understandably vague about what the public good was, since he was largely concerned with vindicating the general competence of the people to discover it. However, he included a number of concrete complaints, all of which concerned the preservation of men's estates from monopolies and from excessive taxation.

His general statement in *Vox Plebis* is worth quoting in full:

'. . . we the people, conceive it our duty, to show unto our governors that good, which by reason of the malignancy of the times and of

[1] *Grand Informer*, p. 11.   [2] *Ibid.*, p. 13.
[3] Cf. Harrington p. 141, below.   [4] *The Grand Informer*, p. 14.
[5] See Joseph Frank, *The Levellers* (Cambridge, Mass., 1955), pp. 98–9 and 118–19, for evidence on authorship.

fortune, we have not been able to do ourselves; to that end, that you our senators ... may put it in practice for the public good. Neither is our opinion to be dispised: for it is a sure maxim, that the people are of as clear judgment in all things that conceive the public, as any, and are as wise, and circumspect concerning their liberties.'[1]

So again it was the rights of private men, principally that of property, that were at stake. If that had not been already established, he made it unmistakable in his most damaging charge against Parliament. It had acted

'... to hold up that common maxim of all oppressing states, which is, that their interest is to maintain the public wealthy, and the particular poor.'[2]

This was an interesting way to express what was wrong, for it was widely supposed that it was impossible for the public to flourish at the expense of legitimate private interests. Private men were supposed to find satisfaction and real benefit in the riches and power of the state. Here, though, was one writer whose main concern was for the particulars, and not for the national treasury.

Another tract, attributed to Overton, only supports the contention of *Vox Plebis*. It was a further call to the community to assert its native rights against tyranny. Again, the only concrete complaints dealt with impositions on estates. Although the public interest, as an expression, did not figure in the text, this was the obvious subject of concern; for the establishment of liberties was described as the '*unum necessarium*', the one thing required to mend the kingdom.[3] Advice to the people regarding the public good was unequivocal:

'... can any man tell better than yourselves, where your shoe pincheth you, and what is most expedient for you to do? Never render your selves so ridiculous as to be led like children and fools by the nose; to be made stalking horses for other men's designs, whose interests are dissonant and inconsistent with yours.'[4]

[1] *Vox Plebis, or the People's Outcry Against Oppression* (1646), p. 67 (BM: E 362). Joseph Frank disagrees with the usual attribution to Overton and suggests Henry Marten as the author.
[2] *Ibid.*, p. 63. Royalists might also express complaints in this form. Cf. Anon., *A Parallel of Governments* ... (1646), p. 6 (BM: E 400).
[3] Anon., *A New-found Stratagem Framed in the Old Forge of Machivilisme* (1647), p. 13 (BM: E 384).
[4] *Ibid.*, pp. 10–11.

The proverb about one's shoe pinching was already traditional by 1640, but it seems only to have acquired political relevance in the Civil War.[1] It could be used only to indicate that those who felt oppression had the most acute impression of how onerous it was.[2] It might support more ambitious claims, as in the above instance, and serve to show that common men, through a knowledge of their ills, might see the public good.

This discussion of the people and the public interest has assumed that there must have been some connection between particular interests and the public interest. The Leveller writings tended to deal in terms of some corporate appreciation of a common good. Since Levellers were certainly not advocates of any group mind, this necessarily entailed some assumptions about each individual's outlook on the public interest. It might only imply that each man had a rational faculty that told him what course of action was just or at least what conditions constituted injustice. This could have been some sort of moral sense that perceived, in a totally disinterested way, what made for righteousness in human affairs. It was perfectly comprehensible to say that the public interest was justice; no one ever seems to have claimed that it consisted in injustice and many writers specifically linked justice and common good. To translate this concern for justice into private interests would be both superfluous and misleading had so many people not introduced the subject themselves. The law of nature enjoined seeking the good of the community and one's own good, but in order to know what these were, all were reduced to citing the grievances of private men. As one nineteenth-century scholar has explained in identical circumstances, one may discuss the public interest in terms of concrete social relations without denying the relevance of justice. In fact, to do so makes the notion of justice more meaningful.[3]

A bent towards the good of the community might be enough when politics was an activity remote from common men; but

[1] See *Outlandish Proverbs: Selected by G. H.* (i.e. George Herbert) (1640), No. 491. A few years later James Howell saw it as an old English proverb. See *Proverbs: Collected by J. H.* (1659).
[2] See John Coales, *A Glasse of Truth* (1649), p. 19.
[3] Eugène Daire, *Physiocrates* (Paris, 1846), pp. IX–X. Daire made this comment to justify an examination of physiocratic ideas.

when they had to provide for the public needs themselves, they had to know what the public interest involved. The Leveller tracts did not deal with elements of national power but with matters very much closer to the private men to whom they appealed. A modern writer, discussing the theme of natural rights in Leveller works, has said that the purport of those passages quoted above was that

'. . . each individual, guided by dependable instinct, has a more exact knowledge than anyone else as to what will best advance his material interests.'[1]

It is indisputable that they were saying this, but they were saying something else as well. On the whole, the passages were directed to describing the public interest rather than private rights and interests. However, in order to give the public interest some content, they showed how it would be secured by caring for particular interests.

Additional insights on the relationship between the particulars and the public may be gleaned from tracts by other obscure men not normally identified with the Leveller cause. Two of these were William Ball and John Warr. Ball was probably quite well known in his own day, for he disputed political questions with such men as Judge Jenkins and Attorney-General Cook. He was probably the same William Ball who wrote royalist literature in 1642 and who tried, unsuccessfully, to contest a seat at Reading in 1645.[2] If Ball deserves any lasting place in histories of seventeenth-century thought, it must be as an exceptionally acute exponent of the idea that political life was a matter of secular interests. This was quite remarkable, for he was conventionally pious and occasionally just as politically naïve as any self-proclaimed saint. But no one, not Parker, nor Milton, managed to state the nature of parliamentary or popular sovereignty with greater force.

Ball was primarily concerned with the people's right to be

---

[1] L. H. Poe, *The Levellers and the Origins of Natural Rights* (unpublished D.Phil. Thesis, Oxford, 1956), p. 213.
[2] Ball's name appears on *A Caveat for Subjects*, a moderate royalist tract. The disputed nomination is described in *The Victoria History of the Counties of England*—Berkshire, Vol. III, p. 361, and in more detail in J. Man, *The History and Antiquities of the Borough of Reading* (Reading, 1816), pp. 224–6.

self-governing, based largely upon the convenience of such an arrangement and not just as a temporary check to tyranny. He brushed aside the objection about not being a judge in one's own case. In place of the legalistic equivocations so often employed on this point, he appealed to the new principle of interest:

'The Commons, Primario, or in the first place are, and ought to be the judges, even as customary tenants are, and ought to be their own evidences; although one man ought not to be judge in his own case, yet all in a kingdom or commonwealth can have no judges of their common interest but themselves, or some amongst themselves, at leastwise no competent judges: and where the common interest is controverted, there, they who have the greatest interests or whom it most concerns ought to be judges . . . and surely the common people in general have the greatest interest in the common interest; and the laws of the land most concern them, wherefor, they, or their representatives or trustees, ought to be judges.'[1]

Far from disabling people from judging a case, the status of an interested party was the only sound basis for making a decision and presumably competence was in direct proportion to the degree of interest. The rules of politics were not those of the law.

Since Ball was concerned with justifying the people's general right to make their own decisions, he was not greatly concerned with specific instances. At any time the people must be deemed competent to decide upon some concrete definition of the public interest. If freedom were not to degenerate to a mere titular possession it had to mean that the people were able to

'. . . determine themselves a general common good, as it shall seem good to themselves.'[2]

This did not neglect the particular interests of individual men, for the people as a corporate body had to regulate their affairs

'. . . so to the particular good of every man, as may not repugn the general good of all; so to the general good of all men, as may not annihilate the particular good of one unjustly or indirectly.'[3]

Even though he coupled this with a plea for the abolition of the 'self-ends' that plagued politics, obviously he placed particular

[1] Ball, *The Power of Kings Discussed* . . . (1649), p. 3.
[2] Ball, *The Rule of a Free-Born People* . . . (1646), p. 43.
[3] *Ibid.*, p. 14.

importance on preserving individual interests. He tended usually to write of 'goods' and not of interests. However, the former term carried all of the meaning of the latter, since he was most insistent that such goods were relative to the desires entertained by citizens at any moment. Some earlier writers had tried to find transcendent value behind the wills of individual citizens. Volition played a greater part in Ball's theory, for he said that

'. . . as beyond the highest heaven there is no mathematical, or further dimension, so beyond a national constitution of government there ought to be no further progression.'[1]

If the public interest were something immanent, dependent upon human interests that were, in a sense, arbitrary, it still had to be conceived in terms that ordinary men could grasp. Since Ball was so concerned with protecting private property rights, the public interest was most intelligible if reduced to the preservation of estates. In his attempts to raise barriers against all governments, this is exactly how he conceived it. For his remarks on what he indiscriminately called '*salus populi*', '*bonum commune*' or the 'common interest' were all triggered by heated disputes about the people's right to seek their 'self-embracing good'.[2] The one instance that he constantly used to illustrate legitimate and direct action to implement the public good was an attempt by the government to dispose of men's 'estates' at will.[3] It would not be sensible to postulate a public interest that encompassed the selfish concerns of all private citizens. In settling on the maintenance of property, Ball apparently thought that he had provided the best possible wedding of private and public interest.

A variation on the theme runs through the writings of John Warr. Warr sometimes spoke the language of Fifth Monarchy and looked towards the day when the 'resurrection of principles will be the death of persons and personal interests'.[4] Still, this long-term goal did not deter him from making some effective

---

[1] Ball, *Power Juridicent and Juritient: or Power of Law-Making and Law-Administering Discussed* (1650), p. 6.
[2] Ball, *State Maxims . . .* (1655), p. 28.
[3] Ball, *Tractatus De Jure Regnandi, & Regni: or the Sphere of Government* (1645), p. 15, *Rule of a Free-Born People*, p. 8, and *Power Juridicent*, p. 12.
[4] Warr, *Administrations Civil and Spiritual* (1648), p. 14.

observations on contemporary politics. Unregenerate man had to be accepted as self-interested. Warr asked only that the various interests on foot be divided into two classes, those grounded upon weakness and those upon corruption. Interests of the first sort could, and must, be 'used' so long as mankind remained spiritually frail. Corrupt and unlawful interests differed from these in taking no account of salvation, and, more significantly, in acting as obstructions to change.[1]

The public interest was never far from Warr's thoughts, though he was not entirely successful in describing it. He made his one vital contribution by showing that the public interest in a popular government was different from that in earlier regimes. Kings had made a 'mystery' of their interest, setting it above the concerns of ordinary mortals; this had to end. Most contemporary governments adopted a middle position, with laws based partly on the king's interest and partly on that of the people; but these, too, were imperfect. They had all neglected the fact that in all systems of government

'. . . the interest of the people is the true and proper interest of that commonwealth; other interests have advanced themselves, pretendedly to exalt this, and yet being once gotton into the throne of rule . . . they bend their utmost endeavour to overthrow it.'[2]

While this identification of the people's interest with that of the public might seem obvious, it was really quite new. The people's good had always been the professed end of government, now Warr's statement showed that this was inadequate. The people had to be given an opportunity to express their interest, a good as understood by themselves. His pointed reference to the traditional doctrine about mysteries of state was typical of the seventeenth-century democrats. Mysteries of state had served to preserve the state and its rulers from enemies, domestic or foreign. Advocates of the people's interest thought more in terms of preserving the rights of private men, and thereby the commonwealth. Thus most of Warr's demands for reform were concerned with enlarging the area of private freedom. He took the degree of respect for subjects' property as the measure of official oppression.[3]

[1] Warr, *The Corruption and Deficiency of the Laws of England* . . . (1649), p. 17.
[2] Warr, *The Privileges of the People* . . .   [3] Warr, *Corruption* . . ., p. 10.

Few radical thinkers can have matched Warr's faith in spontaneous popular action for the public good. He was mildly concerned about the 'provocations' that men received from interests at variance with their own. He gave no answer to these complications, asking only:

'. . . but is truth divided? Is there not one common principle of freedom, which (if discovered) would reconcile all?'[1]

God would lead the people to their freedoms, and this obviously made him optimistic about the possibility of making men more amenable to union in some common good. Strongly rejecting tradition and fundamental law, he placed great confidence in the rationality of the masses. Discussing law reforms, he said:

'. . . if it were possible for a people to choose such laws as were prejudicial to themselves, this were to forsake their own interest. Here (you'l say) is free choice, but . . . the rule of righteous laws are clear and righteous principles (according to the several appearances of truth within us), for reason is the measure of all just laws.'[2]

His vague rhetoric was not wholly that of the mystic. God-given reason could lead men to the common interest if it consisted in protecting the liberties of others like themselves. The whole structure of Interregnum radicalism was reared upon this premise.

These radical democratic treatments of the public interest share two related aspects. The public interest was something closer to the particular interests of private men than had normally been assumed. It consisted not so much in the use of *arcana imperii* to strengthen the state as in those conditions that would protect private rights. Some ventured no further, saying only that the public good was chiefly a matter of removing the most common private grievances relating to security of life and property. When the army and its well-wishers began their assault on Parliament a new theme emerged. Since the public interest was so closely related to shared particular needs, surely private men were adequate judges of it and might seek their own liberty should their representatives fail them.

Like later democrats, those of the seventeenth century tended to move from the position that common men best knew their

[1] *Privileges* . . ., p. 3. [2] *Corruption* . . ., p. 3.

own interests to the position that they might then understand the public interest. They were not concerned with all of a man's private interests, just those that most closely impinged upon public policy. Nor were they very explicit about the interests of single individuals, preferring to ascribe rationality to the public. However, they were obviously implying certain things about individual men. It happened that the individual interests of concern were rights valuable to all, and, indeed, insecure unless all shared them.[1] Securing life and property was the *sine qua non* of further individual fulfilment. The connection between the public interest and those pressing particular interests that could be satisfied by political means was extremely close. Nor can one say that under the circumstances the transition from particular to general interest was unconvincing; though in order to make it a slightly unconventional view of the public interest was useful. This transition must have seemed fairly natural even to men who were not Levellers. John Sadler observed that since every man naturally sought his own good, it was strange that it was so difficult to find. He then proceeded to discuss his proposals for the good of the commonwealth.[2] Presumably the reader was meant to understand that a knowledge of the first should, in some manner, uncover the second.

If an understanding of the public good as essentially the pre-servation of private rights came naturally to Parliament because of its situation, it was even more necessary to those who visual-ized the masses as agents for *salus populi*. Indeed, it is rather difficult to see what other definition they might have offered. National unity and the Protestant cause were all very well, but they were not the sort of national good that private men could do very much about. By comparison, their claims about know-ing how to gain their own liberties, the security of their existing estates and the opportunity to increase these estates, seem quite reasonable.

Naturally, one cannot dissolve all of the prevailing causes into this pattern. Men had fought over opposed views of the

---

[1] This point is made by C. B. Macpherson in order to explain the Levellers' interesting blend of individualism and concern for the community. See *The Political Theory of Possessive Individualism* (Oxford, 1962), pp. 144 and 157.
[2] J. S., *A Word in Season to All Sorts of Well-Minded People in this . . . Nation* (1646), p. 1.

PRIVATE MEN AND PUBLIC INTEREST

constitution, and to some *salus populi* meant fundamental law.[1] Even here, though, private rights, such as property, might intrude. William Prynne attempted an exhaustive description of the fundamental law and found it to consist of two divisions. The first consisted in the protection of various sorts of private rights, foremost of which was that of private property. The other part, dealing with the constitutional laws of the realm, he called a 'fundamental government'.[2] A number of the democrats rejected fundamental law entirely, except in the sense of private rights, which constituted no restraint on the people's sovereignty. Even Lilburne, who was very concerned with procedural changes in the law, was less eloquent about broad constitutional principles governing the organs of government than about private rights.

Not all of the radical ideas on the public interest could survive the political stability that came with the Protectorate. What remained was the assumption that the regime's chief function was the protection of private interests. Pamphleteers did not yet aver that the public interest was a collection of particular ones, but increasingly they insisted that it be construed in a manner that was inclusive of the interests of private men. In this vein Anthony Norwood described the ideal political system as one in which

'. . . the native equality and liberty of every individual member of this commonwealth is indifferently and unanimously submitted to persons elected by themselves, for advancement of every man's private together with the public interest.'[3]

Adherence to the doctrine of private sacrifice for public necessity had become rather grudging in some quarters. A document submitted to Parliament in 1659 contained the concession that sometimes the 'known interest and propriety' of some private men might have to be sacrificed to the public good. However, it concluded irritably

[1] See J. W. Gough, *Fundamental Law in English Constitutional History* (Oxford, 1955), pp. 99 *et seq.*
[2] Prynne, *A Seasonable, Legall and Historical Vindication . . . of the Good Old Fundamental Liberties, Franchises, Rights and Laws of all English Freemen* (1654), p. 54.
[3] Anthony Norwood, *A Clear Optick Discovering to the Eye of Reason* (1654), p. 17.

'. . . that the general invasion of the public interests, should become at any time a necessary means to the promoting of the common welfare (which is to unsettle every man's propriety, for the improving of the common rights) exceeds our apprehension.'[1]

What was striking was not that the traditional principle was affirmed, but the way in which the writer described the public good.

Perhaps the description of men's property rights as 'public interests' needs some explanation. The most probable reason for this usage is that people needed some way of describing those interests of private men that were legitimate and social, rather than private or purely selfish. One might have used the expression 'particular interest' to describe an interest of this sort, but 'private' and 'particular' were normally used together with no apparent attempt to differentiate between them. Someone may have been moving towards such a distinction when he referred to those rights that were the essence of the public good as 'particular and private interests'. He then added that these terms referred to the protection of private property from the government. He was not claiming absolute independence from control in matters of 'private interest as to *meum* and *tuum*, that is to mine and thine'.[2]

The most significant figure to write of the public interest during these years was Marchamont Nedham, journalist, controversialist and most supple of political chameleons. As an official apologist for the Commonwealth, his arguments carry some weight. He was more sophisticated than most of the writers previously considered, and more inhibited, since he was defending the administration. The main respect in which he deviated from other defenders of a commonwealth stemmed from his more detailed treatment of political institutions and policy. Nedham did not assume that the protection of particular interests constituted the whole of the public interest. He appreciated that there was another, though less important, aspect to the public good. This consisted of the use of '*arcana imperii*' or secrets of state for the security of the community. This area had

[1] Anon., *A Declaration of the Christian Free-Born Subjects . . . of England* (1659), p. 12 (B: Wood 610).
[2] R. M., *Speculum Libertatis Angliae Re restitutae: or, the Looking-Glasse of England's Libertie Really Restored* (1659), pp. 5–6 (BM: E 989).

to be left to the executive, which would be immediately responsible to the legislature for its stewardship. He said that there were two ends to government policy, 'public safety' and 'public equity'.[1] Though he neglected to spell out the difference, obviously the former related to national security.

In introducing this subject at all, he demonstrated the deficiencies of other theories that purported to derive the public good from the citizens' understanding of their own interests. But at the same time he insisted upon the subordinate character of the external aspect of the public good. Anyone trying to defend even a diluted seventeenth-century democracy had to be prepared to refute the charge that this form of government could not discharge the state's traditional responsibilities in defence and diplomacy.[2] Nedham stated in a mild form the basic premise of most democrats when he said that laws passed by a legislature were

'... things that have most influence upon a commonwealth, to its ill or well-being ... wherefore matters of grievance being, matters of common sense, and such are obvious to the people who best know where the shoe wrings them, certainly there is no need of any great skill or judgement in passing or applying a law for ease and remedy, which is the proper work of the people in their supreme assemblies, and such as every ordinary understanding is instructed in by the light of nature.'[3]

Those lesser matters requiring the rarer skills of the courtier might be left to him, under suitable supervision.

The major part of the public good then related to matters that might best be handled by inexperienced men who had the one thing necessary—an understanding of their own affairs. One of his chief boasts for a commonwealth was that it alone 'was the only preservative of propriety in every particular'.[4] This followed from the security of 'the people's interest in the govern-

---

[1] *Mercurius Politicus*, No. 16 (19–26 September 1650), p. 262. A number of issues of this paper appeared in collected form in 1656 under the title *The Excellencie of a Free-State*.

[2] See too *A Persuasive to Mutual Compliance under the Present Government Together With a Plea for a Free State Compared With Monarchy* (1652), pp. 26, 32 and 36 (BM: E 655). Francis Osborne is sometimes credited with writing this.

[3] *Mercurius Politicus*, No. 94 (18–25 March 1652), p. 1474.

[4] *Mercurius Politicus*, No. 92 (4–11 March 1652), pp. 1458–9.

ment' and the fact that in Parliament 'every man's particular interest must needs be fairly provided for'.[1] In general, a commonwealth meant less tension between private and public interests. Nedham explained this as arising from

'. . . that apprehension which every particular man hath of his own immediate share in the public interest.'[2]

Not only was his property secured, but he might feel himself a gainer in all national successes. The individual citizen had both psychological satisfaction here and the prospect of direct personal gain.

Nedham certainly maintained the closest connection between private and public interests. His favourite statement about the public interest rose above the problem of relating it to particular interests. He called 'freedom in a successive course of people's assemblies' the interest of the commonwealth. Opposition to this interest, and not to any particular policy, was the criterion for distinguishing a faction. This was an improvement over many contemporary definitions of the public interest. Quite as important, though, were those comments that did involve particular interests, for this approach was much more typical of the age. Nedham's most memorable single comment here referred to the affairs of a commonwealth such as the United Provinces. He commented favourably on the situation where

'. . . the best part of their interest lies deposited in the hands of the people.'[3]

Greater figures, such as Harrington and Penn, were to echo this theme. Indeed, many of Nedham's remarks on the public interest were later to be discussed by Harrington, where some ambiguities became more apparent.

INTEREST AND INTERESTS

The widespread tendency to conceive the public good as the preservation of private interests has been described without much recourse to the idea of 'interest'. The democratic radicals

---

[1] *Ibid.*, pp. 1456-8.   [2] *Ibid.*, No. 85 (15-22 January 1652), p. 1349.
[3] *Mercurius Politicus*, No. 68 (18-25 September 1651), p. 1100. The same issue advertises a collection of several related tracts and letters called *Anglia Liberata* (1651) (BM: E 643) on p. 68 of which this expression appears.

believed that men best knew their own interests and certainly they favoured their acting in terms of it. Nevertheless, interest itself remained a term of abuse to describe the motivation of wicked governors. Gradually, however, the term acquired respectability. Not all aspects of the complex history of this word are material to the issue, but some parts of it are illuminating.

There can be little doubt that the term in its specifically social applications was continental in origin. Since the distinction between new and old associations of the word could be a fine one, it is not easy to trace the process of assimilation. A word already extant in English simply acquired new meanings, not wholly unrelated to the original meanings. Thus interest as legal right, non-legal concern and as influence might all be used in an apolitical sense. Interest as a political guide to princes and statesmen was current in England before 1640, almost invariably in translations from French or Italian.[1]

As far as can be ascertained, it was the Huguenot general and statesman the Duke of Rohan who popularized the term in England.[2] Rohan had referred to 'interest' in most of the contexts relevant to political thought. His best-known contributions dealt with the interest of states, and he used the expression 'interest of England' before it was in general use in that country. The 'interest of the prince' was another of his favourite expressions, though it was perhaps more familiar. Finally, he used interest to apply to the private and selfish designs of private men. This last meaning, the most general of all, was implicit in all of his works, but received special attention only in a minor piece not translated until 1660. Here he observed in typical aphoristic fashion

'. . . that rhetoric which touches not the interests of those we would persuade hath seldom any operation upon them.'[3]

[1] See R. Dallington, *Aphorisms Civill and Militarie* . . . (1613) (from Guicciardini), p. 33; Thomas Wright, *The Passions of the Mind in Generall in Six Books* (1620), p. 204 (quoting Botero); and Leonard Marande, *The Judgement of Humane Actions*, trans. J. Reynolds (1629), p. 20.

[2] See Rohan, *Treatise of the Interests of the Princes and States of Christendom*, trans. H. Hunt (1640). There was a second edition in 1641. A study of Rohan's influence in England is long overdue.

[3] *The Memoires of the Duke of Rohan . . . Together with Divers Political Discourses upon Several Occasions*, trans. G. Bridges (1660), Discourse V, p. 25. A cursory

Rohan's most immediate and obvious influence was surely upon the spate of works on the 'interest of England', which appeared with the Civil War and continued until the end of the century and beyond. Between 1641 and 1659 there were a number of tracts on this subject. While not all of them quoted Rohan, it is surely significant that the title was not used on any English book until his chief work was translated; nor is there evidence of its use in the body of texts. Some, such as Calybute Downing, were not entirely at home with the word, complaining that

'. . . foreign and modern statists take profit for the sense of interest, where honesty is not their principal.'[1]

He mentioned Rohan, but in a neutral way. Later writers, like Thomas Goodwin, were very impressed by Rohan's reputation as a champion of the Protestant cause. Goodwin quoted 'worthy Rohan' who was sound on 'civil interest'.[2] Richard Hawkins, writing on the 'Interest of England', took the French statesman as his basic text.[3] Certainly there were writers on current affairs who used the expression while admitting no debt to Rohan, but even some of them seem to have got it at one remove. Thus Simon Ford, who used it as the title of the companion sermon to Goodwin's, obviously borrowed it from him.[4] William Prynne

survey of English booksellers' catalogues from around the year 1680 suggests that the 1646 French edition of the *Memoires* commonly appeared in libraries then being sold. John Cook, one of the earlier English users of 'interest', quotes from that edition. See *King Charles, His Case* (1649), pp. 32–4.
[1] Downing, *A Discourse Upon the Interest of England Considered* (1641), p. 3. The statist in question may well have been René de Faucigny-Lucinge, who, in treating the motives of princes, said: 'we will then only meddle with profit which we may term interest'. See *The Beginning, Continuance and Decay of Estates*, trans. J. Finet (1606), p. 133. Since he felt the need of defining the term, it was perhaps then a fairly novel part of French political vocabulary. Étienne Thuau's authoritative account of French thought in this period records two of Rohan's contemporaries, Jean de Silhon and Phillippe de Béthune, who emphasized 'interest' before Rohan did. Both published in the years 1631–2. See *Raison D'État et Pensée Politique a L'Époque de Richelieu* (Paris, n.d.), p. 267.
[2] Goodwin, *The Great Interest of States and Kingdomes* (1646), pp. 52–3. See too *England's Interest in the Protestant Cause* (1659), p. 1. The author was probably John Durie.
[3] Hawkins, *A Discourse of the Nationall Excellencie of England* (1657), Part II, pp. 216–23.
[4] Ford, *The Great Interest of States and Kingdomes* (1646).

allowed a reference to the interest of England and its rulers to intrude into his erudite citations from legal history. Scrupulous as always, he cited Rohan as his source.[1]

Writings of this sort are chiefly relevant to the present undertaking because they encouraged the political use of 'interest'. Various theories explaining the importance of such writings have been offered from time to time. Thus 'interest' has been used as a measure of the receptivity of Englishmen to Machiavellian statecraft.[2] This is not entirely convincing. No group more rapidly made the term its own than the preachers, and advice about one's true interest thundered from the pulpit for the remainder of the century. It seems probable that Rohan's stature in England contributed to this great popularity. He had none of the undesirable features of other alien statists, such as Machiavelli. Here was a Protestant stalwart, a relative of the king who had led a rebellion against authority and a political and military sage, whose advice on English liberty might serve the turn of all parties.[3]

As it happened, some of the writers who remarked on the new vogue in political vocabulary were unsympathetic, but they did not impugn Rohan. He seems only to have done the cause good. Critical observations were of two sorts. Firstly, there were moralists who simply bewailed the prevalence of self-interest as a condition, without commenting on the word 'interest'. 'It is an

[1] Prynne, *The Soveraigne Power of Parliaments and Kingdomes* (1643), Part IV, p. 208.

[2] See Felix Raab, *The English Face of Machiavelli* (London, 1964), p. 236. Apart from the strong evidence that it was Rohan who was the immediate influence upon English writers, many users of the term were far from advocating any divorce between religion and policy. Raab was aware that 'interest' was not a word used by Machiavelli.

[3] Since enemies of King Charles made much of his perfidy in abandoning Rohan and the garrison of Rochel in 1628, one might have anticipated a certain coolness towards Rohan by the royalists. At least one of them tried to vindicate this action by alleging faults by Rohan's lieutenants, but he was careful not to attack Rohan himself. See Anon., *Treason's Anatomie or the Duty of a Loyall Subject* (1647), p. 13 (BM: E 427). Most royalists seem to have shared Sir Philip Warwick's opinion that Rohan was a 'very learned and wise statesman'. See *Memoires of the Reign of King Charles I* (2nd edn., 1702), p. 22. A hitherto unidentified manuscript version of the *Treatise* is among the Clarendon papers in the Bodleian. See Clarendon MSS. 130. The Earl of Derby, a prominent royalist, summarized certain parts of the same work, presumably for his own use. See Sloane MSS. 874, fols. 13–16 (BM).

age of interest, great, never greater', thus a critic of the law.[1] Others with a feeling for etymological detail were more specific.

One such writer showed clearly the feelings of those democrats who condemned any form of self-interest on the part of magistrates and yet considered it natural for private men to seek their own interests. He complained of 'state terms of interest, jewels and flowers of the crown' used to elevate prerogative, while in fact

'. . . the great interest (which word is now the only ideal that men fall down and worship) of government and governours is the glory of God and the good of mankind.'[2]

A very interesting passage completed the indictment:

'. . . in a word, words by tract of time degenerate like men. Tirannus once was taken in the better part, when kings were better commonwealthsmen. . . . So was the word Interest, whilst it was of public cognizance, and all Queen Elizabeth's days kept itself sober by drinking English beer till it was made drunk with Fruntiniack and the king and his courtiers by use upon use, and interest upon interest had almost swallowed up the people's principal.'[3]

So in the same passage he managed to convey both the alien origin of interest, in other than the sense of right, and the idea that the demands of the people were derived from some realm that overrode mere sordid interests. The point at issue was royal infringement on the 'public interest' in the name of 'reason of state'. The king wrongly supposed that there was a court monopoly on this sort of reason.[4] Clearly the most important factor in redefining the word interest lay in its application to cases where the old meaning of legal right or concern was not entirely relevant. Interest might then be linked to natural rights or to the people's 'principal'. Most seventeenth-century radicals insisted that the people's interests had to appear in some sort of ethical

---

[1] Charles Cocke, *England's Compleat Law-Judge and Lawyer* (1656), sig. B 2. See too Robert Loveday, *Letters Domestick and Foreign* (1659), letter III, p. 3.
[2] Anon., *No Interest Beyond the Principal, or the Court Camissado* (1648), p. 10 (BM: E 437).
[3] *Ibid.*, p. 10.
[4] *Ibid.*, p. 9. This same complaint about the excuse of reason of state might also be turned against the Parliament. See Anon., *The State of the Kingdome Represented to the People* (1648), p. 7.

dress. Thus the narrow lawyer's meaning of interest gave way to 'interest' in the sense of any right or legitimate claim, and once the legal associations were weakened, it was not easy to say what constituted legitimacy. Hence all claims might be interests.

The sense of unease that greeted interest in its political use might apply as well to national as personal matters. A minister on the Isle of Wight chose to note this aspect, saying:

'Interest hath been a great word among us for divers years and it is so still; and a national interest is sometimes talked of.'[1]

Often interest was redefined, though not in any way that clearly compared the old meaning with the new. William Sedgewicke exemplifies the process of taming the naughty continental term. He felt that in proclaiming the people's interests the army had 'mangled' the true meaning of the term:

'. . . the word interest, which is of a uniting signification, *inter esse*, is to be in, or amongst each other. The public hath its interest in the king, and the king in the public . . . they have the same *esse* or interest, which is to be together in each other.'[2]

Joseph Symonds was less ingenious and more in line with contemporary usage; while thinking largely in a theological context, he indicated the difference between the old legal title and the new interest. Interest, he said, 'in all things is less than possession'; it was a 'state of expectation'.[3] Here he was certainly in error; actually both meanings were current, but the new meaning was as defined by him.

Another took it upon himself to clear 'interest' from its dubious connotations without returning to the innocuous legal meaning. He was trying to justify his own concern for church livings and anticipated a cynical interpretation of his intentions. Moralists would wring their hands and say:

'. . . ah this interest! Whether [sic] it will carry men! How loth you are to plead against it, or let that go in which your gain lies.'[4]

[1] Edward Buckler, *Salus Populi, or a Nation's Happiness* (1658), pp. 23-4.
[2] Sedgwicke, *The Leaves of the Tree of Life* . . . (1648), p. 113, and *Justice Upon the Armie-Remonstrance* (1649), p. 11.
[3] Symonds, *Three Treatises* (1653), pp. 246-7.
[4] Anon., *The Establishment, or a Discourse Tending to the Setling of the Minds of Men About Some of the Chief Controversies of the Present Times* (1653), p. 9 (BM: E 720).

Instead of covering himself with pious disclaimers, this writer faced the issue of seeking one's interest:

'. . . whatever it is that a man hath interest in, if that interest (as he conceives at least) be a just interest, shall he not have liberty to plead for it. . . . Must he pass for a covetous worldling, a self seeker, a lover of his profit, and a carnal interest more than truth . . . because he asks for his own?'[1]

Of course there was no infallible guide to the proper extent of one's interest, but one's own understanding had to be the starting datum.

By the late years of the Protectorate, interest was firmly established in political vocabulary, and had been adapted to general use in all social contexts. Numerous documents show how deep an impression it had made, and how frequently it was introduced into political discourse if only as a pleonasm. The speeches of the Lord Protector no doubt contributed to the vogue; for he used it in a wide variety of senses. In this case, and in others, the word seems to have been almost extraneous, since other words carried the meaning of the passages.[2] Interest had become *de rigueur* for statesmanlike pronouncements, though one wonders if listeners or readers were very much enlightened by its use.

No doubt the increasingly favourable connotation of 'interest' in domestic politics was related to the established place in foreign affairs that it owned to Rohan. Because of Rohan's own concern for the traditional roles of the warrior and courtier, it is more difficult to establish a direct connection with domestic applications of interest. Rohan had always professed the highest regard for the public good and had protested his own innocence of self-love, though he seemed to suspect everyone else! It was not then surprising that an earnest cleric should see no incongruity in quoting this apostle of interest in a work aimed against self-love.[3] Rohan did have a message relating to domestic politics and, as we shall see, his comments on 'interest' were

[1] *Ibid.*, p. 10. Cf. Nathaniel Burt, *An Appeal from Chancery* (1653), p. 1, where the people were urged to remain true to their 'liberties and self-interests'.
[2] See his speech of September 1654 in *Writings and Speeches, op. cit.*, Vol. III, pp. 434-42. The same tendency appears in a tract by Richard Lawrence, *The Interest of England in the Irish Transplantation* (1655), pp. 3, 10 and 16.
[3] John Cardell, *Morbus Epidemicus, or the Danger of Self-Seeking* (1650), p. 31.

applied to that sphere. He held that England, more than all other states, could flourish only if it preserved national unity.[1] This certainly served, in one way, to make his works relevant to men who were more concerned with the internal state of England than with the motions of the European balance of power.

It seems doubtful that the new expressions, such as the 'interest of England', represented any immediate change in the connection between private interests and that of the nation. However, this is exactly what is claimed for them by Charles A. Beard. He has suggested that such terms had associations entirely different from traditional notions about dynastic interest and the will of the prince. The popularity of the new language thus becomes a victory for policies that were more closely related to the concerns of private men than were the *arcana imperii* of the past.[2] This theory is appealing, if only because it suggests a clear pattern in an otherwise muddled course of development. However, it must be qualified in some respects. There was no essential meaning in the expression 'interest of England' that had not been present in references to 'England's weal' and similar expressions. Certainly 'reason of state' ceased to be the opaque cloak for royal ambition that it had once been, but this must be explained by the course of political history and not by changed vocabulary. Beard took a long view of developments and noted that a changed content for the national interest and new language for discussions of it dated from the same period. It is only because he failed to make any clear assertion that he avoided the '*post hoc*' fallacy.

While England's interest might as easily be represented by a prince as by a Parliament, there may have been some connection between changes of language and those of substance. Reason of state and the will of the prince were certainly not notions that could be readily applied to private men. 'Interest' made the journey from the council chamber to the market-place very quickly. This at least meant that the concerns of private

---

[1] *Treatise of the Interests of Princes* . . ., p. 54. Here he assumed that unity was the chief consideration in England's interest. His comments on other states dwelt almost exclusively on matters of diplomacy.
[2] C. A. Beard, *The Idea of the National Interest* (New York, 1934), pp. 15 and 24. The main problem with this pioneering study is that the historical section is very brief and thus compresses too many ideas into too small a compass.

men and those of the community might be described in the same terms, thus perhaps facilitating the process of identifying the two. However, one's claims here must be very modest, bearing in mind that French government and society did not change with the use of expressions such as 'the interest of France'.

The most important remaining stage in the history of the word 'interest' was reached before the Restoration. Interest came to be treated as a social force, in a sense quite removed from any notions of a right that might be possessed by an individual and equally unrelated to the ends of foreign policy. The pioneers here were Charles Herle and Marchamont Nedham. Herle had been one of the first to use the term in a political context. In a later work, published in 1655, he looked back upon the last few years, during which the word had 'much come into use among us'.[1] In its ordinary use, he said, it meant 'concernment' and 'importance' to oneself. He also recognized its meaning as influence, which he called 'power', as in having interest in a friend or a party. Herle's explanation also covered the curious habit of some writers of using 'interest' very much in the sense of the nature or the normal function of a thing. People occasionally referred to the interest of inanimate objects.[2] It was one way of naturalizing the term, by equating it with that law of nature commonly thought to be reflected in the activities and nature of all things. Herle showed his acceptance of this usage when he described interest as 'the centre of everything's safety' and noted that one might then speak of a stone's interest in obeying gravity and staying on the ground.[3]

Quite the most important passage contained his reference to a French proverb, 'interest will not lie'. He understood this as meaning that

'. . . if a man know what is his true interest, he is undoubted true to it.'[4]

In this form the idea might apply to all human affairs; in any

[1] Herle, *Wisdom's Tripos* . . . (1655), p. 169.
[2] See John Saltmarsh, *Dawnings of Light* (1644), p. 2.   [3] Herle, *loc. cit.*
[4] Herle, p. 170. The origin of this maxim is a matter of doubt. Consultation of a number of books of French proverbs of the period has yielded no information, hence it cannot have been very common, if it existed in French at all. The closest approximation in any French work was Rohan's 'l'interest seul ne peut jamais manquer', *De l'Interest des Princes et Estates de la Chrestienté* (Paris, 1638), p. 1.

43

conceivable circumstances, a man would do the best he could for himself. The maxim made no claims about people's capacity to grasp this interest. It was an analytical proposition that simply told one what interest meant. Interest could never lead one astray, since a failure established that the proposed course of action had not been one's true interest. This was not very helpful.

Nedham repeated this maxim, which he attributed to 'politicians' in general. He suggested a double meaning for the expression. One meaning was Herle's; if a man stated his interest correctly and followed it, he would reach his ends. Nedham's primary meaning looked to the position of the observer rather than the political actor. Given the truth of Herle's interpretation, it followed that

'. . . if you can apprehend wherein a man's interest to any particular game on foot doth consist, you may surely know, if the man be prudent, whereabout to have him, that is, how to judge of his design.'[1]

Both Herle and Nedham had their own ideas on the public good, but this is not our concern here. The maxim that they popularized brought the term interest to the forefront of political discourse. It also turned into a commonplace the observation that the actors in political life would seek their interests as they understood them. In this atmosphere new ideas about the public interest become more comprehensible. By the time of the Restoration, self-interest had gained a measure of respectability. For some this constituted an acceptance of the inevitable, for others the predictability of interest became a positive good.

Interest had played one further role in the Civil War. It had made its début with reference to the political designs of kings and then of ordinary men. Before long, the term underwent a further extension in meaning and came to be associated not only with politically relevant concerns but with the groups so concerned. Thus interest went the way of 'common weal' when it stood both for the polity and the good of that polity.

The social basis for this extension in meaning was established as soon as a number of parties appeared on the scene. As long as the king and Parliament were the main protagonists, the war

[1] Nedham, *Interest will Not Lie, or a View of England's True Interest* (1659) p. 3.

might be seen as a struggle between two of the three estates. The bishops, whose status had been a critical issue early in the conflict, enjoyed an anomalous position, sometimes seen as an estate apart, sometimes as part of the nobility. As soon as the populace was drawn into the struggle, the old model of three estates failed as a basis for political discussion. It had been remarkably flexible, referring equally well to three legal orders or to the various ranks of society. One factor that must surely have weakened the idea of estates was the failure after 1642 to agree what the estates were.[1] The idea of estates did not die overnight, but gradually they were being replaced by other units, both in life and in thought.

Peter Heylin, the Anglican historian and divine, saw the decline of the estates as symptomatic of the crumbling of the whole political system. The danger was that the intrusion of new forces into the process of making policy replaced the serene tripartite balance with chaos. Should the '*opinionum multitudo*' be drawn in,

'. . . the differences of opinion, and pretence of interesses, would keep them at perpetual distance.'[2]

[1] On the origins of confusion about what constituted the estates see C. C. Weston, 'The Theory of Mixed Monarchy Under Charles I and After', *English Historical Review*, Vol. 75 (1960), pp. 426–43. The debate continued until the Glorious Revolution. When the estates were restored in their old form, some people still referred to them as interests. See Anon., *The Parallel or, An Account of the Growth of Knavery, under the Pretext of Arbitrary Government* (1679), p. 8 (B: Ashm. 1680). The writer referred to king, lords and commons as 'sober interests'. It was no longer safe to call the king an estate in the casual way of some earlier writers, since this might be used to reduce his authority. 'Estate' was losing its primary meaning so that its use in the old sense had to be explained. Parliament came to be described as 'a body corporate, consisting (according to the first acceptation of the word) of the three estates of the realm'. G. Miege, *The New State of England in Three Parts* (1691), Book III, p. 2. An early eighteenth-century Whig called the practice of distinguishing estates in Parliament a modern French idea, imported from an irrational love of things foreign, and quite unprofitable. See Anon., *Parliamentary Right Maintained, or the Hanover Succession Justified* (1714), p. 52 (B: 8° Rawl. 550). The declining relevance of estates for eighteenth-century politics has been ably discussed by J. R. Pole in his *Political Representation in England and the Origins of the American Republic* (London, 1966), pp. 169–70 and 526–9. He does not consider earlier developments.

[2] 'The Stumbling-Block of Disobedience' (1644), in *The Historical and Miscellaneous Tracts of . . . P. Heylyn* (1681), p. 687.

Another author, of the same persuasion, chose a more obscure idiom in which to make the point. He looked back to an oracular statement by one of the ancients that

'. . . that state cannot subsist where the number of five joined to the number of three, maketh a dissonant, or a discordant harmony.'

Every kingdom, he insisted, 'generally consisteth of three estates, viz. the king or prince, the nobility and the commons'.[1]

The same conditions were greeted with joy by incipient republicans. The demise of the conventional scheme of estates might produce a greater degree of unanimity. Thus reducing three estates to one might mean that there were not 'so many interests to weigh against the public'.[2] Another writer sought much the same arrangement, but with more stress upon the inadequacy of the estates as descriptive tools. The whole concept of estates was open to doubt, since the identity of the estates fluctuated according to the exigencies of political propaganda. Far better, he thought, to view government as 'just so many men, the major part concluding'.[3] For every observer who mentioned the decreased relevance of estates, there were many who simply ignored them. This was a more formidable accomplishment in the early years than after the king and the lords had been formally obliterated.

The example of Thomas Povey of Gray's Inn is instructive in this regard. Owing to its brevity and its anonymity, his work has been entirely forgotten, but it stands as an unexcelled plea for moderation, common sense and compromise in politics. He had nothing at all to say about estates; instead he identified the politically significant units as the king, clergy, nobility, gentry, the City and rural economic interests. The problem was the usual one of somehow discerning the 'public interest', which, in this instance, consisted in getting out of the current difficulties.[4] This interest could be realized if men would just be rational, lay aside extravagant passions and conceits and pursue their interests dis-

---

[1] Anon., *The Distractions of our Times* (1643), p. 2 (B: Ashm. 991).

[2] Anon., *The State of the Kingdome Represented to the People* (1648), pp. 17–18.

[3] J. P., *The City-Remonstrance Remonstrated* (1646), pp. 23 and 27 (B: G.P. 1786).

[4] *The Moderator, Expecting Sudden Peace of Certain Ruine* (1642), p. 13 (BM: E 89). The tract was anonymous, but contemporary sources [BM: E 93 (16); E 462 (24)] identify Povey as the author.

passionately. He proceeded to demonstrate to each of the parties that some tolerable compromise would be in its 'interest'. The people to whom he appealed did not have to be saints:

'... we shall find all or most of these notions to be requisite in every one that will consider and follow his interest as he is an English subject.'[1]

Povey simultaneously asked the various parties to follow their interests and to disavow the political 'passions and conceits' that had divided them. He pictured the economic advantages of peace and compromise; thus appealing to interests that had nothing to do with the slogans of parties.

He revealed the bent of his argument when he attacked the dogmatic constitutional principles held by all parties. With the two chief parties about equal in strength, it was the proper time to negotiate with all participating 'according to their interests'. Since the parties were to look to their interests, this limited the sort of agreement that was possible. The exact character of the agreement could not be described, since it was dependent upon future developments. It could already be said, though, that it was not 'such a truth, as the rigid protagonists of both sides intend'. It had to be understood that

'... state-truth is the brat of imagination, and never had any real being . . . when ambition and interest shall be weeded out of the hearts of men, I will look [for] this purity, this truth.'[2]

There was the same appreciation of the relativity of any public good predicated upon human interests, that Hobbes and his followers were to show. For present purposes, however, Povey is important because he realized that accommodation had to be tailored to the various selfish interests in contention. The public interest was clearly not an absolute remote from particular interests; the reconciliation of these interests was the very stuff of it. Understandably, Povey did not find it easy to say how divergent interests might be combined, so he did not try.

Povey had diverted attention from the formal estates of the realm to the interests of other political units. It was not until 1647 that circumstances made this perspective the dominant one. The change came quite dramatically in June of that year

---

[1] *The Moderator, Expecting Sudden Peace or Certain Ruine* (1642), p. 18.
[2] *Ibid.,* p. 27.

and the agent was Marchamont Nedham, then a royalist pamphleteer. His tract led Civil War argument into a new phase, again
under the shadow of the Duke of Rohan. Nedham saw his
approach as tending to the 'general good', so there is no problem about the relevance of his remarks to that theme.[1] While the
professed aim was the securing of a compromise based on the
interests of the various parties, Nedham's analysis and recommendations were extremely tendentious, since he was in the pay
of King Charles.

He began with the assertion that

' . . no one can take offence, since I state the interests of all indifferently, pointing out to each the way to advance and preserve their
own party, and I shall commend to them what the Duke of Rohan
saith of the states of Europe, that according as they follow their
proper interests, they thrive or fail in success, so the parties now on
foot in the kingdom must look to stand or fall upon the same
ground.'[2]

Thus advice originally aimed at the needs of independent states
came to be applied to interests within a single state. The five
chief parties in the kingdom were to come together in a 'union
of interests'. There was no need for all of them to dissolve their
particular interests in the general good, though they could not
all obtain their mutually incompatible ends. Nedham's emphasis was quite the reverse. All parties should limit themselves to
proper and 'peculiar' interests.[3]

Nedham may not have been quite the first since Povey to
write in this vein. Certainly he was not the last, as his numerous
imitators attest.[4] Few ideas can have been expressed more frequently in the years 1647–9 and again in 1659–60 than that conveyed by the expression 'union of interests'.[5] The vocabulary of

[1] Nedham, *The Case of the Kingdom Stated* (1647), p. 20.   [2] *Ibid.*, sig. A 2ᵛ.
[3] *The Case of the Kingdom Stated* (1647), p. 18.
[4] Certain tracts faithful to Nedham's style may have been by him. One
elaborate survey of 'interests', called *Good English . . .* (1648) (BM: E 441), is
probably his, especially since he praised it in his newspaper. See *Mercurius
Pragmaticus*, Vol. 2, No. 5 (25 April–8 May 1648), p. 8.
[5] Not everyone approved of such a union. Clement Walker saw in Cromwell's efforts to promote a 'union of interests' only tyranny. See *Anarchia
Anglicana or the History of Independency* (1648), Part I, pp. 84–5. Walker called
the various parties in the nation 'public interests', to distinguish them from
selfish, personal interests. See p. 39.

the royal proclamations altered at about the same time. Whereas before Charles had limited himself to declaring his concern for the common good, beginning in September 1647, his offer became that of the 'satisfaction of all interests'.[1] One writer who sought such a union visualized a parcelling out of freedom and safety, saying:

'. . . there is . . . enough to satisfy all parties, all just interests; and there wants only a meeting of ingenious men of all parties and interests, to divide to every one a due portion.'[2]

The great virtue of the slogan of a 'union of interests' was that it suggested all of the right things regarding unity and particular interests, and so by a judicious vagueness on details managed to have it both ways.

Once strong government had been re-established, the tone of this literature changed and it became a matter of reconciling the disaffected to a *fait accompli* in which their interests might be accommodated as far as possible.[3] Those who wrote in this way assumed that most men would not care for the public interest unless something were done to preserve, if not to advance, their own interests. Indeed, a tendency noted before persisted, and appeals were made to immediate personal gain in preference to the various dangerous 'humours' of political principle.[4]

Of course, there remained people who, while recognizing the presence of interests, still hoped that they would cast aside all private aims and love one another. Eventually the interest vocabulary penetrated most persuasions and levels of sophistication. The point was demonstrated when Christopher Feake, the Fifth Monarchist, presented a complicated table of all the 'separate and joint interests' in the land.[5] This turned out to be more a menu than anything else, and he ended his discourse with the happy thought that his party would 'swallow' all the rest.

---

[1] *The King's Most Gracious Messages for Peace and a Personal Treaty* (1648), pp. 75, 88 and 106 (BM: E 438).
[2] Anon., *Propositions for Peace by a Union of Interests* (1648), p. 6 (BM: E 446).
[3] See Anon., *Vox Pacifica, or a Perswasive to Peace: Directed to Each Party and Interest* . . . (1649) (BM: E 1365), and Nedham, *The Case of the Commonwealth of England Stated* (1650).
[4] *Vox Pacifica*, p. 14.
[5] C. Feake, *A Beam of Light* . . . (1659), pp. 53–8.

The death of the Lord Protector brought a return to fluid political conditions and the earlier genre of literature. Nedham remained in the foreground, but he was not alone. Two examples may serve to suggest the tone of later writings. One of the numerous ephemeral news sheets set out the duties of the English Parliament. Chief among them was the preservation of all parties; in their deliberations 'the several interests of the nation they are to respect as land-marks'.[1] General Monck gave even clearer testimony of the sort of appeal that was considered effective propaganda. His mendacious statement of loyalty to the Commonwealth contained a discussion of the many new interests thrown up by the war. He promised to respect them, for

'. . . these interests again are so interwoven by purchases and inter-marriages . . . it may well be taken for granted that no government can be either good, peaceful or lasting to these nations, that doth not rationally include and comprehend the security and preservation of all the aforesaid interests . . .'

The present Parliament was the means of 'comprehending the whole interest of these nations' for it was 'comprehensive of all interests both spiritual and civil'.[2] There could be no better indication that he chose to see the interest of the nation as composed of the satisfaction of a variety of partial interests. Those who wrote of the interest of the nation being dispersed in the hands of the people expressed the same thought.

Having shown that a political scene composed of interests was a common theme, it remains to say what it meant. An interest was not necessarily very different from an estate or a degree of mankind, but there were some differences. Estates, when used precisely in a legal sense, were those divisions of the people of which the constitution took cognizance. In a less technical sense the estates were all of the ranks, and perhaps even all of the professions, in the land. On the whole, estates might be seen as bodies with traditional rights and duties and a certain ascrip-

---

[1] *The Faithful Scout*, No. 9 (17 June 1659), p. 84. The same expression appears in a tract by one of Harrington's followers. See John Streater, *A Shield Against the Parthian Dart* (1659), p. 12.
[2] *A Letter of General Monck's Dated at Leicester 23 Jan. . . . to be Communicated unto the Rest of the Gentry of Devon* (1660), pp. 5 and 6–7 (BM: E 1013).

tive status. One might also suggest with Nedham that the interests in the country adhere to their proper business, but here there was an arbitrary quality about its scope. Interests, in the sense of parties, were self-interested, if they were nothing else; thus they defined their own interests.

It availed one little to ask interests to put aside all self-regard and sink their lot with the public. There had to be some *quid pro quo*. Two answers came to be offered in the Interregnum, both used rather indiscriminately. Government was to take in all interests in the sense of giving all some measure of satisfaction, and certainly by preserving all parties. This was vague, as Povey had shown it had to be. Interest was a conveniently vague term. Preserving an interest in the government might only mean that the government would continue to recognize certain influences; it need not mean that the party involved would have much power.

It was also possible to appeal to the individual members of an 'interest' in a manner above, or below, party. The unloved Dr. John Fell might do both at once. He said that the real national good was not the welfare of one party but of all, and so tried to show how all interests might be secured and advanced. At the same time he insisted that citizens should be considered not as members of various interests but as private men. In this capacity they would then be concerned with such aspects of the general interest as establishing the fundamental laws 'upon which every one's prosperity and liberty are built'.[1]

It was then possible to appeal to two different sorts of interest belonging to the members of any party. No one said more distinctly than Fell that there was a 'common national interest' to be distinguished from particular interests. Yet he also felt compelled to emphasize the need of a ruler whose private interest (i.e. the national interest) least contradicted the aims of particular parties.[2] The whole tract consisted of two sets of conditions that had to be met by any settlement, common interests

---

[1] *The Interest of England Stated* (1659), p. 4. Fell has been generally accepted as the author of this anonymous tract.

[2] Fell, p. 4. Apart from the two factors already mentioned, the other measures that were in the general interest were the settlement of religion, the procuration of a general indemnity, the revival of trade and the attainment of a foreign alliance.

and the claims of particular ones. The two were not perfectly distinguishable, since one of the chief aspects of the common interest was nothing else than giving the greatest possible satisfaction to the various particular interests. He made his task all the more difficult by paying very little attention to considerations such as national defence.

The ambiguity in his approach is no mere product of sterile textual analysis. It was appreciated and exploited by the prolific Nedham, still, as yet, a Commonwealthsman. He seized upon the statement that the public interest was not the interest of one party but of all. This he deemed the most sensible thing in the whole tract.[1] Since the public interest might be seen as somehow the interests of all parties collected, Nedham neglected all those remarks about the components of any 'common national interest', apart from specifically party interests. He proceeded to show by reference only to the various parties and their interests how it was not in the national interest to bring back a king. This approach rested on the tacit assumption that one could specify those partial interests that together exhausted the national interest. This might perhaps follow from the literal sense of some of Fell's remarks, but it wholly violated their spirit and intent. One thing that made Nedham's argument a little more credible was that he added to the list of interests the Neuters, the unorganized and uncommitted. This reduced the 'public' to one party among many. His argument was made all the more credible by his having only to show that all parties could coalesce in a negative policy, though this necessarily implied the positive public interest of maintaining the *status quo*. Clearly, Nedham held that the public interest consisted in the flourishing of trade (identified as the City's interest) and 'satisfaction to all parties'.[2]

In the heat of Civil War polemics men had been forced to adopt the vocabulary and attitudes of individualism. All of the examples cited here bear the marks of controversial literature. In a sense this means that opinions regarding the public interest may not have the same philosophical weight as those conceived in disinterested reflection about the nature of society. Philosophical systems, however tendentious, would have expressed

[1] *Interest Will Not Lie* (1659), p. 4.
[2] *Interest Will Not Lie*, p. 46.

these ideas with greater clarity and consistency. But such appeals were meant to convince, probably did convince many, or they would not have appeared so frequently in diverse forms.

A variety of factors forced the political argument of these years into the relevant patterns. The tendency to conceive of the pressing problems as domestic, the need of relating the interests of governors and governed and the appreciation that the significant political units were interests, all contributed to the pattern. Circumstances caused writers to frame an understanding of the public interest coloured by the requirement that it should be a condition understood by common men and realizable by their activities; less persuasively, they sometimes suggested that somehow a union of interests might encompass all antagonistic forces.

These ideas did not immediately sweep all before them. For one thing, they were not always sensible, being verbal, rather than institutional, solutions. A second factor was that they were functionally limited. They represented the most convenient political weapons for those who wished to justify a more popular form of government or who were trying to persuade warring factions that some solution was possible short of sinking to universal submission before the restored king. The people who used these arguments were usually cast in the role of citizen rather than ruler, upholding the cause of the disaffected, not the side of authority. Nedham the shrill spokesman for a faction used different tones from Nedham the Cromwellian apologist, a Milton for the vulgar. Monck was clearly disingenuous in his claims, but when addressing a public that he conceived to be republican, he did not hesitate to see the national interest as so many particular ones. Royalists in power soon forgot such language. Levellers of all sorts were tempted to simplify political decisions to the level of private ones. Their superiors in a revolutionary regime understandably thought otherwise and looked to the traditional concerns of state. Here were differences in perspective not capable of resolution by mere argument, but only by changing roles.

The explicit disagreement between Parker and his opponents was the same as that between the democratic radicals and the Cromwellian establishment or that between Nedham and Fell. Years later William Penn and John Nalson would be similarly

E 53

divided. One side was prone to minimize the relevance of national power, the other was insensitive to the claims of particular interests, of individuals or groups. This meant that when a party was thrown into the appropriate circumstances it could find a ready-made definition of the public interest. This had not always been so, but from 1640 it was so.

II

HOBBESIAN PERSPECTIVES ON
THE PUBLIC GOOD

THE KING'S INTEREST

A NUMBER OF FACTORS contributed to the growing accommodation between particular interests and those of the public. Certainly the idea of 'interest' as a general social category was relevant, so too was the tendency to analyse society in terms of 'interests'. Both tendencies, however, were to a degree dependent on new perspectives in human psychology.

The seventeenth century saw certain refinements in conventional opinions about the human mind. Emerging in French thought, initially in theological speculation, these ideas were gradually secularized. One looks in vain for satisfactory explanations of their origin, but perhaps the political upheaval of France at the turn of the century may account in part for the cult of the self.[1] However, it was in England that the new preoccupation took root in a way conducive to critical thought about the public interest. The France of Richelieu and Mazarin stressed the subordination of individuals to the dictates of *raison d'état* in ever more compelling terms.[2] In an England where absolutism was to be checked self-interest might more effectively

---

[1] Recent discussions of the rise of this concern include A. J. Krailsheimer, *Studies in Self-Interest from Descartes to La Bruyère* (Oxford, 1962), esp. pp. 1–30, and Anthony Levi, *French Moralists, The Theory of the Passions, 1505 to 1649* (Oxford, 1964), esp. pp. 225–33.
[2] See F. E. Sutcliffe, *Guez de Balzac et son Temps, Litterature et Politique* (Paris, 1959), pp. 190–202 and 252.

challenge the common good, even, as events were to show, in the works of men friendly to monarchy. Political opportunity thus led English thought to conclusions unknown to Balzac's *Prince*, or indeed the *Mazarinades*.

The writers of interest here all wrote about psychological egoism. What is more, they wrote about it in a relatively new way. Now neither an appreciation of the self-interested side of human nature nor frank appeals to it was novel. After all, when clerics of the day spoke about original sin, they were pointing at a number of causes of frailty, high among which was self-love. Few preachers can have doubted that most men were selfish. Similarly, there was a long-standing genre of literature dealing with the various orders of society and the failure of all, or most of them, to contribute to the common good, if necessary at the expense of their own profit. Self-interest had been a hallmark of Machiavelli's work and of his numerous imitators. Machiavelli and his followers, though, imposed certain limits to the prevalence of self-interest. Avowedly statist works concentrated upon the figure of the prince, and whatever leeway may have been allowed him, no corresponding latitude extended to the ordinary citizen, though Machiavelli appreciated the failings of ordinary men. The state, or its personal embodiment in the prince, was placed before the good of individuals in more or less the same way as in the writings of the Christian humanists.[1] Even in the case of the prince, emphasis remained medieval in considering the manner in which he could best execute his function for the common good.

The most noticeable thing about many of the conventional comments on human nature was not that they ignored self-interest but that they failed to examine the possible limits to altruism. Sermons provide a very good index for feelings on this point, for preachers were understandably far more preoccupied with the ills of self-interest than were most other men. Puritan sermons delivered before and during the decade 1640–50 present a confused picture owing to a widespread failure to be precise in de-limiting the scope of the passion. A number of preachers refused to contemplate even the smallest self-regard in such an activity as gaining salvation. Salvation was naturally

[1] For a discussion of this aspect of Machiavelli see H. Hayden, *The Counter-Renaissance* (New York, 1950), p. 423.

the proper end of human conduct, but it was to be sought because it represented God's will for man and not because it was man's will for himself.

Francis Cheynell, in a sermon before the House of Lords, put it this way:

'To say I would not be in Hell, because I would not be tormented, this is the voice of self-love; but to say that I would not be in Hell, because I would not hear my God blasphemed . . . that is noble love.'[1]

The sermon contained the standard praise for those whose every thought was for the common good. Most such works illustrate the difficulty of adhering to an ethic of complete self-abasement, while at the same time appealing to ordinary men. In some of the works recorded here the result was a complete contradiction, since the general plea for virtue contained vague allusions to future plans and pleasures. Either men were to ignore self entirely, in which case such references were extraneous or even an unwelcome temptation to fall from grace, or men were so made that complete suppression of self was impossible. Were this second alternative correct, the extreme self-effacing ethic was pointless. Of course, unusual asceticism on the part of a few saints was a familiar theme and became more familiar with the prominence, during the Interregnum, of Fifth Monarchy Men. But the sermons treated here were presumably addressed to the ordinary unregenerate masses. There seems then to have been a danger of divorcing moral injunctions not only from observed human behaviour but from motives or intentions that could possibly be entertained by human beings.

Frequently preachers avoided any obvious contradiction in their appeals only by failing to stipulate what self-interest involved. They warned men against it and insisted that any self-seeking closed the way to God. At the same time a worthy Independent could describe the search for salvation in commercial terms and advised men to 'trade to heaven'.[2] Though such men

---

[1] Cheynell, *The Man of Honour* . . . (1645), p. 35. Other examples chosen at random are R. Preston, *The Doctrine of Self-Deniall* (1632), p. 121; William Sedgewicke, *Zion's Deliverance* . . . (1642), p. 39; John Benbrigge, *Christ Above All Exhalted* . . . (1645), pp. 5 and 14; and Anon., *The More Excellent Way* . . . (1650), p. 5 (BM: E 1317). The last example is a tract and not a sermon.

[2] Joseph Caryl, *Heaven and Earth Embracing* . . . (1645), p. 25

avoided precise definitions, self-love must have meant desire for gain in this world. Still, some preachers who considered a frank desire for the joys of heaven respectable managed to confuse the question of motivation on other grounds. Sermons that began with an attack on worldly interests could easily end with assurances that God often rewarded his followers with financial success, and indeed did so with a rapidity that made his cause a wise investment.[1]

Considerations such as these cannot account for the new sensibility with regard to self. They do help to explain why Hobbes and others were rather scornful of received opinion and impressed with their own originality. Certainly current thinking about self-interest displayed a good deal of woolliness, but this, of itself, would not produce the sort of reaction seen in Hobbes, for confusions about motivation were very old. The Bible itself provided many. There is some reason to suppose that Protestant thought was more susceptible to this sort of confusion than Catholic theology, simply because Protestants gave a diminished role to works as means to salvation. One still cannot say with complete certainty why so many writers held unreconciled opinions about human nature and why some men chose to pursue the matter further.[2] In matters of this sort the gap between theory and reality must always have been there to some degree, so critical examination of it was dependent on new perspectives rather than on the discovery of new facts. A modern scholar has explained the failure of the schoolmen to analyse self-love and altruism in eighteenth-century terms by referring to their reliance on God to supply men with proper motives. Motivation thus required no analysis.[3] Perhaps the same answer will suffice for a much later period.

The men treated here did not provide for any natural harmony of interests effective in all circumstances. Few people have ventured that far, and none successfully. They did, however, provide theoretical postulates necessary for a reassessment of the relation between private and public interests. The story

[1] See Thomas Care, *Sensuality Dissected; or, the Epicure's Motto, Opened Answered, Improved* (1657).
[2] For a perceptive discussion of this problem see Zevedei Barbu, *Problems of Historical Psychology* (London, 1960), esp. pp. 155–9.
[3] J. J. Reardon, *Selfishness and the Social Order* (Washington, 1943), p. 65.

can begin with Hobbes, who is known to have influenced all or most of the other figures. For present purposes, the important aspect of Hobbes was his view of human nature and the conclusions drawn from it. There has been some disagreement about the correct designation for his theory, though there seems to be no basis for denying that Hobbes placed unusual emphasis upon self-interest.

Normally students have accepted this account of Hobbesian psychology without question, or, as with Warrender, with no very strong dissent. It figures prominently in the political works and is stated there in an uncompromising way. It has been argued, though, that the Hobbesian image of man was less novel than is generally supposed, and that the mechanical account of human nature was both fragmentary and inconsistent with his general position on psychology. The argument relies heavily upon the little known and untranslated *De Homine*. While ingenious, it serves chiefly to uncover new facets about Hobbes's ideas on such subjects as human sociability.[1] This in itself is useful, for we shall see that many writers have had false notions about Hobbes's capacity to appreciate a common good.

This does nothing to discredit the argument that Hobbes was only recording the conventional opinion of the age. However, the answer to this opinion has already been attempted. It was one thing to lament the prevalence of self-love and quite another to accept it as a natural and ineradicable part of human beings. Hobbes did not follow contemporaries in attacking self-interest, so he was not placed in their difficult role of condemning the inevitable. Earlier diatribes against self were radically different, since they proceeded from no coherent theory of the human mind and were thus vague about the critical question as to whether such conduct was a universal pattern.

It was the precision and rigour of Hobbes's thought that distinguished it. He raised the question that was to fascinate early eighteenth-century moralists as well as some seventeenth-century contemporaries both in England and on the Continent, though his own answer was not above criticism. The query was

---

[1] This account is based upon conversations with the author and upon an abstract of the thesis submitted to Cornell University. See B. Gert, 'The Moral Philosophy of Thomas Hobbes', in *Dissertation Abstracts* (Ann Arbor, 1962), Vol. 23, No. 5, pp. 1737–9.

whether any human action could proceed from any intention other than one that was meant in some manner to benefit the actor. Hobbes allowed for variations in men's capacity to foresee their long-term interests, but this did not prejudice the general principle. Perhaps the most extreme illustration of the doctrine was his understanding of pity as

'. . . the perturbation of the mind, arising from the apprehension of hurt or trouble to another that doth not deserve it and which he thinks may happen to himself or his.'[1]

Elsewhere, he explained this sentiment as meaning that pity was strongest for the undeserving victim because men's good opinion of themselves led them to assume that if the innocent could suffer, their own danger was the greater.[2]

Hobbes's significance is also related to the use that he made of these insights. All of this would be sterile as social theory without some consideration of political relationships, as may be seen from the case of La Rochefoucauld. In his *Maximes* he laboured under no illusions about the extent and depth of *amour propre*. Nevertheless, his telling insights were less significant for social theory than they might have been because he largely stopped at the stage of uncovering the determinants of feelings rather than dealing with concrete social activity. Even when he chose to examine clearly defined social relations his interest remained the fashionable trivia of the court. Thus he discussed nothing more important than the reasons why people flattered or praised each other or why they felt elated at each other's successes.[3] His acid comments on human weakness never led him to write about a political system constructed in order to make the best use of it. Thus La Rochefoucauld was distressed, in the usual way, that luxury should have alienated the private interests of men from the public good. He gave the impression that the condition might be remedied if men would but prefer this common good.[4]

---

[1] 'The Whole Art of Rhetoric', in *English Works*, ed. Molesworth (London, 1839–54), Vol. VI, p. 461.
[2] 'Human Nature', in *English Works*, Vol. IV, p. 44.
[3] François, Duc de La Rochefoucauld, *Reflections ou Sentences et Maximes Morales* (Paris, 1692), pp. 56, 93 and 112. The first edition was in 1665.
[4] *Ibid.*, pp. 95–6.

What, then, had Hobbes to say about the common good? The expression did not come very readily to his pen. The two passages where it was most prominently employed dealt with the way in which the social organization of animals differed from that of man. Beasts required no proper political organization, for by instinct they were sociable in that: 'they desire the common good which among them differs not from their private'.[1] He made the same point in different terms, saying:

'. . . among these creatures, the common good differeth not from the private; and being by nature inclined to their private, they procure thereby the common benefit.'[2]

There was a difference of emphasis here, but with comments relating to the activities of sub-rational creatures it is difficult to measure its significance. Certainly the second comment upon animal social life contrasts with the prevailing opinion that the altruism of beasts should serve as a model for men. It may seem as strange to speak of beasts desiring the common good as to imagine their procuring the common good while seeking only their own. The former opinion played an important part in admired texts, such as those of Hooker and Grotius. At least in the animal kingdom Hobbes recognized other standards of behaviour.

Both of these sets of remarks were intended to show that men did not behave in a similar way. They did not desire the common good and their unfettered impulses, with one very significant exception, did not lead to it. Hobbes's argument must be seen as a complete negation of the conventional opinion that men could readily be satisfied in sharing in the common good. The hitherto established position had been that such conduct was desirable to the extent of being a moral duty, thus entailing the assumption that it was possible. Hobbes did not think that it was possible and this is presumably why he did not worry about whether or not it was desirable. The central point as Hobbes put it was that

'. . . man scarce esteems anything good which hath not somewhat of eminence in the enjoyment, more than that which others do possess.'[3]

This was not to say the realization of a common good was not also recognized as beneficial to individuals, but only that men

---

[1] *De Cive*, ed. S. P. Lamprecht (New York, 1949), p. 66.
[2] *Leviathan*, ed. M. Oakeshott (Oxford, 1955), p. 111.   [3] *De Cive*, p. 66.

cared most for those things over which they could assert proprietorship. Obviously a common good would not be common if it were not to be shared.

This tendency to treat the common good as something most easily secured by beasts has apparently been the factor leading some critics to assume that for Hobbes there was no common good.[1] This is untrue. He used the expression in relation to human affairs as he discussed men consenting for the common good 'to peace and mutual help',[2] and he made it the end of the deliberations of councils.[3] On these occasions he did not favour this concept with one of his definitions. People might also have been reassured by Hobbes's statement that, *'ceteris paribus'*, the good of a large number of people was more desirable than that of a smaller number.[4]

In treating the duties of rulers Hobbes defined another expression that served as a much used equivalent to common good or interest. He quoted, with a thousand nameless pamphleteers, the dictum 'the safety of the people is the supreme law'. Safety, he pointed out, was a more substantial matter than mere physical safety; not bare survival, but living delightfully was the end of society.[5] All of this was respectably Aristotelian. He went on to list four components of this public felicity: protection against foreign enemies, domestic order, enjoyment of riches to the degree compatible with public security and, in general, the opportunity to enjoy a harmless liberty.[6] Interestingly enough, one of the aspects of the people's safety was to be measured out by reference to a similar concept, public security. This may not be the luminous clarity sometimes associated with Hobbes, but it does serve to illustrate that *salus populi* went well beyond

[1] D. L. Germino, 'The Crisis in Community', in C. J. Friedrich (ed.), *Community* (New York, 1959), p. 93.

A number of contemporaries also attacked him on this score. In fact, the fear that he had somehow undermined the notion of a common good was a major factor in leading some of them to discuss the concept. See below the treatment of Cumberland, Parker and Tyrrell in Chapter VI. Ralph Cudworth made the same charge against Hobbes, although he offered no careful defence of the common good in *The True Intellectual System of the Universe* (1678), p. 898.

[2] *De Cive*, p. 65.   [3] *Ibid.*, p. 67.

[4] See *De Homine, sive Elementorum Philosophiae Sectio Secunda* (n.d.), Chapter XI, Section 14.

[5] *Leviathan*, pp. 219 *et seq.*; *De Cive*, pp. 142-3.   [6] *De Cive*, p. 144.

physical preservation to embrace the main considerations normally included in the public interest.

Here was room for various components of public safety that in less sophisticated thinkers were dealt with in isolation. Hobbes did not neglect that aspect of the common good that looked to the strengthening of the social tie and, in maintaining the identity of the community, benefited its members without thereby attracting their passionate devotion. But no definition of the public interest couched wholly in terms of national strength would suffice. The psychological lacuna in so many formulations of the common good had been the failure to appreciate the powerlessness of such an idea to win men's passions. To say that part of public safety consisted in personal enrichment and a harmless liberty did then extend one dimension of the concept in the direction of private interests.[1] Others had not explicitly denied the relevance of this factor; they had just failed to mention it. Hobbes did not say that in enriching himself a subject would, in most cases, serve the public as well. He was a mercantilist, if an individualist, and so avoided the extremes of economic liberalism.

Hobbes's theory has been shown to describe a two-dimensional public good resting upon general conditions of stability for social aggregates and upon various forms of individual satisfaction. This is probably the most important source of ambiguity in the idea of a public interest, but it was not the only one. He recognized the traditional distinction between a spiritual and a temporal public good, but after devoting one paragraph to it he chose to leave the matter 'in suspense'.[2] While Hobbes's thought was thus not entirely free from the dualism of a spiritual and a temporal public good, he was primarily concerned with the latter. Hobbes's use of the classical distinction between

[1] Raymond Polin argues that in *Leviathan* Hobbes de-emphasized his original regard for the welfare of subjects. See *Politique et Philosophie Chez Thomas Hobbes* (Paris, 1953), pp. 119–20. This may be true, but Hobbes apparently saw no reason to retreat from his earlier views when, in 1650, he published his *De Corpore Politico*. Here he restated the claims made in *De Cive* with even greater emphasis on the rights of subjects. He dismissed that aspect of *salus populi* concerned with defence by cautioning rulers against aggressive wars. See *English Works*, Vol. IV, pp. 214–20. This emphasis on individual welfare survived in later writings. See *English Works*, Vol. VI, p. 13.
[2] *De Cive*, p. 143.

living and living well suggests yet another pair of categories by which one may treat the common interest. Obviously augmenting national power and prosperity was a different sort of common interest from the scarcely less important aim of improving the quality of social life in a less tangible way.[1] The normal way in which this distinction arose was in connection with the relation between private interests and the public interest. Any extension of the content of a secular common good beyond national survival might give more legitimacy to private interests. Certainly this was true in the case of Hobbes.

The matters discussed thus far concerned what Hobbes called the good or the safety of the people. Owing to the circumstances of his state of nature, the concept of a common good gained meaning only in a particular sort of political order. Hobbes's philosophical egoism combined with his nominalism to produce this result. He kept finding opportunities to emphasize that the 'people' was not a meaningful expression except under certain circumstances. He allowed the conventional use of the term as in the expression 'people of England'. Here it referred to 'a number of men, distinguished by the place of their habitation'.[2] This was without political significance, for the 'people' in this form was merely a geographical expression. The political sense of the term designated

'. . . a person civil . . . either one man or a council, in the will whereof is included and involved the will of everyone in particular.'[3]

In the case of rebellion the people then ceased to exist as a corporate body and degenerated into a multitude. This brought back the state of nature where, with every man claiming his own rights, there was nothing left for the multitude to have a right to.[4] No one who has read the tracts of the popular party could doubt that their neglect of the divisions within the people cried out for such an answer. In attacking the means of financing the parliamentary cause, he voiced a standard royalist jibe.

[1] The modern editor of Spinoza's political writings sees this as an important ambiguity in the idea of a public good. While the ambiguity is no doubt a real one, a number of distinctions on the basis of substantive definitions of the public good suggest themselves. The problem becomes one of holding such distinctions to a manageable number. See B. de Spinoza, *The Political Works*, ed. A. G. Wernham (Oxford, 1958), p. 32.
[2] 'De Corpore Politico', *op. cit.*, p. 145.   [3] *Ibid.*, p. 146.   [4] *Ibid.*

How, he demanded, could the rebels seek to guarantee loans on the basis of the public faith?

'What public faith is there when there is no public? What is it that can be called a public, in a civil war without the king?'[1]

This form of argument displays one of the connections between nominalism and one sort of individualism. The relation may be described in several ways.[2] For present purposes, the most obvious and useful connection would appear to be the tendency of nominalists to reduce abstract concepts and the labels attached to communities to collections of particular and concrete entities. Thus Hobbes insisted that a community had to have concrete embodiment in some few persons, or perhaps a single person, whose particular interest would give substance to the common interest. Inasmuch as Hobbes was concerned with giving substance to the notion of a public, a united council would, in principle, be quite as effective as a king. However, a single ruler was much preferable to a plurality of rulers for another reason.

When Hobbes came to compare the different forms of commonwealth, he expressed one of the seminal political ideas of the period from the Civil War to the Revolution. The prime advantage of monarchy over other forms was the fact that it went much further towards establishing an identity of interest between the government and the public. The king was never seen as anything but a creature of common clay, subject to the same unavoidable self-interest as all other men. Those who made their kings into quasi-divine beings might perhaps exempt them from the normal limitations of the human condition; this was not part of Hobbes's theory, as he made clear:

'. . . and though he be careful in his politic person to procure the common interest; yet he is more, or no less careful to procure the private good of himself, his family, kindred, and friends; and for the most part, if the public interest chance to cross the private, he prefers

[1] 'Behemoth', in *English Works*, Vol. VI, p. 304.
[2] A good source on the connection between nominalism and individualism is Karl Pribram, *Die Enstehung der individualistischen Sozialphilosophie* (Leipzig, 1912). He notes the effect of nominalist thought in weakening the hegemony of the common good (p. 61). However, he is not so concerned with its role in dissolving mental constructs, such as the public, as with its effect in promoting a measure of subjectivism in ethics by weakening ideas of a universal pattern of justice.

the private: for the passions of men are commonly more potent than their reason.'[1]

This would seem to indicate that the private interest of the king would not always be congruent with the public good. Actually Hobbes reached the conclusion that there would be an exact harmony, though he did not make clear whether this was because a monarch's passions led to public benefit or whether his reason could be seen as asserting itself in his own interests. Probably Hobbes would have allowed that both passions, in the sense of strong desires, and reason, in the sense of prudential calculations, combined to procure the happy result. In concrete terms, the harmony followed from the fact that

'. . . the riches, power and honour of a monarch arise only from the riches, strength and reputation of his subjects.'[2]

Hobbes argued the same point in different terms when he took issue with Aristotle's opinion that governments could be classified according to whether they tended to procure the good of the ruler or of the subjects. At this point the difficult question of Hobbes's supposed originality arises. Sheldon Wolin has properly turned his attention to 'interests' as the most rewarding way in which to approach Hobbes. His penetrating analysis makes the point that Hobbes thought not of authority but of a 'public ego', the ruler being nothing more than a 'public institutionalized ego'.[3] One must agree with this interpretation of political individualism, and Wolin's parallel between Hobbes and the Benthamites is an apt one. The most interesting question, though, is to what extent, if any, Hobbes thereby differed from his predecessors and contemporaries. Like most political theorists, Wolin treads carefully here, and while he implies that Hobbes was quite original in positing a public ego, he avoids saying expressly whether the idea originated with Hobbes. Naturally it is a minor point as to whether any single writer on kingship had previously said the same thing; but it is of more relevance to ask how these remarks compared with the views most commonly expressed.

Without trying to contain any such wraith as a climate of opinion, one may still make some observations on English writ-

---

[1] *Leviathan*, p. 122.   [2] *Leviathan*, p. 123.
[3] S. S. Wolin, *Politics and Vision* (London, 1961), pp. 279–80.

ings on the position of the ruler. Many early works discussed the function of rulers without saying much about their private interests and their relationship with the public interest. The writers were concerned either with the extent of the king's jurisdiction over spiritual affairs or with the ways in which he might serve his people by reconciling the needs of policy with those of religion. There had certainly been a strong didactic strain in those books that discussed the duties of the prince. The earliest ones in English, such as Lydgate's edition of *The Falls of Princes*, emphasized the bad end of rulers who neglected the common good. Some later works became more sycophantic in their appeals, and rather than stressing the grisly end of tyrants, courtiers hopefully wrote paeans of praise about the sort of ruler who acted

'. . . as if he were soly and wholly happy in making his people fortunate, and in easing them of the heavy burdens of oppression.'[1]

Authorities on Tudor political thought are agreed that there was a growing tendency to de-emphasize even the possibility of rulers misbehaving, though there are differences of opinion as to the cause. Some interpret this as an increased awareness of monarchy as a service to the governed, others as a consequence of the growth of censorship of social criticism.[2] With discussion of rebellion muted in the late sixteenth century, recourse was had to the ruler's conscience and his goodwill. Few writers before Hobbes deigned to consider the ruler's interests in any detail, since they were strictly subordinated to those of the community. Classical literature, from which Tudor writers drew their ideas, was not lacking in references to prudential concerns that might limit a ruler's ambition. There was the basis of a *quid pro quo* in the ancient idea that no sane ruler would destroy his subjects, for thereby he destroyed his own office. But even this notion appears surprisingly seldom in works that endlessly repeated the obvious in other areas.

The contrast between early works and post-Hobbesian ones

---

[1] George Marcelline, *Epithalamium Gallo-Britannicum* (1625), p. 24.
[2] The first hypothesis was offered, with little supporting evidence, by Lewis Einstein. See *Tudor Ideals* (London, 1921), p. 83. Ruth Mohl's suggestion regarding censorship is more credible. See *The Three Estates in Medieval and Renaissance Literature* (New York, 1933), pp. 141 and 230–1.

may be illustrated by two examples separated by a century and a half. Thomas Elyot, writing in 1531, insisted that a proper prince ruled only for the benefit of his people. In describing tyrants, he said:

'... they ... regard them of whom [they] have governance no more than shall appertaine to their own private commodities, they no better esteem them than other men doth their horses and mules, to whom they employ no less labour and diligence, not to the benefit of the silly beasts, but to their own necessities and singular advantage.'[1]

The same metaphor appeared in a work of 1684 by the Attorney-General of Scotland. George Mackenzie noted, in the prevailing fashion, that the king's interest and that of the people was inseparable. A monarch such as Charles II offered advantages that were most unlikely to come from elected rulers whose interests were short-term ones. This he illustrated by a curious variation on the original metaphor:

'... the one considering the common interest as a tenant does lands of which he takes his present advantage, though he should destroy it; the other caring for it as a proprietor does for his own ground; the one judging it as a man does a hired horse, the other using it as a man does his own.'[2]

Purely rational calculation had replaced restraints of a moral nature. The contrast may be somewhat exaggerated, since not all contemporary defenders of the Stuarts were quite as harsh as Mackenzie, and the attitude reflected here was understandably rare after the Revolution.

There were anticipations of Hobbes's position, but all were of a comparatively mild nature. James I came about as close as anyone in his famous speech before Parliament: 'If you be rich I cannot be poor ...'[3] Edward Forset ended his rhapsody to cosmic harmony with the observation that

[1] *The Boke Named the Governour*, ed. H. H. S. Croft (London, 1880), Vol. II, p. 5. A century later Sir John Eliot subscribed to the same ethic, although he was less vehement about it. See *De Jure Majestatis or Political Treatise of Government*, ed. A. B. Grosart (London, 1882), pp. 65 and 79. A survey of this form of literature is contained in F. Le Van Baumer, *The Early Tudor Theory of Kingship* (New Haven, 1940), Chapter 6.
[2] Mackenzie, *Jus Regium* (Edinburgh, 1684), pp. 57-8.
[3] *The Political Works of James I*, ed. C. H. McIlwain (Cambridge, Mass., 1918).

'. . . the Prince's contentment must be the happiness of the subject and the subject's welfare the security of the Prince.'[1]

However, this most organic of social theorists spoke continually of mutual kindness, which indicated a most un-Hobbesian perspective. There were some men who defended hereditary over elective monarchy on the grounds that concern for posterity would ensure a closer adherence to the public good by the former.[2] However, the implications of this insight into motivation were not spelled out. Finally, Thomas Scot, a politically sophisticated cleric who wrote on foreign affairs, appealed to the king's private good in a number of tracts. Scot dispensed with the idea that rulers must ignore their personal interests, though he continued to put the common interest first.[3] This brief foray into the intellectual history of an earlier period cannot provide any definitive answer to questions about Hobbes's originality. The conclusion is that when compared with a number of earlier writers, Hobbes emerges as the one Englishman who thought the problem of the ruler's self-interest through to its logical conclusion. Others, such as the clergy of Hobbes's own day, used the idea of self-interest when it suited them, but tended to be inconsistent and fragmentary in their treatment of it.

Tudor and early Stuart thinkers had not treated the monarch and the common good in the manner of Hobbes. What, then, of Hobbes's contemporaries? The first point to make is that Hobbes's approach did not emerge full-blown in his earliest works. *De Cive* contained a rather modest statement of the argument. The authority of Aristotle, so often quoted on the necessity of rulers preferring the common good, had indeed been impugned, but only in the most tentative way. Firstly, when Hobbes remarked that the profits and disprofits fell equally upon ruler and subject, he was referring to all forms of government and not just to monarchy.[4] Thus there was no necessary connection here with his later remarks about monarchy; his

---

[1] Forset, *A Comparative Discourse of Bodies Natural and Politique* (1606), pp. 95–6.
[2] Charles Merbury, *A Briefe Discourse of Royall Monarchie* (1581), p. 31, and John Barclay, *The Mirrour of Mindes*, trans. T. May (1631), pp. 108–12.
[3] See Scot, *Vox Regis* (n.d.), p. 14, and *Newes from Pernassus* (Utrecht, 1622) sig. A 2.
[4] *De Cive*, p. 115.

meaning was only that the greatest benefit of government, peace, was indivisible. Further, Hobbes did not claim here that there was any perfect correspondence between the interest of the ruler and that of the people. Instead he admitted that private acts of the sovereign might harm the public. The consolations he offered were the familiar ones that one tyrant would be less onerous than many, and the suggestion that a prince would follow his 'interest' in preserving his inheritance, i.e. the people.[1] It was only with *Leviathan* that the developed 'public ego' emerged, by which time the idea was a very common one in royalist writings. Hobbes's works of 1640 went no further than did *De Cive* and, in any event, were not published for another ten years.

The new emphasis upon beneficial royal egoism may usefully be examined in some of the works of royalists who wrote in the period between the emergence of *De Cive* and *Leviathan*. The question of the king's interest and its repercussions on the public could not have remained in that state of vaguely articulated goodwill that was so marked in earlier English thought. After 1640 it had become distressingly obvious that mutual love was rather a scarce commodity. Still, some royalists managed to combine a suitable truculence with something less than pleas for the ruler's untrammelled ego. Thus Henry Ferne, the *bête noire* of the Parliamentmen, argued from the king's divine mandate, his good intentions and his prerogatives, but not his interests. According to Ferne, all three estates of the realm shared the same 'public interest' and any following of private interest by the king would immediately be checked by the private interest of subjects.[2] Archbishop Usher, a prominent royalist, echoed Ferne's conventional opinions.

There were a great many fleeting references in this period to supposedly Hobbesian ideas, though most of them were both anonymous and too brief to warrant close treatment. Some limited themselves to noting that a king was in no danger of playing the tyrant because his own honour and safety would be casualties in any assault on the people's liberties.[3] Most writers

[1] *De Cive*, pp. 118 and 126.
[2] Ferne, *Conscience Satisfied* ... (Oxford, 1643), pp. 36–7.
[3] See Griffith Williams, *Vindiciae Regum; or the Grand Rebellion* (Oxford, 1643), p. 65; Anon., *Great Britain's Vote* (1648), p. 8 (BM: 100 c. 57).

gave such assurances with the intention of guaranteeing Charles's future good conduct and they did not expressly defend the institution of monarchy in general. Still, they conveyed the theme of the public ego very succinctly by using the idea of the king's interest.

Since the concept of 'interest' is treated at length in other chapters, it is only necessary here to relate the specific uses made of it by the royalists to the general theme of its growing popularity. In 1640 a letter from Sir John Suckling, the poet, to Henry Jermyn had introduced the appeal from interest into the constitutional struggle. Suckling employed the Duke of Rohan's maxims about interest and its infallible power in the realm of domestic policies. In considering the crisis with Parliament, Suckling suggested that the king need only consult 'interest', which he saw as a product of calculation far removed from passion. He continued:

'Kings may be mistaken and councillors corrupted, but true interest alone (said the Duke of Rohan) cannot err.'[1]

This rather unhelpful advice was apparently popular, for the letter was printed under different titles in 1641 and again in 1660.[2] A large number of subsequent royalist tracts relied heavily upon the 'interest' of the prince to allay suspicions about his aims.[3] Admittedly it was one thing to claim that it was the king's interest to give the people reason to trust him and another to suggest that, in looking to his own interest, he would always serve theirs. However, one argument shaded into the other and examples of the latter are also available.

[1] *A Copy of a Letter Found in the Privy Lodgings at Whitehall* (1641), pp. 3–4 (BM: E 163). Another royalist, quoting the same passage, carefully deleted the word 'interest', replacing it with the neutral term 'obligement'. See Anon., *The King's Estate at Present, How Farre he May Dispense with his Royall Prerogative* (1647), p. 3 (BM: E 396).

[2] See *A Letter from Sir John Suckling to Mr. Henry German, In the Beginning of the Late King's Parliament Anno 1640*. The Bodleian copy (G.P. 1678) has a note saying that this was published in 1660.

[3] See Anon., *Three Letters: The First from an Officer in His Majestie's Army to a Gentleman in Gloustershire* . . . (1643), p. 31 (B: G.P. 1368), and Anon., *An Antidote Against the Infectious Aire* (1647), p. 2 (B: A 6.6 Linc.). These differ from tracts such as that by Williams only in that they stressed 'interest' as a guide to the king.

One author closely paralleled *De Cive* in his argument. He insisted that

'. . . self-love and interest is the most natural and predominant of all man's thoughts and inclinations and inseparable from any, which no other affection in us is.'[1]

The condition afflicted all governments, but it was most easily channelled into socially useful courses in monarchy, for

'. . . he is more likely to have care of a kingdom that is to leave it to his posterity, than he that hath only his own being to provide for out of it and can . . . run away with the public wealth when his reign is almost at an end.'[2]

The same point had already been made in picturesque fashion, without using the word 'interest'. Bishop Bramhall argued from the dubious assumption that a single ruler would be more readily satiated in his appetites than could many. Slightly altering his approach, he insisted that as a matter of agrarian economics, the tenant with a long tenure was more restrained in the use of his land, and so by analogy an hereditary monarch would discipline himself by expectations of future rewards.[3] Though such suggestions would have appalled Elyot, men in this later age saw nothing incongruous in treating the subject–sovereign relationship as a special case of the conservation of natural resources. Both of the authors just mentioned supported the theory that an ideal political system was one in which a single ruler procured the common good while seeking only his own. Not all pamphleteers who stressed the idea of interest held such extreme views. Some noted only that the interests of king and people were mutual, without emphasizing unalloyed self-interest on the part of the king.[4]

The king's interest was most clearly asserted by two opponents of Henry Parker, the parliamentary champion. These were Dudley Digges of All Souls and Bishop John Maxwell. Allen credits Digges with applying Hobbesian doctrine, and certainly

---

[1] W. J., *A Dissection of All Governments or an Answer to a Pamphlet Entitled the Privileges of the People* (1648), p. 6 (BM: E 545).
[2] *Ibid.*, p. 11.
[3] [Bramhall], *The Serpent Salve* (1643), p. 91.
[4] Anon., *Certain Material Considerations Touching the Differences of the Present Times* (1642), p. 11 (BM: E 246).

his distinction between the law of nature and the right of nature suggests some knowledge of *De Cive*.[1] Digges was equivocal on the main issue in that he strongly denounced 'policy' and Machiavellian practices, while simultaneously advocating great freedom for the monarch to follow those policies dictated by his rational self-interest. According to Digges, the king's interest had to be that of the public, because, unlike lesser men, he had nothing to gain from any lapse in state-security. He did little to develop the theme, except to add, in medieval fashion, that the head of the body politic could not hope to thrive by the consumption of the members.[2] The interest of the king was construed rather narrowly as 'strong state security'.

This was unexceptional political theory, but he presented it against a background of purely Hobbesian psychology. He directed his comments on human nature to subjects and only by implication applied them to all men, monarchs included. Pleading for subordination to a common good just did not work, for, as he said,

'. . . naturally we love society below ourselves, for the end of it was to convey us such and such goods, and that which is loved in order to something else is less amiable.'[3]

Still, he contrived to reconcile self-interest and regard for one's neighbour, observing that 'in our enemies' wounds our souls will bleed to death'.[4] Was this to serve as a warning to monarchs as well? One was not told.

No such doubt applied to his views about the secular interests of the sovereign. Certainly he began by paying lip service to the traditional idealization of a benevolent and disinterested ruler. Power should properly be placed in the hands of public persons who were 'more unconcerned in the decisions'.[5] Little more was heard of such a lofty theme in seventeenth-century debate, in fact, it did not even survive the tract in question. He criticized those who wrote as though a king must never speak for his own interest, but should accept what was good for the

[1] J. W. Allen, *English Political Thought 1603–1660* (London, 1938), Vol. 1, pp. 500–1.
[2] [Digges], *The Unlawfulness of Subjects Taking Up Arms Against their Sovereigne* (Oxford, 1643), pp. 20 and 74.
[3] *Ibid.*, p. 123.   [4] *Ibid.*, p. 52.   [5] *Ibid.*, p. 8.

public as good for him. Digges was not quarrelling with this identification of interest, but he wished to leave the king the initiative in seeking his own interest. This made the public interest, and not that of the king, a by-product and ensured that the king would benefit if there were any discrepancy between the two. Digges denied that it was just to expect the king to practise passive self-abnegation. This might be appropriate for other citizens who were represented in Parliament. But the king had no proxy, and had to be responsible for expressing his own interests.[1] Far from being silenced with respect to his private interest, the king, of all men, was the one who might most safely exercise it.

'It always was the master policy amongst the wisest legislators to grant to them the greatest power of government to whom the preservation of the present state would be most beneficial, because then private interest were the same with the public.'[2]

This may well have been the general practice, but it had not been the admitted theory upon which earlier political life had been based.

Digges proceeded to take a closer look at the idea of the public interest in the form of *salus populi*. He allowed that it represented a desirable condition, but he queried the Parliament's understanding of what it entailed. The great danger lay in over-stating the substance of *salus populi* to exaggerate the extent to which individual interests were to be cared for. Alternatively the danger might be seen as emphasizing the satisfaction of personal, rather than social, interests. He took strong exception to Parliament's claim that the king had a duty to confer upon the people 'all kind of political happiness'. If taken literally the king was bound

'... to promote every particular person to all kinds of political happiness ... to advance all to honours, offices, power, command.'[3]

In place of this extravagant definition, Digges offered a severe

---

[1] *Unlawfulness ...*, p. 143.

[2] [Digges], *An Answer to a Printed Book, Intitled Observations upon Some of His Majestie's Late Answers and Expresses* (Oxford, 1642), p. 117. This was a more direct statement of the point than Hobbes was to provide until the publication of *Leviathan*. See, *op. cit.*, pp. 122-3.

[3] *An Answer ...*, p. 15.

version in terms of 'protection', narrowly interpreted as physical safety.

John Maxwell was another royalist who explored the problems raised by the cry of *salus populi*. His chief work contained a long exegesis of the maxim '*salus populi suprema lex esto*'. *Salus populi* involved the good of both king and the people, thus, despite the frequent use of '*populus*' to describe only the vulgar, this was an improper interpretation.[1] Indeed, there need be no assumption at all that the good of subjects was the prime end of all government, in some forms of government it was but a secondary consideration, 'not the principal end, but the external and adventitious'.[2] The ruler might well obtain the people's good, because in their peace and plenty he found his own.[3] If the good of the prince and people were the same thing, it might seem to matter little whether the king actively sought the public interest or his own private interest. However, the argument was about the prerogative and the power of deciding in what measures the public good consisted. Maxwell followed Digges in giving the king maximum discretion in such matters. While the king would not rationally assume that loss to the people could be his gain, still, any abridgement of his interests to their supposed good was unthinkable.[4]

After all, he insisted, it was not '*faelicitas populi*' that the king was bound to secure. Again, Parker's ill-advised comments about promoting all subjects to perfect happiness proved highly vulnerable to a *reductio ad absurdum*. Interpreting Parker's formula to be that the public safety consisted in the promotion of private goods, Maxwell chose to stress the safety of the whole community in a sense very close to the normal meaning of reason of state. He divorced the moral obligation associated with the maxim from the details of day-to-day law-making, expressly saying that *salus populi* might have little to do with the 'interest' of individuals or laws made for their private good. All such considerations might be set aside as the king used his prerogative to preserve the community.[5] The physical survival of the state thus made legitimate that arbitrary

---

[1] [Maxwell], *Sacro-Sancta Regum Majestas* . . . (Oxford, 1644), pp. 159 and 175.
[2] Maxwell, *op. cit.*, p. 158.   [3] *Ibid.*, p. 159.
[4] *Ibid.*, p. 170.   [5] *Ibid.*, p. 176.

government that had been opposed in the name of private rights.

If Maxwell had any egregious weakness it was his penchant for excessive detail; he simply refused to let well enough alone. Thus he piled argument upon argument as he grasped any available stick with which to belabour his opponents. This meant that the various lines of attack were not clearly related to one another, if they were not contradictory. This is best illustrated by his tactics in discussing what was meant by the 'people'. He was never able to decide whether to accept Parker's vocabulary and thus take the people to mean the body of the citizens (in which case their safety was not the supreme law), or to insist that 'people' meant king and people. Sometimes he did the first, sometimes the second. Similarly, he resorted to the original meaning of *'salus populi'* as it appeared in Ulpian, but he used his learning to obscure the argument. First he said that this original meaning only applied to private interests in a secondary way, the conservation of the species taking precedence over that of individuals. But he also made the more extreme claim that Parliamentmen were writing of 'the singular and peculiar good of everyone singly', which was Ulpian's definition of the private, as opposed to the public, realm.[1] This would seem to make the royalist's *'salus populi'* entirely irrelevant to the welfare of private persons, except as they benefited from the preservation of the state.

Implicit in Maxwell's book was a distinction between the good of the people (or even of the people and king) and *salus populi*. This was what allowed him to dwell upon the safety of that aggregate called the community at the expense of all particular interests and all forms of public welfare other than physical safety. When he attacked the slogan of *salus populi* he denied that it was synonymous with the 'public good of prince and people'.[2] Elsewhere, he made the mistake of appearing to identify *'salus populi'* with the joint good of king and people and with forms of private welfare not immediately connected with the defence of the kingdom.[3] The trouble was that he was trying to accomplish two different things with the same set of arguments: firstly, to state the doctrine of the 'public ego', and secondly, to discredit the prevailing meaning of *salus populi*. Thus he introduced too many related concepts and did not

[1] Maxwell, *op. cit.*, p. 174.   [2] *Ibid.*, p. 176.   [3] *Ibid.*, p. 159.

adhere consistently to his distinctions between them. Either he should have made no such distinctions or better ones. At least one contemporary assailed him for lack of clarity.[1]

For both Digges and Maxwell the Hobbesian theme of royal self-interest answered the main requirements of stable government. However, their comments on 'salus populi' both contrast with those of Hobbes and throw additional light on his theory. Polin has observed, rather cryptically, that the public interest in Leviathan could not be expressed in the same terms as were private interests since it was not 'de même ordre'.[2] Still, he insists, Hobbes could already have advanced the maxim of the Utilitarians that the public interest was but the sum of private ones, but he refused to adopt the shallow optimism on which it was based. Similarly, Polin draws a parallel between Hobbes and the later liberals, based on the manner in which both assumed that the good of each would accord with the common good.[3]

Several questions arise here. What is the point of associating with Hobbes a view of the public interest that he never accepted, i.e. the utilitarian one, especially when Polin tells us as much himself? Why emphasize the point that the good of each would accord with the common good, when in some sense this was claimed for every political theory? These seemingly irrelevant observations do point to certain relatively novel aspects of Hobbes's thought. Hobbes indeed stressed the convergence of the interest of each with that of all in a different way from most predecessors. He was not satisfied with the analytical proposition that in the welfare of the whole the parts would realize their prosperity in some undefined sense. With Hobbes, the public interest went a long way towards taking in individual interests, though many Parliamentmen would have quarrelled with his priorities in ranking such interests. His 'public safety' was a richer concept than it was in Digges and Maxwell, for he said unequivocally that states existed for the welfare of the members, while they did their best to deny it. Hobbes was not promising to promote all men to every happiness. Nevertheless, the conditions listed under the heading of public safety were closer to the ideas criticized by Maxwell than to the pure reason-of-state version.

[1] Samuel Rutherford, Lex Rex (1644), p. 226.
[2] Polin, op. cit., p. 126. [3] Ibid., pp. 126 and 115.

All this means only that Hobbes raised the problem of the public interest, but did not solve it entirely in accord with individualistic premises. No matter how much one reads into those aspects of the public safety that dealt with individual liberty, it remains true that Hobbes never saw the public interest as merely the product of converging or conflicting individual interests. When Hobbes came to ask what the public interest involved, he placed more weight upon the satisfaction of individual interests than did many others, but the mechanism whereby this desirable condition was realized was the action of one, and not many egos.

Whatever Hobbes's originality in positing a public ego, the 1640s saw a number of works which did not obviously rely upon him and took the idea rather further than had his published writings. Charles himself introduced the limiting factor of his own interest in various of his pronouncements and many others did the same thing for him. It seems useful to show how the debate of these years gave rise to statements of a Hobbesian sort. One of Milton's main points in *Eikonoklastes* was his rejection of the argument that the king was bound by his own and his children's interest to seek the welfare of his subjects. This, he said, applied equally to all hereditary monarchs and had deterred few of them from misusing their powers. He further noted that all men were enjoined to honest dealing by their interests, if salvation were considered an interest, but that this check had not been very effective.[1]

Joseph Jane has been identified as the author of a reply to Milton, appearing after the king's death. On the point about the weakness of divine sanctions on human conduct, Jane gave a less ambiguous and more secular answer than the supposed atheist Hobbes. Charles was referring here only to 'humane or civil interest which men are apt to judge strongest'.[2] Divine rewards and punishments had no place in his theory. Civil interest was a sufficient guide for a king, though members of Parliament might not safely be trusted on this basis alone. Milton had demanded whether the king's appreciation of his own interest were actually being offered as an adequate means to the public good. The answer was an unequivocal 'yes':

[1] [Milton], *Eikonoklastes* ... (1649), p. 6.
[2] [Jane], *The Image Unbroken* ... (1651), p. 74.

'. . . if the King comprehend his own advantages, it is sufficient for the common good of the three-nations.'[1]

The nature of Jane's book required clandestine publication, so there is no record of the date when it appeared. Had it been after January 1650–1, it might have benefited from the argument of *Leviathan*, but by this time there was no longer any need to rely upon Hobbes.

Sir Robert Filmer, best known for his patriarchial theory of monarchy, was one thinker who seems to have had his theory sharpened by the insights of Hobbes. *Patriarcha*, which seems to have been composed before 1640,[2] made only passing reference to the prudential nature of royal concern for the public good. The most relevant comment was his quotation from the remarks of James I, quoted above. Filmer's arguments for leaving the king unhindered in exercising his prerogatives turned upon the unconvincing assumption that the law of nature bound fathers and kings to protect their charges. Specifically, the law enjoined kings to ratify acts of their predecessors in office in matters relating to the public good. He clearly said here that kings must remember that the public interest had always to be put before the private, for the

'. . . profit of every man in particular, and of all together in general, is not always one and the same.'[3]

This was a most significant statement, for it suggested that the two forms of profit might *sometimes* be identical. In different circumstances Filmer was to argue precisely that point.[4]

The tone of Filmer's political writings altered as well as he strove to eliminate traditional fetters on the royal interest. Thus he tried to use Aristotle to show that there could be no form of government entirely for the governor's benefit, hence rendering Aristotle's comments on tyranny irrelevant. This he considered to be established on the grounds of Aristotle's remark that a master's function could not survive the destruction of the servant. While it was possible for particular men to suffer under

---

[1] *Ibid.*, pp. 118–19.
[2] *Patriarcha and Other Political Writings*, ed. P. Laslett (Oxford, 1949), p. 3. All future references are to the Laslett edition.
[3] *Patriarcha*, p. 96.   [4] See below, p. 226.

certain governments, in all forms the people in general found 'benefit and profit'.[1] In another work he ignored any alleged contradiction in Aristotle and said simply that

'. . . not to regard the common good, but to reign only for himself, is the supposition of any impossibility in the judgement of Aristotle.'[2]

Since he discussed Hobbes at some length in the same work, he was obviously in a position to benefit from this more powerful thinker. Hobbes, of course, had provided a discussion of this exact point in Aristotle in his *De Cive*, though his argument did not depend upon any distortion of the text.

The theory of the public ego is really only relevant to this discussion of the public interest because it led a large number of writers to consider the latter idea. Some few royalists moved directly to a consideration of this question without first defending self-interest on the part of the king. The most noteworthy such effort was by Robert Sanderson, future Bishop of Lincoln. His lectures delivered in the Oxford Divinity School in 1647 constitute an unusually fine example of the conventional, royalist understanding of the public good. It was unlike that of Parliament and had still less in common with the views of radical democrats. However, it typified the opinions of those conservative gentlemen who were, as yet, unconcerned with the problem of universal self-interest.

Sanderson's intention was to vindicate the royal prerogative in the face of strident appeals to *salus populi*. Unlike some others, Maxwell, for instance, he avoided any confusion between '*salus populi*' and the good of the community in some broader sense. Sanderson used 'common good' or 'public interest' as equivalents to *salus populi*.[3] In analysing such concepts, he treated their two parts separately. Thus he claimed that 'public' referred to the king and people and not to the people or commons alone. This was by now a standard argument and warrants no close inspection. More important, however, were his remarks about

---

[1] *Observations upon Aristotle's Politiques . . .* (1652), p. 204.
[2] *Observations Concerning the Original of Government* (1652), p. 259.
[3] Sanderson, *Ten Lectures on the Obligation of Humane Conscience, Read at the Divinity School at Oxford, in the Year, 1647*, trans. R. Codrington (1660), p. 311. Even after the translation the Latin version of these lectures went through many editions.

what the 'safety' of the public entailed. The rebels had denied in theory and practice that obedience to the laws established was the prerequisite for any common good. His understanding of safety was that

'. . . the commonwealth may flourish in peace and safety, and that all private men, according to their measure and degrees, may partake, rejoice in the public happiness, in a word, that they may be all inservient to the common good.'[1]

He was very explicit about why this disagreement had arisen. The king's enemies assumed that their private rights took precedence over all else. Sanderson not only condemned this opinion but also exposed his own presuppositions with unusual candour:

'. . . if any man finds his dignity or liberty affronted, or injured in some small thing, nay, and if it be in a great one, he is not presently to complain that he hath endangered or lost his safety; for every hurt or blemish is not directly opposed to the safety of anything . . .'[2]

Especially, it seems, it did not entail the destruction of the commonwealth. His opponents had

'. . . such an interpretation of the safety of the people, that unless every one of the lowest degree of citizens be altogether secure from all unjust force and unrighteous domination of some superior or other there shall be no public peace at all. The safety of the commonwealth is then indeed in danger, when by the incursions of exotic enemies, or by the depredations of wicked citizens . . . unless some timely help be provided, the city and country will be destroyed.'[3]

Sanderson had a different scale of priorities. For him, the most vital consideration was the protection of the state from foreign aggression.[4] The only proper grounds for any deviation from the laws was the imminent destruction of the state by enemies foreign or domestic. In that event extreme measures were to be taken, but only at the discretion of the king.[5] Reason of state was then the essence of the public good and private

[1] Sanderson, p. 311.   [2] *Ibid.*, p. 340.   [3] *Ibid.*, p. 353.
[4] *Ibid.*, p. 172. He identified the other two aspects of the public safety as the promotion of justice and the protection of commerce.
[5] *Ibid.*, pp. 361–2.

advantages even of the majority of the citizens flowed from the safety of the state. They must not compete with it.

Hobbesian ideas about the self-interest of the king had become firmly established by the end of the Civil War. Great as their popularity was, another sort of argument, that of Sanderson, was perhaps even more popular, being widely accepted among the royal pamphleteers. Men might differ in their degree of emphasis on the royal ego, but no orthodox royalist could afford sincerely to accept the parliamentary interpretation of *salus populi*. Both in its substance and in the means of effecting it, this idea was entirely alien and this remained true even when the king publicized his desire to satisfy all interests. There were strong indications in Hobbes of an outlook that differed from that of conventional royalists, for his theory of human nature would not allow him to ignore the selfish designs of private men. His purposes were different from the average pamphleteer, so one would not expect him to limit himself to sneers at *salus populi*. However, it was left for others to examine the common interest in the light of Hobbesian self-interest.

A COMMUNITY OF INDIVIDUALS

The people to be considered here had several characteristics in common. All of them wrote substantial, serious books on political philosophy. They had their own causes to promote, but they were also interested in understanding the problems of politics that events had made so apparent. Thus they had a certain independence of outlook not found in most of the contemporary literature. In their various ways, all had been influenced by Hobbes, the two who actually quoted him perhaps less than the two who did not. Whatever their association with Hobbes may have been, all of them suggested new applications of his doctrines about self-interest.

Anthony Ascham is the one member of this quartet who was not a thoroughly committed monarchist, in either its Stuart or Cromwellian forms. Ascham was a Commonwealth diplomat, but by the very nature of his political outlook owed strong allegiance to no political system except that which existed *de facto*. He shared Hobbes's view of man and in some ways put it to the same theoretical use. Though he quoted Hobbes a number of times, his work was no mere imitation, and he disagreed in places with the master. Another intellectual influence may have been the Duke of Rohan, mentioned by Ascham both as a writer and as a man.[1] It may have been significant that the term 'interest' appeared in Ascham; it was used in the sense of a general social force and took no article, as in the statement

'. . . interest makes Gods as well as kings, and laws for heaven, as well as laws for the earth.'[2]

This was characteristic of Rohan, and of very few others widely read in England at this time.

The distinctive mark of Ascham's writing was his practice of examining social duties in the light of man's self-interest. He emphasized the matter of physical safety at least as much as did Hobbes, and, indeed, seems to have done so more, since it was the major theme in his work. The right to life was the basic claim and led to another, that of property necessary to sustain life. In this connection he referred to a 'common right or natural community', but the concept had none of the connotations of the common good, which was so often described in such terms. This common right amounted to no more than the justice of appropriating from another's goods enough to sustain one's life. While to the Marxist the denial of any such right might appear a more perfect embodiment of economic individualism, Ascham's view was individualistic none the less.

Reversing a strongly held idea, he utterly denied the primacy of community over individual interests. The statement about using another's goods emerges not as an idealized form of primitive communism but as potentially anarchical right, to be exercised, in some circumstances, at the expense of another's preservation.[3] One statement by Ascham may have been unique in English thought up to that time; certainly most men would have held the exact opposite to his remark that

'. . . nature it self [was] more intent to the preservation of particular than of public bodies, which are made out of particulars, and as

[1] Ascham, *Of the Confusions and Revolutions of Government* (1649), pp. 112 and 191. The first edition of this work appeared in the previous year. The edition of 1649 had nine additional chapters.
[2] *Ibid.,* p. 154.   [3] *Ibid.,* p. 164.

much as may be for the particular ends and preservation of each singular.'[1]

The problem was how much 'may be', and here Ascham was silent. Clearly, though, his individualism went beyond that of Hobbes, for Ascham asserted as strongly as possible the primacy of individual over common interest, without paying any attention to a public ego to integrate society. At times he gave the impression that his interest in a crude physical survival, had led him to reduce the pretensions of the state to the level of a private army holding possession of the persons of individuals.[2] With such an extreme position, one can hardly wonder that he was sceptical of the efficacy of early training, the arts of diplomacy and the claims of religion to bring selfless benevolence into the world. All such devices broke against the hard fact that all men wanted the same few scarce items.

One recent commentator has suggested that Ascham and others may have been led to their opinions by a growing disenchantment with a political situation where all parties claimed with equal vigour to speak for the common interest of the community.[3] Certainly Ascham dealt the common interest some heavy blows, and in this he was not alone. At this time cynicism about professions of regard for the public interest had become fairly common. It was natural for supporters of the king to try to puncture the more inflated claims for *salus populi*, but others did so as well. Two examples of contemporary opinion should suffice:

'. . . the most dangerous designs of public ruin and particular interests have always been fomented under the most plausible species of public advantage.'[4]

'. . . when you discover in any man more than ordinary pretensions of zeal to the public good . . . you may then, I say, be sure that party . . . is such an one as mislikes his present condition.'[5]

In the minds of some citizens talk of the common good sug-

---

[1] Ascham, p. 44.   [2] *Ibid.*, p. 4.
[3] I. Coltman, *Private Men and Public Causes* (London, 1962), pp. 23–5.
[4] Anon., *Vox Militaris* . . . (1647), p. 1 (BM: E 401).
[5] Anon., *A Copy of a Letter Written to an Officer of the Army by a True Commonwealthsman* (1656), p. 14 (B: Wood 626).

gested radicalism of a most dangerous sort. A modern parallel would be the situation where an association with 'peace' slogans might, in some circumstances, suggest political extremism. One royalist resorted to verse, each line of which recorded some social ill to be avoided. One stanza reads as follows:

> From such as still aim at the public's good,
> From those that have two faces under a hood,
> From a reformation founded in blood,
>   Libera me.[1]

It was not unusual then to question the good faith of those who were too ostentatious in proclaiming their regard for the public interest. Ascham went further and claimed that the preservation of the community did not deserve that primacy traditionally accorded to it. Thus he came much closer to undermining the conventional notion of a public good than Hobbes ever had. Ascham differed from his contemporaries in his marked disrespect for political order as such, an attitude more extreme than simple hostility to some form of government. Of course Ascham's treatise was unsatisfactory because he said little about the exact limits of individual duties to the community. This reflected the fact that he was not trying to describe the normal routine of social life but men's actions during the confusions and revolutions of government. From certain comments about the permanence of strife, one gathers that he meant some of his observations to refer to political life in general, but still the perspective was very much coloured by the immediate situation.

Ascham was perhaps the author of another work that dealt differently with the problems of politics. It has been confidently asserted that he wrote the chief theoretical defence of the Rump.[2] If this is so, he apparently managed to suppress some of his more extreme opinions when he had to justify political authority. His earlier emphasis upon self-interest and unavoidable conflict is not easy to reconcile with the statement that the government would be based on

---

[1] Anon., *A New Litany for These Times* (1659) (B: Wood 483).
[2] 'E. Philodemius', Γενεσις ... *The Original and End of Civil Power* (1649). The editors of one modern reprint take it for granted that Ascham was the author, but such certainty seems unwarranted. See W. H. Dunham and S. Pargellis (eds.), *Complaint and Reform in England 1436–1714* (N.Y., 1938), p. 640.

'. . . a wise conspiration of several different notes into one sweet and harmonious tune of common interest.'[1]

However, other thinkers had adopted a new tone as political conditions changed. For all his apparent disenchantment with public life and its responsibilities, he did serve the Commonwealth as a diplomat until his assassination in Spain.

Several passages in the tract are similar to Ascham's earlier opinions. Thus, while he defended the people's right to overthrow tyranny, the writer appeared to have no strong attachment to popular government. He had none of the animus against monarchy that one sees in Milton, for instance. This writer simply said that the power of the people might be collected into the hands of 'one or more persons' for purposes of administration. He mentioned Hobbes, at a time when his works were still not widely quoted, although it is hard to tell what he thought of him.[2] The passage that most smacks of Ascham was the one where he discussed the meaning of '*salus publica*' as the foundation of all politics. It meant that government was

'. . . for the safety and benefit of the whole, and every individual (the general being but as it were, a constellation of particulars) in their distinct nature, rights and privileges.'[3]

This was precisely the sort of argument that one did not usually find in an apology for established institutions. While it might be generally allowed that, in a sense, the community was only a collection of particular men, conservative writers used this point to show how all particulars would be protected when the community was safe. Normally, of course, they did not describe the community in these terms at all, for they were not prepared to go further and say that the good of the state was that of the particular members. Ascham did say this, showing clearly that the public safety was the protection of private rights. Ascham was not the only person to say this, as we have seen; many

---

[1] *Original . . .*, pp. 6–7.
[2] *Ibid.*, p. 15. This passage plainly states that Hobbes was an important thinker. There is an additional comment, seemingly critical of his views about human nature, although the syntax of the sentence might make it refer equally well to Cicero.
[3] *Ibid.*, p. 10.

democrats, and some other people who had been influenced by Hobbes, used the same approach. Nevertheless, few writers, up to this time, had expressed the point in quite the same way. The best previous example occurs in a passage already quoted from *The Confusions and Revolutions of Government.*

Ascham had dismissed in a sentence the role of religion in effecting a degree of harmony between private and public interest. Others, no less individualistic, took the religious sanction more seriously. Hobbes himself was firmly committed to celestial self-interest, and remarked that only men 'without discipline' would fail to weigh the profit and loss of a future life in their present calculations.[1] The doctrine later to be called theological utilitarianism was already current, and in a sense had always flourished, though one has to allow for differences in emphasis. People like Hobbes called self-interested the activity of seeking salvation, while earlier thinkers, as noted before, were less concerned with classifying all actions according to their degree of self-interest.

The same consideration played an important part in the writings of others who were influenced by Hobbes. One hesitates to speak of a Hobbesian school, for there was never any time in the seventeenth century when opinion would tolerate an obvious admiration of Hobbes as a political thinker. The universities seem to have been especially severe with his confessed admirers.[2] Nevertheless, there were men who followed Hobbes in his main conclusions, even though they may not have thought it politic to admit it.

One of them was Thomas White, the author of a number of works on theology and of one important book on politics. White was a notorious Catholic. After a career as a teacher of theology at Douay and Lisbon, he returned to England, where he flourished on controversy to a great age.[3] Hobbes knew him, but if

---

[1] 'Behemoth', in *English Works*, Vol. VI, p. 231.
[2] Ferdinand Toennies records the persecution of one Oxford admirer. See 'Contributions à L'Histoire de la Pensée de Hobbes', in *Archives de Philosophie*, Vol. XII, Cahier II (1936), p. 100. See too *The Recantation of Daniel Scargill Publickly Made Before the University of Cambridge* (Cambridge, 1669) (B: Wood 608).
[3] For details of his life, the best source seems to be Robert Pugh, *Blacklo's Cabal Discovered* (1680). Pugh was working on a life of White, but apparently it never appeared.

we are to believe John Aubrey, White interested him very little owing to his lack of aptitude for geometry.[1]

Human nature presented an essentially Hobbesian aspect to White. 'Man,' he said,

'. . . being a rational creature . . . desires to know that the work prescribed for him is good, that is, good for him.'[2]

Accordingly, White believed that men were best governed when left free to proceed by their own inclinations. He realized that this would not always be possible, but he saw any neglect of the basic principle as nothing less than a denial of man's rationality and his humanity. To a large extent, he equated self-interest and rationality, since each in its perfection obviously involved the other. Strangely enough, in his theological writings, White appears to have subscribed to the casual usage of the ordinary pamphleteer in associating 'interest' with irrational passion.[3]

His book was ostensibly written to support established authority, but the most interesting sections were only concerned with this in a secondary way. White's unconventional approach here was to ask how men could ever be expected to do anything unless it was to their advantage. Such questions hovered in the background of most tracts written to secure obedience, but his merit was that he said bluntly, even shockingly, what other men only implied. White looked with frank astonishment at the long tradition of calling upon men for absolute self-sacrifice. In order to act, men required some motive, and a complete disregard of self seemed to supply none. Even the actions of the most ascetic holy man of Asia had to be fitted into the limits of human behaviour. The universal law was that one would only scorn one set of pleasures, in order to enjoy, with greater certainty, another set. To perform any action with no thought of self was extremely irrational, and against nature.[4] This was certainly self-interest, but thus far had no particular political relevance. One cannot emphasize too much Warrender's point that there

[1] *Brief Lives*, ed. A. Clark (London, 1898), Vol. I, p. 369. Wood, on the other hand, records a much closer relationship between the two. See A. Wood, *Athenae Oxonienses*, ed. Bliss (London, 1817), Vol. III, Cols. 1247–8.
[2] White, *The Grounds of Obedience and Government* (1655), p. 5.
[3] *A Contemplation of Heaven* (Paris, 1654), p. 60.
[4] *Grounds . . .*, pp. 55–6.

is a vital distinction between self-ends in relation to early matters and to those of another life.[1] Much of the confusion of seventeenth-century writers might have been avoided had they always admitted the differences between social and religious self-interest.

Fortunately, White discussed his theme in its political applications, although this did not involve dropping the question of salvation and its place as a universal interest. In a far more direct way than Hobbes, he was led to examine the critical concept of a public interest and its status in a community of egoists. The vital chapter posed the question 'why a man is to hazard himself for the common good'.[2]

He began by observing that of course there was some recompense, for the good of the whole reflected upon the part. At this point the schoolmen had generally stopped. With White, it was only a starting-point, for

'. . . in morality the reason of all action is the good obtainable by it which if less or not greater than what we hazard and peradventure, lose in the attempt, it is no good nor can it be a rational motive of such an action. We ought therefore to seek out this great good.'[3]

This involved a critical appraisal of traditional doctrine. White chose Aristotle to illustrate its shortcomings, since his dictum on the subject had been endlessly quoted in the medieval version '*bonum commune divinius est quam particulare*'.[4] This was an obvious target to a nominalist such as White. He allowed that were there some 'platonic idea' of particular goods that might be termed the common good, then the statement might be comprehensible. However, he assumed that Aristotle did not mean that, since he had rejected the theory on which platonic ideas were based. White undoubtedly rejected it too.

White understood that the notion of a common good was accorded a certain superiority over particular goods by virtue

[1] H. Warrender, *The Political Philosophy of Hobbes* (Oxford, 1957), p. 221.
[2] *Grounds* . . ., Chapter X, pp. 67–78.   [3] *Grounds* . . ., pp. 68–9.
[4] In his role as an heretical theologian, White was also a philosopher. He had a particular animus against Aristotle and apparently it was he who converted Sir Kenelm Digby to what was then known as the 'atomicall philosophy'. See Pugh, *op. cit.*, 'Epistle to the Catholic reader'.

of its universality. He appreciated as well the quality of infinity in the life of a commonwealth when it was compared with a single citizen. All this he allowed to be 'very august and lustrous'. Significantly, he did not deny the real excellence of the common good, but he chose to discuss its apparent qualities with a faintly ironic air. His real source of complaint was Aristotle's treatment of the connection between individual and social goods:

'. . . when . . . I see the same great master teach us that good is the same with desirable, and every one's good, what is desirable to him; I find it an intricate labyrinth of equivocation wherein we endlessly err, while we think that good taken in common should be accounted good, truly and properly.'[1]

The parallels that suggested themselves to White were illuminating. Aristotle's position was akin to expecting a man to rejoice at being robbed because it was of some good to the robber. He further illustrated the impossibility of looking to some universal good unrelated to one's own, asking:

'. . . who would be so wild as to bend any strong labour here in England to profit the king of Persia or Siam, if he expected no good to reflect on himself by it?'[2]

Indeed, according to the premises, one could just as easily substitute the King of England for those distant potentates. His examples showed clearly that there was no objection to Aristotle's equation of a man's good with what he desired (i.e. his interest); it was only that specious individual good hidden in the general good that bothered him.

The quixotic activities mentioned in the examples were only a slight exaggeration of the common practice of dwelling upon the common good without asking about personal profit. White's whole point was that one always had to ask 'cui bono?' On the basis of his rigorous nominalism, then

'. . . to cry the common good, is a mere deceit and flattery of words; unless we can show that the common good is as great to us as we make it sound.'[3]

---

[1] *Grounds* . . ., pp. 70–1.   [2] *Ibid.*   [3] *Ibid.*, p. 71.

Thus far the argument would seem to have been aimed at discrediting the very notion of a public good, although this was not the intention. The initial impression was only strengthened by his statement that 'we must see who are the common whose welfare is to be preferred before private interests'.[1] However, he did not proceed to examine social forces in the manner of some later writers.

This was so because of the task that White had set himself. His main concern had been to criticize the misconception that one could possibly ignore one's own good while seeking a common one. It had not been to ask what sort of an entity this common good was, though it was understandably difficult to separate the two questions entirely. Misunderstandings about how people could be expected to behave easily led to false assumptions about the common good, the supposed end of their endeavours. The conclusion to White's narrowly defined task came with an introduction of religious considerations to solve worldly problems. In the nature of things, some conflict between immediate secular interests and the common good was inevitable. Thus a sufficient motive to seek the common good was dependent upon a 'rational apprehension' of some future life where earthly accounts would be balanced.[2] Much of White's work then became as much an argument for the existence of God as it was for the authority of the magistrate. It was, in a sense, an argument from design, in this case the design not of the universe but of the human ego and the concessions that had to be made to it in order to have social order. It remained true that one should prefer the common good to one's own, in so far as one looked only to satisfaction in this world, and the 'should' was both an ethical and a prudential one.

White's contribution was not then as radical as one might first think. His point did have political implications though, for having made his plea for organized religion, he took a further look at the concept of a common good. The insistence that discussion of the concept only made sense to those who were to act for it, when their interests really were included, was of general application. It could point to eternal rewards, but its implications need not end there. Obviously White was not confident in securing adequate obedience with only heavenly rewards to

[1] *Grounds* . . ., p. 153.   [2] *Ibid.*, p. 75.

provide an incentive.[1] He discussed the common good in relation to secular affairs and offered purely worldly incentives to sustain it.

One of his observations was quite conventional except that it involved a Hobbesian denial that a subject could claim rights against the commonwealth. He wrote:

'. . . whoever understands what common and particular signify, easily understands that the common and particular are not two; as the part and the whole are not two, because the part is included in the whole.'[2]

Stated in this way, the proposition came dangerously close to Aristotle's contention, for it seemed possible that an individual's supposed good might disappear into the good of the whole, without his having any assurance of personal benefit. Another statement might seem to say the same thing as the previous one, but with an important change in emphasis.

'The end of the subject in his obedience, immediately, is the public good or the good of the commonwealth; a further though more cordial and deep in the subject, is the good he is to receive out of the commonwealth being well, which is nothing else but that the particulars be so.'[3]

This statement did not conclude with a self-evident fact. At least it had not been self-evident to the numerous writers who thought of the good of the commonwealth in terms of national security or the furtherance of God's will, neither of which was generally seen as identical with the welfare of a collection of particular persons. Especially this was so in the case of the writers who insisted that the preservation of the whole dwarfed into insignificance the interests of particular members. White's departure from such views was one of perspective; it did not even mean that he ignored reason of state and maintenance of political independence. But he translated it into Hobbesian terms. He valued public peace more than anything else; he

[1] White did not greatly emphasize punishments as effective sanctions. In fact, one of the orthodox complaints about his theology was that he diluted the pains of hell. See *A Letter by G. L. to Mr. And. Kingh* (n.d.) (BM: C 38, a.41).

[2] *Grounds . . .*, p. 131.   [3] *Ibid.*, p. 97.

sought a quiet life rather than honour.[1] Obviously he expected others to have the same values, for his clearest measure of when the 'common good' could be seen to dictate preserving the government was

'. . . when the merchant, the husbandman, the tradesman, with their appendices, are in an undisturbed practice of their functions.'[2]

This was certainly the sort of common good of which the common man might have a 'rational apprehension'.

White appreciated that there was a decided difference in perspective between his position and that of conventional dicta about a common good. In a minor work he foreshadowed the argument of his *Grounds of Obedience*. Undoubtedly the good of particulars had to yield to that of the community, but that did not close the issue. When one spoke of the good of creatures, it might mean either that of the whole mass of them or some particular ones. In any event, the 'good of a creature must of necessity be suitable to its inclination'.[3] This was a most important statement, for it established that 'good', to White, meant the same as 'interest' for some of his contemporaries. His main point became apparent when he claimed that

'. . . where there is no prejudice to the common, the good of the particular is truly good; and its best, absolutely best, not only to the particular, but to the common; since the good of the common is compounded of the good of every particular, and is so much better, as all particulars are better.'[4]

The other participant in the dialogue demurred. Such a notion was very hard to absorb, for "tis so strange to what I have hitherto been taught'.[5] The character who spoke for White allowed that this was so, but added:

'. . . yet I do not conceive you have been taught anything contrary.'[6]

White's point of view was far from revolutionary, since it consisted largely in providing an unusually careful justification of

---

[1] *Grounds . . .*, p. 117.　　[2] *Ibid.*, p. 154.
[3] *Rushworth's Dialogues* (Paris, 1654), p. 236. White claimed to be the author only of the preface and the fourth dialogue. He seems to have written them all, however, and William Rushworth, if he existed, had no part in the work.
[4] *Ibid.*, p. 249.　　[5] *Ibid.*, p. 251.　　[6] *Ibid.*

traditional precepts. Egoistic men were to have their good 'carried' by the common good, just as their liberty was to be found in the interstices of the law.[1] He took the argument that in realizing the public good, private interests were satisfied, and chose to emphasize the converse, that the satisfaction of private interests was itself the common good. In carrying the analysis farther than most other thinkers, he at least posed the problem of the common good by stressing the interests of individuals. Despite his unorthodox formula for the public good, its compatibility with individual interests required the higher principle of salvation.

Significantly, though, he suggested circumstances where purely secular considerations could effect the necessary harmony. In rejecting classical writers as guides to understanding what was involved in a common good, he made some very important concessions. The dictum about preferring the common good had been coined in a social environment that was no longer relevant. The reason was that writers such as Aristotle had been thinking of popular governments

'. . . where plainly the common good was the good of them who were to reward the causes of it so that it was no wonder the common good should be so highly exhalted and cryed up: where it was the particular good both to them to whom it was commended, as also the commanders themselves . . .'[2]

The statement seems to absolve Aristotle from the charge of confused thinking and places the odium upon his followers, who perpetuated an anachronism. However, surely it was a most damaging admission for any defender of one-man government, for it implied that the problem of the common good would disappear were all interests to gain access to the government. He had thus put the case of the middle-class radicals of the early nineteenth century, without trying to discredit it.

The systems in question were heathen, of course, but he never said that this disqualified them. The only answer that was implied was that White accepted the government of the day, and it allowed for no such easy reconciliation of public and private interests. Harmony in a system with a chief magistrate (he avoided the title 'king') lay in the congruence of his interest with

[1] *Grounds . . .*, pp. 130 and 127.   [2] *Grounds . . .*, p. 72.

that of the public. All private citizens apparently had ulterior motives in any ostensible sacrifice for the common good. But the obligation of the chief magistrate was perfect in the sense that there was no antithesis between his private interest and that of the public. He insisted that the ruler must not act for his own interest rather than for the good of the commonwealth.[1] However, his further insistence that the ruler was, for this reason, morally superior to his subjects seems perverse. The ruler was not exempt from self-interest, he was simply in a position where his prosperity, honour and security were best provided for by keeping the commonwealth safe and prosperous.[2] Since, within the terms of his argument, it was not possible for a rational ruler to deviate from his own understanding of the public good, the source of his moral superiority was difficult to see. His virtues came from his social situation, and not from any refined moral awareness. White seemed closer to the truth when he implied only that the ruler's function was the most admirable, because of the social benefits that he conferred.[3] His clearest single statement of the relationship between the ruler and the common good was that

'. . . because the common good is the very private good of the commander, therefor it is not related to any other private good of the same nature; and so it is not commanded or limited by any other, as in the subject it is by the end of his idioticall good.'[4]

White had more to say about discovering the common good. Justice, so frequently offered as the essence of the common good, was no help in its discovery. Justice, in the lawyer's sense, was a mere 'platonic idea', abstracted from the inevitable 'circumstantial occurrences' that plagued government.[5] Rulers should forget about Justinian when trying to discern the public good; much more helpful were either

'. . . the science of politics, or the certitude of faith and tradition, which are the only two rules a high government hath.'[6]

The ruler would obviously consult his own interest too, but here he was concerned with the sort of knowledge that would make the public ego effective. Pragmatic calculation was the way to

---

[1] *Grounds . . .*, p. 80–1.   [2] *Ibid.*, p. 81.   [3] *Ibid.*, p. 78.
[4] *Ibid.*, p. 98.   [5] *Ibid.*, p. 139.   [6] *Ibid.*, p. 173.

that public good that consisted in the well-being of the particular citizens.

White's book was a clear indication that the traditional dicta about the common good were being questioned. His was not an individualism that promised great new opportunities for concrete social activity, but like most kinds of individualism at this time, it did allow men to keep what they already had. More than most men, White was aware of the benefits of leaving people to pursue their concerns in tranquillity. Like Hobbes, he saw political liberty resting in the silence of the law. One of the most interesting things about White was that he divorced his religious rewards for compliance with the public good from his idea of the good itself, which was wholly secular.

As a Roman Catholic controversialist, and rather an unorthodox one at that, White cannot have been very influential. He could not even claim to express the political views of English Roman Catholics, though one contemporary critic felt that White and other Catholics were more likely to conceive the world in terms of self-interest than were others.[1] Though undoubtedly quite well known as a person, his theory of politics failed to excite much interest. His book was correctly interpreted as a defence of Cromwell and not of Stuart legitimacy; thus his work was largely discredited.[2] The one full-scale critique was by Roger Coke, better known for his writings on commerce. It was not impressive. Coke objected strongly to White's emphasis upon rational self-interest and countered with an incoherent attempt to divorce the will from the understanding, thus separating interest and reason.[3] He passed over the

[1] William Ball, *State Maxims* (1655), p. 2.

[2] See Anon., *Evangelium Armatum, A Specimen, or Short Collection of Several Doctrines and Positions destructive to our Government Both Civil and Ecclastical* (1663), p. 58 (B: Wood D 26); T. R., *A Letter from a Gentleman to his Friend in London* (1660), p. 24 (BM: C 38, a.41); and Anon., *Ursa Major and Minor . . .* (1681), p. 19 (B: Ashm. 1680). White was aggrieved that he should have been branded as anti-monarchical, but some of his comments on the restored Stuarts were notably cool. Thus he remarked pointedly that no government, once dispossessed, had any right to restoration unless it clearly accorded with the public good. His loyalty to all governments was then obviously conditional. See letter to Sir Kenelm Digby, 29 April 1663(?), (BM: Add. MSS. 41), 846, fols. 84–5.

[3] Coke, *A Survey of the Politicks of Mr. Thomas White, Mr. Thomas Hobbes and Mr. Hugo Grotius* (1660), Section II, p. 2.

important chapter on the common good with the observation that it might well have great merit, but that he intended to leave it undisturbed. In White's philosophical egoism he saw individualism, and feared that the practical effect of his doctrine was to release all men from conventional social restraints.

White was not an entirely original thinker; he owed much to Hobbes. However, his quarrel with Aristotle was probably his own and not that of Hobbes. Certainly he showed considerable ability in developing certain points that were only implicit in Hobbes, if they were there at all.

Hobbes also precipitated interesting reactions elsewhere. John Hall was the author of a massive five-hundred-page book on government that appeared in 1654. He identified himself as a resident of Richmond in Surrey, and has since been known to bibliographers as Hall of Richmond to distinguish him from several better-known Halls writing upon politics at this time. He was an educated man, but seems to have left no trace in the universities or the Inns of Court. Nothing else is known about him, but he did write an interesting book.[1]

Hall's book owed a great debt to Hobbes, although ironically it began with a disclaimer regarding sources, similar to that in *Leviathan*. Hall was technically correct in his claim that he quoted from almost no sources but the Bible, but the whole argument was studded with borrowings from Hobbes. On goodness and pleasure, liberty and dominion he followed Hobbes to the letter.

The central assumption about self-interest being the key to human behaviour was developed in very much the same way as by Hobbes or White. Government had been established for the particular ends of men and it could survive no longer than it could appear to personal interests, for men could recognize no higher good than their own.[2] The whole problem of government

---

[1] The only promising clue regarding his identity is Aubrey's reference to one Hall, who, with White, was a great friend of Sir Kenelm Digby. Aubrey, *op. cit.*, p. 227. Aubrey thought that this Hall, like White, was a Jesuit, which our author certainly was not. See John Hall, *Of Government and Obedience as they Stand Directed and Determined by Scripture and Reason* (1654), pp. 210–11. Hall wrote another book called *The True Cavalier* (1656), which is helpful only because it shows that he accepted Cromwell for typically Hobbesian reasons. See pp. 128–9.

[2] *Of Government . . .*, p. 28.

was that of using 'policy' in order to make egoistic men pursue their own welfare to the benefit of others. Purely disinterested benevolence was irrational and unnatural, so that while benefiting others, men would have to be following their own interests, or they would lack any will to act. Such comments, of course, only raised the classical difficulty of cataloguing the determinants of human behaviour. What one man called self-interest, another would call altruism.

Hall came closer to the facts of social life in presenting the case for monarchy. Those who sought popular forms of government were naïve in their assumptions about human nature, for

'. . . after the vulgar manner, to dream of public-spirited persons or public souls (meaning such as have no private interest) is not only untrue, but could it be, it would, instead of benefit, be the ruin of that whole state. For through the distracted endeavours of so many voluntary public undertakers, the whole would perish by degrees, and while each particular failed, for want of due self-regard, the whole would fail by consequent.'[1]

Far more even than Hobbes, Hall emphasized the prevalence of opinions opposed to his own. The ills of the world had led men to assume self-interest ('*philautia*', to him) to be unlawful. Even those who deemed it natural and unavoidable somehow fancied that its force prevailed at the beginning, but not at the end, of human enterprises. This, he pointed out, was simply muddled thinking

'. . . as though the end and design of each action, must not, in all voluntary and intelligent agents, be before any attempt thereof: or, as if any reasonable creature, could out of self-regard begin any thing, which, in the issue, he did forsee would prove otherwise.'[2]

In fact, any tendency to prefer another's interest to one's own was not only irrational but sinful. This odd-sounding statement referred to the impiety of ignoring divine rewards and punishments, and not to any anarchical individualism. For Hall assumed that man was to some extent socialized by calculations of the effect of his activities on salvation.

He did not place as much reliance upon this sanction as had White, perhaps not as much as had Hobbes, whose comments

---

[1] *Of Government . . .*, p. 98.   [2] *Ibid.*, p. 98.

on the matter were not as specific, and hence difficult to compare. White had sometimes written as though all self-regard in social life were to be overruled by that more refined selfishness that looked to salvation. Hall chose to argue the same basic point in more general terms. He wrote of a judicious ordering of pains and pleasures, punishments and rewards, both worldly and eternal, that could be used to produce the common good. Despite the initial discussion of theological utilitarianism and the oppressively pious tone of the closing chapters, Hall said very little of hopes and fears about salvation as a harmonizing agent. He said correspondingly more about secular incentives and sanctions. It was certainly not unusual for writers on politics to note that government had a role here; everyone who discussed the need for government after the fall of man had some such consideration in mind. Hall was more explicit than most, for it had not been usual for men to come to grips with the perennial problems of politics in terms that stipulated how men were to be led to serve the public through the pursuit of their own interests. His remarks on the need to lead men to the common interest by 'policy' epitomized the contribution of the Hobbesian writers. Though perhaps they said the obvious, they said it more clearly than had their predecessors.

Hall thought that pain and fear were more powerful emotions than pleasure and hope.[1] Nevertheless, men needed encouragement through rewards, for it remained obvious that 'the common ass is ill saddled'.[2] At this stage of the argument he had nothing to say about the nature of the rewards. He turned instead to consider the institutions of government. The grand question here was the debate between commonwealthsmen and royalists about the respective merits of their systems. Hall used all of the common arguments against popular government, and included a few that were not frequently heard. Thus he claimed that popular government stumbled on the fact of human disagreement, for if it claimed to allow the majority to have its own way in matters of equal concern to all, there remained the problem of judging what matters properly fell into that category.

His nominalism rebelled against the common cry of the parliamentary party that a community could harbour no sinister

[1] *Of Government . . .*, p. 450.   [2] *Ibid.*, p. 99.

designs against itself. He could see no community, but a collection of oligarchs, who claimed to speak for the common good
and equated the commonwealth with themselves. In reply, he
followed Hobbes in going behind the façade of a public interest:

'. . . but if men would well consider it, these terms of commonwealth
and public good are but bare politic notions, not being creatures
capable of address or interest: and that they are not otherwise
manageable, or to be represented or collected into a sum or total,
than as related to the persons therein intrusted.'[1]

In other words, a public good had to be treated as the private
interests of some people. If the rulers were divided in their interests, it was not sensible to identify the public good with their
private interests.

Though here Hall was primarily concerned with displaying
the unpalatable reality that lay behind the notion of a common
good in a democracy, he had more positive things to say about
it. From the inconveniences of democracy, he passed on to the
virtues of monarchy. His argument was more elaborate than
Hobbes's treatment, but Hobbes was probably his model. Hall
made interesting use of an idea closely akin to the medieval concept of *dominium*. The whole trouble with parliamentarians
was that they were committed in varying degrees to the different items of business, their efforts waxing and waning with the
extent to which their personal interests were involved. The convenience of having a single ruler was that he had an adequate
incentive to procure the common good, on all occasions. His
immediate concern in all matters of policy Hall called a 'whole
interest'.[2] The good of the public just happened to coincide with
the private interest of any rational monarch, and so in seeking
his own good he served the public.

It was perfectly natural for private men to prefer their own
interests to the neglect of all else. This was often inconvenient,
for

'. . . every particular property is but parcel of the public . . . if that
public have not a person of whole and equal interest herein, and
thereby of whole and equal in the particulars thereof, how can the
whole be duly regarded?'[3]

The stress upon the proprietary nature of the king's position

---

[1] *Of Government* . . ., p. 93.   [2] *Ibid.*, p. 94.   [3] *Ibid.*, p. 135.

might seem outmoded, but this was certainly what Hall meant, as will be shown below. Like White, he denigrated the conventional notion of justice. Men had usually erred in assuming that somehow justice could exist in the abstract before it was realized in concrete cases.[1] Distributive justice in the allocation of riches, offices and arms and the setting of all social priorities could be left to the self-interest of a ruler who stood to profit from an efficient organization.[2] This was the only meaningful embodiment of justice.

The discussion of general problems of public policy was contained in the chapter called 'Of the Publike Good, Common Good or Commonweal'. Having already vindicated individual self-seeking in general terms, he began by trying to liberate the interest of the national state from any restraints arising from more inclusive communities, such as Christendom or humanity. He drew an exact parallel between the claims of individuals *vis-à-vis* the state and states *vis-à-vis* humanity. In both bases the preservation of the larger unit was immediately dependent upon the welfare and interest of the component parts.[3] In applying consistently the principle that only through the self-seeking by the parts was the whole vitalized, Hall displayed the paradox of an age that gave prominence both to necessity of state and to individual self-interest.

When he had justified national ambitions, he turned to domestic aspects of the common good. He did not make the distinction between domestic and foreign interests in the exact way sometimes attempted. Since he had a good deal to say about trade in this chapter, it was easy to pass from one sphere to the other, since commerce was relevant to both. This might seem to be a minor point, but it is of interest that Hall had almost nothing to say about national strength in the reason-of-state tradition. He conceived of national happiness in terms of 'the general notion of pleasure',[4] something more easily attributed to individuals than states. The common good involved 'collecting the

<hr/>

[1] *Of Government . . .*, p. 150.   [2] *Ibid.*, p. 160.
[3] *Ibid.*, p. 158. A similar idea was Ascham's contention that the sovereignty of a nation state followed from its being considered as a single individual with all of the autonomy that was thereby implied. Cf. Ascham, *op. cit.*, p. 71.
[4] *Of Government . . .*, p. 158.

happiness of each kingdom into a total'. This could only be done by maximizing the number of citizens who benefited from any given policy. The idea was simpler than the famous 'greatest happiness of the greatest number', but it was not dissimilar, as his explanation shows:

'. . . as the happiness of a whole kingdom must (collectively considered) be greater than the happiness of any single person or order in the same, so must the happiness of one kingdom increase above that of another in proportion, as the persons by them made happy do differ in number.'[1]

The subject as well as the ruler had an important role in securing the public interest. Hall's discussion of commerce consists of a strange blend of crude mercantilist ideas and others of a more liberal nature. Like almost everybody else, he recognized certain aspects of foreign trade requiring regulation in the national interest. In domestic trade he was still conscious of a national stock that might be spoiled in a general scramble, but on the whole he advocated *laissez-faire* in that area. At worst, most such abuses would only transfer goods from one group of subjects to another, without having much effect upon aggregate national stock. Because of his earlier claim that national happiness was proportionate to the extension of individual felicity, this should have been a matter of concern. Probably he just assumed that calculating differential utilities was impossible.

Hall was intrigued by the way in which most domestic commerce proceeded smoothly because men were able to prosper by providing for each other's wants. Largely because of this, he advocated an open market, saying:

'. . . authority interposeth but in few cases with success: and in my judgement, in the silence of authority, they are under no rule but of their own consciences; namely of the rule of do as thou wouldst be done unto.'[2]

There is some doubt about how seriously he meant the reader to take this internal sanction, for he had already observed that this admirable ethic simply did not work, citing as an instance that a man buying a horse could not be expected to pay the owner what the buyer would like to get for it were it his.[3] Economic

---

[1] *Of Government . . .,* p. 159.   [2] *Ibid.,* p. 163.   [3] *Ibid.,* p. 141.

activity could not function upon such a basis. In buying and selling the agents might trust to their own skill to benefit themselves as they could. As far as he was concerned, where there was no trust, there could be no cheating, and if one were to measure the illegality of a trade by the proportion of gain, the least profit should also be unlawful.

This freely functioning self-interest did not harm the public. Could it also be a positive benefit? The answer was 'yes'. In alleging detriment from various trading practices, men too often assumed that the consumer's interest was paramount, but was the seller not also a subject? If laws were passed for some, but not all, aspects of commerce, then the law was partial. Should all commodities be subject to control, principally in price, the situation was still unsatisfactory,

'. . . since the gain might as well have gone round; by my enhancing proportionally my commodities to him or others as now our losses do, as being all of us low rated.'[1]

The case for freedom and inflation was a partial one, since Hall was only concerned with certain kinds of economic regulation and he took a shopkeeper's view of what commerce was all about. But with these qualifications his work remains a fine specimen of economic individualism.

Hall raised a fascinating point in connection with the conventional exhortations against commercial practices. Just as all anti-monarchical books were written by discontented subjects,

'so few writers of moral or political duties are tradesmen or sellers, but all buyers: and so, for their interest sake, having not regard to the equal justice of the thing itself, would have them bounded and not themselves.'[2]

The analogy with Monarchomach literature was not a very happy one, nor was the argument wholly convincing. Nevertheless, it stands as a rare instance of perception about the social basis of the anti-individualist ideology.

The laws of the market were treated here as part of a political theory, and this is why the subject has been dealt with in this chapter and not alongside other economic writings. Hall integrated his economic thoughts with his political theory very

---

[1] *Of Government* . . ., p. 163.   [2] *Ibid.*

neatly. Like anyone else, a monarch could be seen as running a commercial venture, selling a service, as it were. Thus, if all other callings were left free to charge what the market would bear, surely it was unfair that the ruler should be 'rated' by others. Thus the absolute monarch was quite justified in raising the price of protection and discriminating among his customers according to the effort needed to protect them and perhaps also in accord with the differing interests men had in protection.[1] This was surely an extreme case of viewing the function of governing as a property right.

This point has implications for an understanding of Hobbes. The discovery that, for all his authoritarian views, he was an individualist is not new.[2] Unfortunately commentators have been embarrassed by an inability to point out satisfactory examples of his individualistic opinions. The point of view was contained in observations about man, and not about economic activity. Hall, surely his closest unacknowledged follower, showed just this close connection between economic individualism and absolute monarchy. Indeed, he used arguments for the former to bolster the latter. This was the public ego with a vengeance!

One other representative of royalist opinion had interesting things to say about the public interest. The scholar, Matthew Wren, entered the history of political thought as an effective literary opponent of Harrington. He had very little to say about one of the major themes treated here, the interest of the king. Wren disliked the mechanical conception of government apparent both in Hobbes and in the republicans, for he preferred a monarchy that was more an 'animate body' than an 'engine'.[3] With such presuppositions, one would not expect him to adhere closely to the Hobbesian system, though he defended *Leviathan* against some trifling criticisms by Harrington.[4] Wren's

[1] *Ibid.*, p. 164.
[2] See C. B. Macpherson, *The Political Theory of Possessive Individualism* (Oxford, 1962), p. 62, and B. de Jouvenel, *Sovereignty*, trans. J. F. Huntington (Cambridge, 1957), pp. 238–40. The latter writer seems to exaggerate the opposition to claims for Hobbes's individualism.
[3] Wren, *Monarchy Asserted; in Vindication of the Consideration upon Mr. Harrington's Oceana* (Oxford, 1659), p. 159.
[4] [Wren], *Considerations on Mr. Harrington's Commonwealth of Oceana* (1657), pp. 7, 9 and 41–2.

remarks on royal self-interest were fragmentary and inconsistent. On one page he portrayed kings as benevolent and disinterested arbiters. On the very next page he was not so sure and added that even when a prince's laws seemed most partial to his own interest, it might be condoned since he was probably still preserving the public peace. In this event, public and royal interest were identical.[1]

Wren's most important contribution was his searing critique of some of Harrington's ill-considered utterances about the common interest of mankind. Some of Wren's points will be noted in the treatment of Harrington and need not be mentioned here. Briefly, he rejected the authority of both Hooker and Grotius for the existence of anything corresponding to a common interest of mankind. Their arguments from the design of the universe were, at best, only weak analogies. Wren had absolutely no patience with explanations of human behaviour that depended upon factors drawn from the world of nature. Like Hobbes and White before him, he strenuously denied that the behaviour of animals was analogous to that of men. Whatever might be true of beasts, men did not recognize, or respond to, any common interest of mankind. As far as this work went, Wren's position seemed to be quite simple, the notion of a common interest did not make sense when defended on the basis of any innate propensities in man.[2] While he limited himself to saying that Harrington's arguments for a common interest more excellent than particular ones was 'infirm', the general tone implied that such a thing was a chimera.

His next exchange with Harrington produced a different emphasis and introduced a qualification. He was no happier with the latter's reasoning, but the nature of his objection to a common interest was put in different terms. His key statement was that

'I must always assert that, though originally in the state of nature ... there was no common interest of mankind distinct from the parts taken severally ... yet since the institution of government, men are obliged besides, nay in some cases, above, their own private to advance the public or common one.'[3]

[1] *Monarchy Asserted . . .*, p. 12.   [2] *Considerations . . .*, pp. 20–1 and 32.
[3] *Monarchy Asserted . . .*, pp. 49–50.

The odd point about this was that his opponent had never said anything about a state of nature, and indeed had said a good deal that related quite unambiguously to the common interest under a civil government. Nor had Wren himself previously mentioned any state of nature. Thus Wren was making use of the very ambiguous notion of a state of nature to express his disagreement with Harrington. This disagreement did not relate to the question as to whether men had behaved in a certain way in some distant past, it turned on differing conceptions about human nature. Wren refused to allow that men sacrificed themselves for society in any spontaneous or disinterested way. They simply obeyed the laws that preserved society, something that was 'the interest of every private man'.[1]

Wren's position on the common interest emerges as individualistic in a Hobbesian sense, with all of the limitations that this entailed. It was necessary to discard all vague references to the common interest of mankind, for he recognized each man's unwillingness always to prefer the common interest without external compulsion. Thus he epitomized the Hobbesian contribution to the theory of the public interest. It was not to gratify every interest of every person but to admit fully and frankly that there was a problem that could not be banished by hopefully attributing any false altruism to human beings. As an alternative to Harrington's ideas, Wren offered only a straightforward account of the social convenience of obedience, combined with the conventional argument from the private interest of the ruler. Wren is unsatisfactory as a social theorist only because he used his great capacity to uncover obvious flaws in Harrington, rather than offering a carefully developed theory of his own. Apart from defining the public interest in formal terms as the will of the prince, his only comment as to its content was that it involved conditions whereby

'. . . justice may be impartially administered and every man preserved in the enjoyment of his own.'[2]

The writers grouped together here had only certain tenets in common and they were not consciously a school. Filmer once referred to the existence of a 'party' including such divergent

---

[1] *Monarchy Asserted . . .*, p. 50. [2] *Ibid.*, p. 12.

figures as Selden, Grotius, Ascham and Hobbes.[1] Actually, about the only common factor among all four was that they all belonged to that great segment of humanity whose views conflicted with Filmer's.

It remains true, though, that Hobbes was the most prominent of several men who looked closely at the social implications of self-interest. Many minor figures went no further than to write about the 'public ego'. Others, with a concern for precision in treating self-interest, were led naturally to question the ancient injunction to prefer the common good. In order to say what processes were involved in preferring a common good, it was generally necessary to give an unusually clear explanation of what the concept of a common good meant. On questions like this, Hobbes was perhaps the most reticent of the major figures. As far as can be ascertained, White, Hall and Wren were the only writers in the Interregnum period to devote an entire chapter of a book to an analysis of the public interest.

None of these men reached the conclusion that individuals could, in all circumstances, follow their understanding of their own immediate interests and still serve the public. But of course, as will be explained in due course, no sane man ever made such a claim, and even those who appear to have come closest to the extreme position were thinking about particular contexts. Writing about government in general, as Hobbes did, was the surest way of avoiding an excessively optimistic theory of harmony. In such circumstances it became ludicrous.

Two important contributions emerged from the works treated here. The theory of the public ego led to a new formulation of the main problem of government. Political systems had to secure an identity of interest between rulers and ruled. The general idea was certainly not entirely novel, but the normal vagueness about the scope of self-interest in political life had obscured the point. The second contribution was the attempt to define the public interest in terms of individual interests, rather than emphasizing factors such as national power. Sometimes this involved no more than stressing very emphatically the degree to which particular interests were cared for in the common interest. It was no longer enough for moralists to say how excellent

[1] 'Directions for Obedience to Government in Dangerous or Doubtful Times', in *Works*, p. 231.

general interests were in comparison to private ones. At the very least, one had to be more specific about what was to be done for particular interests. There were strong disagreements about the relative merits of competing definitions of the public interest. Perhaps the difference between preserving the community and promoting individual subjects to happiness by allowing them to accumulate property was only one of emphasis. But to at least some seventeenth-century men it was a significant distinction. The most pronounced Hobbesists chose the more liberal formula and so allied themselves with many writers on the popular side of the Civil War. By contrast, the more conventional royalists defended an older version of the public interest. They would continue to do so after the Restoration.

Some recent studies of Hobbes's influence have concentrated upon him as a target for criticism and abuse in the Restoration.[1] One prominent historian has gone so far as to speak of his complete lack of relevance for the intellectual climate of the second half of the century.[2] Hobbes, of course, had many ideas and some of them were uncongenial to the new age, just as they had been uncongenial to the old. However, the two central themes of this chapter represented the wave of the future, not a backwater. Hobbes's idea of the public ego was immediately accepted as quite orthodox by many defenders of kingship. His followers' views on the public interest constituted a more subtle and difficult point, but it too was gaining the day. Both of these arguments might prove useful to a republican such as Harrington.

[1] J. Bowle, *Hobbes and his Critics* (London, 1952), and S. L. Mintz, *The Hunting of Leviathan* (Cambridge, 1962). Mintz emphasizes (p. 147) Hobbes's failure to influence his contemporaries.
[2] H. Trevor-Roper, *Historical Essays* (London, 1958), p. 242.

III

ALTRUISM AND INTEREST
IN HARRINGTON

HARRINGTON IS A major bridging figure in the emergence of new perspectives on the public interest. Complex, obscurely worded and curiously ambivalent, his thought captured the notions implicit in many other writers and presented them on a canvas sufficiently large to repay close analysis.

Harrington's lasting fame was built largely on the theory of the balance of property; it is only of peripheral importance here. Instead, the numerous and sometimes baffling remarks on human nature, social conflict and the all-important concept of 'interest' will claim more of our attention. Emphasis cannot be confined to those general passages relating to the public interest, for matters as diverse as Harrington's cosmology and the mechanics of his utopia are important to the central theme. Too many contemporary references to the public interest failed to explain the writer's basic assumptions. Whatever defects his work displays, Harrington has the supreme virtue of placing his ideas in a meticulously defined political process. This affords the best opportunity to assess the nature and consequences of the republican enthusiasm for a popularly derived common good.

With Harrington, as with Thomas Hobbes, a view of man played an important part in the political theory. Indeed, it will be argued that the basis of human motivation in Harrington's system was for all practical purposes very similar to the Hobbesian model. Harrington followed fashion in proclaiming his distaste for Hobbes. At the same time he applauded the latter's insights on human nature as 'the greatest of new lights'.[1] Recent discussions of Harrington have certainly not emphasized his thoughts on human nature, although it is difficult to agree with the contention by Mrs. Shklar[2] that the author himself avoided all mention of the subject. If one admits the eloquent testimony of the institutions of Oceana, it might be more appropriate to complain of an embarrassment of riches. For it would appear that there was some confusion, or at least uncertainty, in Harrington's position, not unlike the 'Adam Smith Problem' posed by German scholars in their attempts to reconcile Smith's ethical writings with his economic assumptions. Though we lack an orderly account of the mental processes governing the inhabitants of Oceana, scattered throughout the political writings lies ample material to justify the author's comment that 'the form of government is the image of man' (499).

This image of man in its most general form was expressed in the commonplace that he is both a sensual and a philosophical animal. In terms no less conventional, man's soul 'is the mistress of two potent rivals, the one reason, the other passion' (44).[3] The main question to be answered here is the degree to which

[1] *The Oceana and Other Works* (London, 1747), p. 259. All further references, hereafter inserted in the text, are to this edition.

[2] J. N. Shklar, 'Ideology-Hunting: The Case of James Harrington', *American Political Science Review*, Vol. 53 (1959), pp. 662–92, at p. 673. It is even more difficult to discover the grounds of the remark that this opinion was generally entertained by students of the subject. One of them has accused Harrington of lacking intuitive insight in describing human nature, but a poor description is still an attempt. See A. E. Levett, 'James Harrington', in F. J. C. Hearnshaw, *Social and Political Ideas of the Sixteenth and Seventeenth Centuries* (N.Y., 1949), p. 198. Another has noted that Harrington explained history in terms of social forces, rather than on the basis of more human factors, but again, this does not constitute complete neglect of human nature. See J. A. Pocock, *The Ancient Constitution and the Feudal Law* (Cambridge, 1957), p. 146.

[3] For a discussion of the conventional nature of these remarks see S. B. Liljegren, 'James Harrington's Oceana edited with Notes', *Skrifter Vetenskaps-Societeten*, Vol. I (Heidelberg, 1924), pp. 244–5. The one unconventional note seems to be Harrington's unqualified condemnation of the passions. Other Englishmen, writing at an even earlier date, saw the passions as forces for good as well as ill. See Thomas Wright, *The Passions of the Minde in Sixe Books* (1620), pp. 17–18, and Edward Reynolds, *A Treatise of the Passions and Faculties of the Soul of Man* (1640), p. 45.

Harrington contemplated political actors being moved by self-ish or altruistic considerations. Commentators on Harrington would appear to have assumed his adherence to the former view without considering certain remarks that fail to cohere with it.[1] Since 'reason' and 'passion' were the only psychological categories employed by Harrington, we must begin with these terms, trying to discover just what he meant by them.

Reason in individuals was identified with human judgment, inventive capacity and moderation, the passions, with a brutish mode of life and unhappiness (499, 44). Not surprisingly then, Harrington felt himself committed to deposing the passions and advancing reason (252). At one time moralists would have linked reason to political obedience and social altruism, while the passions would be seen as promoting anti-social conduct. But Harrington as a student of Hobbes was aware that reason had no necessary connection with altruism.

Reason appears as a possible enemy to the public good in a passage where Harrington paraphrased Grotius to the effect that:

'. . . tho it may be truly said that the creatures are naturally carry'd forth to their proper utility or profit, that ought not to be taken in too general a sense; seeing divers of them abstain from their own profit either in regard of the same kind, or at least of their young . . .' (46).[2]

In a subsequent defence of his stand, Harrington asked rhetoric-ally:

'. . . does it therefore follow that the eminent degree of reason, wherewithal God hath endowed man, must in him deface that natural affection and desertion in some cases of private for common good, which is apparent even in beasts?' (251).

Since 'natural affection' was conventionally used as an equiv-alent for the passions,[3] Harrington seems to have tied his plea for the common good to human propensities that his programme

---

[1] See, for example, R. Polin, 'Economique et Politique au XVIIe Siècle: L'Oceana de James Harrington', *Revue Française de Science Politique*, Vol. 2, No. 1 (1952), p. 27.

[2] Cf. *The Law of Warre and Peace*, trans. Clement Barksdale (1655), Preface, sig. [3^v].

[3] See Liljegren, *op. cit.*, p. 245.

was intended to remove. The situation was the more confused by his perverse insistence upon saying that action of the altruistic sort was the product of one form of reason, the reason of mankind, as distinguished from the reason of a private man (46). This paralleled Harrington's use of reason in the psychologically irrelevant area of 'reason of state'.

What sort of mental phenomenon was this natural affection, then, and how could it be integrated into the picture of human nature? One could perhaps extricate the author from his (probably unrecognized) difficulties by assuming that there was something different from both the reason of a private man and the passion or 'appetite' that was supposed to be the sole mover of beasts. This would serve to qualify and complicate the description of human nature and the attempts to differentiate animal and human conduct. Actually, natural affection received no psychological explanation at all, but a political one, couched in terms of the emerging key to political life—interest.

Harrington had no compelling need to concern himself with altruism based either on sentiment or on anything else. With the introduction of interest, 'the mover of the will' (241), reason and passion disappear as distinct determinants of human behaviour, for interest encompassed them both (46, 253).

In order to master the chaos of Harrington's vocabulary, some explanation of this many-sided term must be offered. Polin's interpretation,[1] quoted approvingly by Shklar,[2] that interest, to Harrington, meant only property interest, seems to be doubly inaccurate. He recognized both other objects of interest and other meanings of the term 'interest' besides profit.[3] Viewed analytically, all other interests might well be protected by the distribution of land. But it is one thing to emphasize the importance of this factor for the social structure and another to assume that all interests were reduced to that in property. As we shall see, Harrington was aware that ordinary men had 'interests' that had no immediate connection with

[1] Polin, op. cit., p. 27.   [2] Shklar, op. cit., p. 673.
[3] Interest was sometimes restricted in meaning to the desire for wealth; this was especially so in France. See Jean de Silhon, De La Certitude des Connaissances Humaines (Paris, 1661), p. 105, where the author complained about this fact. However, Harrington is the last person to credit with giving the word a single, unequivocal meaning.

property of any kind. Interest made most sense when applied to the concerns of individuals, and here it had as its object all the variety normally found in human designs. Harrington had also said that all government was interest (498), but it would be nonsense to claim that this meant that government *was* property. Polin's position is useful in showing how Harrington extended the meaning of a concept in new directions, but the equation of interest with economic gain is wrong either with respect to individuals or to larger social units. Much of this chapter could be seen as an essay on the meaning of interest, and some aspects of it must await consideration of Harrington's treatment of the common interest. For the present, interest will be considered only in relation to individuals.

The most fruitful source of ambiguity follows from the use of reason as equivalent to interest, but not exhaustive of the meaning of the latter. Harrington quoted Hobbes's dictum that 'as often as reason is against a man, so often will a man be against reason' (46). By way of mitigating the dangers of this situation, he then continued, 'but there be divers interests and so divers reasons'. There followed the discussion of natural affection as a means of neutralizing self-interest and a threefold classification of reason and interest, only the first item of which, the reason or interest of a private man, is relevant here. As well as admitting that there was a diversity of interests, Harrington might also have confessed a rather different ambiguity, that he used 'interest' in a number of different ways.

When applied to individuals, the term lay open to one classical ambiguity, noted in modern studies on interests.[1] In its role as mover of the will it referred to what people actually did want, and hence was equivalent to 'intention' or 'desire'. But it could also be used, and was also used, to suggest what people ought to want were they to maximize their utilities. Here interest meant a desirable state of affairs rather than an intention actually entertained by people. Generally the two were seen as coinciding, as evidenced by Harrington's ironical jibe at an opponent—'the interest of the people is not their guide but their

---

[1] See C. W. Cassinelli, 'The Concept of the Public Interest', *Ethics*, Vol. 69 (1958–9), pp. 48–61, and B. M. Barry, 'Public Interest', *Supplement to the Proceedings of the Aristotelian Society* (1964), pp. 1–18.

temptation!' (24)[1] However, Harrington betrayed an awareness of the distinction in using the expression 'true and real interests' (491). Here he suggested that the people might not see
their interests, in this case, political freedom, but he quickly
rejected the thought. In fact, the same passage contained a re-
affirmation of the capacity of ordinary men to see their interests.

The passage serves only to show that the people's good was
not entirely subjective. In theory, if not in practice, they might
have an 'interest' without recognizing it. The distinction had no
operational value; it just established that it was not the recognition of some good that made it an interest. Harrington had no
need to stress this fact because he was confident that in most
instances citizens would be motivated in accord with their long-
term secular benefit. There was no appeal here to calculations of
benefit arising from the state of the soul in an after life. Some
faith in men's capacity to discover their own advantage was
necessary in a treatise that avoided mere exhortations to be virtuous and placed realistic limits on the degree to which they
could be expected to consider remote and social over immediate
and personal interests. In the event of a discrepancy between
what one might call people's 'real' interests and their desires,
the machinery of Oceana would break down, for there was no
clear criterion by which to identify interests other than the
testimony of the actors themselves. Harrington made no allowance for persistent and widespread irrationality.

Another use of interest involving a qualifier was 'private interest'. The 'interest of a private man', in some passages, had no
sinister connotation at all; it was simply 'private reason' (46).
Elsewhere, however, 'private interest' was damned a 'mire' (44),
'the constant bane of the public' (146) and the 'corrupter of
religion' (449). From these unambiguous marks of distaste it is
obvious that private interests were selfish designs that tended to
harm the public. 'Private interests' did not necessarily mean the
same thing as falsely conceived interest, for Harrington was
quite aware that an individual might have designs opposed to
the good of the community which, when realistically appraised,
were also to his own benefit. Thus he poured scorn on the
hoary argument that a king, or the head of any smaller com-

[1] By this, he meant, of course, that the people's interest was indeed their
guide, not a mere temptation.

munity, could be deterred from seeking his own interest by the realization that his welfare was related, in a less immediate fashion, to the good of the community (588–9).[1] This in itself would provide sufficient reason not to use the argument from true interest as a means of controlling self-assertion.

We are still left with the problem of doing something about the 'mire' of private interest. The answer seems to have been that the selfish motives associated with self-interest were to be retained and the environment manipulated in order to remove occasions for public detriment. The distinction between legitimate interest and private interest would then be reduced to differences in their respective consequences. It would have been helpful to the reader had Harrington distinguished more precisely between destructive and innocuous self-interest; his own indecision on such questions seems to be the best explanation of this omission.

When Harrington first raised the matter of self-interest, he suggested something rather more complex than that offered above. He had just made his remarks about natural affection leading men to the common interest of mankind,[2] but the elliptical argument obviously left him dissatisfied. So he proceeded again to take up Hobbes's statement about men preferring their interests to reason, just as if the first attempt at an answer had never been ventured (46). The second stage of his argument was couched in the following characteristically opaque language:

". . . wherefore unless you can show such orders of government, as like those of God in nature, shall be able to constrain this or that creature to shake off that inclination which is more peculiar to it, and to take up that which regards the common good or interest; all this is to no more end, than to persuade every man in a popular government not to carve himself of that which he desires most but to be mannerly at the public table . . . (46).

[1] As we have seen (pp. 101–5 above), Wren, whom he was criticizing here, was rather moderate in defending the royal ego, since he thought in terms of benevolence on the part of the king, and not just of rational conduct guided by his long-term interests. On this matter Wren must be counted as slightly old-fashioned.
[2] The argument is not very clear at this point, but, construed in the light of the corresponding section of the *Prerogative*, this interpretation seems reasonable.

Institutions, then, were to control self-interest. Apparently Harrington had rejected homilies as a means of leading men to embrace a common good, though his almost impenetrable syntax leaves just a little doubt about this. In the quoted extract he explicitly noted man's dominant self-interest, hence he must have appreciated that better manners at the public table were dependent on something more than giving a gentle push to already strong altruistic propensities. The case does seem strangely over-stated; for, as subsequent analysis will suggest, the institutions of Oceana did not so much cause an inclination to be shaken off as limit opportunities for its harmful exercise. Thus his language served to disguise the discontinuity between the two arguments.

Before passing on to an examination of political institutions, there remains one further ambiguity regarding their function. Harrington unmistakably proclaimed his faith in the power of institutions, saying:

'. . . give us good men and they will make us good laws is the maxim of a demagogue, and is . . . exceedingly fallible. But give us good orders and they will make us good men, is the maxim of a legislator, and the most infallible in the politics . . .' (75–6).

The basic point was stated even more succinctly in the post-humously published *System of Politics* and in the *Political Aphorisms* of 1659 where the presentation of the essence of his thought contrasts with the cluttered detail of *Oceana*.[1] Such a position was relatively rare in the ranks of republican thinkers both before and after the publication of *Oceana*. Had Harrington no other accomplishments to his credit, his feat in raising political discussion above fatuous pleas for good men would be worthy of recognition, and has, in fact, been recognized.[2] The possibility arises, however, that what he had given with one hand he took back with the other. True, institutions, rather than human nature, were seen as the proper starting-place for reform, but

[1] In the former, we learn that 'good orders make evil men good, and bad orders make good men evil' (500). The expression may well have been borrowed from Machiavelli, see *The Discourses of Machiavelli*, ed. C. J. Walker (London, 1950), Vol. I, p. 217.

[2] See H. F. R. Smith, *Harrington and his Oceana* (Cambridge, 1914), p. 46, and P. Zagorin, *Political Thought in the English Revolution* (London, 1954), p. 143.

the improvement in human nature was apparently only deferred. Was the natural inclination to self-interest, then, only a temporary aberration, to be removed as men came to be fashioned in a new mould?

This issue illustrates perfectly the manner in which Harrington was poised between alternative views of man and society, and thus it merits as careful an examination as the meagre material allows. Presumably self-interest would have to disappear were it incompatible with men being good; thus the meaning of making men good assumes some importance. Actually Harrington decided that virtue was compatible with men's pursuing their interests within a properly constructed system. The Archon of Oceana, who undoubtedly spoke for his creator, said:

'. . . we are not so to understand the maxim of legislatures, which holds all men to be wicked, as if it related to mankind or a commonwealth, the interests whereof are the only straight lines they have to reform the crooked; but as it related to every man or party, under what color soever he or they pretend to be trusted apart from the whole . . .' (165–6).

Presumably 'interest' here may be read as self-interest, since the context shows that the Archon was speaking of men's concerns as they understand them themselves. The most intelligible explanation of the co-existence of virtue and self-interest is Harrington's assumption that rational action was normally virtuous, virtue being understood as in the above quotation: as conduct conducive to the good of the community, or at least not destructive of it. Reason and interest were also linked, so it was not surprising that interest and virtue were equated, almost by definition. Sometimes the connection was weakened to the level of an empirical generalization, as when Harrington claimed that

'. . . wisdom and honesty are all one: and tho you shall find defects in their virtue, those that have had the fewest have ever been, and forever shall be the wisest . . .' (322).

This left open the question as to whether rational or wise actions were always virtuous.

One other factor may help to explain the morass of undefined terms. Harrington did, in fact, contemplate some reorientation in human nature, though not in any sense that would dispense with rational self-interest. As late as the *System of Politics* which Toland dated as 1661,[1] Harrington insisted that

'. . . the more the soul or facultys of a man (in the manner of their being infus'd into the body of a multitude) are redin'd or made incapable of passion, the more perfect is the form of government . . .' (499).

This comment supported the earlier one about constraining men to throw off their unreasonable selfish inclinations. If some educative role were accorded the political system, his faith in the triumph of reason over passion would make more sense. *Oceana* did contain a fleeting reference about people coming to understand their own happiness, once instructed in it (166–7), and there was a further, and more concrete, mention of education as the 'plastic art of government' followed by plans for the training of the youth for citizenship (172). This involved no direct allusion to any withering of the passions, but he did suggest that the man not trained to 'relish' the laws 'spits fire and blows up castles' (171–2). The general idea was not foreign to moralists of the early eighteenth century, some of whom stressed how habit might eventually transform selfish action compatible with the public good into action undertaken to further this good.[2]

It thus comes as a surprise when, in *The Art of Lawgiving*, he renounced any need for the atrophying of the passions, denying that

'. . . the equality of a government was pretended to be such, as should make a crooked man straight, a wicked man good, or a passionate man a philosopher.'

Rather, was it not, he demanded,

'. . . sufficient to prevent any influence that wickedness or passion in a man or men, may have upon the government?' (463).

One is grateful to his tenacious critic Wren for having provoked this outburst. Considering that he continued to express himself in the old vein in his last, as in his first, work, there is no room for any development of views here. Either this was what

[1] See Toland's life of Harrington, prefaced to *Works*, p. XXXI.
[2] See E. Albee, *A History of English Utilitarianism* (London, 1902), pp. 76–7.

he meant all the time or his attitude throughout was ambivalent. If the first position is to be accepted, one can only say that Harrington discovered a remarkably obscure way of saying that goodness was to be restricted to men's actions in the political arena and that such virtue involved no refinement of passions in any conventional sense. The comment about men's retaining their full complement of passions seems particularly incongruous with the other remarks about the passions, and perhaps the hyperbole about making passionate men philosophers was intentional. The original position seemed to contemplate nothing so spectacular as this, but rather a growing tendency for men to follow habitually the ways of reason with all its attendant good for society. It does seem possible that Harrington was simply not certain whether his system was self-sufficient or whether ultimately it rested upon a certain mutability of human nature. The modern reader of Harrington sympathizes with Wren's frustrated cry that attacking his opponents' arguments was comparable to driving the Irish from a bog.[1] Sometimes one has the impression that the reason which was to redeem men from passion and vice was a personal quality equivalent to virtue, and sometimes it lay in the workings of the system that came closest to right reason, which left obscure the precise impact upon the individuals constituting the system, although their actions and mental processes would certainly be affected. By sliding easily from reason as virtue to reason as calculation to reason as the fulfilment of justice (for this, as we shall see, was the content of the right reason embodied in popular government), Harrington obscured, perhaps even to himself, the extent to which his system was predicated upon the mutability of human nature.

The remarks treated here reflect a basic uncertainty about the processes involved in reconciling self-interest with social good. In addressing himself to this question, Harrington gave several answers without differentiating clearly between them. An examination of the form of government advocated by Harrington provides a detailed commentary on the basic insight that 'if a man be to judge upon his own case he resolves upon his interest' (509). Perhaps understandably, *Oceana* was less well provided with discussions of interest and its social control than

[1] M. Wren, *Considerations on Mr. Harrington's Commonwealth of Oceana* (1657), p. 57.

were a number of the shorter works. In *Oceana* the constitutional details were set out. In some later versions many irrelevant embellishments were omitted, as Harrington concentrated on defending his general position against critics.

One of the main virtues claimed for a commonwealth was that, if properly constructed, no individual or group would possess both the interest and the capacity to disturb it with sedition (52). Harrington noted that liberty, power and riches were the three 'interests' that caused sedition.[1] While he certainly tended to pass over the interests of weak and harmless people, Harrington tried to show how satisfaction in these respects might be made general (260). For present purposes, this section of his work is useful in indicating that order was to be preserved by giving satisfaction to all men who might be dangerous if thwarted. The process had nothing to do with any communion with the interest that was the reason of mankind.

In so far as there was any psychological explanation of the orderly conduct of the masses, it consisted in an instinct of self-preservation. This instinct Harrington identified with the aspect of human reason known as experience. The unsatisfactory account of human nature is especially well illustrated here, since Harrington was never sure what moved the unreflective masses. Sometimes he credited them with no more than a purely sensual response to stimuli (515), and sometimes he implied that they might be quite discerning (490). Whether the masses would discover their interest by instinct, or, as previously suggested, through education, matters little. Harrington was sure that they would find it.

The motivation of rulers was a matter for closer consideration, for on them rested the onus for the well-being of the polity. All of the familiar constitutional gadgetry of Oceana was directed towards harnessing their self-interest for social purposes. This was in accord with the usual republican tendency to suspect the interest of rulers, while applauding a measure of self-regard on the part of subjects. Harrington might have been more explicit about the ends to be served by some of his constitutional devices. This has led, for instance, to an interpretation of the rota as an example of his unrealistic faith in the inexhaustible

[1] This provides an effective refutation of the assumption that Harrington had a purely economic conception of 'interest'.

supply of good men prepared to serve the republic.[1] But Harrington had said 'let the rulers of Oceana be dishonest if they can' (322). It was certainly the deficiencies of all, and not their virtues, that made the undertaking necessary. The related technique of separating the functions of government had the same intent behind it. The only remarkable aspect of this idea was that it again assumed universal self-interest in a more pointed manner than did some reformers.[2]

Another vital consideration was the relationship between the legislators and their constituents. The basic premise here was that

'. . . the result of all assemblies goes principally upon what they conceive to be their own interests' (477, 606).

The legislature had to be one that could 'never contract any interest other than that of the whole people' (48). One normal motive to be tender to the interests of constituents was lacking, for immediate re-election after the expiry of one term of office was forbidden (98–9). The necessary identity of interest sprang from the arrangement whereby the legislators were to embody in their own persons the economic and regional interests of the people. Harrington denied that ordinary men made political decisions on the basis of any perfect understanding of the public good (44, 515), and quite clearly the 'mean persons' who represented them in the 'prerogative' chamber shared their limitations (519). There was, naturally, the one difference that members of the legislature were in a position to seek the good of others, since it was inextricably linked with their own.

On the general relationship between representatives and represented, Smith's observation that Harrington had no idea of a local mandate from constituents would seem to be correct, though not because this would be a complete anachronism.[3] Harrington went to considerable lengths to open channels of

[1] G. P. Gooch, *English Democratic Ideas in the Seventeenth Century*, ed. H. Laski (New York, 1959), p. 253.
[2] See *The Speech of the Rt. Hon. Nathaniel Lord Fiennes* . . . (1658), p. 13 (BM: E 934), from which one would gather that a separation of powers was primarily an administrative convenience.
[3] Smith, *op. cit.*, p. 51. Certain radicals already thought in such terms. See Anon., *Certain Queries Lovingly Propounded to Mr. William Prynne* (1647), pp. 3–4 (BM: E 398).

communication between the legislature and the outside. Understandably most of the effort went into securing a basic harmony
of interests. If the representatives truly embodied the interests
of the masses, they would generally gain sufficient guidance
from their own interests. This was what led Harrington to his
elaborate schemes for representing property, numbers and also
regional interests. He defended the local connection of the
senators in some detail, emphasizing how important it was to
link them directly to the population (483).

For all this care, there still remained some problems.
Harrington seems to have felt that the interests of the representatives might not always suggest the proper matters for their
attention. One can perhaps accept his reasons for believing that
the legislature might lack any motive to harm the public, without seeing quite how it was to discover what the public wanted.
There was no problem about resolving issues in terms of the
interests in the prerogative; the question was one of suggesting
issues. This must be the explanation for his elaborate schemes for
popular initiative. It involved the right of tribes (the local con-
stituencies and administrative areas) to petition the senate, and
such petitions were privileged, guaranteed a hearing (96).
Unofficial petitions were also envisaged, and these were to be
referred to a committee which would select issues for debate
(127). Such arrangements constituted a certain advance on the
practice of the day of which Harrington was critical (491–2).[1]
In a characteristic touch, Harrington added an officially spon-
sored forum, not unlike his own Rota Club, which was to give
a sympathetic hearing to all suggestions from private men (128).
Further consideration of these rather facile plans for expressing
the people's interest must await the discussion of how the public
interest emerged.

Another interesting and relevant feature of the political
system of Oceana was the place given to parties, or, in the more
typical parlance of the day, 'factions'. It seems reasonable to
assume that the greater the scope allowed such manifestations

---

[1] While the Long Parliament claimed to speak for the people, it was not
enthusiastic about hearing from the individual members of the public. The
years 1647–8 saw a great many radical pamphlets claiming abridgement of
the right of petition. At this time Parliament took action against 'tumultuary
petitioning'. See *Journals of the House of Commons*, Vol. 5 (1646–8), p. 567.

of diversity, the more realistic the original recognition of the role played by self-interest. An understanding of Harrington's views on social conflict is also important in its own right; as we shall see, various misinterpretations of his thought stem from a neglect of this factor. His views certainly require clarification, owing to his tendency to refer to the 'people' in a corporate capacity. Such expressions certainly suggest the 'great unity' attributed to the public by some republicans,[1] who naïvely imagined that a common interest would spontaneously emanate from the inchoate mass. Some servants of the Good Old Cause deserved L'Estrange's scorn, but Harrington was not one of them.

His strictures against faction were usually directed against the unopposed control of the government by a single party.[2] Complaints of this sort are not peculiar to the seventeenth century, nor are they symptoms of naïveté. Faction was described as a vice of the few and it was associated with oligarchy (446). Thus his real concern was not so much disunity as government in the interest of a narrow party.

This is demonstrated in his position regarding parties arising in the normal course of political life, normal, at any rate, for the Interregnum. Recognizing both religious and temporal parties, he treated them for all practical purposes as identical (260). Such divisions were of concern only in the absence of a 'common ligament of power sufficient to reconcile or hold them' (73-4). The onus was on the framers of the commonwealth to supply the means of avoiding any dangerous consequences.

Harrington was scarcely enthusiastic about the presence of parties, but he indulged in remarkably little moralizing on the subject. If he appreciated how good men might despair at such divisions (76), he no less appreciated how they might be driven to perpetuate them (542). Of the commonwealthsman, he said, 'if he excludes any party he is not truly such' (74). This tolerance extended not only to people such as repentant ex-

---

[1] The expression is from Roger L'Estrange, *A Plea for Limited Monarchy* (1660), p. 2.
[2] Even Fink, who seems to overstate Harrington's desire to avoid the formation of parties, concedes that these remarks were directed against government by a single faction. See Z. S. Fink, *The Classical Republicans* (Evanston, 1945), p. 65.

royalists but also to those who remained militant, for whatever was to become of royalists in the long run he was prepared to contemplate with equanimity their dominating the legislature. In that event, he remained confident that they would still not overturn the system of government that alone could offer permanent guarantees of their personal liberty and estates (220) (447). Such a group would only be more dangerous if excluded from political activity (76).

On this issue, more perhaps than on any other, Harrington addressed himself to a particular controversy within the general crisis of his age. His point of view was almost unique among republicans and he was especially identified with it and criticized on that score.[1] When pressed by opponents to show how popular government could avoid anarchy, he sought support in the capacity of the ancient Hebrew commonwealth to transact public business while torn by divisions (416). He resorted, too, to the argument that factions in such commonwealths were bloodless, in contrast to the situation in monarchies (419). One remarkable fact is that, though the Venetian model from which Harrington drew was clearly designed to prevent the formations of factions,[2] this function of the institutions of Oceana was never mentioned.

The most searching contemporary criticism of this theory was that by Matthew Wren, who stressed its insouciant disregard for the harsh facts of social conflict.[3] Such objections might seem warranted in view of the tendency, already noted, to treat the public as an homogeneous unit. Various remarks about the people knowing their own interest certainly leave one with a rather superficial impression of society. In his rebuttal, Harrington failed fully to answer the charge, relying more upon rhetoric than reason. Nevertheless, he was prompted by Wren to admit that government policy did largely involve such controversial subjects as 'the regulation of trade' and 'privileges of corporations' (590). His answer was that such disagreements could be

---

[1] John Rogers, *A Christian Consertation with Mr. Prin* (sic), *Mr. Baxter, Mr. Harrington, for the True Cause of the Commonwealth* (1659), p. 59, and Anon., *The Private Debates, Conferences and Resolutions of the Late Rump* (1660), p. 8 (BM: E 1019).

[2] Fink, *op. cit.*, p. 32.

[3] M. Wren, *Monarchy Asserted* . . . (1659), pp. 12-13.

contained by the political system, as witnessed by the experience of the Dutch commercial republic, where a volatile economic life was judged compatible with political stability. Was it reasonable, he asked, to view disputes between 'tanners and clothiers' as comparable to the barons' wars typical of monarchy? As before, he drew the line between tolerable and intolerable conflict at the point where violence threatened and showed a decided preference for bourgeois over aristocratic virtues. The whole exchange, involving no more than a paragraph on either side, showed an understanding of social forces that all too rarely found its way into political discussion. Of course, Harrington was a country gentleman and was not particularly conversant with commercial life and its political repercussions. Still, Macpherson did well to explode the myth of Harrington's thoroughgoing commercial naïveté.[1] He was aware of sources of conflict that could survive the establishment of an equal commonwealth. In his description of the government of the capital, Emporium, he granted corporations their traditional representation (170). Hence he was also familiar with the interest of the commercial community in government. Nor did he overlook the existence of clergymen and lawyers within the legislature, both of whom were in a position to write their professional interests into the laws (432). Harrington provided no reason for assuming that the conflict of interest between lawyers and the public would be ended by the new government, though the structure of the legislature would inhibit the lawyers' efforts to further their professional interests.[2]

Interpreters of Harrington have pointed to his lack of emphasis on social conflict.[3] In this connection it should only be noted that beyond showing why conflict would not overthrow the system, it was no part of his task to labour the topic, thus turning minds to the possible defects of popular government. For a very sophisticated view of the public interest, all that was lacking was some explicit recognition that the system could not function

[1] See C. B. Macpherson, *The Political Theory of Possessive Individualism* (Oxford, 1962), p. 175.
[2] Smith has noted (p. 65) that Harrington did not expressly exclude lawyers from the legislature. This was surely not an oversight, as implied by Smith, but a consequence of the general process of neutralizing sinister interests by counter-pressures instead of suppressing them by law.
[3] Shklar, *op. cit.*, p. 664.

freely without a considerable degree of conflict. The admissions with respect to economic life were deficient only in a failure to relate them concretely to the working of the political machinery. For him to have contemplated political parties, even on the eighteenth-century model, would have necessitated too daring a leap beyond the political facts of his age. It is very important to correct such misinterpretations about social conflict in Oceana, for they have led to further misunderstanding of Harrington's views on the public interest.

Both of the considerations thus far treated relate to the central problem of the public interest. The image of human nature and the institutional setting in which this nature was to function were the basic ingredients from which Harrington produced his definition of the public interest. Taken together, these two sets of remarks suggest that Harrington was in possession of a variety of methods for harmonizing individual designs and the public good. Natural affection, reason cultivated by education and a judicious arrangement of institutions were all available for the task. It now remains to examine the manner in which the public interest was to be discovered.

The term 'interest', already analysed in relation to individuals, was also applied to the concerns of aggregates such as the state and humanity. Here there were three different concepts, closely related, but not precisely the same in scope and emphasis. The three were: the 'reason (or interest) of state', 'the common interest of mankind' and the 'publick interest' (sometimes called the 'national interest'). These various terms must be sorted out.

The reason of state was variously defined by Harrington as 'the interest or error . . . of the ruler or rulers' (46), 'the administration of a government' (512) and 'that in a kingdom or commonwealth which in a family is called the main chance' (512).[1] Less convincingly, in view of the traditional connotations of the term, he called it 'fair play' (512). Presumably, then, it was public policy that was being considered, though the reference to 'administration' might lead one to think that it was the activity of policymaking and not the policy itself that was of concern. This latter is a perfectly intelligible definition of the public

[1] The only known commentary on reason of state in Harrington is C. J. Friedrich, *Constitutional Reason of State* (Providence, 1957), Chapter 3.

interest, conceived in terms of procedure and process, but it was not Harrington's definition here.

One oddity is that Harrington had a tendency to equate two quite different sorts of phenomena under the one rubric of reason of state, a confusion paralleling that previously noted in his treatment of the interests of individuals. Thus the concept referred to the range of policies that could maintain the *status quo* or render it even more favourable for a state. However, when referring to those states lacking a healthy congruency between foundation and superstructure, Harrington allowed for a variety of reasons of state, one for each of the contending groups in such a divided state. Thus it became an interest of states or estates in a different sense. Here, then, reason of state ceased to be a maxim pointing towards a political condition to be realized by the government and became the interests or desires of groups of individuals. Presumably this multiplicity of conceptions about the safety of the state could be found even in a properly constructed state, for, as one of the definitions shows, he did allow for the possibility that rulers might err in formulating their reason of state. The then current ideas about reason of state would lead one to think in terms of a single set of policies rather than conflicting conceptions.[1] This was doubtless owing to the degree to which political vocabulary reflected the practice of monarchies and hence the designs of the prince. Harrington appears to have been familiar with the writings of the Duke of Rohan, who was prominent among writers on this theme.[2] The interest that commanded princes was his main concern. This interest was a single one, limited to one person. In Harrington's system everyone was commanded by interest, thus there was more scope for divergences on the question of reason of state. Reason of state was not a very common term in England in this period, not nearly so common as 'public interest'. True, Parliament had ventured to use the term early in the century[3] and Parker's writings in 1642 had given it a prominent place.

[1] Meinecke's classic study of the concept makes no mention of an approach such as Harrington's, though it does not deal with English thought in any detail. See F. Meinecke, *Machiavellism*, trans. D. Scott (London, 1957).

[2] Harrington referred (p. 189) to a 'French politician' who claimed that England was invulnerable except through self-destruction. This was surely Rohan, who quoted this statement, sometimes attributed to Elizabeth I.

[3] See G. L. Mosse, *The Holy Pretence* (Oxford, 1957), pp. 12–13.

However, to most supporters of the Good Old Cause it smacked of royal machinations,[1] and so all parties, royalists included, had become hesitant about using it in any favourable sense.

One other factor in Harrington's unconventional use of the term might be his concentration upon reason of state in domestic policy, rather in relation to foreign affairs, which appears to have been the focus of most writings on the subject. In choosing to emphasize the domestic applications of reason of state, Harrington realized that he was in an area more susceptible to disagreements than was foreign policy (513). Nevertheless, there were other works which used the concept to cover aspects of domestic policy relevant to the preservation of the state, but few went behind the formal structure of government policy to suggest the existence of a variety of interpretations.[2] Naturally, the pamphlet literature of the Civil War dealt with disagreements about the best way of preserving the nation. It could reasonably be argued that this was what the war was all about. However, when making the point, members of the Roundhead party preferred to think in terms of preserving the people, rather than the state. The basis of the struggle was frequently seen as a dispute about the 'public interest'.[3] Harrington's peculiar distortion of traditional notions may best be seen as a reflection of the insistence pervading all his work, that what was good for the community must in some way be reconciled with what the people really wanted. Many years later the theme would find memorable expression in Halifax's claims for a 'natural reason of state', an 'undefinable thing' recommending itself to private citizens.[4]

The relationship between the reason of state and the public

[1] Even Marchamont Nedham did his best to dissociate himself from the term. See *Mercurius Politicus*, No. 60 (24–31 July 1651), p. 959, and No. 108 (24 June–1 July 1652), p. 1690.

[2] The similar expression 'mystery of state', normally associated with rulers, was sometimes applied to the activities of groups of private men. See Anon., *A Wonderful Plot or Mystery of State* ... (1647) (BM: E 393).

[3] See *A Remonstrance of his Excellency Thomas Lord Fairfax ... and of the Generall Councell held at St. Albans the 16th of November, 1648*, p. 14. When Charles I was condemned and executed, the official reason was not reason of state but the people's 'public interest'. See 'An Act for the Abolishing the Kingly Office', 17 March 1648–9, in C. H. Firth and R. S. Rait, *Acts and Ordinances of the Interregnum, 1642–1660* (London, 1911), Vol. II, p. 19.

[4] 'The Character of a Trimmer', in *The Complete Works of George Savile, First Marquis of Halifax*, ed. Sir W. Raleigh (Oxford, 1912), p. 60.

interest was never made explicit. Harrington did explain that the reason of state varied both in the content of policies and in the people in whose interests the policies were executed, according to the form of government. The actual content of these policies was more carefully elaborated for flawed systems of government than for his own form of stable democracy. In the short chapter in *A System of Politics* devoted to the reason of state he noted a number of the tactics characteristic of Machiavellian guides to princes, but dismissed reason of state in the favoured political system with the comment that here it dictated a course of action 'to preserve the form intire' (513). Though this might seem a somewhat narrow, constitutional definition of the public interest, it is quite in accord with the modern definitions already mentioned. Indeed, it would appear that in a properly constructed democracy the reason of state and the public interest were substantially the same. When defining the reason of state in terms of interests, Harrington had said that it consisted of the interests of the rulers, these being the prince, the nobility or the people (46). Recalling that he endlessly affirmed that his system of government would realize the interest of the people where others failed, it must follow that, for these limited purposes, public interest and reason of state were identified. In a sense, reason of state was the broader generic term since it was a part of all systems, but there was no meaningful public interest except in popular government, since elsewhere the public was not served. There was even a slight difference in emphasis between the concepts in the case of an equal commonwealth, since reason of state suggested matters primarily related to preservation of the state, while a public interest could be involved in a greater range of issues.

The concept of the 'common interest of mankind' has already been mentioned. It was only elaborated on two occasions, the second being intended as a clarification of the first, and was casually introduced in a very few other places. The initial statement was that there was

'. . . a common right, law of nature or interest of the whole; which is more excellent, and so acknowledged by the agents themselves, than the right or interest of the parts only . . . (46).

This passage arose in the preliminaries of *Oceana* where

Harrington was discussing man's nature with the intention of proving how the Hobbesian portrait of egoism could be reconciled with something other than the Hobbesian form of government. A more elaborate version of the same position is found in the first book of *The Prerogative of Popular Government*, written against his able opponent Matthew Wren.

Before trying to ascertain the meaning of these passages, it is instructive to consider the arguments by which Harrington tried to establish the existence of such an interest. The analogies inherited from Hooker and Grotius pointed in both cases to instances of 'natural affection' in beasts and (in Hooker alone) to evidences to a harmony directed towards the good of the whole, seen even on the part of inanimate objects. Hooker had alluded, somewhat obscurely, to rocks flying upwards upon occasion 'to relieve the present distress of nature in common'.[1] Understandably, Harrington chose the more plausible analogy and stressed that if beasts were capable of altruism, surely men also responded to a common interest, that of mankind. In the *Prerogative* Harrington denied attempting to prove any causal connection between behaviour on these different levels, but contented himself with saying 'as we see it is with creatures . . . so we find it to be with man' (252).

He appealed to the testimony of human beings, making much of the fact that the civil laws based upon man's nature recognized such an interest, and hence a propensity to follow this interest must be embedded in human nature. The actual statement was that men, by their nature, must then 'acknowledge' such an interest. But mere acknowledgment would really be of no avail, unless men were guided by it. Harrington's words blurred the precise relationship here, as indeed he had to, if he were to cling both to Hooker and to Hobbes. Finally, he resorted to the example of a criminal, who, being put to death, was not so treated in order to further his own interest, nor to comply with the interests of any other single man. Hence the interest involved must be 'a common interest of mankind distinct from the parts taken severally' (252).

Now this welcome return to concrete political fact rests rather uncomfortably at the side of arguments drawn from the sup-

[1] *The Works of that Learned and Judicious Divine Mr. Richard Hooker*, ed. J. Keble (Oxford, 1888), Vol. I, (Book I, Ch. III), pp. 211–12.

posed altruistic side of human nature. Harrington had suggested the latter avenue in saying that

'. . . man, who tho he be evil, gives good things to his children, will work hard, lay up, deny himself, venture his life for his little commonwealth . . .' (252).

The statement just quoted appealed to a form of benevolence on the part of men, whatever the difficulties (duly pointed out by Wren[1]) of deriving from familial affection a common interest of mankind. However, the legal example simply entailed the obvious truth that there were occasions when the conduct of an individual had anti-social consequences, something admitted by even the most passionate proponents of a natural harmony of interests. One must agree that in execution of a thief the action proceeds as a public concern, for that, then as now, is the essence of public as opposed to private law. But the example failed to illustrate any person preferring the public good to his own. The criminal presumably had no choice in the matter, for there is no trace in Harrington of the far-from-obvious position of some modern idealists that criminals will their own punishment. It is also true that members of the public could reasonably be expected to eschew, in their own interests, the activities thus discouraged.[2] Thus the remarks on human nature showed altruism without reaching any interest of mankind and those in the example, a form of common interest devoid of altruism. This discontinuity between the arguments may be traced to a seeming failure to decide what exactly he was defending. The quotation from Hooker was both an exhortation in traditional terms to prefer the common good and an argument drawn from the divine plan of the universe to support the contention that in a variety of contexts the more social and more general good was actually preferred. Some of the arguments brought forth by Harrington suggested that he was sufficiently the captive of a traditional vocabulary to write at times as though the realization of a common interest were dependent upon men consciously seeking that good and sacrificing their own interests to it. Upon occasion he emphasized the existence of the common interest

[1] M. Wren, *Monarchy Asserted*, p. 47.
[2] M. Wren, *Monarchy Asserted*, p. 50. Thus, again, Wren has made the relevant point.

of mankind, without connecting it to any altruistic impulses.

The relationship between the common interest of mankind and the public interest has yet to be described. In *Oceana* Harrington mentioned an interest of mankind 'more excellent . . . than the right or interest of the parts only' (46). In his *Prerogative* the same point was reiterated in the form that 'there is a common interest of mankind distinct from the parts taken severally' (252). There is no reason to suspect any change in meaning, despite the different phrasing. Both the actual words of the second statement and the sense of the example of the criminal leave the reader with no conclusion but that Harrington was dealing with a common interest distinct from the private interest of any single person. Blitzer, the only commentator to treat the relevant passages, has interpreted them to mean that there was a common interest

'. . . distinct from the sum of private interests, that is a "general will" rather than a "will of all".'[1]

Such an interpretation would lead to an apparent contradiction in Harrington, as will be noted below. The interpretation overlooks the significance of the word 'severally' introduced to clarify the earlier phrase in *Oceana*, 'the interest of the people'. In seventeenth-century English the word had the same meaning as it has today; it signified 'individually', 'apart from the others'.[2] Actually these statements were not really concerned with the sum of private interests but with private interests in isolation.

The meaning of the two statements and the nature of the relationship between the common interest of mankind and the public interest are both made clear by an appreciation that the first concept was one with ethical connotations. 'Common right' and 'law of nature' were employed as synonyms for the interest of humanity (46). Here is additional evidence of the almost endless ambiguity of the term 'interest'. The identification of interest with legal right had a long and respectable history. Here, however, Harrington had identified it with the moral rightness basic to the idea of natural law. This should not

---

[1] C. Blitzer, *An Immortal Commonwealth* (New Haven, 1960), p. 145. Pages 137–49 are a commentary on the passages of concern here.
[2] *Oxford English Dictionary* (1961), Vol. 9, s.v. severally.

be surprising in an age when claims of legal right based on pre-scription were giving way to arguments from natural right. An earlier discussion of 'interest' has demonstrated how the term might serve new causes not founded on legal right.[1] Grotius was probably the immediate source of the equation of common interest and natural law. The translator of his work rendered a passage in the preface in terms of an 'interest . . . of the whole', otherwise called the 'law of nations'.[2]

Whatever the reasons for the use of 'interest' in this connec-tion, it seems certain that the interest of mankind was a moral law only rarely attained by the interests and actions of indi-viduals. In fact it was not wholly realized in government policy genuinely in the interests of the whole community, as in a demo-cracy. Harrington claimed only that 'the interest of popular government' (i.e. the public interest in a democracy) 'came nearest to the interest of mankind' (46, 155, 509). One such comment underlined the ethical nature of this interest of man-kind in the words:

'. . . law in a democracy holds such a disproportion to natural equity as the interest of a nation to the interest of all mankind . . .' (509).

Thus the interest of the public could only approximate that of mankind because the latter was a moral ideal unattainable in public policy created on the basis of human interests. While one might think that the interest of mankind simply took in the concerns of an area larger than a single state, actually it was not a geographical concept at all. It was a condition of natural equity imperfectly displayed in the operation of private and state interests. The interest of mankind was, then, significantly different from interests of states and individuals, even though Harrington tried to give to those interests of which he approved some of the ethical connotations inherent in the 'interest of humanity'.

Once it is established that the 'interest of mankind' might differ from the 'public interest' in scope and content, one may evaluate Blitzer's assumption that Harrington had contradicted himself. Blitzer has insisted that Harrington first introduced a traditional conception of the common good and later chose the difficult formula of a 'sum of private interests'. Harrington

[1] See p. 40 above.   [2] Grotius, *op. cit.*, sigs. [6ᵛ–7].

undoubtedly implied the latter view of the public interest on at least two occasions. The argument of *Oceana* was expressed succinctly in the claim that

'. . . the people taken apart are but so many private interests, but if you take them together they are the public interest' (155).

A minor polemic called *Policaster* was even more explicit:

'. . . if a man know not what is his own interest, who should know it? And that which is the interest of the most particular men, the same being summed up in the common vote, is the publick interest' (590).

All this is confusing, but Harrington was perfectly consistent within his own terminology. Two explanations are now available. The predicates applied to the public interest and the interest of mankind referred to different, though related, concepts. Thus what was said of one did not automatically apply to the other. Secondly, as has been shown already, Harrington did not say that the common interest was distinct from and superior to the sum of particular interests; his examples, and the literal meaning of the text, mean something else. This is not to say that suggesting a superiority of the common interest of mankind to that of all individuals was wrong, but rather extraneous to the purpose of the writer. Since the public interest of a single state failed to attain the perfect justice that was the interest of mankind, all particular interests necessarily did the same. However, Harrington did not spell this out.

It is worth noting that this most difficult of passages found few parallels in seventeenth-century literature. It was quite common to insist that men prefer the common good before their own, but rarely did anyone claim in this way that there was a common interest of some sort, distinct from particular ones. Most writers must just have assumed this to be the case. Moreover, there was an excellent reason for limiting oneself to the moral injunction, instead of analysing the difference between the two sorts of interest, for Harrington demonstrated the ambiguities inherent in such statements. One has to refer to a work of the next century to find an exactly parallel passage, and the author was a self-acknowledged follower of the 'great Mr. Harrington'. Thomas Pownall, one-time Governor of Massachusetts, wrote an original treatise against the social atomism usually found in social contract theories. He suggested, with a wealth of metaphor, the way in which interests were connected within society. This led him to remark that there was an interest of the community 'distinct from that of the particular constituents, considered as separate and independent'.[1] This passage demonstrates how Harrington's ambivalent position might be used to combat extreme individualism, while, at the same time, it confirms the interpretation given here of the original.

The idea of the common interest of mankind belonged to that part of Harrington's political thought that was derived from Hooker and Grotius. Thus it seems worth while to consider the place of those arguments in the intellectual history of the age. While this cannot tell us anything more about Harrington's use of this material, it can suggest the reason behind the obvious incongruity between some of Harrington's concrete proposals and the language in which they were made.

Harrington's borrowings from Hooker and Grotius were quite clearly part of a waning cosmology. Prior to this time it had been the fashion to integrate social duties into the order of the universe. It had been part of the medieval passion for analogy, an effort to simplify a complex environment by postulating an artificial uniformity. Discussions of social duty had adopted the form of proofs of the existence of God, in that the same pattern was discerned in natural phenomena and in human affairs. Of course, it had long been accepted that there was one hierarchical order throughout creation. This meant that every part of creation had a fixed place. However, philosophers had also discovered a pattern for deviations from the natural order. Heavy objects, they said, obeyed a physical law of nature in coming to rest on the ground, but on occasion they might fly upward. Similarly, men sought their own comfort, but, given some necessity, they too might depart from their normal state. It was quite in accord with the hitherto prevailing mentality to see a single law at work in such disparate situations as the filling of a vacuum in the physical world, the care of an animal for her young and the self-sacrifice of individuals for the public good. The basis for this doctrine, as it was used in the seventeenth

---

[1] Thomas Pownall, *Principles of Polity, Being the Grounds and Reasons of Civil Empire* (1752), p. 68. Pownall's admiration for Harrington was expressed in the first edition of this work. See *Treatise on Government* (1750), pp. 58–9.

century, was probably Aristotelian, but the origin does not really matter. In Harrington we witness its death, not its birth. Prior to Harrington, the same metaphors, virtually the same vocabulary, had been present in works by some of the most prominent thinkers of the age. Bacon had insisted that there was a twofold good in relation to everything in the universe, one good pertaining to itself alone and another as it was a part of some greater unit.[1] In such matters men were to take for their model those stones that, upon occasion, went up,

'. . . forsaking their duty to the earth in regard of their duty to the world.'[2]

A host of lesser writers joined Bacon in this conceit, all of them saying substantially the same thing.[3] Doubtless it was as common on the Continent as it was in England.[4]

After Harrington, however, the idea to seems have become far less common, at least in relation to discussions of the public interest. Very few examples have been discovered and these are quite perfunctory in comparison to the earlier profusion of detail.[5] It seems probable that this was more than a mere change in literary taste. One of the few later examples that appeared after Harrington was in a work by Sir John Monson, which, by the author's own admission, was written in 1641.[6]

There can be no certain answer to this problem, but clearly

[1] F. Bacon, *The Two Bookes of the Proficiencie and Advancement of Learning* (1605), sig. tt.$^{r-v}$
[2] *Ibid.*
[3] See W. Willymat, *A Loyal Subject's Looking-Glass* (1604), p. 21; William Pemble, *A Summe of Moral Philosophy* (Oxford, 1632), p. 2; Anon., *Touching the Fundamental Laws . . .* (1643), p. 8 (BM: E 90); T. Warmstry, *An Answer to Certain Observations of Mr. Bridges* (1643), p. 47; Edward Reynolds, *Self-Deniall: Opened and Applied in a Sermon* (1645), p. 25; Anon., *Heutonaparumenus, or a Treatise of Self-Denyall* (1646), p. 37 (B: Pamph. C 74); D.I.R.H., *A Looking-Glasse for the Parliament* (1647), p. 19 (BM: E 427).
[4] See E. Moliner, *A Mirrour for Christian States*, trans. W. Tyrwhit (1635), pp. 192–3.
[5] See David Lloyd, *Modern Policy Compleated* (1660), Part II, p. 5, and Edward Stephens, 'A Caveat Against Flattery, and Profanation of Sacred Things to Secular Ends', in a collection of essays with the general title *The True English Government* (1689), p. 19.
[6] Sir John Monson, *A Discourse Concerning Supreme Power and Common Right* (1680), pp. 49–50.

the intellectual climate had become less favourable to such explanations of social behaviour and social duties. It is tempting to give some credit to Matthew Wren's devastating critique of this aspect of Harrington's thought. Statements such as those quoted by Harrington dealt with what was then loosely called natural law. In the seventeenth century there was increasing dissatisfaction with the imprecise nature of this concept. Quite a number of writers on political and moral subjects echoed the complaint of John Donne that the term was

'. . . so variously and unconstantly delivered, as I confess I read it a hundred times before I understand it once.'[1]

Since natural law meant so many things, it is not surprising that the dissatisfaction about current usage lacked uniformity, but one observation was most prominent. There was a tradition, originating with the lawyers of ancient Rome, of applying the concept indiscriminately to man and beast alike, and sometimes, by extension, to inanimate objects. Donne's objection was against this practice of employing the idea both in human and non-human contexts. Some commentators struck particularly at the analogies linking human behaviour and geological abnormalities. It was misleading to say, as some had, that the law of nature was so strong that not only sensitive creatures, but

'. . . inanimate beings were elevated by it, even as the very stones did knit and unite themselves to the building of the universe.'[2]

No doubt the disappearance of the conceit stemmed, at least in part, from such criticisms. An unwillingness to apply concepts such as justice to animals was not incompatible with using animal behaviour to emphasize human duties. This is what Grotius did when he denied that beasts were capable of obeying a law in any sense analogous to human behaviour, while still allowing that both humans and animals performed the same acts determined by the law of nature.[3] However, the more

---

[1] Donne, Βιαθανατος. *A Declaration of that Paradoxe, or Thesis, that Selfe-homicide is not so Naturally Sinne, that it may never be Otherwise* (n.d.), p. 36.

[2] This expression was quoted by two authors who objected to such arguments by correspondence. See N. Culverwel, *An Elegant and Learned Discourse of the Light of Nature* (1652), pp. 36–7, and, less clearly, John Heydon, *The Idea of Law . . . whereunto is added the Idea of Government* (1660), p. 115.

[3] Grotius, *op. cit.*, p. 5.

sensible course seemed to be to sever the two spheres completely.

One may also place this tendency in a broader cultural framework. The dissolution of the Elizabethan world-picture has attracted a great deal of attention especially from students of literature. Part of this process has been described as a growing estrangement between man and nature, such that it was difficult to describe them in similar categories. As one scholar put it:

'. . . for scientific description the human element is felt to be an adulteration, whereas the Elizabethan universe was recognized as the grand design of God for man.'[1]

This tendency to sunder the human from other spheres of reality has been differently expressed as a change in the understanding of natural law. From a moral rule imposed upon man from without, natural law came to be a mere description of actual human behaviour. The element of constraint was weakened and the specifically and uniquely human aspects of this law were emphasized.[2] This, too, could have no effect but to destroy the foundation of social duty as expressed by Hooker and Grotius.

The passing of this cosmology is of the utmost importance for social philosophy. It meant that henceforth the relationship between the individual and the community would have to be described much more closely and in social terms. No longer would it be sufficient to attribute one pattern of behaviour to rocks, animals and citizens. Particular interests and their place in the general interest could now be treated free from a lot of extraneous material. Indeed, it has to be treated in different terms, for the form of the older explanation of social duties was becoming unfashionable. This affords the best explanation of the ambiguities in Harrington's remarks on the public interest. In the language of one recent study, he was an 'empiricist'.[3] However, on this issue, he had tied his most explicit statements to the vocabulary of a waning tradition, the earlier notion of

[1] S. L. Bethell, *The Cultural Revolution of the Seventeenth Century* (London, 1951), p. 56.
[2] See Michael Macklem, *The Anatomy of the World, Relations Between Natural and Moral Law from Donne to Pope* (Minneapolis, 1958).
[3] See W. H. Greenleaf, *Order, Empiricism and Politics, Two Traditions of English Political Thought, 1500–1700* (Oxford, 1964), Chapter XI.

'order'; little wonder, then, that such passages seem inconsistent with the rest of his thought.

The material from Hooker and Grotius played a relatively minor role in Harrington's general description of government. It would have played a lesser role still had Wren not chosen to query Harrington's comments on cosmic order. Wren had seized upon what almost amounted to an aside in the preliminaries of *Oceana*. It was, however, at a critical point in the exposition of his general theory and one of the most vital passages for an understanding of the public interest. Harrington's reply consisted of a point by point defence against all the miscellaneous criticisms, ranging from fundamental objections to the political machinery of Oceana to picayune aspects of the governments of Israel and Rome. Harrington's main concern in these polemics is indicated by the fact that in the chapter of the *Prerogative* devoted to the common interest, only the first part dwelt on that topic, and he soon launched into a discussion of political mechanics, related only in the most tenuous way to the question at issue. The important point is that neither Harrington's republicanism nor Wren's royalism was directly involved in the clash, and neither writer took pains to integrate the point in dispute into their respective theories of government. The only connection between the comments on the interest of mankind and Harrington's general theory lay in the desirability of establishing that monarchy, or government in the interest of a single man, was further removed from the justice associated with natural law than was democracy. Oddly enough, this was one contention that was not explicitly argued in the somewhat academic exchange with Wren.

In treating the common interest of mankind we discovered what the public interest was not; it is now appropriate to ask what Harrington thought it was. The result of the many is the wisest result, we learn,

'. . . because every man has an interest what to choose, and that choice which suits with every man's interest, excludes the distinct or private interest or passion of any man, and so comes up to the common and public interest and reason' (253).

The essence of this remark is the classical liberal view that the raw materials for discovering the public interest are the concerns of private men as understood by these men themselves. This position was by no means universally accepted and there were certainly difficulties in the way of sustaining it. The interests were to be so joined that the resultant collection of forces was something other than the triumph of some selfish designs over others. The manner in which this feat was to be performed taxed the ingenuity of all those social thinkers who had transcended naïve pleas to prefer the common good.

In describing Harrington's solution one must bear in mind that he was referring chiefly to the proceedings of legislative bodies. The assumption throughout was that the interest of the public could be represented in a legislature. While this was a perfectly conventional position, Harrington's novelty lay in his denial that the political system had previously secured the necessary identity of interest and his faith that his system could provide it. All the comments directed to the problem then had a double significance, first, with respect to the personnel of the legislature, secondly, in relation to the public at large.

It was, of course, the prerogative that was to be the chief focus for popular influences. Here, for one accused of attributing too great a unity to the people, Harrington seems to have given considerable scope for the diversity of interests to be found on matters of public policy. Certainly there were confident references to the people's interest, but it is clear that the people were not expected to be all of one mind on political issues. Had this been so, the statement that the system 'took in all interests' would be meaningless (76). Similarly, there would have been no real purpose behind the proposal to create equal units to return legislators, nor the special insistence that the maximum practicable size of the prerogative was also the optimum (519). Thus the problem of discovering the public interest was narrowed in scope to the operation of a legislature representing all interests and seeking occasional inspiration through various channels of communication with the public.

The crucial problem remained that of transforming the inputs of diverse private interests into a public interest. The process of summing up interests to produce the public interest was revealed in decisions by majority vote. Harrington did face the problem of designating the will of a mere majority as the public interest, though his answer was not altogether satisfactory. He treated the process of discerning the public interest as analogous to that of verifying the perception of objects (590). Such an approach to the problem almost certainly betrayed the influence of the natural law tradition, for a similar appeal to the reliability of the 'outward senses' is found in Grotius, in the same preface from which Harrington had already quoted. Grotius had been concerned with inferring from the common practice of various peoples certain eternal laws of justice. The problem faced by Harrington was more difficult, for generally acknowledged maxims of right conduct or universal promptings of conscience were inadequate guides for the making of public policy. Through a failure to consider the actual nature of the decisions to be made by an assembly, Harrington's words lent a misleading objectivity to the content of the public interest. Without knowing the nature of his metaphysical views, if any, it is impossible to grasp the full force of the parallel. While Grotius had assumed that all those who were normally equipped humans could perceive the law of nature, Harrington contented himself with the comment that the decision of the majority could be deemed 'most authentick' in an uncertain world (590). Elsewhere he recognized the fallibility of all human ordinances (254, 480). Harrington's more cautious use of the Grotius analogy is understandable, when one recalls that the public interest was not precisely the same as the law of nature, but on the whole came closer to it than the interest of a single ruler or any other small proportion of the population.

There was no suggestion in the defence of the majority principle that the minority had to recant. Surely Blitzer is correct in saying, in another context, that Rousseau's solution would not have appealed to Harrington.[1] But how, then, was the minority to be satisfied? In the first description of the public interest quoted from the *Prerogative* there was a specious plausibility in the use of 'every man', first distributively, when he stated that each man had an interest behind his vote, and then collectively, when we learn that the choice must suit 'every man's interest' (i.e. that of all men). The language gave an appearance of logical rigour, when, of course, there was none. The fact that each man participated in the decision was no guarantee that each would be pleased with the result. There remained the

[1] Blitzer, *op. cit.*, p. 145.

problem of explaining in what sense the result could be deemed to be in the interest of the losers.

In an age when justification in terms of one's 'real will' was unknown, the closest comparable argument appealed to the profit to be derived even by the opponents of a measure, if the whole community profited from it. For all his occasional rhetoric about instinctive altruism, Harrington never used that argument, and it seems unlikely that he expected self-interested men of limited vision to acquiesce without some concrete good which they themselves could value. One of the proudest boasts made for *Oceana* was that

'. . . the government . . . goes altogether upon consent, and happens not only to fit private to public, but even public to private utility' (298).

Thus Harrington's basic individualism precluded any solution based upon some 'true interest' that might not move the wills of the individuals involved.

A partial answer to the problem of the minority lies in the scope given for compromise and manoeuvre within the legislature. Senators could, of course, debate issues, and thus minorities would be given a hearing. The supporters of a motion defeated by the prerogative could also hope to effect some compromise, for any proposal by the senate failing to pass the prerogative was to be returned to the senior body for amendments and further debate (445). Any minority within the senate at least had within its power the capacity to initiate new motions at any time. In the case of those members of the prerogative who found themselves in a minority against the declared will of both chambers, there could only be the consolation that the greater number of the representatives of the lower orders had agreed with the aristocratic chamber. Hence men's economic concerns would probably not suffer through class exploitation.

In the end, this fact, and not any express reliance upon the arts of political compromise, explained the role of the minority.[1] Only by placing great weight upon the people's concern to pro-

---

[1] See Polin, *op. cit.*, p. 36. To allow this is not to concede that the only object of 'interest' was property in land. This would be to confuse the basic conditions protecting vital interests with the interests themselves.

tect the existing distribution of property could Harrington have claimed that all interests were satisfied. There is ample evidence to support the view that he did place such emphasis upon the agrarian. It was seen as ensuring an identity of interest between the two chambers (261) and as being 'satisfactory to all interests' (290). From an earlier version of the latter point it is obvious that here 'all interests' referred to 'all parties' and not all individuals (236). The confusion of Harrington's comments on decisions by majority vote can then be traced to the enormous importance of maintaining the balance. This led him to note how all parties and almost all individuals could agree in defending the agrarian. The very fact that he could contemplate divisions within the legislature suggests that Harrington was aware that most decisions regarding the public interest would not involve that foundation of the political order, the agrarian. Still, he carried over into a discussion of other issues his optimism regarding the identity of interests on that key point.

It is quite apparent that the result of every vote of the legislature could not be in every legislator's interest in the same sense, since some gained their immediate objectives and some found fulfilment only in the knowledge that their overall stake in the political order was protected. One need only refer to the various comments on sedition to appreciate that self-interest could counsel acceptance by the minority, who

'. . . perceiving that they cannot impair the common interest, have no other interest but to improve it . . .' (254).

However, the nature of the interests being served remained demonstrably different. Had Harrington made the distinction between immediate, strongly felt interests and less personal and more remote ones, his remarks would have been much clearer. Such a subtlety was not dependent upon the intricacies of any hedonic calculus, but was found in the work of contemporaries who were comparatively unremarkable as political thinkers.[1]

Harrington doubtless realized that he had failed to show convincingly how all men could have their immediate interests served on any controversial issue. Certainly the comparable

[1] See John Durie as quoted above, p. 15.

passage in *Policaster* made no attempt to assert the impossible, and here he retreated to the position that the majority interest was the interest of the public (590). It is not really surprising that Harrington should have attempted what he did. His whole position rested upon the claim that his commonwealth would secure the interests of all and the public interest was derived from those of individuals. Thus the temptation to see every interest as equally gratified on every issue was considerable. Much the same outlook was revealed in his remarks about the interest of a family, where he insisted that the interests of a majority of the members constituted the family interest, or else the family did not know its interest (107). Here, instead of over-looking the fact that individuals all had numerous interests of varying intensity, he had resorted to another ambiguity. A family could not know its own interest in the same sense as could an individual, since the family was a different sort of entity and existed only through the persons of particular members. Like most of the other republicans, he tried to relate the rationality shown by individuals in pursuing their interests with the emergence of a national interest. This leap from private interest to public good might appear to be the result of attributing an unreal personality to aggregates such as a family or a state. In point of fact, the conclusion followed from his habit of treating interests in the same way as the units to which these interests were attributed. If each man knew his own interest, then some larger unit (all men taken together) knew its interest.[1] Thus stated, the proposition was unsound; fortunately Harrington supplemented his bad logic with a careful analysis of political forces. This is illustrated by considering his Rousseau-like suggestion that the decision of the legislature excluded the 'distinct or private interest or passion of any man'. This is really less of a mystery than are many other passages. In both chambers the whole range of competing interests had finally to be reduced to a vote for or against the motion, and the motive behind a member's choice did not matter. The legislators could quite easily approach their task in a self-interested way and still procure a result that avoided the triumph of any selfish interest. Harrington's treatment of party has already provided the basis for an answer. He was concerned less with the existence of

[1] See *Works*, pp. 166–7 and 590.

private interest than with its unopposed existence. Throughout all his writings the emphasis was to exclude the domination of politics by the interests of one or a few men. While the laws might not satisfy every interest, neither were they likely to ignore the major interests represented in the legislature. The carefully designed scheme of representation was meant to ensure a favourable result no matter how unscrupulous the members of the prerogative were.

Discussion thus far has been aimed at showing how self-interest and the common weal were reconciled in Harrington's thought. The answer has taken the form of explaining how the common interest came to be known, and how policies in accord with it were put into effect. It might be objected at this point that the wrong question was asked, and that what was required was some definition of the common interest having both concrete content and a degree of generality useful for application to all the facets of public policy. Actually Harrington provided a multi-level view of the public interest and came as close as any of his contemporaries to demonstrating the complexity of the concept.

At the most abstract level of treatment he saw the public interest as a first approximation to the common interest of mankind, or natural law. Dealing in somewhat more concrete terms, he endorsed Wren's statement that the public interest was that

'. . . justice be impartially administered and every man preserved in the enjoyment of his own' (590).

This version was contained in the same paragraph as that couched in terms of a summing up of interests, and there was no incompatibility between the two. Some confusion about Harrington's thoughts on the public interest may be traced to a failure to grasp that saying how the public interest was to be discovered or maintained was not quite the same thing as saying what it was. Although Harrington failed to explain that he was applying various sets of predicates to the concept, he certainly did just that. Admittedly the public interest is best understood in terms of a continuing process, rather than as a static condition. But in our own day the author of one of the more behavioural studies on the subject has recognized the need of some notion, such as justice, to describe the content of the public interest, claiming all the while that this justice is a fiction useful in the process of balancing particular interests.[1]

One may distinguish how something is produced from the thing itself. A definition in the language of natural law still did not explain how the public interest was realized. Earlier thinkers, such as Hooker, assumed that it was a matter of kings and subjects searching their consciences, hence the process of summing up interests was irrelevant. Harrington contemplated no such thing. In his theory justice and common right emerged largely as a by-product of self-interested activity and was not derived from either revelation or moral self-examination.

Much of the remaining confusion about interests and the public interest in Harrington's thought derives from the fact that it is difficult to know just how much agreement within the community he deemed either possible or necessary. The use of the earlier tradition of 'order' definitely emphasized unity of interest, and certainly he saw the maintenance of the agrarian as a 'common interest' (265). It was not, however, *the* common interest in the sense that it exhausted the meaning of the concept, though it certainly constituted a general state of affairs that included other matters that were also beneficial to the community. Broad as the balance of property was, it was not all-encompassing, and Harrington mentioned other social relations, quite independent of it, as very profitable to the public.[2]

Remarks by several commentators suggest a failure to appreciate how fluid and variable the idea of the public interest was, thus they have not recognized the degree to which the concept might simultaneously be described in different ways and on different levels of generality. Because most citizens had to be in favour of the distribution of property, they did not have to agree about everything else. The comment by one scholar that Harrington postulated 'a universal, uniform public interest of all citizens'[3] requires some amendment. After all, Harrington described the process of legislative decision-making in terms of discovering the public interest, and here there was no uniformity of opinion.

---

[1] See H. R. Smith, *Democracy and the Public Interest* (Athens, Ga., 1960), pp. 145–59.

[2] See the remarks on usury, *Works*, p. 256.

[3] R. Koebner, *Die Geschichtslehre James Harringtons* (Breslau, 1928), p. 4.

Polin takes the same approach. After attributing to Harrington the opinion that the public interest was the distribution of property in land, he observed, quite correctly, that it was an inadequate definition. It neglected the important truth that governments had to define the public interest by political decisions, not once, but over and over again.[1] This is true, but one can hardly pillory Harrington for neglecting the day-to-day business of determining the public interest. In treating it as the decision of a legislature whose members were interested in preserving the existing power structure, he gave ample scope for flexibility. There was no need to specify what policies were in the public interest; defined in formal, positive terms, it was whatever the legislature said it was.

Another criticism turns, in part, on a one-dimensional view of the public interest. One charge was that Harrington leaves the public interest 'hanging . . . in the air' because he did not know what all men ought to want.[2] Levett added, alternatively, that Harrington felt that he did know what men actually wanted; they wished to preserve the balance of property. However, this was a highly personal interpretation and it failed to explain what made the public interest 'more reputable' than private interest.[3]

A distaste for Harrington's alleged insensitivity to moral values has produced ill-founded criticisms. It seems unfair simultaneously to complain of an undefined public interest and one defined too narrowly in terms of a policy that happened to appeal to Harrington. The whole point of presenting the institutional context of Harrington's observations has been to show that he did not leave the public interest hanging in the air. His treatment of the relationship between legislators and constituents linked proceedings in the legislature with social forces outside it, and the legislature was clearly the forum where the public interest emerged. Harrington never contemplated an endless series of votes on the general balance of power and property, and to this extent his remarks on the balance of property remain divorced from the descriptions of law-making. However, this serves only to emphasize that there were various

---

[1] Polin, *op. cit.*, p. 38. This follows, of course, from his earlier misunderstanding about the meaning of 'interest'. See above, p. 112.
[2] Levett, *op. cit.*, p. 197.   [3] *Ibid.*, p. 201.

public interests. Only one, the balance of property, was stressed, since it was the foundation of the polity. The others, at a lower level of generality, were to be specified as the occasion arose. Levett's criticisms illustrate how one misunderstanding about the theory, the assumption that the balance was the sum and substance of the public good, might generate others.

Once it is established that the public interest could involve values and interests on a wide range of matters, it becomes clear how this public interest might be deemed more reputable than private interests. People normally feel that a common interest is more worthy of pursuit than the interest of a single person, and Harrington subscribed to this opinion. While it is true that early individualists were usually unconcerned about the sort of spiritual common good favoured by Levett, this writer has overlooked their merits.

Curiously enough, most misunderstandings about the new ideas on the public interest arise through a failure to relate these views to the protection of property. In the case of Harrington, too much attention has been paid to this factor, for his remarks on the public interest are distorted if seen as relating solely to the balance of property. Early republicans had the same concern for the rights of private persons without elaborating the desire into a law of social development. In others there had been a similar emphasis on representing property in Parliament, the same assumption that a regard for private interests in property was the basis of a genuine common interest. Of Harringtonians, those who were obviously greatly influenced by the theory of the balance of property said the same things about the public interest as those who ignored it.

One anonymous disciple in the former category clearly expressed the connection between the balance of property and the common good. Because the great bulk of property was in the hands of the people, as opposed to the nobility, therefore 'the greatest interest' was in their hands. Men who were aware where the balance of property lay should be elected to Parliament, for then the public interest could be advanced 'in a genuine natural way', free from violence.[1] He took for granted that

[1] Anon., *Some Grave and Weighty Considerations Humbly Proposed to the People to Direct them in the Choice of their Representatives* (1658), p. 14 (B: Pamph. C 106).

148

the commons of England would be sensible of their own interests. He also accepted the principle that

'. . . such laws and administrations, will best comport with the nation's [interest], as are framed according to the interest of revenue in land.'[1]

This was a good deal more subtle than the crude statement that the preservation of the balance was the public interest, something which no Harringtonian seems to have said. Another tract of the same genre advocated basing government on

'. . . the rights and propriety of the people (who together are the greatest proprietors in the lands and interests of the three nations).'[2]

This would produce a system where no one interest was 'rampant', but all were 'passant'.[3]

One republican, describing himself as a friend of Harrington, took no interest in the agrarian and was severely critical of the aristocratic bias behind the senate of Oceana. As far as he was concerned, a single chamber would suffice because the lower house on Harrington's model would take in all interests. This was obvious in that

'. . . the whole interest of the nation is taken in to constitute this supreme power, every county, city, and considerable borough, . . . send in competent numbers to secure their interests, no sort of men but have an interest going there.'[4]

Representatives could be trusted because they could not secure their own benefit without benefiting all others. All that was needed was

'. . . so many, and no more, as may among themselves, be well informed of their own and the people's interest (being universally the same) . . .'[5]

This did not mean that all men had to think alike on all

---

[1] *Ibid.*, p. 14.
[2] Anon., *The Plain Case of the CommonWeal* (1658), p. 14 (BM: E 972).
[3] *Ibid.*
[4] Anon., *The Grand Concernments of England Ensured* (1659), p. 25 (BM: E 1001).
[5] *Ibid.*, p. 47.

issues. Indeed, like Harrington, this writer stressed the need for diversity within the legislature, though he felt that the nation could make do with a smaller group than Harrington wanted, and he asked

'. . . why five hundred or thereabouts being equally distributed for elections according to the interests of every part of England, should not as well preserve the interest of mankind?[1]

In this way the supreme power would be placed in such hands 'wherein the whole interest of the nation is combined'.[2] The last word, with its associations of collecting separate interests into a total, was faithful both to a thinker like Ireton and to Harrington. In terms of concrete policies this writer saw the common interest as including various matters, such as religious toleration and the improvement of trade. His most explicit remark was that 'the defence of property is the common interest of this nation'.[3]

These fugitive tracts from the chaotic final years of the Commonwealth added little to Harrington's scheme. However, they serve to emphasize his connection with prevailing forms of republican thought. People influenced by Harrington might alter their vocabulary in certain respects to incorporate the argot of *Oceana*. But Harrington's teaching on the public interest could easily be integrated into current ideas on the subject. His remarks had been more extensive, and hence gave ample opportunity for internal contradictions. Nevertheless, they were substantially the same as those of less prolific republicans.

Harrington's thoughts on the public interest have now been weighed in relation to each other, to the body of his political works and to the thought of his republican contemporaries. His treatment is frequently difficult and elusive, qualities which are more apparent in the discontinuities between the occasional philosophical flourishes and more mundane descriptive material and in the author's excessive zeal in the use of the term 'interest'. If the hypothesis offered here is correct, the factor most conducive to ambiguity was Harrington's position as a thinker caught between two traditions. The older, that of Hooker, emphasized self-abnegation and a cosmic natural law. These figured in Harrington's writings, but such references seem

---

[1] *The Grand Concernments* . . ., p. 49.   [2] *Ibid.*, p. 39.   [3] *Ibid.*, p. 12.

almost to be interpolations.[1] The individualism with which Harrington has been associated led to a view of public policy firmly rooted in an appreciation of the strength of rational self-interest. The public good was thus based upon the interests of individuals, although it was not a condition that could be equated with any interest in isolation from the others. Thus there was a public good distinct from that of particular citizens taken individually. However, it differed from that of earlier doctrine, for this public good emerged from the expression of private interests; only by consulting them could it be known.[2] Appeals to any law higher than human concerns had been minimized.

It would appear neither necessary nor possible to say what Harrington really meant, if that involves rejecting his adherence to one of these traditions. Indeed, it is quite understandable that Harrington should not have separated the two strands of thought, for they lent a useful ambiguity to those critical passages where he had to make the difficult transition from individual interests to common interests, armed only with the faith that the people, properly organized, could not fail to secure the people's interest. At such points reference to innate altruism, an ethically conceived common good transcending personal interests and a system that would make men 'good', could only be of service.

The agrarian and the balance resulting from it provided one common interest in Oceana. Apart from that, harmony could be secured either by exhorting men to prefer the common good or by postulating a common interest that 'stoops to every man's peculiar one',[3] as Wren put it. For Harrington, the public interest was meant to stoop to the level of man's self-interest, while much of the language in which the process was described referred to the former solution of raising men's desires to the

---

[1] It is unnecessary, however, to join one commentator in finding 'secret writing' in Harrington. See W. T. Bluhm, *Theories of the Political System* (Englewood Cliffs, N.J., 1965), pp. 341–2. As we have seen (pp. 132–4 above), the two sets of remarks were not as incompatible as one might think and there is no reason to suppose that Hooker was invoked only to disguise the real message.

[2] Koebner (p. 15) makes the point effectively by referring to 'massegeben Interessen'.

[3] M. Wren, *Considerations*, p. 22.

level of a common good prescribed by natural law. There were bridges between these positions: specifically, the equation of reason with virtue; the ambiguous meaning of 'interest', one sense of which denoted 'right', and the close association of the interest of the people with natural law. The reason why the present interpretation has assumed the primacy of the more individualistic of the positions is that one could not construct the political institutions of Oceana on the basis of altruism and old-fashioned ideas of natural law, but were all such references deleted, the basic structure would be in no way impaired.

Not the least of Harrington's merits as a political thinker lay in his having dealt with the public interest in terms relevant both to Hobbesian self-interest and to popular government. He combined the appreciation of human limitations, and even of the prevalence of social conflict typical of many royalists, with the aspirations of such 'democratic' thought as the period afforded. His theory may be seen as putting liberal ideas about the public interest to a demanding test. Though Harrington failed to produce a wholly coherent description of the public interest, he did raise the important problems in a strikingly modern way. This, in itself, represented an advance beyond both orthodox republican thought with its insistence upon human virtue and royalist opinion centred upon the wise legislator. Harrington's efforts gain in stature in comparison with these denials that there was any problem at all.

IV

CONSCIENCE AND INTEREST
AFTER THE RESTORATION

THE PERIOD BETWEEN the Restoration and the Glorious Revolution has never attracted much attention from students of political theory. Those in search of the giants have rightly passed over those thirty years, viewing them as an interlude between the brilliant confusion of the Civil War and the era of Locke. No amount of research is likely to afford us the view of a village Hobbes; it is undeniable that there was a decline both in the quantity and the quality of political discussion, a fact owing as much to the growth of consensus in some areas of policy as to the increasingly effective censorship.

There were, nevertheless, certain themes that ripened into theoretical significance. Two of these, the analysis of society in terms of interests and an increased awareness of the social implications of self-interest, were related to each other in the closest way. Both were plainly manifested in the toleration controversy, a major issue that called into question the whole structure of society. It was not the only issue of the day, but it was much more promising for the social theorist than was the struggle over the dispensing power or other supposed parts of the royal prerogative. Instead of dreary, and frequently inaccurate, lists of precedents, the quest for religious freedom called forth thoughts on the relationship between private wants and public needs, the problem, that is, of the public interest. Arguments for liberty of conscience provide a particularly good index of changing opinions because the issue was a long-standing one with relatively few important changes in the general circumstances of the case. Hence, changes in the nature of arguments serve as fairly useful indicators of changed perspectives.

The literature on this subject has naturally been approached from a purely political viewpoint. This seems reasonable, since the matter was frequently treated as a political one, that of reconciling the divergent aims of groups of citizens organized on a religious basis. Thus, while one may accept W. K. Jordan's warning not to expect to find 'articulate self-interest' in the literature,[1] the caution relates best to those who seek a purely economic interpretation of claims for spiritual freedom. Obviously few, if any, were prepared to argue solely on that basis, for the problem was not just economic. However, there could be no comparable objection to treating religious liberty as a political problem, and men wrote quite freely of their own interests and presented arguments even more frankly directed at self-interest in others. While economic considerations might be tangential to toleration, public order was not, and some writers chose to emphasize only political factors, although most argued on a variety of levels. It was true as well that religious persecution took the form of civil disabilities and impositions on men's estates. While this might not be plausibly described as a purely economic problem, it constituted another secular consideration.

The court had long viewed the problem in terms of policy rather than the evangelical side of religion, though theoretical justification understandably lagged behind practice. Following the Restoration, however, the most politically sophisticated discussion came from spokesmen of the persecuted sects. There was also a shift in the mid-seventeenth century from works written by churchmen and couched in theological language to those of a more secular cast, frequently by laymen. The increased attention paid to the unfortunate repercussions of intolerance upon trade is well known. Quite as important as references to the commercial importance of the Presbyterian was an appreciation that political order might be sustained by an equilibrium among the various religious parties. The dramatic chapter in the religious struggle lasting from 1660–89 brought into the accepted tradition of discourse ideas about the clash of interests

[1] W. K. Jordan, *The Development of Religious Toleration in England*, Vol. IV (London, 1940), p. 341.

in society that previously had been confined to the more cynical of the 'mirrors' of princes and to the widespread revulsion at the tactics of Jesuits and Machiavellians. After the Restoration subjects were in the unaccustomed position of counselling their rulers to tolerate a plurality of competing religious groups, using as an inducement a variation on the old formula of divide and rule.

The argument was not entirely novel before the 1660s, but no document with quite the same vocabulary and meaning of the later tracts has been discovered. From the ruler's perspective, the clearest literary evidence of an acceptance of the maxim of *divide et impera* was put into the mouth of Charles I by the churchman John Gauden. The author of *Eikon Basilike* had the royal martyr advise his son to beware of exasperating factions, for, in the much-quoted words,

'. . . connivance and Christian toleration often dissipates their strength, whom rougher opposition fortifies, and puts the despised and opposed parties into such combinations as may enable them to get a full revenge.'[1]

The essential difference between this point of view and that espoused by the victims of persecution was that Gauden (or Charles) was Machiavellian, in the pejorative sense, in considering the problem only in terms of maintaining the ruler's power. While finding it impossible to neglect this matter, later versions of the basic idea were to emphasize much more both the claims of the various 'factions' and their role in securing the good of society while seeking only their own.

Another of the influential policy arguments for toleration was of a much earlier date and nominally Roman Catholic in inspiration. In his important *Liberty of Prophesying*, Dr. Jeremy Taylor, chaplain to Charles I and ultimately a bishop, included a section on the propriety and prudence of a prince tolerating several religions within his dominions. To support his positive conclusions Taylor could find no better text than that provided by Jacques Auguste de Thou (d. 1614), the *Politique* historian and statesman. The relevant passage was:

Haeretici qui pace deta factionibus scinduntur, persecutione uniuntur contra rempublican.'

[1] *Eikon Basilike* (1648), Chapter 27, p. 241.

This Taylor somewhat loosely rendered as follows:

'If you persecute heretics or discrepants, they unite themselves as to a common defence. If you permit them, they divide themselves upon private interest; and the rather, if this interest was the ingredient of the opinion.'[1]

This was far removed from the sentiment normally ascribed to Catholics in the often hysterical 'scare' literature of the period—as far removed as the positions of sovereign and subject. It should be added that de Thou was not an orthodox Catholic; in France he had been subject to suspicion for his too tender regard for Huguenots.

It is certain that de Thou remained an influence on sophisticated thought after the Restoration, and some who perhaps had not read the original were familiar with Taylor's translation.[2] For those to whom even Taylor may have seemed an abstruse writer, there appeared in 1660 a very slight but representative extract from de Thou's chief historical work. It expressed his leaning towards a balance of religious parties, though it was not the section quoted by Taylor.[3] Of the numerous references to de Thou in the more learned writings of the period, almost all from Protestant sources were quite unqualified in their praise, the most common compliment being that he was a most reliable witness on the French wars of religion. Many English authors cited him as an historian, without actively subscribing to his political solution to the religious problem. Thus Milton had been a great admirer of 'Thuanus', but made no reference to his statist's approach to religion. In order to gain acceptance, ideas of this sort had to be reconciled with the ever-present slogan of a

[1] *Liberty of Prophesying* (1647), p. 213. This section of Taylor's book was reprinted in 1687 and 1688 under the title *Toleration Tolerated*. Taylor gave no reference for the passage from de Thou, which is strange, for other quotations from him were carefully documented. The preface to de Thou's history contains sentiments similar to those quoted by Taylor, but the exact words do not appear. See *Historia Sui Temporis* (Paris, 1604).

[2] See J. H. M. Salmon, *The French Religious Wars in English Political Thought* (Oxford, 1959), p. 127. Here the author notes de Thou's considerable influence around the year 1670. There is no mention of his ideas on religious parties and their control.

[3] See *An Extract out of Thuanus his Preface to his History . . . Concerning Toleration of Differences in Religion* (1660), by C. H. (B: Vet. A 3, e.609).

united 'Protestant interest'. They also had to be dissociated from the divide and rule formula, popularly supposed to be the creed of seditious Catholic subjects. All of this no doubt reduced the usefulness of such arguments even after the Restoration.

The advocacy of both Taylor and Gauden smacked of the court. The policy arguments introduced by them did not bulk large in their respective works; Taylor used many other considerations of a more spiritual nature and placed his most significant comment in a work dealing with a wide range of matters. Gauden's advice was also nicely set off by a remark in the immediately preceding paragraph about not tolerating factions, thus neutralizing some of the effect. Perhaps significantly, neither man was closely identified with the argument, for Taylor simply quoted de Thou, while Gauden published anonymously. Such efforts only appear significant when contrasted with those contemporary champions of toleration.

Of all the religious groups involved in the toleration struggle, the Roman Catholics appear to have had the most pronounced bent towards political arguments for liberty. By the Restoration the Catholics' claim to be a bulwark against the triumph of Puritanism was already old. An anonymous tract of 1604 contained vague intimations of a balance of forces by which the Church of England was to be strengthened by the checking of Presbyterian ambitions.[1] The closest parallel in the writings of Protestant Dissenters was probably the approach of Henry Jacob, who made much of the fact that religious freedom was for the common good and the safety of the state.[2] Perhaps analysis of a specifically political sort was not uncommon, but surviving evidence is scarce. Charles Herle, always a sensitive barometer of political opinion, recorded the fact that some people discussed the problem of religious diversity in terms of a

[1] See *A Supplication to the King's Most Excellent Majestie wherein Severall Reasons of State and Religion are Briefly Touched* (1604), p. 4 (B: Wood 511). Allen found this work uninteresting, for the quaint reason that its argument was only one from expediency. See J. W. Allen, *English Political Thought 1603–1660*, Vol. I (London, 1938), p. 209. Most scholars treating the subject have failed to appreciate just how rare and remarkable arguments from expediency were.

[2] [Jacob], *To the Right High and Mightie Prince, James . . . an Humble Supplication for Toleration . . .* (Middleburg, 1609), pp. 23, 30 and 41.

balance of forces. He rejected the idea, however, and, relying upon the nautical vocabulary then favoured for discussions of public affairs, insisted that 'a ship is never so well ballasted in her two equal sides, as in her one entire bottom'.[1]

The displacement of the Church of England in the Interregnum seems to have silenced political arguments for liberty of conscience in most quarters. However, the Roman Catholics reflected the political vocabulary of the age by their use of 'interest' as a guide towards a solution. The Catholic lawyer John Austin went beyond the unexceptional idea that men whose beliefs were tolerated would respond by being good subjects from gratitude. In an argument directed to the government of Cromwell he claimed that self-preservation and a desire to consolidate gains already won would prevent Catholics from using their religious liberty as a foundation for political supremacy. They would be

'. . . bound by their own interest (the strongest obligation amongst wise men) to live peaceably.'[2]

Since the Catholics were normally regarded as an emanation of a foreign power, no petition dealing only with the inherent justice of their case was likely to receive a favourable reception. This doubtless explains why they led in the use of 'interest' as the basis of accommodation.

Some few Protestants did descend to political realities in the period prior to 1660, but these were very few. Classical treatises on the subject of toleration, such as that of Busher, were silent about any political dimension. One of the most interesting anticipations of later argument appeared in an anonymous tract whose author argued that all religious sects would try to maintain a general toleration once it were established, something which could not be done but by maintaining all similarly situated groups.[3] More typical of the early genre were the Baptists, who dismissed the problem of raison d'état with the observation that princes should deem that policy most conducive to national

---

[1] Herle, *A Payre of Compasses for Church and State* (1642), p. 17.
[2] Will. Birchley (i.e. John Austin), *The Christian Moderator, First Part* (1651), p. 19.
[3] [William Walwyn?], *Toleration Justified & Persecution Condemned* (1646), p. 14 (BM: E 319).

safety that was approved by God.[1] Thus they translated the whole matter of political interests to a higher sphere.

The distinctive mark of much Restoration literature was precisely the willingness to discuss liberty of conscience in the language of politics. References to justice and divine will were not absent, but increasingly men appealed to interests, that is, to what men wanted and, in their more rational moments, thought possible. These questions were largely independent of what was just or holy. An anonymous tract, tentatively dated 1660, set the new tone. Conformity in religion was not possible, nor, if possible, could it be counted upon to procure 'unity of interest'. But this unity of interest was just what was needed, for

'. . . they are strangers in the affairs of the world, who have not learnt that Interest and not religion, makes all the great enmitys and amitys both public and private.'[2]

Even more to the point was a work attributed to Sir Peter Pett, a man of affairs who was certainly no stranger to the world. His main point was that most writers on religious organization seemed unaware of the 'incurable defects of human nature'. To treat the topic realistically, one had to discuss 'political interest'.[3] This dictated a policy of religious freedom extending to a number of parties. In such circumstances the various parties were unlikely to know each other's strength, and this difficulty of calculating the nature of the opposition would preserve the peace. Each group could be relied upon to respect the freedoms of all others. Separated by their animosities, none would join together except to preserve the common liberty. Pett referred to schemes for toleration as 'models'.[4] The term fits Restoration proposals very well, for very often they consisted of a portrait of

[1] See T. Monck *et al.*, 'Sion's Groans', in *Tracts on Liberty of Conscience and Persecution 1614–1661* ed. E. B. Underhill for the Hanserd Knollys Society (London, 1846), at p. 376.
[2] *Second Thoughts or the Case of a Limited Toleration* (n.d.), p. 7. Lord Clarendon has been proposed as the author. See S. Halkett and J. Laing, *Dictionary of Anonymous and Pseudonymous English Literature* (London, 1929). Vol. V.
[3] R. T. (i.e. Peter Pett), *A Discourse Concerning Liberty of Conscience in which are Contain'd Proposals About What Liberty in this Kind is now Politically Expedient to be Given* (1661), pp. 1–4.
[4] *Ibid.*, p. 1.

society with careful attention paid to the disposition and probable behaviour of the constituent parts.

Dr. John Owen, late of Christ Church, Oxford, made an observation very similar to Pett's in the course of defending 'interest' as a guarantee of the *status quo* following a toleration. His case rested upon the assumption that

'. . . to surmise the acting of multitudes, contrary to their own interests . . . is to take away all assurance out of humane affairs.'[1]

Here was notice that 'interest' had ceased to be the unfailing enemy of social order; on occasion it might serve to bolster it. Owen was not very concerned with the mechanics of balancing parties. He thought his case sufficiently established on the claim that the government erred in trying to keep Dissenters weak and poor. A better way to secure national strength was to

'. . . preserve industrious men in a peaceable way of improving their own interests.'[2]

Owen's most effective work from the viewpoint of political theory included the claim that religious persecution served only to reduce the number of citizens associated with the 'civil interest' of the nation, thus weakening it.[3] This anticipated a theme later argued in detail by William Penn, who, as a student, was much influenced by Owen.

There was no scarcity of toleration tracts in the sixties, for though the censorship under Roger L'Estrange dealt harshly with republican propaganda, there was no comparable restriction upon the expression of essentially political views under the cover of treating ecclesiastical organization. John Corbet, a Presbyterian polemicist, was one of the earliest in the field. His concrete proposals were hardly striking, being shared by most Presbyterians. He was much more concerned with accommodation between the established church and his own than with a genuine liberty for all, though the latter idea was not altogether

[1] [Owen], *A Peace-Offering in an Apology and Humble Plea for Indulgence* (1667), p. 33.
[2] [Owen], *Truth and Innocence Vindicated in a Survey of a Discourse Concerning Ecclesiastical Polity* (1669), p. 77. For his remarks on balancing parties see pp. 297–8.
[3] [Owen], *Indulgence and Toleration Considered in a Letter unto a Person of Honour* (1667), pp. 7–8. Owen is the accepted author of all these tracts.

absent. The really interesting facet of his work for present purposes was the constant emphasis on the religious question as one involving the reconciliation of divergent interests. He depicted Comprehension, or the policy of enlarging the church establishment to include Presbyterians, as a coalition of interests based upon the necessary principle of self-preservation. In all his writings Corbet strove to establish the substantial nature of the Presbyterian 'interest'. 'This interest will never vary from itself,' he assured the government,

'. . . this interest . . . is not like a meteor which after a while vanisheth away, but is of a solid and firme consistence like a fixed constellation.'[1]

Interest, far from being a shameful *arrière-pensée*, was elevated as a guarantee of orderly and responsible conduct. His party, unlike the Catholics, had no foreign attachments and wished only to secure their 'interest' at home. Once having done so, 'duty and interest' would bind them against all refractory behaviour.[2] Corbet made much of the need of broadening the 'interest' of the government and the Church of England, for a narrow, 'contracted interest' could only spell weakness.[3]

Corbet did not refrain from making the conventional charge that his opponents were moved by 'perverse self-love' or 'particular carnal interest'. However, since the quality was present, he chose to pander to it, treating the situation as a 'question of interest'.[4] Having 'asserted the interest of the universality in opposition to the advancement of a particular interest', he then turned to 'the particular concernments of the king, of the nobility and gentry, and of the episcopal clergy'.[5] His treatment could hardly have silenced all objections, since the message to the last three was essentially that their position would not deteriorate; there was no convincing demonstration of positive advantage.[6] Very much the same argument was repeated in a later work, where the erstwhile estates were referred to as 'interests'. The ambiguity of the word interest is evident here, for he

---

[1] Corbet, *The Interest of England in the Matter of Religion* . . . Part I (1661), p. 43. See too Part II, p. 181. The two parts are paged consecutively.
[2] [Corbet], *A Second Discourse of the Religion of England* (1668), pp. 12 and 38.
[3] *Interest of England*, Part II, p. 155.   [4] *Interest of England*, p. 178.
[5] *Ibid.*, pp. 188–9.   [6] *Ibid.*, pp. 252–9.

both wrote of king, clergy and nobility as 'three important interests of the kingdom' and he also insisted that his scheme would be acceptable, 'these three important interests being known aright'.[1] Interest could obviously thus be used either as a synonym for party or for the aims or good of that party.

Corbet by no means neglected the public in his treatment of lesser interests. In fact, sometimes one would almost think that considerations of national strength and the good of the Protestant interest (to which end he quoted Rohan) were the only important ones. As his *Second Discourse* put it:

'. . . the good of the several parties is best served by . . . the good of the universality.'[2]

This was not wholly representative of his overall position, however, for the strength of the analysis lay in the recognized necessity of proving how the good of the nation was inextricably interwoven with that of the Presbyterians. This task led him to consider

'. . . such a common-good as belongs to all sorts of men, by whom a public weal consists.'[3]

As already suggested, this condition was to be achieved by granting the Presbyterian demands.

One weakness in the case was a failure to say anything convincing about the interests of some sorts of men, since he neglected to consider the state of religious interests other than the two main ones. Presumably all Protestants were to gain liberty of conscience, since he observed that the religious establishment under the proposed comprehension would be sufficiently broad to 'control all parties', even if some remained outside it. Plainly Corbet saw a variety of parties in religion as legitimate and even unavoidable. Ideally they should not exist, but irremediable defects in human nature produced them. The best thing to do was to ensure that they did not turn into political factions, something which they were not by nature.[4]

If Corbet was comparatively frank and perceptive in political matters, his opponents were no less so. One critic refused to allow that the Presbyterians were as momentous in the balance

---

[1] [Corbet], *A Discourse of the Religion of England* . . . (1667), pp. 40 and 48.
[2] *A Second Discourse*, p. 4.   [3] *A Second Discourse*, p. 2.   [4] *Ibid.*, p. 11.

of the nation as they claimed. He dwelt upon the 'divided interests' of Dissenters, and on this basis claimed with perfect candour that there was no political necessity of recognizing any such demands, for their lack of unity served to render them fairly inoffensive.[1] This position rested upon the same assumptions as did later arguments for toleration, but rarely were such sentiments so cynically expressed by one not desirous of toleration. However, it was simply the situation of the writer that made the statement striking; the model of society suggested by his remarks was becoming fairly common in polemical literature.

A new sophistication marked the toleration tracts published in the late 1660s. A concentration of works around 1667–8 coincided with the fall of Clarendon and doubtless indicated renewed hope on the part of the sects that their old enemy would no longer torment them. Now for the first time spokesmen for persecuted groups advocated the dark designs of policy as being in the interests of governed and governors alike. Some such works showed a new sympathy for the Roman Catholics and included the suggestion that they should be included in any toleration. This complicated the mosaic of affected interests and perhaps made the idea of balancing interests a more natural solution than it had been when there were fewer interests involved. However, this could not account wholly for the new vogue in argument, for many people in the previous twenty years had advocated liberty of conscience without considering 'interests' at all.

One of these tracts has been attributed to David Jenkins, the noted Welsh judge.[2] Authorship does not matter very much, and for present purposes it will be convenient to treat both the

---

[1] [Richard Perrinchief], *A Discourse of Toleration* . . . (1668), p. 30. Cf. [Samuel Parker], *A Discourse of Ecclesiastical Polity*, 3rd edn. (1671), pp. 158–60. Parker discussed the possibility of balancing religious factions, but dismissed the idea as impractical.

[2] Jenkins is normally credited with writing *A Proposition for the Safety and Happiness of the King and Kingdom* (1667), since the preface was signed with his name. A subsequent work, *A Defence of the Proposition* (1668), contained the claim that it was by the author of the *Proposition*. This tract has always been accepted as the work of the Presbyterian minister John Humfrey. Probably he wrote both of them, as the Bodleian catalogue suggests. Authorities differ as to the date of Jenkins' death, but if the *D.N.B.* is correct, he died in 1663.

Proposition and its defence as the work of John Humfrey. While the tone of Humfrey's work varied a good deal, from one tract to another, the emphasis in these writings was on political realities.

While he deemed liberty of conscience a good thing in itself, most of the author's energies were devoted to selling the plan to the government. The main proposal was epitomized with only slight exaggeration as the strategy of the Roman general who marched his troops away from a besieged city, only to return when internecine struggles had weakened the watch on the walls.[1] Toleration was the prerequisite for civil order, for only by that expedient could the various factions united against prelacy be divided. So long as persecution continued, these factions had, of necessity, to 'combine their interest'. To the hypothetical objection that the Oxford oath performed the divisive function adequately in separating those who would and would not take it, he had a ready answer. He noted that the common interests of Dissenters outweighed such minor irritants:

'. . . while their combined interest is all one, the dividing them in their single interests and little angers, is but multiplying parties against you.'[2]

Interest of state dictated a judiciously maintained balance, for,

'. . . if such factions are considerable and equal, a neutral kind of un-concernment and indifferency, makes the chief magistrate strong, while he keeps his interest in all of them.'[3]

Despite the prolonged treatment of the interests of the government and ecclesiastical establishment, Humfrey was primarily concerned with furthering the interest of his own party. However, at every stage in the discussion he reverted to the happy dispensation whereby the good of the religious parties harmonized with that of the government. Obviously toleration was sought for groups other than his own, though the exact scope was not made clear. If the attrition of general proselytizing tended to undo the Independents or Catholics, this seemed all for the best.[4] But the essential point was that political benefits would only follow if they were left free to pursue their interests.

[1] *A Proposition*, p. 37.   [2] *Ibid.*, pp. 40–1.   [3] *Ibid.*, p. 41.
[4] [Humfrey], *A Defence of the Proposition;* . . . (1668), pp. 99–100.

The position of the magistrate, one of *tertius gaudens*, was stated in a number of ways. In some of these passages the idea of a balance of interests became clearer, for he dropped his confusing insistence that factions would have to be 'equal' in some undefined sense. One typical excerpt will suffice:

'. . . when there are any sects that are considerable in their rooting and numbers, if they be banded in common interest against the laws, while they are put in force against them, I think, indeed, they are dangerous . . . but if they be disbanded into their single interests by toleration, there is no more fear of them; but the supream magistrate is become so much stronger, to wit, in the strength of all of them for himself, and of each one against another.'[1]

Humfrey dismissed the common objection that some people sought sinister designs behind a façade of conscience. Such pretexts presented no danger, he assured the reader, for liberty of conscience would serve to dissociate other Dissenters from those plans, which had previously flourished on artificial alliances.[2] This portrait of a congeries of atomized interests seems to have been unique in the controversy up to that time, at least in the degree of refinement and elaboration of the central theme.

His writings are also noteworthy for an unusually good appreciation of the paradox that liberty of conscience produced both a useful fragmentation of interests, which, united, might be dangerous, and a general interest in maintaining the new *status quo*. Thus he insisted that there would be no problem of public order under toleration, for the government would be strengthened by a new 'universal interest' against both insurrection and invasion.'[3] This constituted an improvement in clarity over some of the earlier works on toleration, one of which had suggested that basing toleration on a 'coalition of all interests' was somehow different from balancing the interests of the various parties.[4] Humfrey made it clear that broadening the basis of the government's support by winning over all of the main interests was not inconsistent with dividing the religious 'interests'.

Apart from his obvious adherence to a balance of interests to

---

[1] *A Defence* . . ., p. 103.   [2] *Ibid.*, p. 70.   [3] *Ibid.*, pp. 99–100.
[4] See J. V. C. O., *Amsterdam: Toleration or No Toleration* (1663), pp. 5–6. This rare tract is not in Wing. The copy consulted is in the library of Trinity College, Cambridge.

secure the public good, Humfrey also discussed this concept in a slightly different context. Since a defence of religious liberty involved clashing with established laws, such claims might be countered by the same arguments used against republicans and other advocates of popular government. In the course of attacking such repressive measures as the Five-mile Act, Humfrey observed that private citizens might disobey a law obviously against the public good, without violating their consciences. He was not thereby justifying rebellion or even popular control of law-making. He allowed that the magistrate might judge what the public good was for purposes of making the law, while the subject would judge for purposes of obedience. To make his point he chose the homely example of waggoners who were hindered in making a living by ill-considered regulations. Such people might ignore such a law with good consciences.[1] One test of a law was if it 'hath not root enough upon the public utility to maintain itself against private encroachments'.[2] A law really for the public good would gain much support from private men for their own interests. The absence of such support made the law a dead letter. He was very hostile to those thinkers who elevated the monarch's honour over the public good, for he insisted that 'the good of the people in their public capacity is the good of the commonwealth'.[3]

Bishop Simon Patrick answered Humfrey. His complaint was that Humfrey had revived the old cry of '*salus populi*', with the old radical interpretation. He understood Humfrey to mean that God made every man judge of his own actions, therefore he was able to judge the public good. His answer was that

'. . . if he can show me the necessary connection of these two and that the former infers the latter, I shall acknowledge that he is a deep man. But they seem to me so widely distant, that one can never pass from the one to the other by the longest train of consequences.'[4]

Patrick then proceeded to use Sanderson's famous lectures to

[1] [Humfrey], *A Case of Conscience* . . . (1669), pp. 5–6. (B: Pamph. C 126).
[2] J. H., *The Obligation of Human Laws Discussed* (1671), pp. 111–12.
[3] *The Obligation of Human Laws Discussed* (1671), p. 130. In the same passage Humfrey used 'common interest' as an equivalent to the people's good.
[4] [Patrick], *An Appendix to the Third Part of the Friendly Debate* (1670)—Postscript, p. 189, misnumbered 185. As the title suggests, Patrick had a disconcerting tendency to express himself in a series of afterthoughts.

dispose of such doctrines. This dispute was not primarily about the meaning of the public good, but how it was to be known. However, the debaters were in disagreement on the first score as well. Patrick insisted that a law might be in the public interest, although some particular persons were damaged by it.[1] Humfrey could not deny this, but he adopted the position that a law truly in the public interest would be sustained precisely because it benefited particular persons. Only the fact that both men were primarily concerned with the problem of obedience and conscience kept their disagreement about the nature of the public good in the background.

Humfrey was an able thinker with a taste for political ideas. Some of his other writings show a remarkable familiarity with the classics of political thought both of the past and of his own time. His main source of inspiration, however, seems to have been another toleration tract of 1667. While Humfrey did not wholly agree with its emphasis, he still felt that he had to justify treating liberty of conscience in terms of political forces after the subject had already been so thoroughly dealt with. In discussing toleration, Humfrey quoted Gauden, an unnamed French historian, on the policy of Henry IV and 'one worthy knight who was the author of the papers called *Liberty of Conscience*'.[2] The historian was probably de Thou; the worthy knight was certainly Sir Charles Wolseley, the figure to whom we now turn.

Wolseley had been an active political figure in the Interregnum. Out of favour with the restored Stuarts, he rusticated himself and acted as a vigorous advocate of toleration for the next thirty years. There is less evidence of special pleading here, and whatever his religious loyalties were, they did not lead him in the direction taken by Corbet and Humfrey. Instead of Comprehension, his aim was a thoroughgoing liberty of conscience, with no special status for Presbyterians.

Wolseley stated the merits of a balance of interests in the strongest terms:

'. . . so many divided interests and parties in religion, are much less dangerous than any, and may be prudently managed to balance

[1] Patrick, *op. cit.*, pp. 211–12, misnumbered 207–8.
[2] J. H., *The Authority of the Magistrate about Religion Discussed* . . . (1672), p. 31. Elsewhere his praise was less restrained. See *A Case of Conscience*, p. 12.

each other, and to become generally more safe and useful to a state, than any united party or interest whatever.'[1]

Quite what was intended by the latter part of the statement is not certain. Though there was no more than a hint of dis-establishment feeling, the Church of England seemed to be treated as one party among several. Clearly, he went beyond the position that divisions in religion were a sad but unavoid-able fact, although this idea itself still had some battles to win. He expatiated on the political value to the sovereign of having countervailing forces in society, forces which could only be in-tended to check the established church.

For the prince there was the assurance that liberty would not produce unity among the parties, for that was the child of perse-cution.[2] The *status quo* could be freely left to the interests of the parties, with the single qualification that the balance had to be managed. By this he presumably meant that the state might bring pressure upon the Church of England. Since he clearly assumed that liberty of conscience would be a permanent condi-tion, it is difficult to see how royal leverage could much affect the other sects; but this church, with its legal privileges, still had something to lose. All interests would benefit from the arrange-ment. He particularly insisted that alienating the Nonconform-ists could never be the basis of a 'true national interest'.[3]

There was little here that Humfrey had not already said, and perhaps it would have been more natural to find Wolseley quoting Humfrey than the reverse. The most significant and original point was his insistence that limited conflict had a genu-ine value that was lost in a united religious establishment. It is also significant that Wolseley's position on the balance of inter-ests was reproduced in an unusual number of other tracts, either by him or by plagiarists.[4] Clearly Wolseley's work made an

[1] [Wolseley], *Liberty of Conscience the Magistrate's Interest*, p. 53. This tract is appended to another called *Liberty of Conscience Upon its True and Proper Grounds Asserted and Vindicated* (1668).

[2] Wolseley, *Liberty . . . the Magistrate's Interest*, p. 64.   [3] *Ibid.*, p. 58.

[4] See *A Few Sober Queries upon the Late Proclamation for Enforcing Laws Against Conventicles* (1668) where query XLI followed the exact words of Wolseley's statement on the balance of interests. Others include Anon., *A Modest Answer to Dr. Dove's Sermon Preached at Bow-Church* (1682) (B: Pamph. C 158), and Anon., *Reasons Humbly Offered Proving it is Inconsistent with the Interest of England that the Civil Magistrate Should Put the Penal Laws into Execution Against*

impression on his time, although it is not easy to say why this was so.

There were few other tracts worthy of notice in this period. One Anglican survey of 'factious' doctrines on toleration dealt only with Corbet, Humfrey and Wolseley.[1] The writer had over-looked a few minor targets,[2] but most people who discussed toleration in political terms said little, and nothing original. A major figure such as Andrew Marvell alluded to the benefits of a balance of interests, but characteristically let his remarks take the form of a personal jibe at Samuel Parker.[3] Peter Walsh, a Roman Catholic apologist, was also aware of the political con-siderations involved, and also skirted the topic. Walsh seems to have been inhibited by the reputation for deep political intrigue that surrounded men of his faith. Thus he ostentatiously dis-claimed the importance of 'private or civil interest' and even appears to have been trying to reopen that debate between 'policy' and 'religion', supposedly resolved some decades before with the recognition of the importance of policy. He managed to convey the essence of de Thou's message, but in the most innocuous way consistent with making the point intelligible.[4]

A modern scholar has observed that there was a dearth of valuable political literature in the seventies.[5] The decade began with devious manoeuvring by Charles to better the lot of the Catholics and ended with the hysterical ephemera written about the Popish Plot. There was an hiatus in the flow of inter-esting political argument, at least in the first half of the decade, but a portent of change was the appearance, in 1675, of the first major political work by William Penn. There followed a long series of treatises on the benefits, largely political, of a universal

---

Protestant Dissenters (1682) (B: G.P. 1126). This last was just another edition of Wolseley's original tract.

[1] 'Abraham Philotheus', *Anarchie Reviving or the Good Old Cause on the Anvile* (1668) (B: B 1.4 Linc.).

[2] See Anon., *The Judgement of a Good Subject upon His Majestie's Late Declara-tion for Indulgence of Tender Consciences* (1672), pp. 5–7 (B: C 12.4 Linc.), for a sophisticated understanding of a balance of interests.

[3] Marvell, 'Rehearsal Transposed', in *Works*, ed. A. B. Grosart, (London, 1873), Vol. III, p. 193.

[4] [Walsh], *The Advocate of Conscience Liberty* (1673), p. 33.

[5] Caroline Robbins, *The Eighteenth Century Commonwealthman* (Cambridge, Mass., 1959), pp. 26–7.

liberty of conscience. While not as indefatigably prolific as George Fox, Penn ensured that mere lack of numbers would be no barrier to an exhaustive presentation of the Quaker argument. Penn was so prominent from this time until the revolutionary settlement that it will be convenient to treat his writings in a body without rigorously adhering to chronology. This involves no danger of isolating his political theory from the events that gave rise to it; whatever embarrassment the tangled events of 1687-8 may have caused others, Penn's goals remained perfectly consistent throughout. His large armoury of arguments contained some which, if not wholly inconsistent, at least appealed in widely different terms. However, the various themes are scattered fairly uniformly throughout his writings.

Corbet, Humfrey and Wolseley had all discussed liberty of conscience in terms of the national interest. They had all been concerned, as well, with giving a measure of consideration to the various partial interests involved. The general argument here was that the national interest could not be considered in isolation from some, at least, of the particular interests. Their specific proposals differed, but all thought in terms of broadening the foundations of the government's support by a toleration. Unless other interests were taken into consideration, the government would remain weak, with the better part of the people in sullen opposition.

From the point of view of political theory their work was defective in failing to examine notions such as 'interest' and the 'public interest' with any degree of care. They snatched at whatever slogans were available. Rohan was useful, because everyone knew that in one sense it was in the interest of the English nation to foster unity and to present a united front to foreign enemies. It also seemed reasonable to say that the public interest was a more genuine entity if policies in its name gained the support of most of the citizens. As far as the church establishment was concerned, unity came first, and an enforced unity was superior to that different sort of unity produced through indulging consciences. The case for toleration badly needed some statement of priorities; some explanation in terms of the primacy of individual rights and the national benefit, even in national strength, to be derived from honouring these rights. This was the contribution of William Penn.

The earlier Quaker writings provide no close continuity with Penn. While the forbidding volume of this literature precludes any categorical statement, the general tenor of early Quaker writings on toleration was piously naïve and apolitical. The dominant theme that emerges is the inherent goodness and godliness of liberty of conscience. Self-interest appeared as a vice of most men, from which Quakers were alone free.[1] It was, of course, his Quaker beliefs that led Penn to renounce any reliance upon oaths as a guarantor of political order. Since this factor was still taken seriously by some, its repudiation would naturally lead any astute thinker to seek out some alternative. Still, other Quakers shared his feelings on oaths, but not those on interest. Penn's later espousal of the cause of the Catholics would also have served to lead him to disregard the social sanction of oaths, for it was then a common tenet of all Protestants that Catholic casuistry allowed them to break faith with heretics. Thus oaths were a weak basis for the argument. Since his religious antecedents were scarcely models of *Realpolitik*, one must assume that in his role as a man of the world, and his dual capacity after 1681, as ruler on one continent and subject on another, Penn acquired his outlook.[2]

Penn's contribution to political thought chiefly consists in having translated current problems into the language of interest. All his proposals, but most importantly that of toleration, were brought to the bar of interest and there harmonized with the ends of individuals as well as the needs of the state. It seems reasonable, then, to attempt to discover what 'interest' meant for him. Penn obliged with a substantial discussion of just this point in one of his early anonymous tracts. One can do no better than to quote him:

'. . . the word interest has a good and a bad acceptation; when it is taken in an ill sense, it signifies a pursuit of advantage without regard to truth or justice. . . . The good signification of the word, and

[1] The numerous works by George Fox, the elder, and Francis Howgill provide ample evidence of this tendency.
[2] Penn had always had connections at court through his father, the admiral. He also became a courtier in his own right, if rather an unconventional one. Penn's close and complex relationship with James II has been sympathetically re-examined by Vincent Buranelli. See *The King and the Quaker* (Philadelphia, 1962).

what I mean, is a legal endeavour to keep rights, or augment honest profits, whether it be in a private person or a society.'[1]

The significance of the definition is that it plainly indicated, even in the respectable version of the term, that it was a recognized good actively pursued by individuals. There was no attempt to introduce the passive cousin, 'true interest', whereby what men really sought was cast aside in favour of what they ought to seek. The explanation for this does not involve attributing any cynicism to Penn's character. Though obviously a deeply religious man, he suspended, for purposes of political debate, all considerations of ultimate personal good in the sense of salvation. It was by invoking the welfare of men's souls that more authoritarian thinkers tended to supersede worldly concerns. Penn made no appeal to an ultimate, supramundane rationality. This is not to say that he dignified the passing fancy of a moment with the 'good' meaning of interest, but any tempering of legitimate self-indulgence was to be by a rational expectation of terrestrial rewards.

The various strands in Penn's definition were further illuminated in succeeding paragraphs:

'Civil interest is the foundation and end of civil government . . . the good of the whole must needs be the interest of the whole, and consequently the interest of the whole is the reason and end of government.'[2]

The essence of this statement was at this time fashionably expressed in the maxim 'interest will not lie'. Penn proceeded immediately to pour content into this interest:

'. . . none can stumble at the word good for every man may easily and safely interpret that to himself, since he must needs believe; tis good for him to be preserved in an undisturbed possession of his civil rights according to the free and just laws of the land, and the construction he makes for himself will serve his neighbour, and so the whole society.'[3]

---

[1] 'One Project for the Good of England' (1679?), in *A Collection of the Works of William Penn* (London, 1726), Vol. II, p. 682. The original bore no date, but an answer to it was published in 1680.

[2] William Penn, *One Project*, p. 683.

[3] *Ibid.* In this connection, perhaps it is worth recording the opinion of a modern scholar. He claims that the attitude that each man must judge the public interest for himself is a peculiarly American one. H. Cleveland and

The sentiment, and indeed the very words, are familiar. Not only are they reminiscent of Harrington's efforts, but the passage seems to be a paraphrase of all those Commonwealth Republicans who founded the common interest on each man's concern for preserving his personal rights. Whether or not this was a question of direct influence or the result of the similarity of Penn's circumstances to theirs cannot be established. Certainly Penn quoted no earlier sources for his opinions.[1] In developing his theme from individualistic premises, Penn would find this position a natural one, scarcely avoidable for anyone trying to relate the interest of the state to individual interests. No amount of enumeration could suggest the variety of individual interests of a personal sort, and any facile assumption that mere reason of state led to individual satisfaction was distasteful. Thus a promising solution was to discover some socially acceptable condition that was also the course dictated by the vital interests of private men.

This led to the formula in terms of the preservation of rights. It was not just a matter of maintaining the *status quo*, for the phrase about augmenting honest profits left scope for individual striving, and as we shall see, this interpretation was borne out by Penn's treatment of the toleration issue. Harrington had written of interests being summed up; Penn did not employ the same expression. He did, however, make clear that the interest of the state was correctly seen as the interests of individuals. 'The whole,' he affirmed, 'takes in all parts.'[2]

Much the same point was made by a subtle play upon the word interest. Penn argued that by persecution the government undercut the basis of its own strength, for the interest of the government was as large as the mass of people supporting it. It was a fatal error to allow the civil interest of a people (i.e. the basis of its loyalty to the government) to be narrowed by the

H. D. Lasswell (eds.), *Ethics and Bigness* (New York, 1962), p. XLII. Penn's statement might seem to support this theory, but others, including Humfrey, had already said much the same thing.

[1] Buranelli's assertion that Penn took the term 'interest' from 'John Harrington . . . one of Penn's favourite sources', does not invite much confidence. See Buranelli, *op. cit.*, p. 129. Penn is credited with a knowledge of *Oceana* largely on the basis of the constitution provided for Pennsylvania. See E. C. O. Beatty, *William Penn as Social Philosopher* (New York, 1939), p. 9.

[2] *One Project*, p. 683.

ambitions of one party. In this context the remark could refer either to the Church of England or to the Catholics, who gained by the harassment of one group of Protestants by another. This led to the observation that

'. . . since the civil interest lies as large as the people of that interest, the people must be preserved in order to preserve that common interest.'[1]

While this comment may have owed something to the common notion that a nation flourished in direct proportion to the size of its population, this was not the only implication. Earlier thinkers who had visualized the interest of state as diffused among the people had expressed the same thought.

If the meaning of interest to describe the designs of individuals was tolerably clear, this could not be so readily said of the interest of the government. In suggesting that the government broaden its interest, that word bore very much the connotation of 'influence', one of its accepted seventeenth-century meanings. The government flourished in proportion to its influence over the mass of citizens. Certainly this was not the normal meaning of the 'interest' of a government. Penn himself gave the conventional understanding of the concept when he referred to 'civil interest' and said that it consisted in

'. . . the preservation of the free and legal government of it [the state] from all subjection to foreign claim.'[2]

While nobody would question that the two ideas were related, it remains true that the maintenance of territorial integrity was not coextensive in meaning with responsiveness to all domestic interests.

One might think that Penn had thrown his case away to embrace the cause of conventional reason of state. However, he had already said that each private man could adequately interpret the good of society, because each man knew his own interest in preserving his liberty and property. He had some trouble in suggesting that the preservation of private rights and the maintenance of national strength were really the same thing. The ambiguous use of 'interest' was one way of equating these two things. It had crept in at the very point where Harrington

[1] *One Project*, p. 685.   [2] *Ibid.*, p. 686.

had been forced into clumsy equivocation, at the vital juncture between the interests of the individual citizen and that of the whole, as represented by the government. Penn was saying that the state-interest of self-preservation (or the interest of the government) could best be pursued if the body of the people could identify their interests with that of the government. He took it as a necessary truth that these two interests were inseparable, on the common-sense grounds that the preservation of the constituent parts of the nation was essential to national preservation. Most calls for unity and religious uniformity had stressed how necessity of state dictated doing everything possible to strengthen the nation and the Protestant interest. Such people assumed that preserving the nation was the preservation of its people as well. Penn had clearly reversed this traditional statement of priorities, saying that since the civil interest grew in proportion to those of that interest, the preservation of the people's interest was the necessary condition of securing the common interest.

Apparently he had not thought it sufficiently convincing to say that national strength was more a function of the satisfaction of various partial interests than it was of their repression. Thus he introduced the dual meaning of interest.[1] There was one interest of the state in being strong and independent and another interest that consisted in the domestic influence of the

---

[1] Arguments in this form were not unusual in the seventeenth century. Writers often leave one with the impression that they were constructing arguments in the knowledge that their force depended upon the ambiguous use of words. 'Interest' was ideal for such purposes, because it had so many meanings. A good example of the technique occurs in a tract where the writer discovered the common interest of the nation by joining the personal interest of the Prince of Orange with the electoral interest of the magnates who had brought him to the throne. In this case, 'interest' meant two different things. The interest of the Prince was treated as a personal concern, i.e. interest in the conventional sense. When discussing the 'interest' of the men responsible for the Revolution, this pamphleteer said that they had controlled events 'by that interest they had in them', adding, 'by this, their interest, they will as certainly be elected again'. See Anon., *The Common Interest of King and Kingdom in this Confused Conjuncture, Truly Stated* (1688), p. 2 (BM: T 692). The writer was clearly referring to interest in the sense of influence, an application already common in connection with elections, and destined for much greater use in the eighteenth century. See R. Walcott, *English Politics in the Early Eighteenth Century* (Oxford, 1956), p. 155.

government, this influence, or 'interest', being measured by its respect for private rights. By passing rapidly from 'interest' in one sense to 'interest' in another, he implied that there was something more than an empirically verifiable connection between the two. The connection approached the certainty of a truth by definition. Penn's feat here consisted in broaching that aspect of a national interest that dominated all others as far as Tories and Anglicans were concerned. He freely admitted the importance of national strength, but still managed to dissolve the common interest into the interests of individual citizens. The twofold meaning of interest served to capture the bastions of state power for individualism.

The most remarkable aspect of this tract, apart from its emphasis upon the nature of a common interest, was that it concentrated upon the way in which the interests of individuals were involved in the struggle for liberty of conscience. Quite often writers suggested that persecution was an unwarranted attack upon men's liberties and estates, but Penn went further to relate these liberties to the public good. This should not obscure the fact that most discussions of the toleration question by Penn and others dealt with particular interests of another sort, those of groups. These, too, might be used in various ways in order to maintain the public interest. Indeed, some of the remarks already quoted from Penn were meant to apply both to single individuals and to religious groups.

In the passages just treated, Penn had chosen to ignore the uncomfortable fact that liberty would not necessarily unite all interests behind the government. To mollify the Church of England he had stressed the enhancement of national strength that toleration would bring. The established church was tempted by 'the power of interest and that self-interest too'.[1] By emphasizing the claims of property, Penn had suggested how the construction placed by each man on his civil interest might serve the whole society. But there remained problems in the relationship among the various religious interests and between each one and the government. He had indicated one path to order and unity in the interests of men as claimants of natural rights, but he also had to consider them as members of antagonistic parties. *One Project* was well suited for displaying Penn's

[1] *One Project*, p. 688.

individualism, but it was deficient on detail as to the manner in which the public good was to be sustained. Would the Church of England really be strengthened by the removal of a measure of its legal protection? If the Catholics delighted in internal dissention, why should they welcome a general toleration?

Much of Penn's work provides another perspective on the interests of the day. While it did not involve any denial of the possibility of a 'united civil interest' under a general liberty of conscience, allowance was made for various means of achieving this result. The very nature of an interest meant that Penn could appeal to interests of various sorts in order to sustain the government and the freedom of citizens. His model of society was based upon the remarkable paradox that political unity was dependent upon diversity in religious belief and a certain tension between the various sects. In his earliest politically relevant writings Penn had already begun to think in terms of a configuration of religious parties that would provide the conditions necessary for a settlement. He expressed his thoughts in a document sent to a German prince. The gist of the message to this persecutor of Quakers was that toleration was the only politically rational course because

'. . . it rendereth the prince peculiarly safe and great . . . because all interests, for interests sake, are bound to love and court him.'[1]

Another early tract pointed to the possibility of combining a certain unity of interests with a fruitful diversity, or even a large measure of conflict among them. He made the point effectively by remarking that in seeking unity of opinion in other-worldly affairs, that unity essential for social life was being impaired.[2] Even this was not an entirely adequate rendering to the theme, and in later works he was more insistent on the element of conflict. In this same early tract he admitted one of the formative influences on his social thought, as he quoted Gauden's comment about disuniting potentially seditious groups.[3]

[1] A Letter to the Prince Elector Palatine of Heydelberg reproduced in 'Travels in Holland and Germany' (1677), *Works*, Vol. I, p. 75.
[2] 'The Great Case of Liberty of Conscience Pleaded' (1670), in *Works*, Vol. I, p. 455.
[3] *Ibid.*, p. 462. There are other references to this passage scattered throughout his writings. Penn was also familiar with de Thou's work. See *The Reasonableness of Toleration and the Unreasonableness of Penal Laws and Tests* (1687).

The full array of policy arguments appeared in Penn's best-known and largest work on domestic politics, *England's Present Interest Discovered*. The major problem posed here was that of

'. . . allaying the heat of contrary interests, and making them sub-servient to the interest of the government, and consistent with the prosperity of the kingdom.'[1]

It is clear from the context that Penn envisaged no radical re-pression of interests, although he went out of his way to placate the government. He justified toleration by a great array of con-siderations including the claims of natural rights. Presbyterians had tended to concentrate upon publicizing the size and im-portance of their 'interest'. The less impressive weight of Quaker interest combined with Penn's individualism to produce this emphasis upon rights. He condemned persecution mainly as an unjust invasion of private property; an invasion which also had the effect of reducing men's incentive to acquire pro-perty. This ultimately weakened the state for it impoverished it and drove out useful citizens.

The main recurring theme was that the polity could remain healthy with

'. . . superiors governing themselves upon a balance, as near as may be, towards the several religious interests.'[2]

While he could appreciate the logic of stifling new opinions when such action was supported by the public and was the interest of the government,

'. . . it cannot be so, where a kingdom is of many minds, unless some one party have the wisdom, wealth, number sober life, industry and resolution on its side, which I am sure is not to be found in Eng-land.'[3]

This was not a cry for disestablishment. However, Penn did insist that the government would have to lean on the English people rather than on the church, for only the former included

p. 14. This is one of many anonymous tracts not included in the *Works*, but now recognized as by Penn.
[1] 'Englands Present Interest Discovered' (1675), in *Works*, Vol. I, p. 672.
[2] *Ibid.*, p. 692.   [3] *Ibid.*

'the strength of all interests'.[1] The state was still expected to have some preference for the Church of England, though he never said how this was compatible with the condition that it should not outweigh all the other parties, for this would 'break the balance'.

It is of no concern here to determine how the church establishment was to survive the exigencies of the balance, which, in the absence of an answer, is just as well. Penn's essential task was done when he had shown that interests were neutralized when held in a state of equilibrium. The use of the idea differed from earlier comments by de Thou or Gauden in looking to the advantages of such an arrangement to all parties and not just to that currently in control of church and state. He appealed, for instance, to the Presbyterian's need for other religious parties to allow him to balance himself against the ruling power of Episcopacy. This involved having the other sects free to participate in public life and to be available as potential allies.

The model presented here usefully complemented the perspective of *One Project*. It involved looking at the repercussions on the government of self-interested activity by the various religious parties. At the same time Penn could justifiably view the parties as united in their civil interest in that all would have a stake in maintaining the *status quo*. The distinction between a union of interests in one sphere and conflict in another was certainly made more intelligible by Penn's practice of differentiating carefully between 'the distinct interests of religion and policy'.[2] All parties could support the government of church and state while competing for primacy, or, at least, adopting a defensive posture towards each other in order to preserve their gains. Far from detracting from the efficacy of the political union, this balance of interests was the essence of it, the essential condition without which survival of the parties, and hence loyalty to the state, would be jeopardized. One might suggest that Penn's distinction between religious and civil interests was not quite so clear as he sometimes suggested, for the claims for

[1] *Ibid.*, p. 704.
[2] Philo-Britannicus (i.e. Penn), *The Great Question to be Considered by the King and this Approaching Parliament* ... (*c.* 1680), p. 3 (BM: 816 m. 1).

religious liberty were inextricably tied up with the right of personal safety and property, and nowhere more so than in Penn's own writing. However, the basic point was clear enough.

Later versions of the central thesis admitted of tactical departures from the scheme. In another tract Penn chose to describe the social scene under religious liberty in most idyllic terms. He visualized the wolf and the lamb (not identified) as lying down together and considered the peaceful condition of flowers growing on one bank a convenient simile. The parties were described as loving one another.[1] Still, he did not forbear from quoting the classical reason-of-state advice by Gauden. Very much the same attitude appeared in another tract, normally ascribed to Penn, which was published at about the same time. There was only one mention of 'interest' and the usual quotation from Gauden. These writings were really no indication of any waning of his enthusiasm for sophisticated analysis. In the latter work he explained his reticence on the subject, referring the reader to his major contribution of that year, one wholly devoted to the political treatment of toleration.[2]

A Persuasive to Moderation was the most exhaustive attempt to calculate all interests and to suggest how all might be reconciled. Penn constructed it as a gloss on the maxim 'interest will not lie'.[3] In a state, as in a ship, men would seek the safety of the whole by seeking their own. The natural dictates of self-preservation would suffice. He held that even men in the throes of extreme religious commitment could be relied upon to be sufficiently rational:

[1] *Considerations Moving to a Toleration and Liberty of Conscience* (1685), p. 3 (B: A 16.2 Linc.).
[2] 'A Defence of the Duke of Buckingham's Book' (1685), in *Works*, Vol. II, p. 722.
[3] *Works*, Vol. II, p. 727. This maxim might still be considered seditious when applied to the activities of private men, which was the point in Dryden's satire on the Whig's supposed faith in the people:

> The reason's obvious: Int'rest never lies,
> The most still have their interest in their eyes,
> The pow'r is always theirs, and power is ever wise.
> (*The Medal*, 1682, 11. 88–90)

Only a few years later Bunyan used it innocently enough as an established English proverb. See *The Work of Jesus Christ* (1725), 1st edn. 1688, p. 34. For the use of the proverb in an economic context see below, p. 215.

'. . . though all parties would rejoice [*sic*] their own principles prevailed, yet every one is more solicitous about its own safety than the others verity. Wherefore it cannot be unwise by the security of all, to make it the interest of all as well as the duty of all, to advance that of the public.'[1]

All persuasions would be drawn to the government by the power of interest, for not only were men less factious if well treated, but the government sustained that balance by which the weaker groups survived, though it did not really create it.

Penn anticipated the obvious objection that to attempt to base national unity upon encouragement of limited conflict seemed anomalous. His answer moved him to indulge in an uncharacteristic profusion of metaphor. Hannibal's army with its internal balance between native and foreign units was an inappropriate parallel, but he offered it. Nature afforded a more revealing model:

'. . . we see all heat consumes, all cold kills; that three degrees of cold to two of heat, allays the heat but introduces the contrary quality, and overcools by a degree: but two degrees of cold to two of heat, makes a poize in elements and a balance in nature.'[2]

Though this could hardly have impressed the Royal Society, it doubtless served its purpose in making an old idea respectable, while giving it new meaning. Should one party be sufficiently shortsighted to attempt to crush another, the 'balance at home' (an obvious allusion to the more common concept of a balance in Europe) would take effect.[3]

Penn took particular care to note that this arrangement was far from a mere aid either to the monarchy or to the Church of England. The model conceived here was also a more complex and flexible one than that of some Presbyterians, who thought in terms of a confrontation between a powerful establishment and all the rest. While earlier he had been uninterested in the fate of the Roman Catholics, or even quite hostile to them, here he insisted upon their being given full rights of conscience and

[1] *Works*, Vol. II, p. 727.
[2] *Ibid.*, p. 741.
[3] The parallel between the balance among nations and that within them appealed to writers of the day. See Anon., *Three Great Questions Concerning the Succession and the Dangers of Popery* . . . (1680), p. 16 (B: 4° W. 74 Jur.).

accorded them an important role in the scheme of mutually checking forces.

Even before the campaign by James II for Catholic emancipation, Penn had adjusted his appeal to the prevailing winds.[1] The Anglicans were seen as the central mover of his balance, holding a mean position between the Nonconformist and Catholic extremes. That church was to be prepared to throw its weight at all times to the side of the weaker party. As was often the case in such writings, there was no satisfactory discussion of details that were rather important for an understanding of the general principle. How, one wonders, would the church 'lean' towards one party, if it were not in a position to revoke or grant privileges? Did Penn contemplate an alliance to influence the government or was he thinking only that a belligerent party would be inhibited when it realized that much social power in the form of wealth and numbers could be arrayed against it? The text gives no answer. Upsetting the balance would bring sanctions and the possibility of conflict, but one is not told in what forum it would take place. In any event, Penn felt that all parties would accept this role for the Church of England, as neither Presbyterian nor Catholic could hope for as sympathetic an arbiter if the other held the scales.

The prime concern here was to suggest some sort of moving equilibrium among what Penn called the 'three considerable church-interests'. At the same time some appreciation of broader implications also came to light. A model adjusted to prevailing circumstances was but a particular instance of a more generally applicable principle. It was in this spirit that Penn observed that

'... they are neither few, nor of the weakest sort of men, that have thought the concord of discords a firm basis for government to be built upon. The business is to tune them well and that must be the skill of the musician.'[2]

[1] Penn published his most anti-Catholic tract in 1679, as he succumbed to the hysteria of the Popish Plot. See 'England's Great Interest in the Choice of This New Parliament', in *Works*, Vol. II, pp. 681–2.

[2] 'A Persuasive to Moderation' (1686), in *Works*, p. 741. The expression *'concordia discors'* was used in arguments for toleration before Penn began to publish. For an early example by an English Catholic see J. H., *A Letter from a Person of Quality to a Principal Peer of the Realm . . . Occasioned by the Present*

Apparently the beneficial results of opposed self-interests could be realized throughout the political system. Unfortunately, apart from this tantalizingly brief reference, there was nothing to indicate Penn's thoughts. He may have been thinking of the classical precepts about dividing ambitious courtiers, or the comment may have been related in some relevant way to the contemporary scene. Certainly few ideas can then have been more in vogue than that of balance, borrowed from the still novel discoveries in mechanics.[1] So various were the uses made of the idea that it would be dangerous to infer too much from a bare allusion; still Penn's grasp of the social significance of the *concordia discors* did appear to transcend conventional advice about restraining cabals.

The theme was little altered in another of Penn's major tracts. There was the same insistence that 'duty, principle and interest' all pointed towards an acceptance of his proposals. As before, he was plainly most concerned with men's efforts to preserve their acquired gains rather than to increase them, though within the religious context of his remarks there was doubtless provision for strengthening a party rather than merely maintaining its identity against all opposition. He stressed that interest was neither a passive nor a static thing:

'. . . interests change as well as times, and 'tis the wisdom of a man to observe the courses, and humour the motions of his interest, as the best way to preserve it.'[2]

The fruitful tension among the competing interests remained much as before except that now the balance involved four parties apart from the Church of England. Earlier he had thought in terms of fewer parties, but in *Good Advice* he paid particular attention to the place of the Catholics in the balance.

Debate upon the Penal Laws (1611, really 1661), p. 12 (BM: T 2230). See too a broadside marking the royal declaration for liberty of conscience, *Discors Concordia, or Unanimity in Variance* (1687) (B: Ashm. H 24).
[1] For a brief discussion of the prevalence of this notion see James E. King *Science and Rationalism in the Government of Louis XIV* (Baltimore, 1949), pp. 51–2. Many seventeenth-century sources used the expression to convey the meaning of state or condition, as in 'the balance of our affairs'.
[2] 'Good Advice to the Church of England, Roman Catholic and Protestant Dissenter', *Works*, Vol. II, p. 764.

Penn also stressed the enduring nature of the balance, parties being less mortal than men.[1]

In Penn's most interesting observation he turned away from the immediate situation to dwell briefly upon the general nature of social conflict. Holland had long served as an inspiration to proponents of toleration. Penn wanted to open public offices to all men regardless of religion, but he was embarrassed by the fact that the Dutch followed a less permissive policy, since they reserved control of the government to members of the established church. Penn tried to excuse Dutch practice while, at the same time, showing that their situation was unique. Holland, he said, was a small, economically exposed trading nation without the resources of England. This precarious position made the government very careful in treating other interests, and the interests not directly represented in government were equally careful in their means of opposing the government. Thus the economic efficiency needed to keep Holland from ruin precluded the 'national disorder' involved in introducing different religious parties into the government.[2] The implication was that England had both a wider margin of error and greater need of giving political power to minority religious interests. Presumably the intrusion of men of all persuasions into government would not affect the position of the Church of England.

Penn's contribution to the deluge of pamphlets following the Declaration of Indulgence of April 1687 was not very important for purposes of political theory. As a Dissenter who enthusiastically grasped the offer of liberty, his main concern at this time was to reassure both fellow Dissenters and Anglicans on the question of the Papist menace. There was no need to recant any of his theories about the use of social power, but certain aspects of his earlier ideas were de-emphasized. Thus he must have deemed it impolitic to stress the continuing struggle among all churches, concentrating instead on the new possibility of strengthening the Protestant cause against any onslaught by the liberated Catholics. This was not a major concession, but it was reflected in a changed tone. He took unusual pains to note how the temporary alliance with Popery for the passage of a toleration Act would dissolve once this object had been gained. All

[1] *Good Advice*, p. 769.   [2] *Good Advice*, p. 773.

Protestants could then unite interests in their common distaste for Catholicism. The picture of Quakers soon to be united with the established church in 'affection and interest' was comprehensible in the light of conditions, but would have seemed out of place in some of the earlier writings.[1] Similar considerations must have prompted him to say that the 'common union and interest of all parties in a league of mutual liberty' was much superior to the clash of factions that had existed to date.[2]

Another theme more in keeping with his previous statements was the security lent to any settlement by the predictable reactions of parties moved by interest. The proposed toleration was not only the 'true interest of the Roman Catholics, but they think so'.[3] He regularly made similar avowals for the other parties. To banish the bogey of the Catholic's policy of *divide et impera*, he pointed out how this could best have been accomplished under a religious repression as one Protestant destroyed others. He interpreted the Catholic support for indulgence as a repudiation of their more sinister ambitions.[4] A note of incoherence here, for Penn could not resist insinuating his favourite point about the benefits of competing interests. Thus, in a curious *volte-face*, he described a toleration as dividing the Dissenters from the Church of England. If it was the interest of the Catholics to divide the Protestants, they could not think it wise to unite them, which they would do if the Catholics were thought to be against toleration for all.[5]

These final comments on liberty of conscience did provide the occasion for some clarification of Penn's thoughts on interest as the prime mover in political activity. He had begun his discourses on the subject by distinguishing between two meanings of the word, though the line between the favourable and unfavourable meanings did appear perilously fine and certainly many times he seemed to be recommending policies on the

[1] *A Letter from a Gentleman in the Country . . . Upon the Subject of the Penal Laws and Tests* (1687), p. 9.
[2] *Some Free Reflections Upon Occasion of the Public Discourse About Liberty of Conscience* (1687), p. 14 (BM: T 763).
[3] *The Great and Popular Objection Against the Repeal of the Penal Laws and Tests . . .* (1688), p. 10.
[4] *Ibid.*, pp. 10-11.
[5] *Ibid.*, p. 12.

grounds of both at once. At times he had said hard things about interest as a motivation, once damning 'interest or faction' as 'the only true heresy'.[1] However, if anything, his attitude had softened in the later writings.

He refrained from making the common charge that interest prevented the Church of England from granting liberty. His strongest form of criticism was contained in remarks about the superiority of the general good to the 'narrow advantages of a party'.[2] In point of fact he was prepared to argue that the interest of the church pointed towards his policies of a harmony of interests centred on the balance, but apparently the following of one's assumed interest was not *prima facie* grounds for condemnation, even in the event of miscalculation. He readily allowed the Anglican taunt that interest lay behind the Dissenters' claims for freedom and asserted that this being their interest they might follow it.[3] In the event that two parties were unalterably opposed in their interests as they understood them, the larger should prevail.[4]

Interest was never lauded as the ideal grounds for settlement, just as the best possible. God had chosen to place men in a situation where their interest led them to conclusions that 'virtue and wisdom' should have taught them long ago. Until God sent miracles on 'higher principles of union' men were advised to act upon the lower, but secure basis of interest.[5] This was perhaps no cause for rejoicing, but the great virtue of agreements based on interest was their permanence.

'For whatever be the morality of any party, if I am sure of them by the side of interest and necessity, I will never seek or value an ensurance by oaths and tests. Interest is the choice men naturally make and necessity compels submission from the unhappy subjects of her power.'[6]

[1] 'An Address to Protestants' (1679), in *Works*, Vol. I, p. 816. This was written during Penn's anti-Catholic period, hence the great emphasis upon Protestant unity.
[2] *Three Letters tending to Demonstrate how the Security of the Nation Against All Future Persecution for Religion Lies . . . in the Establishment of a New Law for Universal Liberty of Conscience* (1688), p. 12 (BM: T 1685).
[3] *Some Free Reflections*, p. 7.
[4] *Ibid.*
[5] *A Second Letter from a Gentleman in the Country . . .* (1687), p. 12.
[6] *The Great and Popular Objection*, p. 16.

In the comparative calm of the nineties Penn held fast to this opinion. He said then:

'Interest has the security though not the virtue of a principle. As the world goes it is the sure side.'[1]

Its influence was rendered legitimate, if not wholly palatable, by the fact that 'we are tied down by our senses to the world'.[2]

One continuing source of ambiguity was the exact area of human experience covered by the term interest. Several times he contrasted it with religion.[3] He also set it apart from 'inclination', presumably because the latter implied an emotional attachment rather than a choice based upon rational calculations of worldly gain. In this latter discussion the term seemed to have an almost wholly economic connotation.[4] The contrast with religion is particularly noteworthy, because Penn had been arguing all the while for liberty of conscience as he wrote of interest. This indicates the general bent of his thought. While holding things of the spirit in high regard, he primarily appealed to men's desires to maintain or better their state in the world. Had he been interested only in inner peace for himself and others, he might have said less about 'interest', although the Quakers' need to testify to their faith makes it difficult to separate religious belief from external circumstances. As it was, Penn appealed to the fact that Dissenters wanted political influence commensurate with their economic importance, as well as increased encouragement as traders.[5] Although 'interest' was, at best, a slippery, unmanageable concept, Penn gave it an unusually clear and consistent meaning. It was, as he once said, 'a strange thing'.[6] It was strange indeed; for he had shown how, given the opportunity, it would lead men to the national good. Throughout Penn's writings 'interest' related to concerns about civil status and worldly opportunities. To emphasize his

[1] 'Some Fruits of Solitude in Reflections and Maxims Relating to the Conduct of Human Life' (1693), in *Works*, Vol. I, p. 828.
[2] *Ibid.*
[3] 'Some Fruits of Solitude in Reflections and Maxims Relating to the Conduct of Human Life' (1693), in *Works*, Vol. I, p. 828.
[4] 'Advice of William Penn to his Children', in *Works*, Vol. I, p. 900.
[5] This point was especially stressed in a tract of 1677. See *A Commentary Upon the Present Condition of the Kingdom and its Melioration*.
[6] *A Third Letter from a Gentleman in the Country* ... (1687), p. 7.

meaning he frequently wrote of 'civil interest'. Occasionally he mentioned a religious interest, but this was obviously not the primary application. Interest unqualified by any adjective meant worldly interest.

Penn's overall aim was best expressed by himself when he said that he was seeking a principle 'to adjust our several interests upon'.[1] Again and again he insisted that his solution provided, in the language of the day, a sufficiently broad bottom for all of the interests of the kingdom. He could harangue his colonists rather platitudinously about preferring the common good and his economic views were far from undiluted individualism. Nevertheless, Penn brought an engaging realism to the main social problem that he chose to treat. Of course the general good was his aim, professed and, no doubt, real. But he did steadfastly insist that it be reconciled with individual and group interests, a reconciliation for which he had an attractive and ingenious formula. Though the general good was the 'touchstone' for all human affairs, he promptly added that it could not be attained without the 'general satisfaction of all parties.'[2]

One of the few scholars to take Penn seriously in his role as a social theorist has failed to take him seriously enough. Beatty correctly judged that Penn's special contribution to the toleration controversy was not just the *divide et impera* of the cynical politician. His complaint was that

'. . . in arguing for a balance amongst the ruled and unity among the rulers Penn was an opportunist rather than a philosopher.'[3]

The point is debatable on several grounds, not the least of which is the writer's view of the function of social philosophy. Neglecting such imponderables, however, a very important point is that Penn never made any such clear distinction between the rulers and the ruled as is implied. He was quite happy about carrying religious interests into the House of Commons in the persons of representatives of all persuasions. He also accepted the existence of parties with quite as good grace as did almost any of his contemporaries.[4] Naturally a degree of unity had to be present among the rulers as long as a single man, the king, played a central constitutional role.

[1] *Some Free Reflections* . . ., p. 11. [2] *Three Letters* . . ., p. 26.
[3] E. C. O. Beatty, *op. cit.*, p. 53. [4] 'Some Fruits of Solitude', p. 838.

True, Penn might have said more about the ideas of constitutional balance which were already part of orthodox political opinion. Had he done so, it might have involved de-emphasizing the major novelty in his social theory—that social forces in the shape of interests should be largely self-regulating through mutual limitation. Formal organs of government had been asked to evacuate that area of social life then most open to heated conflict, and by so doing they would release forces requisite for a happy equilibrium. To be sure, there had been suggestions of manipulation of the balance chiefly by the Church of England, but Penn had always been conspicuously reticent about what this really entailed. The negative contribution provided by the relaxation of state control was much more clearly explained, because much more important.

The excuse for a close examination of these scattered essays in advocacy has been that they represent the most highly developed answer of post-Restoration England to the perennial problem of conflicting interests. Most unreflective men, and many who thought a good deal about social problems, eschewed all forms of conflict. Without embracing conflict as a good in itself, Penn did suggest how under the proper conditions society could heal itself.

Were Penn's tracts unique, were there no parallels in contemporary literature, his work would still be important and interesting. The fact that there was a wealth of similar argument only enhances his importance as the most prominent spokesman for the distinctive approach of the period to the toleration issue. How many of the companion works may be attributed directly to Penn's influence, and how many to the fact that others reacted to the same circumstances is impossible to say. Persuasive evidence for the latter hypothesis follows from the fact that a number of tracts quite similar in design antedated his earliest writings. Penn was, without doubt, one of the most prominent participants in the toleration struggle and he was mentioned by name frequently in libellous fashion, more often than any other contributor.[1] Surprisingly, relatively few

[1] As early as 1673, the Earl of Castlemain singled out Penn as the major champion of toleration. See Anon., *A Full Answer and Confutation to a Scandalous Pamphlet Called a Seasonable Discourse*, p. 24 (B: A 5.16 Linc.). See too Thomas Comber, *Three Considerations Proposed to Mr. William Penn* (n.d.), and

Anglican sources specifically took issue with Penn's 'interest' model of society. Perhaps this was because until early in the eighties the Presbyterians, with their characteristic argument, had been most prominent. Many of the exhortations to bolster the Protestant interest by striving for religious unanimity may have been aimed at the Quaker writer, but this can only be supposition. One who did address himself directly to the issue, as stated by Penn, said:

'. . . there are no parties in this or any other nation so exactly poised, that they have equal numbers and interests.'[1]

Penn's output during this period was probably only surpassed by those who wrote newspapers, and these efforts were slanted far more towards trivia than were Penn's discussions of social principles. Of course in making any assessment of Penn's relative output and influence, one must remain aware that he was not averse to putting his name to a fair proportion of his works, while anonymity disguised the identity of many other writers. But few quoted him directly, perhaps because men preferred to demonstrate their learning by using de Thou, or because of a natural desire to avoid identification with the unpopular Quakers.[2]

Between them, Humfrey and Penn had largely exhausted the possibilities of a balance of interests and a public good consisting in the satisfaction of particular interests. Those who first came to the subject after 1680 often wrote important works, judged by the needs of the day. However, from the viewpoint of social theory they must be classed as epigoni; the most interesting things had already been said. Great figures such as the Duke of

Anon., *Some Queries Concerning Liberty of Conscience Directed to W. Penn and H. Care* (n.d.) (B: C 11.11 Linc.).

[1] Anon., *An Argument for Union Taken from the True Interest of . . . Dissenters* (1683), p. 13 (B: Ashm. 1227). While he was almost certainly writing against Penn, he misunderstood him. The conditions for a successful balance were not nearly so stringently defined by Penn.

[2] Thus Francis Bugg, who had a special animus against Quakers, wrote an introduction to Wolseley's tracts, which were much inferior to the similar writings by Penn. Bugg's edition was called *De Christiana Libertate* (1682). Albert Warren was one obscure figure who explicitly praised Penn's theory of a balance of interests. See *An Apology for the Discourse of Humane Reason* (1680), p. 89.

Buckingham and Halifax, the Trimmer, entered the war of words but they had no new insights to offer. Occasionally the literature contained echoes of Penn, as when George Care said, in a nice aphorism, that toleration 'restores society instead of unity'.[1] In these years the word 'duty' became almost an appendage of 'interest' and that proposal was a poor one indeed that could not be supported on both grounds, although sometimes the task of combining the two strained the talents of writers and the credulity of their readers. After various unconvincing attempts to relate the Catholic ambitions of James II to the interests of the established church, one pamphleteer concluded lamely that the true interest of the church was to stand or fall with its duty.[2] It was easy to express commitment to Penn's approach to the toleration issue and even to his concrete analysis, without relating proposals to the public interest. One Roman Catholic found the essence of Penn's doctrine in two sentences. In order for a government to be secure, its policy had to be 'comprehensive of all interests'. Were toleration granted, God would have reason to be pleased with 'the harmony that ariseth from that discord'.[3]

A clearer example of the political priorities in Penn's thought was the complaint of a writer favourable to the Quakers, that persecution consisted of malice masquerading 'under the specious titles of reason of state'. He rejoiced that the one factor that reduced the damage of the penal laws was the Englishman's high regard for liberty and property. Each man hesitated to jeopardize others in this respect, for in so doing he endangered his own.[4] Here in reduced form was the antithesis offered by Penn. On one side were false claims of reason of state; on the

[1] G. C. (George Care), *A Reply to the Answer of the Man with no Name* (1685), p. 27. Cf. Penn, *Works*, Vol. I, p. 455.
Others who wrote favourably of balancing interests included Edward Whitaker, *An Argument for Toleration and Indulgence as it is the Interest of States* . . . (1681), p. 15; Henry Care, *The King's Right of Indulgence* . . . (1688), p. 40; Richard Burthogge, *Prudential Reasons for Repealing the Penal Laws* . . . (1687), pp. 9–10, and James Paston, *A Discourse of Penal Laws in Matter of Religion* (1688), p. 31.
[2] Anon., *The True Interest of the Legal English Protestants Stated in a Letter* (1687), p. 6 (B: Ashm. G 12).
[3] N. N., *Old Popery as Good as New* (1688), pp. 5 and 18 (B: Ashm. 1018).
[4] A. N., *A Letter from a Gentleman in the City to a Gentleman in the Country About the Odiousness of Persecution* (1687), pp. 25–6 (B: C 9.5 Linc.).

other the prospect of preserving the interests of private men, which was the true way to ensure national security.

The problem in interpreting the mass of writings on liberty of conscience is that so few of them contained any detailed political analysis. It appears that explicit acceptance of the balance of interests was largely a function of the detail in which the political overtones of religion were examined. Most Nonconformists who devoted a good deal of space to the theme reached broadly similar conclusions, but the majority passed briefly over the whole matter leaving no clear indication of what political structure was desirable or possible. A balance of interests was quite compatible with what, from another perspective, was a condition of social unity founded mainly on goodwill. Following Penn in his most idealistic passages, Giles Shute wrote both of a union of parties based on general affection and a vaguely defined balance. From his standpoint, keeping up the tests was to follow the maxim 'Divide to strengthen', which was incomprehensible.[1] Obviously it was not incomprehensible to Penn, if one defined properly who was being divided and what was being strengthened. Thus some men probably had much the same concrete proposals as Penn, but avoided the element of paradox in the *concordia discors*.

Understandably, even those members of the Church of England who favoured a more tolerant regime were less vociferous than people who actually suffered under the penal laws. Nevertheless, there were books arguing for liberty of conscience by men who were Anglicans, and these became more numerous after it became clear that James II wanted a toleration. Such writers had little to say about the interests of subjects. Any consideration of Episcopalian thought must take into account the fact that friends of the *status quo* in church and state were forced into a painful choice by the designs of King James. If the advocacy of those who had chosen the crown rather than the church was unenthusiastic, it was because the royal caprice had thrust them into the arms of a distasteful cause. Their reluctance to analyse society in Penn's terms thus followed from the fact that Anglicans looked upon the situation from the perspective of established institutions. More important than any of the liberal Anglicans were those writers who upheld church and crown

[1] G. S., *A New Test in Lieu of the Old One* (1688), pp. 32–3 (B: Pamph. 188).

before there was any need for a choice between them. It is important to ask what Tories and Anglicans were saying about toleration and the public interest, for only then does Penn's position appear as a radical alternative.

The response of the anti-toleration forces to the problem of social conflict may be gathered from a very few examples drawn largely from Roger L'Estrange and John Nalson. The first was a licenser of the press, who apparently saw it as his duty and pleasure to refute any seditious opinions that managed to get published; the other was an ambitious clergyman.

L'Estrange set the pattern for semi-official argument in 1661 when he took issue with Corbet. The latter had been so presumptuous as to attempt to weigh the relative claims of Anglican and Presbyterian in the balance of the nation. This sort of comparison was entirely unacceptable to the church, and at that time, to the king as well. L'Estrange was prepared, up to a point, to view English society as a congeries of interests.[1] Allowing that the Presbyterians were a major 'interest' in the land, he was still not prepared to assign to the party any political role or any effective influence on policy. This was only in part based upon the numerical insufficiency of the Dissenters, though he joined others of his persuasion in insisting that their claims about their size and power were grossly exaggerated. The chief reason given for rejecting their pretensions lay in the fact that they undermined 'the common interest of the king, nation and the Protestant cause'.[2]

Since an early stage of the onslaught involved a rebuke to seditious factions hiding their private designs behind a façade of common good, this immediately raised the question as to what rationale he had for the Anglican and 'Tory' stand. It was, in fact, no other than this same common good defined in convenient terms. For these purposes he identified the public interest not with the articulate desires of any public or with the interests of the various groups but with the *status quo*. He refused to take seriously charges that privilege existed without adequate foundations, simply because unprepared to see his party as one among others.

[1] See L'Estrange, *A Momento Treating of the Rise, Progress and Remedies of Seditions* (1682), *passim*.
[2] L'Estrange, *Interest Mistaken* ... (1661), p. 84.

Rather, the contest was between 'the law and a faction'.[1] Elsewhere, he added:

'. . . the law is our common resting place and the main foundation upon which we are all to bottom. The law is an impartial judge.'[2]

Of course, such a statement was wildly specious, for it was a simple refusal to look behind the law, which itself was a product of social forces.[3] Any party became a faction if it contravened traditional wisdom; it was doubly damned if it laid its case before the 'mad, brutish rabble'.[4] The conservative case entailed an intense hostility to self-interest on the part of the subject. This is admirably illustrated by the aplomb with which the cleric Richard Perrinchief accused Dissenters of minding their own interests to the injury of the public. In his opinion, citizens forfeited their opportunities to remind rulers of their needs, if the complainers were 'partisans'.[5] L'Estrange was less restrained, saying that

'. . . he deserves to be expelled humane society that narrowly prefers his little dirty interest.'[6]

Clearly the dispute was not merely one of different policies being offered in the public interest, but involved different conceptions of what the concept 'public interest' meant. The Tory position had been relatively consistent since the opening volleys of the pamphlet war in the 1640s. While the popular side had striven, with variable success, to render coherent its slogan of *salus populi*, the royalists had held that there were certain rigidities in the social system not amenable to change by popular sentiment. There is a further parallel with the earlier literature

[1] *Interest Mistaken*, p. 109. Indicative of his outlook here was the unembarrassed appeal to 'reason of state' as the justification for official policy. See, *ibid.*, pp. 82 and 108. Anglican clergymen used the concept gingerly and few even of the purely political arguments for repression were as frank as that of L'Estrange. An exception was Nalson, who also appealed to reason of state. See *The Common Interest of King and People* (1678), p. 113, and *The Present Interest of England* (1683), p. 32.
[2] Ibid., p. 139.
[3] As pointed out by A. A. Seaton in *The Theory of Toleration under the Stuarts* (Cambridge, 1911), p. 120.
[4] L'Estrange, *Interest Mistaken*, pp. 112 and 125.
[5] *A Discourse of Toleration* (1668), p. 35.   [6] *A Momento*, p. 87.

in that again it was the conservative side that made explicit the difference in assumptions.

L'Estrange seems to have realized, however dimly, that he and his opponents used terms in different ways. One of his favourite jibes, couched in the crude raillery of his newspaper, was that enemies of king and church were given to using ambiguous generalities. One such was 'common good' or '*salus populi*', which he claimed was meaningless, until related to the interests of the monarchy.[1] He made fun of all proposals in the name of 'this phantome commonly called the People'.[2] His answer to one opponent was they were concerned with different publics, 'the one for the public of the people, and the other for the public of the Prince'.[3] Certainly, the public good had little to do with individual rights. For L'Estrange it seems to have meant peace, trade and satisfactory relations with foreign states.[4]

While few writers had more to say about 'interest' than those bulwarks of the crown, Nalson and L'Estrange, there was no room beyond the council-chamber for any beneficial self-interest. Both quoted Rohan and the interest of the prince, but both equally decried self-interest on the part of subjects.[5] Nalson frankly admitted that his views went contrary to what the Dissenters deemed their interests to be. He merely used the point popularized by Hobbes and Joseph Glanvill, that men were usually unable to distinguish between truth and their own interests. This allowed him to avoid any serious consideration of the interests of disaffected parties. It was necessary only to instruct them to 'lay aside the clog of self-interest'.[6]

Nalson's political theory was constructed around the conventional and conservative interpretation of the public interest. He wrote that it was only reasonable that

[1] *The Observator*, Vol. II, No. 211 (2 February 1684-5), and Vol. III, No. 196 (31 July 1686).
[2] *Ibid.*, Vol. II, No. 211, and Vol. III, No. 67 (3 August 1685).
[3] *Ibid.*, Vol. II, No. 44 (14 April 1684).
[4] See L'Estrange, *The Nation's Interest in Relation to the Pretensions of His Royal Highness the Duke of York* (1680), p. 17.
[5] For references to Rohan see Nalson, *The Present Interest of England* (1683), p. 3, and three tracts by L'Estrange, *Interest Mistaken*, p. 82, *A Momento*, p. 46, and *A Reply to the Second Part of the Character of a Popish Successor* (1681), pp. 11–12.
[6] [Nalson], *The Project of Peace* (1678), p. 25.

'. . . private opinion should confine itself to private breasts . . . and not be allowed to walk abroad to affront authority, no more than particular gain is suffered to undo the public stock.'[1]

He correctly saw that some of his opponents sought political expression for their faith in the form of parliamentary representation. Breaking the monopoly of sanctioned religion might involve the introduction of 'polyarchy' into the state. He made this connection on other grounds that those who alluded vaguely to an affinity between Presbyters and republicans. The point was that given the political ambitions of religious interests,

'. . . where the government is elective and mutable, every several party will endeavour to make such an interest in all elections, as to have a considerable number of the governors of their persuasion.'[2]

Nalson's thought was dominated by a divorce between two things that Penn and others had tried to join—national and personal interest. His argument followed exactly the same course as those directed against Henry Parker some forty years before. Thus he discounted the particular claims of citizens in favour of such general conditions as peace and religion. Penn had not denied the importance of such community interests, he had just insisted that their realization depended upon considering private interests. Nalson also vigorously distinguished between desires and interests.[3] It is very probable that this same Nalson was the author of an anonymous attack on Penn's *One Project*. He expressed Penn's position quite accurately as being that

'. . . the good of the whole (. . . meaning all the parts and members of society) is the civil interest of the whole.'[4]

Correctly assuming that Penn had not meant his remarks about preserving the state from foreign enemies to constitute the essence of his idea of the public interest, he took Penn to task for claiming that the public interest was nothing more than the 'quiet possession of civil rights'. In offering an alternative point of view, Nalson gave primacy to the good of souls and the

[1] *The Project of Peace*, p. 170.
[2] *Ibid.*, p. 196.   [3] *Ibid.*, p. 317.
[4] *A Seasonable Corrective to the One Project for the Good of England* (1680), p. 2. The attribution is that of the Bodleian catalogue.

'church interest' (singular) which gave institutional form to the public good.[1] Individualism is not incompatible with a concern for spiritual values. But, Nalson's emphasis on preserving community standards blunted the edge of Penn's individualism and laid the basis for his competing definition of the public good. Though he chose not to dwell upon the alternative, it obviously stressed the real good of citizens and the spiritual health of society.

It may seem odd that Nalson failed to argue against Penn's individualistic distortion of the doctrine of reason of state. The most probable answer is that Penn's treatise was rather too subtle and ambiguous to analyse effectively in a political tract. It was easier for the Quaker leader to perform his manipulation of concepts than it was to criticize his position. Actually Nalson had already written another, much more substantial work, where he had defined the common interest in purely secular terms. While secular, it was no more friendly to particular interests as Penn understood them. By this reckoning, the common interest of society consisted in protection from foreign powers, the maintenance of domestic peace and the distribution of justice.[2] Penn's special concern for the maintenance of private rights was relegated to a sub-category of the task of preserving domestic order. To men of Nalson's persuasion, the common good chiefly consisted in preventing foreign invasion or domestic disorder. Unity was the value to which all others had to give way.[3]

It was natural, in view of his authoritarian bent, that Nalson should have given little scope for any spontaneous activity on the part of the citizens in this quest for the public good. They were to be the passive recipients of the monarch's blessings. In one overgrown sentence he spelled out the essence of Tory political thought in an age of self-interest philosophies:

'Hereditary monarchy . . . has no separate interest, or distinct design from the good of the public; for whether it be peace, plenty, glory,

[1] *A Seasonable Corrective . . .*, p. 2.
[2] Nalson, *The Common Interest of King and People* (1678), p. 48.
[3] See M. D., *A Seasonable Advice to all True Protestants in England* (1679), p. 12 (B: G.P. 1046). This is another excellent example of the standard appeal to Dissenters to sink their private interests in the common interest and to unite in the name of national strength.

o   197

riches, trade, war, happiness or misfortune, the people can have none of these in general, but the Prince must have his share of them too, so that the Prince cannot be miserable and his people truly happy, nor the Prince happy whilst his people are really miserable and therefor a monarch in consulting the safety, honour, welfare, peace and prosperity of his people, does at the same time consult his own interest in every one of them: and this must of necessity oblige him to act vigorously and constantly in all his endeavours for the attainment of their ends.'[1]

Significantly, he looked to the actual sentiments of the king and the 'true' interest of the citizens.

Nalson may well have been the author of another tract that recalled quite vividly the arguments of the 1640s. The author complained that seditious elements were always reading too much into the 'public good'. It did not mean that

'. . . no subject whatsoever, no not the poorest, the weakest, the meanest, may be wronged or injured by such as are his equals or superiors in the world.'

The safety of individual citizens was sufficiently cared for if the government guarded against 'invasions of foreign enemies' and 'home-bred domestic villanies'.[2] This was but a paraphrasing of Sanderson's lectures of 1647. It may well have been directed against Penn; there is no way of knowing. The writer assumed that the objectionable interpretation of the common good was very common. Unfortunately, the parallel with the period of the Civil War is exact and more outraged complaints have survived than the supposedly numerous provocations. No doubt, the writer was not thinking of writings as explicit as his own, but of conventional Whiggish allusions to liberty and property. Tories of this sort caricatured the popular case, so that it becomes difficult to know what the original claims had been.

Nalson and similar Tories were not innovators in political thought. Their function, like that of the Cavalier apologists in the Civil War, was to underline the unorthodox nature of some of the new notions about the common interest. There was a perfectly sensible, if illiberal, idea behind Tory pronouncements on the public interest. Nalson took as his starting-point the assump-

[1] *The Common Interest of King and People*, p. 109.
[2] Anon., *Salus Populi or the Case of the King and People* (1681), p. 6 (B: G.P. 1126).

tion that since it was impossible to satisfy all parties interested in any issue, one should just ignore interests other than those identical ones of king and nation.[1] The wisdom of the ages was behind the claim that all particular interests would thereby find fulfilment. The approach did not lack sophistication in its recognition of the prevalence of social conflict. Nor did it require any elevated misconceptions about human nature, except with reference to the rationality of rulers. The trouble with it was that at the same time as it recognized the irreconcilable nature of many human demands it left no scope for the particular interests of individual and group.

There was no effective dialogue between the two sides largely because both were writing propaganda. Texts, such as that of Gauden, which Nonconformists adapted to their own purposes were undoubtedly familiar to all. Many opponents of toleration were prepared to quote that section of *Eikon Basilike* that warned of gratifying factions, while they passed over in silence the passage in the same chapter that suggested in rudimentary form a balance of interests. L'Estrange himself was quite aware of the benefits of releasing one faction to check another, and he toyed with the idea that one might more readily tolerate a divided religious party than a strong, united one.[2] He never became a consistent advocate of the *concordia discors*, however, and, when converted by force of circumstances to the cause of liberty, he contented himself with the observation that if liberty was the Nonconformist's interest, it was unfortunate that this interest went unsatisfied.[3] It would have been interesting to observe Nalson's reaction to 1687, but he had died in the previous year.

Several other studies of the seventeenth-century idea of religious liberty have ended with a treatment of Locke, viewing his three letters on the subject as the culmination of a long process.[4] Compared to Penn and some minor figures, most of Locke's writings on the subject hovered far above the facts. His works were not political in emphasis. However, while he treated the

---

[1] *The Project of Peace*, p. 189.
[2] L'Estrange, *Toleration Discussed* (1673), p. 299.
[3] *An Answer to a Dissenter* ... (1687), p. 14.
[4] The two standard works are Seaton, *op. cit.*, and H. F. Russell Smith, *The Theory of Religious Liberty in the Reigns of Charles II and James II* (Cambridge, 1911).

CONSCIENCE AND INTEREST AFTER THE RESTORATION

problem of religious freedom and public order on a philosophical plane, he still had the same priorities as had Penn. In an early unpublished work he wrote of the merits of allowing all religious interests to balance each other.[1] At the same time he observed primly that he would not elaborate, since this theme related to the magistrate's interests, not to his duty.[2] He might have added that it was equally concerned with the interests of many private men.

He certainly did not neglect these interests, and in treating them, presented the liberal interpretations of the public good. In refusing indulgence to consciences, the magistrate deserted his chief function which was

'. . . the preservation, as much as possible, of the property, quiet and life of every individual being.'[3]

In his most famous work on toleration he restated the point more clearly. Like Penn, he implied that private interests need not be sacrificed to national strength, nor need the two be alternatives, for were sufficient care paid to accommodating private interests, the nation would inevitably be strong. Here he described the magistrate's duty as being that

'. . . provision may be made for the security of each man's private possession; for the peace, riches and public commodities of the whole people, and, as much as possible, for the increase of their inward strength against foreign invasions.'[4]

Locke was not nearly so explicit as Penn had been and he did not explain the significance of the order in which he detailed the government's responsibilities. Nevertheless, it seems no accident that his priorities were those of Penn, not those of Nalson.

The compromise of 1689 was not the end of toleration as a political issue. The struggle merely entered a new, and less dramatic, phase. The alternative positions in relation to the public interest continued to be stated in this context. Objections to the liberal definition of the public good continued to appear,

[1] See 'An Essay Concerning Toleration' (1667?), printed in H. R. Fox Bourne, *The Life of John Locke* (London, 1876), Vol. I, pp. 174–94, at p. 192.
[2] *Ibid.*, p. 186.   [3] *Ibid.*, p. 185.
[4] *A Letter Concerning Toleration*, ed. J. W. Gough (Oxford, 1948), pp. 152–3.

but such criticisms were mild. One friend to liberty of conscience gently chided natural-right theorists for being confused. The case for liberty of conscience might be better put if one began with the common good and showed how it consisted in maintaining natural rights,

'. . . because the natural rights, in many circumstances of a particular member is much more difficult to determine, than the general good of a collective community.'[1]

The anonymous critic saw an excessive concentration upon particular interests as very common. Probably it was; for the very next year there appeared a perfect example of the sort of argument of which he had complained. In the course of defending religious liberty, the Rev. John Jackson dwelt on the nature of law. A common, but inadequate, basis of law, was the

'. . . will of political societies consenting to what may most advance each their own particular interest and power.'

This was a 'Machiavellian notion'.[2] That disposed of the national interest in terms of power. The true foundation of public policy was

'. . . the community, from whose consent alone all power is naturally derived, . . . for the preservation of their natural rights, which is the public good.'[3]

The term 'community' might cause ambiguity, but he carefully restated the proposition to avoid all misunderstanding:

'. . . the public good being nothing but the natural rights of private particular persons, entering into society to preserve them by such means as they shall judge best for the whole.'[4]

Even advocates of persecution in the early eighteenth century seem to have avoided the earlier elevation of national power over particular interests. A bulky treatise directed against Locke contained a definition of the duties of government that was very like Locke's own. It consisted in

[1] Anon., *An Equal Capacity in the Subjects of Great Britain for Civil Employment, the Best Security to the Government* (1717), p. 5 (BM: 110 f. 60).
[2] Jackson, *The Grounds of Civil and Ecclesiastical Government Briefly Considered* (1718), p. 3.
[3] *Ibid.*, pp. 7–8.   [4] *Ibid.*, p. 7.

'. . . the security of the civil interests, i.e. the lives, liberties and possessions of the subject; all of which may be comprehended in one word, the public civil good.'[1]

The writer defended persecution, not because it was necessary for national strength but because anything, such as heresy, which might displease God might cause Him to defeat those purposes for which government had been instituted.[2] Whatever men thought that the public good was, they could always find reasons for doing what they wanted. The ideas of Penn and Locke were by then less the attitude of a party than a piece of common intellectual property.

After the revolutionary settlement the idea of a *concordia discors* lost some of its urgency, but it still occurs in political literature. Only one observation on the later history of the idea seems necessary. Beginning in 1701, John Shute, later Viscount Barrington, published a series of tracts on liberty of conscience and the interest of England. Barrington fully subscribed to the conventional notion about balancing religious parties and he used it in various ways.[3] However, he also gave it a purely secular and political interpretation. Toleration preserved not only the balance of religious interests but also the balance of the constitution. Of course, the British Constitution was now frequently described in terms of a balance between the organs of state. Everyone knew that this was the basis of the subject's liberty. However, Barrington dispensed with a purely constitutional balance and added the balance of social forces familiar in arguments for toleration. He managed this feat by establishing the connection between the Whigs and the dissenting interest. Thus he argued that any weakening of the Dissenters, as by further persecution, would also weaken the Whig party. The Whigs, in turn, stood for certain principles which must be preserved in order to maintain freedom.[4]

[1] Henry Stebbing, *An Essay Concerning Civil Government as it Stands Related to Religion* (1724), p. 46.
[2] *Ibid.*, p. 83.
[3] [Barrington], See *The Rights of Protestant Dissenters in Two Parts* (1705), Part II, pp. 41–2 and 48–9.
[4] [Barrington], *The Interest of England Considered in Respect to Protestants Dissenting From the Established Church* (1702), pp. 29–30. There were two more editions in 1703, and in 1701 there had appeared a less elaborate version with the title *An Essay Upon the Interest of England* . . .

Most remarkably, Barrington did not restrict his loyalties to his own party but to the party system, for he insisted that if either of the two parties was permanently weakened the liberties of England would be destroyed by the other. In his view,

'. . . the constitution of England consists in a balance of parties; as the liberties of Europe do in a balance of powers.'[1]

He said as clearly as possible that the 'general good' was dependent upon this balance of parties.[2] Adam Ferguson and Burke could add little to this insight.

Again the toleration question had evoked the claim that the public good was dependent upon the pursuit of self-interest. If Penn's insistence upon the rights of private men gave content to the public good, the *concordia discors* showed the way to this good. People who said that the public interest was the protection of private rights did not necessarily subscribe to any balance of interests for the health of society. The two ideas were quite distinct. However, they complemented each other most effectively, since both showed how the public good might be reconciled with private interest. Thus they contributed to that remarkable paradox of political argument, that some of the people who were most insistent on creating a genuine common good were equally adamant that this entailed looking to the interests of private persons.

For several reasons the question of toleration has been particularly useful for exhibiting current ideas on public and private interests. It was an area peculiarly immune to the conventional means of controlling individual self-interest. It was difficult for those in authority to appeal for passive obedience as a step towards salvation and the securing of one's permanent interests. Dissenters were in a position to reject their rulers in church and state as authoritative guides to their eternal interests; had they been acceptable in this capacity, there would have been no controversy.

In another respect the question was well suited to arguments from interest. This seems to have been one of the very few issues during the century where the analysis of behaviour was largely prospective. It was a matter of asking what sort of reactions

[1] *Interest of England . . .* (1702), p. 31.
[2] *Rights of Protestant Dissenters . . .*, Part I, p. 73.

could be expected on the part of rational men placed in a set of defined conditions. Political argument has traditionally been directed towards the past rather than the future. Men discussed ancient rights, not current needs; they looked to oaths, pacts or expressions of God's will at some time in the past in order to explain future conduct. The official defence of the Cromwellian regime in the years 1649–50 dealt almost entirely with such matters. Even the arguments from interest in 1647–8 and in 1659 had been based on rather a static picture of political forces and had not tried always to present to affected groups a convincing treatment of their interests. It was all too easy to say that acceptance of certain conditions was the interest of a party by *force majeure*, since otherwise it would be destroyed by the authorities. In the case of toleration it was vitally important to know how men would construe their own interests. Mere passivity was not always enough, for the balance was dependent upon parties actively defending their interests.

Whether or not one calls this pattern of argument individualism does not matter much. These works may have given a larger place to men acting in concert than did some of the classic texts of individualism, but this can only be taken as a sign of their cogency. Writers like Penn produced *livres de circonstances*, not formal social theory. For this reason they did not find it convenient always to say the same thing in a perfectly consistent way. The growing concord between private and public interests existed as a social theory only through such opportunists. In fact, it probably showed itself to best advantage in such circumstances, since an exhaustive examination of the theme was apt to uncover difficulties. Nevertheless, Penn and others had a meaningful approach to the public interest, one that was gaining supporters in other social contexts as well.

V

ECONOMIC ARGUMENT: THE PUBLIC INTEREST QUANTIFIED

COMMERCE, MAINLY DOMESTIC

THE CLASH BETWEEN national power and private interest touched economic as well as constitutional issues, although modern misconceptions about mercantilist thought have somewhat obscured the parallel. The tyrant's plea of necessity might find its equivalent in economic paternalism, while economic individualists sought to use that property sanctioned by civil rights. The necessary conditions for such a state of tension were the same in both spheres of activity; before it could exist, some measure of legitimacy had to be accorded to private interests. If ordinary men were largely excluded from the avenues of political power and so unable to protect their interests by political means, the public interest might well seem adequately described in terms of national power. Should economic life be conceived as the fulfilment of mutual duties for the betterment of an organic community, private and public interest were likewise in different and incompatible spheres.

As soon as the inevitability of self-interest in economic life came to be appreciated, the basis for individualism was laid. A recognition of its all-pervasive character did not necessarily constitute approval, but it did make it increasingly difficult for moralists to demand a degree of community spirit that was obviously absent in the real world. It was easy to see in necessary behaviour, respectability. Moralists might reject self-interest and all its works, but they were not concerned with describing social processes. When seventeenth-century writers began to treat economic life in terms of causal relationships, few assumed any other mode of behaviour than that of the economic man. That model alone provided some degree of predictability.

The relationship between private and public interest has traditionally been described in terms either of an artificial or a natural harmony of interests. Before the seventeenth century it would scarcely be relevant to speak of either form of harmony, since legitimate private interest was not yet part of the picture. Students of early moral dicta regarding economic life have been unanimous in observing that the public good was then removed from the plane of private interest, so that, as one has put it:

'The idea that, after all, private good makes for public good seems not to have occurred to these critics of their time. Private interest, to them, could only be the foe of public interest.'[1]

Though emphasis varied, some of the earliest surviving remarks about the common weal preached a most uncompromising ethic. The farther removed the authors were from commercial life, the more rigorous were their demands. Laud once said:

'. . . if any man be so addicted to his private interest that he neglects the common state . . . he wishes peace and happiness for himself in vain. For . . . he must live in the body of the commonwealth and in the body of the church.'[2]

This certainly emphasized duty rather than profit, but it was irresponsibly permissive in comparison with some statements. Many writers suggested not only that one had to have a care for the public but that one should have no other. Indeed, personal concerns might appear quite unreasonable. Clement Armstrong complained that:

'No man in England never seeketh for no common weale, but all and every for his singular weale.'

Far from accepting this situation, he deemed it contrary to the whole scheme of the universe, for

[1] R. Mohl, *The Three Estates in Medieval and Renaissance Literature* (New York, 1930), p. 325.
[2] Quoted by H. Levy, *Economic Liberalism* (London, 1913), p. 89.

'. . . what other right hath God put into the head of every one man, but only the right of common weale of all the members in his body. What man can say by the office of his mouth, feeding all the members in his body to give to one hand more than to another or to one finger or to any one member more than to another . . .'[1]

He recommended this undiscriminating altruism to all men, and not just to rulers.

Aegrement Ratcliffe laboured the same organic analogy to the same purpose. Ambitious man forgot that policy looked to the preservation of the whole body and not that of any particular person. He forgot, too, the commands of God

'. . . who hath created him a seelie member of the huge and mighty body of humane society, and appointed him his distinct charge, not to be exercised to his own particular, but to the relief and common maintenance of the universal body.'[2]

Possibly some modern interpreters may sometimes have exaggerated the conservatism of early moralists, for they were not always so clear as those just quoted. In complaining of the abuses of the ruling class, one prominent preacher said:

'. . . they shall differ nothing from the craftesmen which apply an occupation to get their living upon, and not to the intent to profit the commonwealth.'[3]

This has been interpreted as a complete rejection of self-interest in all occupations.[4] While this would be quite in accord with the tone of the whole work, Crowley was not actually concerned with the social duties of small men, but of the great, and while he showed no enthusiasm for the profit motive among the lower orders, it was not his purpose to condemn it.

[1] Clement Armstrong, 'A Treatise Concerning the Staple and the Commodities of this Realm' (c. 1530), in R. H. Tawney and E. Power, *Tudor Economic Documents* (London, 1924), Vol. III, p. 114.
[2] *Political Discourses* (1578), sig. A III. See too William Perkins, 'A Treatise of the Vocations or Callings of Men', in *A Golden Chaine* (Cambridge, 1605), p. 919, and Anon., 'How the Comen People May be set to Worke an Order of a Commenwelth', in R. Pauli, *Drei Volkswirthschaftliche Denkschriften aus der Zeit Henrichs VIII* (Gottingen, 1878), p. 53.
[3] Robert Crowley, *An Information and Petition Agaynst the Oppressours of the Pore Commons of this Realm* (1548), sig. A III.
[4] W. G. Zeeveld, *The Foundations of Tudor Policy* (Cambridge, Mass., 1948), p. 212.

Two isolated instances of a more modern note appear in six-teenth-century literature. Significantly, both belonged to that small number of books that were concerned more with the nature of English government and society than with any narrow form of social pleading. Still, in discussing contemporary issues, such sources exhibit some of the urgency found in later treatments of the public good.

Thomas Starkey recorded a conversation, real or imagined, between Cardinal Pole and Thomas Lupset in which they touched on the various issues of the day. Pole advanced the seemingly innocuous proposition that the prosperity of the individual citizen and the state rested in the same conditions, so

'. . . if we can first find out that thing which is the wealth of every particular man, we shall then consequently find out also what thing it is in any city or country we call the very true commonweal.'[1]

Bearing in mind that Pole had already said that self-love often destroyed communities, Lupset replied that if

'. . . the common weal rise out of the particular weal of every one then every man ought to study to maintain the particular weal to the setting forward of the common. And so that which you noted before to be the destruction of every commonweal, now by this reason and ground should maintain the same.'[2]

Pole then modified his argument; inordinate self-regard was destructive and men were often blind to the connection between private and general goods, or they would not be so rashly self-interested. He concluded that the common weal

'. . . is nothing else but the multitude of people, the number of citizens in every . . . country.'[3]

This was rather an oblique way of stating the claims of national power, but it still represented a capitulation. He was saying that every unit was important, but not that every interest was beneficial.

Another famous dialogue, written either by Sir Thomas

[1] 'A Dialogue Between Cardinal Pole and Thomas Lupset', in *England in the Reign of King Henry VIII*, Early English Text Society (London, 1878), pp. 32–3.
[2] *Ibid.*, p. 33.   [3] *Dialogue . . .*, pp. 45–6.

Smith or by John Hales, touched upon exactly the same question.[1] One participant observed that

'. . . every man is a member of the common weal, and that that is profitable to one may be profitable to another if he would establish the same feat. Therefore that that is profitable to one and so to another may be profitable to all, and so to the commonwealth.'[2]

The rejoinder by the next speaker was the voice of tradition, authority and the author. One could not presume that what was good for one was good for another or for all; rather one had to say that

'. . . that thing which is profitable to each man by himself (so that it is not prejudicial to any other) is profitable to the whole common weal.'[3]

Without this qualification, he added, robbery and murder would be justified. This hardly disposed of the problem, for the terms were too broad to provide guidance in areas of policy where less objectionable private interests were being advanced. In fact one is left with the impression that the author purposefully left the matter in suspense, for an unconvincing argument had been disposed of by one scarcely less vulnerable. Perhaps this apparent doubt may be accounted for by the topic that sparked the debate—enclosures. On this issue the theory of individualism enjoyed its earliest triumph, as we shall see shortly.

Neither book provided a satisfactory explanation of the relation between private and public interests. Nevertheless, they presented the classical liberal approach to the public interest in a way suggesting that it may already have been current in discussion of social policy. Nor was either author very sympathetic to this idea, yet both sought some formula for a common good that was compatible with particular interests. The individualist's outlook was not yet the norm, for society was still visualized as an organic hierarchy.[4] The necessary relationships between

[1] *A Discourse of the Common Weal of this Realm of England*, ed. E. Lamond (Cambridge, 1929). The pendulum has now swung towards Smith as the author. See M. Dewar, *Sir Thomas Smith, A Tudor Intellectual in Office* (London, 1964), pp. 53–5.
[2] Lamond, p. 50.   [3] *Ibid.*, p. 51.
[4] For a brief treatment of this point see Helen C. White, *Social Criticism in Popular Religious Literature of the Sixteenth Century* (New York, 1944), p. 245.

parts and wholes might easily lead one to conceive of a common good as so many private ones, but it could not carry great conviction until society was commonly seen as a collection of single units. Further, without the specifically economic mechanisms of harmony, the idea remained just a sterile logical possibility. It was important to show in terms of economic causation how one man's interest might relate to another's; any explanation that skirted the facts of economic life was unsatisfactory. These works had already established that the problem was not a matter of reconciling a private interest with an abstract common good embodied in the state. Thomas Smith, in particular, saw the issue as that of harmonizing private interests with each other, from which harmony proceeded the common good.

Historians of economic thought have correctly pointed out that the most extreme ethic of self-effacement was not that of orthodox mercantilism which assumed that private men would naturally and rightly seek their own profit. This insight serves well for purposes of describing economic theories and renders ridiculous the vision of economic man springing full-blown from the brow of Adam Smith. However, there were good reasons for paying continued lip service to the older ethic. While men might very well realize that clear analysis of economic life was dependent on assuming self-interest to be predominant, argument often required protestations of altruism. An ethic based upon one's duty to God and to the commonwealth might provide arguments against self-interest without defining the common good. It was only necessary to identify a selfish intention in order to discredit a course of action. The argument for a free market had the same virtue in that it often consisted in saying that if things were left alone all would be for the best. At the same time this approach might be rather vague about what the common good was; it did not matter, for it was produced largely without conscious effort.[1]

It was more difficult to tell men that self-seeking was not shameful, thus encouraging such activity, if some people were still denied the pursuit of satisfaction. This involved saying what

[1] The incalculable nature of the greatest happiness of the greatest number has been advanced as one reason why the Benthamites were partial to a measure of laissez-faire. See G. Myrdal, The Political Element in the Development of Economic Theory (London, 1953), p. 43.

the common good was, for private interests could no longer be discredited by their selfish character and had to be judged by their consequences. Surely it was the difficulty of judging these consequences that led many writers in the first half of the seventeenth century to condemn certain proposals, simply because they were obviously self-interested. Merchants themselves frequently fathered schemes that they claimed were solely for the public good. Sometimes the results could be amusing, as when one worthy merchant appealed to Parliament to improve trade, while denying any special concern for the merchant's lot. The merchant, like all other men, was to

'. . . employ his utmost endeavour to the general good and not to have the least thought on particular or private ends.'[1]

Special incentives to various categories of merchants were carefully set apart in a series of verses appended to the tract. Thus the writer honoured all of the necessary conventions, while allowing no room for misunderstanding by those who most stood to benefit from his plans.

Once it had been established that the merchant was primarily concerned with his own profit, the arrangement came to be seen as providential. A number of writers were obviously intrigued that the organic pattern of society based upon duty and restriction to one's calling might be restated in terms of universal self-interest. It is hard to agree with an observation in Viner's splendid study to the effect that this idea was very rare. Quite a number of writers were very clear in their espousal of the so-called 'intermediate' position that self-interest was a beneficial force, though in need of channelling for optimum results.[2]

One rather typical mercantilist observed how happy was the situation of a nation with merchants whose

'. . . care of their own profit, is so necessarily interwoven with the care of the commonwealth's and its good, that to themselves and to their country, their labours . . . do bring in thus mutually, not only a commodity, but also an honour.'[3]

[1] John Battie, *The Merchant's Remonstrance* (1648), p. 6.
[2] Jacob Viner, *Studies in the Theory of International Trade* (New York, 1937), p. 99. Viner's bibliography is invaluable.
[3] Lewes Roberts, *The Merchant's Mapp of Commerce* (1638), p. 21.

In a later work he returned to the peculiar relevance of social duty to the merchant. Men were not born for themselves, he said, most actions carried good intentions either to the public or to private people. In this connection he praised the valiant soldier who wore his sword to defend himself, but was ever ready to draw it for king and country, and the skilled lawyer, who learned the law to defend his own rights, but was equally prepared to defend the rights of others. Finally he turned to

'. . . the judicious merchant, whose labour is to profit himself, yet in all his actions doth therewith benefit his king, country and fellow subjects.'[1]

It was an inexact parallel, for in both the other cases, curious as they were, there was at least a suspicion of altruism. Only in the case of the merchant was self-love truly and perfectly social.

For all this, Roberts was writing within the context of regulated trade. He anticipated the growing group of merchants who, in the second half of the century, insisted that outright prohibition, even of harmful imports, was unwise. Rather, he favoured allowing the merchant to seek his own profit in bringing them in, but with a high tariff to increase revenue and to limit vice to those who could afford it.[2] This indicates that already there could be some notion of a limited harmony of interests between the merchant and the state. The former was left free to do as he wished, while the burden of the high duty fell upon the consumer. For Roberts, the merchant's interest already coincided in large measure with that of the prince, although, compared with later writers, Roberts thought very little about the merchant's impact on other interests within the state. Adam Smith himself sympathized with some regulation of harmful imports and qualified his free trade doctrine on that point.[3] In such circumstances the text-book progression from an artificial to a natural harmony of interests becomes unreal. Even early in the seventeenth century there were some notions of spontaneous harmony, while later theories of a natural harmony may well be

[1] *The Treasure of Traffike* (1641), pp. 1–2.
[2] *Ibid.*, pp. 39–40.
[3] *Inquiry into the Nature and Causes of the Wealth of Nations*, ed. E. Cannan (London, 1930), Vol. I, pp. 424–32.

exaggerated by some commentators.[1] While it is clearly unwise to see every petty scribbler as groping painfully towards the insights of classical economics, it is no less an error to overemphasize the gap that separated mercantilist and liberal thought.

Another fine example of the theme of harmony occurs in a pamphlet by a fierce Tory who paused in his argument for passive obedience to ponder the nature of society. Original sin had left men largely devoid of charity but still with needs that could only be cared for by mutual services. Sin made government necessary and at the same time released compensating social forces. The following passage expresses the essence of his thought:

'. . . in order to the supplying these necessities cupidity hath taken the place of charity, and effecteth it after a manner which we cannot enough admire, and whereunto the ordinary charity would not arrive. For example, you see spread all over the country, persons who are ready to assist you when you travel. . . . What could be more admirable than these persons, were they animated by charity. But it is cupidity which maketh them act. . . . Where is that charity, which is contented to build a house for you. . . . Cupidity will do, and cheerfully too. What charity will run to the Indies for medicines, stoop to the meanest employments, and not refuse the basest and most painfull offices? Cupidity will perform all this without grudging.'[2]

Indeed any apparent paucity of such observations might best be explained by the very fact that the benefits of self-love were so widely appreciated that it was unnecessary to discourse at length on its merits. Many writers must simply have assumed that self-interest was the *sine qua non* of commerce and there were few to dispute the worth of commerce. Another politically conservative tract contrasted the morals of political and economic

[1] The traditional analysis of individualism in terms of natural or artificial harmony may well be the work of Halévy. See Shirley L. Letwin, *The Pursuit of Certainty* (Cambridge, 1965), p. 146 n. On the second point see Lionel Robbins, *The Theory of Economic Policy in English Classical Political Economy* (London, 1952), pp. 25, 28 and 56. Some of the more extreme claims for a spontaneous harmony of interests may even have antedated Smith. See Anon., *An Essay on the Improvement of the Woollen Manufacture* . . . (1741) (B: G.P. 869), and Anon., *A Letter to the Author of Considerations on Several Proposals for the Better Maintenance of the Poor* (1752) (B: Vet. A 5 e. 2967).
[2] Anon., *The Grounds of Sovereignty and Greatness* (1675), pp. 19–20 (B: B 2.1 Linc.).

life. The true subject was expected to be loyal and to seek the 'common interest'. He should bear in mind that 'true loyalty is so little swayed by interest that it is its own contentment'.[1] The author assailed the vulgar idea that all men were guided by self-interest, which was true with respect to

'. . . neighbourhood and private commerce, but never . . . owned by men of any understanding to extend to the public.'[2]

When John Eachard wrote his retort to Hobbes, he put the facts of economic life in more favourable terms. His parody of Hobbesian solemnity is perhaps the only genuinely funny political document of the period; it is also revealing. His point in ridiculing Hobbes's dramatic portraits of self-interest was not to deny the reality of such phenomena but to reduce the subject to proper proportions. He observed that the cash nexus would necessarily govern more relations than would love, since the latter sentiment would scarcely sustain the butcher or the blacksmith.[3] It was all very well to see life as perpetually darkened by the cloud of interest, but there was always the possibility that Restoration England would render the terrible word innocuous. Eachard must have enjoyed describing a 'close covenant' with a shoemaker, in which

'. . . for FEAR of catching cold, I took the shoes, and for FEAR he should never see me again he took my money.'[4]

Only a little 'artifice of language' was needed to drive all things on to the 'common shore of interest'. 'Interest,' he concluded reassuringly, 'is a word innocent enough, but only when it crosses equity and reason.'[5]

All but the most rigidly traditional mercantilists were prepared to find virtues in the rational pursuit of interest. Neither William Carter nor Andrew Yarranton could be accused of being excessively liberal on questions of economic policy. The former was a wool merchant who was the most prolific of all the

---

[1] Anon., *The Demeanour of a Good Subject, in Order to the Acquiring and Establishing Peace* (1681), p. 31 (B: Ashm. 729). Wing attributes this essay to one Thomas Godwyn.
[2] *Ibid.*, p. 32.
[3] Eachard, *Mr. Hobbs's State of Nature Considered* (1672), pp. 130–1.
[4] *Ibid.*, pp. 151–2. [5] *Ibid.*, p. 156.

literary opponents of exporting unwrought wool, the latter has been called, albeit incorrectly, the father of the 'infant industry' argument for protective tariffs.[1] Both leaned heavily on the social usefulness of intelligent selfishness. Yarranton assumed that changes in economic policy had to be justified in terms of private interests of affected parties and this he did at great length. Carter occasionally bewailed the current lack of altruism and public spirit, but he never asked men to be charitable in any way that was prejudicial to themselves. Instead he insisted that there was not enough rational calculation in economic affairs, for men frequently deprived themselves of gain simply in order to exclude others as well.[2]

These two proclaimed their doctrines to the refrain 'interest will not lie'. Applied to commerce, the maxim had changed in emphasis from its initial use in political literature.[3] It no longer meant only that people would follow their interests as they saw them, or following their true interests would profit. Now the maxim also held out the hope that men would see what their interests were. Carter insisted endlessly that men should be able to see their interests. Those who opposed his schemes were obviously resolved to 'cross the proverb' and

'. . . by a piece of wit to make it appear that it is not always true, that interest cannot lie.'[4]

Yarranton displayed the new emphasis when he joined the maxim to another of more ancient origin, saying:

'I know where your shoe pinches; and its a truth that interest will not lie.'[5]

Such interests did not entail freedom to engage in all forms of profit-making for the aim of these writings was to lead men to

[1] See P. E. Dove, *Account of Andrew Yarranton, the Founder of English Political Economy* (Edinburgh, 1854), p. 74.
[2] W. C., *England's Interest by Trade Asserted* (1671), p. 43.
[3] For some time 'interest' had referred both to a person's designs or desires and to his real welfare as perceived by another. However, the proverb had been interpreted in terms of the latter meaning of interest. See above, pp. 43-4.
[4] 'The Reply of W. C.', in *A Summary of Certain Papers About Wooll as the Interest of England is Concerned in it* (1685), p. 32 (BM: 288 e. 32).
[5] Yarranton, *England's Improvement by Sea and Land*, Part II (1681), p. 209.

understand that their interests would be served by certain reforms.

Trade and the public interest might be treated in two settings, domestic and foreign. In many respects the settings overlapped both in life and in thought, but they were distinguishable and involved different problems. Modern references to the triumph of self-love over social usually mention both levels of commerce, drawing indiscriminately from both the symptoms of a new social attitude.[1] This is quite legitimate if only it is appreciated that all such writers were not toiling in the same cause. Certain restrictions on commerce were being lifted at the same time as others were imposed. There were many writers in the seventeenth century who advocated the removal of petty, irritating regulations since they favoured a few sweeping laws designed to secure a favourable balance of trade.[2] Thus the tide of individualism did not advance simultaneously on all fronts. Writers might make very far-reaching claims in order to carry some limited demand for freedom. Most studies in the history of economic thought have looked for theories and found in the seventeenth century either crude traditionalism or disappointment. Should one examine the texts as forms of argument often limited in function to gaining short-term assent for particular policies, those attitudes known as individualism stand out more clearly.

There was, however, progress from restrictive to liberal views about the public interest. This need not be measured solely by the increasing frequency with which liberal views were aired. To this must be added the qualitative changes relating to the contexts in which such ideas were employed. Attempts to identify economic individualism in the sixteenth century must rely largely upon demands for an uncontrolled domestic market.[3] If comparable themes were not common in the next century, it was surely because the government was no longer very interested in policing such aspects of trade. One of the most critical

[1] See the commentators on Joseph Lee quoted below, p. 221.
[2] See G. S. L. Tucker, *Progress and Profits in British Economic Thought 1650–1850* (New York, 1960), p. 18, and E. Heckscher, *Mercantilism* (London, 1955), Vol. I, p. 300. Tucker records this theme in the literature, Heckscher, the actual trend of administration.
[3] See the examples quoted in H. M. Robertson, *The Rise of Economic Individualism* (Cambridge, 1933), pp. 71–3.

areas in the mid-seventeenth century was the matter of enclosures. Here restraints were still onerous and thus the debate was spirited.

The enclosure question is particularly well suited for consideration because it was resolved, in terms of debate at least, before the end of the century. Demands by landlords for permission to enclose might be countered on two fronts. One obvious approach was to state the claims of the poor and the duty of charity before personal profit. This factor was rarely ignored, but interestingly enough, some of the better-known works against enclosure placed very little reliance upon it. The requirements of public order might be endangered by idleness resulting from enclosures,[1] or depopulation might be seen as impairing the nation's capacity for defence,[2] but the welfare of the poor as people, rather than as components of national power, was relegated to an inferior position.[3] Certainly the opponents of enclosure might easily refute the argument that the dispossessed were either not injured or did not deem themselves to be injured. Those in authority might still veto a move to enclose on grounds such as the tendency to produce depopulation. Official documents suggest that decisions had to be made in the name of an inarticulate mass with no knowledge about proceedings or conscious interest in them. The Privy Council in 1631 defended its suspicion of enclosures by saying that they were

'. . . very hurtful to the commonwealth although they bear a fair show of satisfaction to all parties.'[4]

Opponents were then placed in the position of defending a good unassignable to particular persons against claims to legitimate profit by the all-too-concrete landlords. The enclosers

---

[1] R. Powell, *Depopulation Arraigned* (1636), p. 35.
[2] Lamond, *op. cit.*, pp. 49–50. And Powell, *loc. cit.*, p. 32.
[3] Such expressions of concern for national power contrast with the argument of a very late plea against enclosures. Here the author insisted merely that it was more advantageous to benefit many than the few, better for 'three men to have six pence a day each, than for one man to have eighteen'. John Cowper, *An Essay proving that Inclosing . . . is Contrary to the Interest of the Nation* (1732), p. 24.
[4] Quoted by M. Beresford in F. J. Fisher (ed.), *Essays in the Economic and Social History of Tudor and Stuart England* (Cambridge, 1961), p. 58.

had another advantage in debate. One of the standard measures of national prosperity was the value of lands expressed as so many years' purchase. He who improved his land might very well portray himself as enriching the nation through his enterprise. After all, he owned the land, a part of the nation, and so his prosperity might be visualized as redounding to the national stock in a manner precluded to merchants and others equally bent on self-enrichment. It was certainly with this in mind that a memorandum of 1607 said that in enclosures 'the good individual is the good general'.[1]

Not all would-be enclosers neglected long-run considerations, though a certain myopia in this respect was surely advantageous to them. One specifically said that in defending this policy he kept in mind 'three generals'. He managed to show to his own satisfaction how all three national considerations, flourishing of native commodities, trade and national safety, could only be improved. At the same time he specifically considered the interests only of those citizens who were directly involved with the common lands. Thus in respect to those citizens who claimed rights in the commons, he would endeavour to 'preserve each man's particular interest'.[2] His scheme would benefit 'each particular man's interest, and so to the commonwealth in general'.[3] There were then two alternative routes to the common good, that through promoting general unassignable goods and that through private profit. Since both positions appeared here in the same work, they were plainly not incompatible, although most writers concentrated upon one or the other.

It was not a great step from here to one of the most famous documents of seventeenth-century individualism. Joseph Lee was a Leicestershire clergyman who came to the rescue of the enclosers when they were being hard pressed by a fellow clergyman. His philosophy, with all of the ambivalence typical of this literature, was summarized in one sentence:

[1] Quoted by A. F. Chalk, 'Natural Law and the Rise of Economic Individualism in England', *Journal of Political Economy*, Vol. 59 (1951), pp. 332–47, at p. 339.
[2] Silvanus Taylor, *Common Good: Or, the Improvement of Commons, Forrests and Chases by Inclosure* (1652), p. 12. The editions used were those of the Library of Congress and the Bodley. The latter copy bears the date 1692.
[3] *Ibid.*, p. 12.

'. . . it is a duty incumbent upon all that are members of the commonwealth, as they have means and opportunity, to the best of their understandings and abilities, to endeavour the advancement of the public benefit, which is but the summa totalis of all the particular items.'[1]

Lee apparently saw as equivalents two statements that were rigorously distinguished in traditional morality, for clearly the second half of this sentence clashes violently with the first.

IN HIS OPINION, PAST PRACTICES IN LAND UTILIZATION HAD BEEN 'to the great prejudice of the commonwealth in general, as well as of the owners in particular.'[2]

It would then seem that the second condition might have followed from the first, but actually he reversed the causal relation as his next such statement showed. Here he complained that these practices had been

'. . . to the prejudice of the owners in particular, and of the commonwealth which proportionately suffers in every man's loss.'[3]

The wisdom of the ages had been confuted; now it might be claimed that there was little point in looking to the ship of state if all of the passengers, or even some of them, were in personal distress. By their intransigence, the poor were hindering

'. . . a double benefit to the owner in particular, and consequently in proportion unto the commonwealth in general . . . for upon such enclosures the price of the land could not be trebeled unless a treble profit might be raised. And this, for as much as concerns the commonwealth in general, is evident by experience, because upon enclosure, the proportion of taxes is accordingly raised above the rate, which they were formerly at.'[4]

Here was one basis for linking private and public interest; the national treasury would benefit from the inflated land values. His chief argument though was more abstract and neglected the technical details of the harmony between private and public interest. It was enough that private men agree 'upon a

---

[1] Pseudomisus (i.e. Lee), *Considerations Concerning Common Fields and Inclosures* . . . (1654), p. 3. (B: Gough Leicest. 7). Two of the three tracts attributed to Lee, are anonymous, but there seems to be no need to assume, with some students of enclosures, that there was more than one author.
[2] *Considerations* . . ., p. 10.   [3] *Ibid.*, p. 11.   [4] *Ibid.*, p. 30.

course (as of enclosure) for the general good of them all'.[1] Here the common good was not measured by the state of public revenue, but was the product of the wills of private men. A common good of this sort had not been much talked of in economic debate, but of course it had already become common in political speculation.

Lee had first suggested that an increment in land values would be a general benefit and he pointed out that those unfortunates who felt themselves prejudiced were a minority. He ended by assuming that enclosures, which would not depopulate, would not harm even the poor and thus public benefit was assured, for

'. . . if injurious to no private person, and profitable to them all, it must needs be beneficial to the commonwealth, which is but the summa totalis of sundry persons as several figures.'[2]

He recognized no public detriment but that which could be ascribed to single persons.

Lee made two further defences of the enclosers. He reaffirmed his great regard for the public good and denied that he cherished any selfish ambitions that might cause public detriment. Even his most conventional expressions of social conscience remained faithful to his original outlook. He allowed that there was no good reason why a man should use his land longer than his use was in accord with the natural fitness of the land. However, while this might seem to be a limitation on the rights of property, it was really no concession at all, for he refused to dissociate the two functions of public utility and private gain. He saw no point in posing any conflict between rational estate management and the common good:

'I know of no reason why any man should please himself in the usage of his land, both to his own hindrance, and to the prejudice of the commonwealth the prosperity whereof should be every man's desire, care and endeavour, as well as his own.'[3]

Lee had refuted all claims for objective prejudice to the various affected interests. In his opinion, the clergy, poor, cottagers,

[1] *Considerations . . .*, p. 28.   [2] *Ibid.*, p. 39.
[3] Pseudomisus, *A Vindication of the Considerations Concerning Common-Fields and Inclosures* (1656), p. 38 (B: Gough Leicest. 7).

tenants and owners all stood to gain. He still had to deal with the objection that enclosure caused mental distress to those adhering to traditional standards of behaviour. His opponent had remarked that enclosers sought 'filthy lucre' and not God's glory. Lee's answer doubtless shocked some contemporaries:

'It is a very strange principle and unheard of paradox that nothing can be done to God's glory which tends to man's profit.'[1]

Perhaps it was unreasonable, but it was certainly not unheard of; little else had previously been heard.

Lee's most important statement of principle was first quoted by R. H. Tawney, and there seems to be little doubt that most writers who mention Lee know him only from that one quotation.[2] It was not an unfair summary of his case, though the argument was slightly exaggerated in comparison with more sober statements that might be gleaned from the same work:

'. . . the advancement of private persons will be the advantage of the public: if merchants do buy an advantageous commodity, hath not the commonwealth an advantage thereby as well as themselves? If men by good husbandry . . . do better their land, is not the commonwealth enriched thereby? So whatever benefit we make to ourselves, tends to the public good.'[3]

He did not mean the last sentence in a literal fashion, since he was prepared to call some self-interest objectionable. He stigmatized the graziers who opposed his policies as self-interested, without any conscious irony.

Lee was not yet typical of all economic thought. For instance, he claimed more for the merchant than many merchants were prepared to claim for themselves. However, if one compares his approach with the rest of the surviving tracts advocating enclosure, some quite remarkable conclusions emerge. Others were perhaps less adamant in their individualism, but many clearly favoured enclosure for the same reasons as Lee. Their

[1] *A Vindication of the Considerations Concerning Common-Fields and Inclosures* (1656), p. 41.
[2] *Religion and the Rise of Capitalism* (London, 1926), p. 259. See Heckscher, *op. cit.*, Vol. II, pp. 322-3, and L. C. Knights, *Drama and Society in the Age of Jonson* (London, 1957), p. 151.
[3] Lee, *E'vraeia rov 'Aypor, or A Vindication of Regulated Inclosure* (1656), pp. 22-3.

moderation may easily be explained; after 1656 there was little articulate opposition.[1] While the practice of drawing conclusions from an author's reticence may be dangerous, the evidence is impressive. The pattern was the same. An author would record the great inconveniences 'both to private and public' through a failure to enclose.[2] This meant that lands returned not one quarter

'. . . of that profit either to private or public, which they are respectively capable of.'[3]

The obvious inference was that benefit to the landlord was proportionately reflected in benefit to the public, since such writers wrote of the national interest and gave no other yardstick than the increased value of lands.

Discussion of enclosures fused almost imperceptibly into general recommendations for land improvement. A number of writers assumed that their function was to publicize improvements in technique and they just took for granted the beneficial nature of enclosures. Even treatises almost entirely technical in nature could harbour the same individualistic premises, as in the case of a work intended to promote the use of a new form of fodder. After mentioning the various interests that might be affected by innovations in land use, the writer conceded that some men might sustain a real or apparent loss through a rationalization of husbandry. Still, this could not prevent landlords from improving their holdings,

'. . . which of common right, every man may do . . . if the public receive no prejudice thereby.'[4]

This was no effective qualification, because he had already taken as axiomatic that the improvement of lands 'proportion-

---

[1] See J. E. C. Hill and E. Dell, *The Good Old Cause* (London, 1949), p. 422.
[2] Samuel Hartlib, *A Discovery or Setting out of Land, as to the Best Form* . . . (1653), p. 3.
[3] *Ibid.*, p. 3. Sir Richard Weston, *A Discourse of Husbandrie* . . . (1654), p. 2, and Samuel Hartlib, *The Compleat Husband-Man* (1659), pp. 41–2. Weston may not have intended to support a policy of enclosure, but Hartlib used him for that purpose.
[4] Anon., *St. Foine Improved, A Discourse Shewing the Utility and Benefit which England hath and May Receive by the Grasse Called St. Foine* (1671), p. 13 (B: Ashm. E 16).

ately improveth the stock and riches of the nation'.[1] Having demonstrated that the landowner's profit was inextricably tied to that of the nation, he might well have stopped. However, he relentlessly set out to prove that no one could lose by his schemes:

'. . . neither doth any particular man suffer any injury . . . for if he did, the law would do him right.'[2]

Such writers were then more acute and consistent than they sometimes get credit for. One could justify such a policy by showing the connection between the landlord's profit and that of the public, with the latter measured by some general consideration, such as national defence or revenue from taxation. However, once having insisted upon the merits of private profit, they obviously thought it incumbent on them to show that a public good involved the private good of all concerned. Thus an argument beginning with an alleged harmony between one private interest and that of the public might end by assuming that the best description of the public interest was the satisfaction of all private ones. The two ideas were not identical, and they were not inseparable, but they might readily occur together.

The same point of view appears in the work of John Houghton, journalist and genial purveyor of patent cures. He defended enclosures and various other economic changes on the assumption that 'no one will dispute a profit'.[3] However, he was singularly vague as to whom they were profitable. He was a free-trader in most respects, though he did not assume that any automatic harmony prevailed on all occasions. Once, when writing of politics, he complained that 'public and private interests do seldom quadrate'.[4] Still, he felt that the elusive harmony obtained in enclosures and he chided those experts, such as John Evelyn, who wrote only of technical matters while ignoring interests:

[1] *Ibid.*, p. 2.   [2] *Ibid.*, p. 13.
[3] Anon., *England's Great Happiness or a Dialogue Between Content and Complaint* (1677), p. 4 (B: Pamph. C 139). Houghton claimed to have written this tract and there is no reason to disbelieve him.
[4] *A Collection of Letters for the Improvement of Husbandry and Trade*, Vol. 8, No. 178 (27 December 1695).

'When there was only an enquiry, what was the way of propagating timber-trees Mr. Evelyn taught it the world much beyond what any writer had done before. But in cases where the public good results from the good of every particular, as it does in this, it ought first to be cleared that the planting timber-trees was beneficial to the planter. . . . For every man to be a faithful steward to his land, must put it to that use that will bring most money.'[1]

Here the previous relationship was reversed, and it was claimed that in cases where the public interest was a collection of private ones, it was only sensible to appeal to such interests. Lee's time had caught up with him. By the beginning of the next century the author of a large book on husbandry dismissed objections to enclosure, saying that the obvious increase in rents that it brought should banish all disputes.[2]

Lee's logic cannot be improved by showing that he was no singular, isolated figure. It is important, though, that private and public good were so easily reconciled in this context. One might then assume that wild men possessed by the most extreme principles abounded at this time. The correct conclusion, though, would be that the principles, however common, were unremarkable when put into their context. Very sober men might argue as Lee had, and while the century saw no general enclosure act, enclosers received aid and comfort from the statute book. A Restoration statute which accepted the encloser's priorities said in its preamble:

'Forasmuch as the encouraging of tillage ought to be in an especial manner regarded and endeavoured, and the surest and effectualist means of promoting and advancing any trade, occupation, or mystery, being by rendering it profitable to the users thereof . . .'[3]

---

[1] *Ibid.*, Vol. 2, No. 36 (7 April 1693).

[2] J. Mortimer, *The Whole Art of Husbandry* (1707), p. 1. A contemporary, James Puckle, took it for granted that enclosures 'improve our lands and enlarge our products . . . and thereby in proportion add to its [the nation's] wealth and treasure'. *England's Path to Wealth and Honour* (1700), p. 30. Captain Walter Blith was perhaps one of the last enclosers to worry very much about depopulation and other such general interests. Still, he had no convincing proposals except to rely upon the self-interest of the landlord. See *The English Improver Improved* (1653), pp. 77–8.

[3] 15 Car. II. 7. The language of statutes and proclamations is rather too formal to record changed attitudes towards individualism, although Cunningham was confident that a close study of statutes from the first half of the

Lee would doubtless have gone further to question the use of advancing any trade unless it profited the practitioner, otherwise the assumptions were similar.

While the land question afforded the best possible occasion for individualistic formulations of the public interest, there were others. It was a projecting age and there were a number of proposals of other sorts that entailed some discussion of social consequences. Many extraordinary schemes were proposed as being in the public interest; for what projector would claim anything else? Some of the most important of these writings dealt in one way or another with means of stimulating credit.

Few such works could avoid the question of what the public interest was. In domestic trade this was no easy matter, for it was rather difficult to introduce an external standard based on the safety, or even on the prosperity, of the nation. There was no simple tabulation of the king's profit as measured by customs revenue, or that of the nation as told by the balance of trade. Of course some aspects of inland commerce might be discussed in terms of their effect on the foreign trade balance, but this was not always possible. Thus the public good was often seen as the preservation or the advancement of various private interests. Writers increasingly resorted to the idea that a genuine public good must not harm any private interests and indeed should advance them all. An acknowledgment made only with the greatest difficulty was that equally legitimate interests might be unalterably opposed. A favourite way of resolving the difficulty was to bring a moral disqualification against one side. Thus when it was unavoidable that planting fruit trees would harm the brewing industry, or prohibiting stage coaches, the drivers, these interests had somehow to be discredited. The best reason for denying these groups equal satisfaction with the majority of private men was that their activities were morally harmful or their persons degraded.[1] Mere numerical weakness was

century would reveal an increased concern for the satisfaction of private interests. See W. Cunningham, *The Growth of English Industry and Commerce in Modern Times* (Cambridge, 1912), Vol. II, pp. 17–18.

[1] See Samuel Hartlib, *A Designe for Plentie By An Universall Planting of Fruit-Trees* (n.d.), pp. 15–16, and Anon., *The Grand Concern of England Explained* (1672), p. 40 (B: G.P. 1119). See too Thomas Culpepper, *A Discourse Shewing the Many Advantages which will Accrue to this Kingdom by the Abatement of Usury* (1668), p. 28.

not always enough; such interests had to be further tainted.

Even that sinister figure the usurer received unusual consideration. A number of writers who advocated a reduction of the interest rate insisted that the usurer could find alternative means of investing his money that would be no less profitable. Such a reform might cause inconvenience to some, but the advocates stoutly affirmed that it would operate 'without the least diminution to the estate of any man in particular'.[1] John Cary went so far as to claim that a low interest rate would so swell the usurer's volume of business that he could scarcely afford not to press for it.[2]

Even people who were most authoritarian in their political opinions adopted a more liberal understanding of the public good for purposes of economic argument. In his best-known tracts, Robert Filmer derided the new idea that the public interest concerned as much the interests of ordinary men as it did the king's. Nevertheless, on entering the usury controversy on the permissive side, he adapted his views to suit the circumstances. An opponent had attacked usury as detrimental to the commonwealth, without bothering precisely to locate the injury. This was a standard form of argument and was based on two value judgments. The first was the ancient doctrine that excessive interest was unethical and the lenders parasites; the second was the assumption that cheap credit was generally good for trade. High interest rates raised prices and reduced the velocity of circulation of money, or so it was thought. Filmer attacked precisely that general, unassignable good that low-interest men must have deemed most obvious and impervious to criticism:

'... Indeed he would persuade us that to lend to the rich is to enable him to oppress the commonwealth, and so consequently the poor. But he doth not show how the commonwealth can be wronged by usury, and yet no particular be first oppressed.'[3]

Fenton, his opponent, had his priorities all wrong, though he adopted the argument best suited to his bad case, for

[1] Francis Cradock, *Wealth Discovered* (1661), p. 35. For a similar instance see William Potter, *The Key of Wealth* (1650), p. 60.
[2] Cary, *An Essay Towards the Setling a National Credit*, ... (1696), p. 9.
[3] Filmer, *A Discourse Whether it May be Lawful to Take Use for Money* ... (1678), pp. 34-5.

'. . . because he sees that in some cases he cannot show how any particular person is oppressed by usury, therefor he flies for sanctuary to the commonwealth to hide himself in the crowd.'[1]

This was less than fair comment, but it shows admirably how one might now argue that real detriment to the public had to involve immediate, personally felt injuries to identifiable individuals. If some people clearly gained and no one could make a convincing case for his own loss, the presumption had to be that the public had gained. If there was any one quality that united the more effective tracts advocating individualism it was this one. Public good and ill had to be related to the fortunes of private men; if causal relationships could not be traced to this conclusion, references to the public interest were not very meaningful. Filmer's position stressed the particular and the concrete, but it was short-sighted in refusing to contemplate those real interests that could not easily be made articulate. Fenton's understanding of the public good was traditional, economically conservative and the only possible one for certain situations. It was also a most irritating restriction to those who were understandably aware of their own interests and feared sacrificing them to an abstraction.

After the Restoration variations of Filmer's attitude were commonly expressed, though there is no way of knowing whether it was the most prevalent view. One promoter voiced the exasperation that awaited everyone trying to justify plans in the name of the public good. In keeping with the new vogue of seeing this good as that of every single man, his proposals for expanding credit had been challenged as failing equally to accommodate all men. 'Nor nothing else under the sun,' he answered, for a coach going to Bristol was of no help to those travelling to York.[2] It was perfectly true that those without any goods or credit could not expect an immediate benefit from it, yet they might eventually reap some gain, for the general improvement in trade would benefit thousands.[3]

When a similar scheme a few years later brought the charge

[1] *Filmer*, p. 35.
[2] R. Verney, *England's Interest, or the Great Benefit to Trade by Banks or Offices of Credit in London* (1682), p. 20.
[3] *Ibid.*

that it might benefit particular men and not the nation, its champion used an argument of quite unusual crudity. He set out to show how his banks of credit would profit the nation, the crown and the people. Actually he did not bother to distinguish among these ill-assorted categories. He assured the king of consideration, without stooping to details, and treated the people and the nation as one entity, presumably on the assumption that the riches of a nation were its people.[1] He also identified private and public gain. Without any special feeling of intrepidity, he said quite frankly:

'. . . the nation is one great family; a particular person gets, the nation gets.'[2]

Perhaps he would have wished to be understood in the manner of the modern welfare economist who says that there is a net gain if the particular interests profiting from any measure may compensate the losers and still profit. Of course one might simply argue that the membership of private men within the community meant that their gain was that of the community, and some said just that. However, this was the most arrant opportunism and most unconvincing unless some attempt were made to show that there were no private losses offsetting private profits. Both in domestic and in foreign commerce the argument from private gain invited proof that other private interests were preserved or improved. Whatever H. M. meant, his comment reveals that the mercantilist idea of a national family with a common stock was not necessarily a bridle on private ambitions. It could be turned to quite the opposite purpose. Despite their reputation to the contrary, many mercantilists were not just concerned with the aggregate dimensions of the national product but also with its distribution. Hence H. M.'s statement may have taken for granted a general harmony of interests among the various particular interests in the nation. A discussion of this theme is best left until it can be placed in its most familiar context, in relation to foreign trade.

[1] H. M., *England's Glory* . . . (1694), p. 20 (BM: 523 b. 28). The British Museum catalogue suggests that William Paterson was the author, but Sir Humphrey Mackworth, who was also interested in banking schemes, seems a more reasonable choice.
[2] *Ibid.*, p. 17.

COMMERCE, MAINLY FOREIGN

Most seventeenth-century discussions of the merchant looked to the foreign trader as the prototype. One reason for his greater dignity was the vital nature of his function. It was possible to dismiss retailers as simply passing money from hand to hand, but the foreign trader enriched the nation, often, as xenophobic mercantilists gleefully recorded, by impoverishing others. Foreign trade clearly related to the foundations of national power. English writers were mightily impressed with the achievements of the Dutch, who had made trade their reason of state, and beginning in about 1650 many Englishmen proclaimed that trade, above all, was the interest of England.[1] Once it had been established that the interest of England was involved, the ubiquitous Duke of Rohan came to figure in economic literature. Of course he could have no useful message in terms of technical economic advice, but his name could still not be overlooked when interests were being discussed. A paper by the Eastland Merchants used his authority, saying that it had been an observation of

'. . . a great man in his time, that the ill success which did attend princes and states in their great affairs, did generally arise through the mistake of that which was their true interest.'

This, the company continued, was serious indeed,

'. . . for as it is natural for every thing to tend to its proper centre, so it is as natural for every man to pursue (tho' by different ways and means) that which he apprehends to be his proper interest.'[2]

Foreign trade was one area where a measure of agreement

[1] See Benjamin Worsley, *The Advocate: or a Narrative of the State and Condition of Things Between the English and Dutch Nations, in Relation to Trade* (1652), p. 9; Henry Robinson, *Certain Proposals in Order to the People's Freedom and Accommodation* (1652), p. 10, and R. Baker, *The Marchant's* [sic] *Humble Petition* (1659), p. 4 (B: G.P. 1524).
[2] *Reasons Humbly Offered by the Governour, Assistants and Fellowship of the Eastland Merchants, Against the Giving of a General Liberty to all Persons . . . to Export the English Woollen Manufactures* (1689), p. 3 (BM: 8248 bb. 26). For an even less likely instance of Rohan's influence see the broadside, *A Proposal for Raising Sixty Thousand Pound per Annum . . .* (c. 1700) (B: B 8.22 Jur.).

about what policies constituted the public interest was possible. There might be differences of opinion about how a favourable balance of trade might be measured, or even about the possibility of measuring it, but everyone allowed that it was a good thing. Economic liberals would point out that all exports were paid for by imported goods, but they too recognized that finding a market for English goods was essential. The crude bullionist and the man who said only that exports had to equal imports agreed on certain basic conditions upon which national prosperity depended, however much they might differ as to means. This modicum of agreement does not mean that analysis must be limited to the various means for achieving the public good, for there were also alternative or supplementary definitions as to what that good was. Thinking in terms of the balance of trade did not preclude discussion about satisfying private interests. It only meant that arguments in the latter form would not dominate the field as they did in controversies about inland trade.

The relationship between the merchant and the public good received memorable expression in several publications of the East India Company written by Thomas Mun. The essence of the matter was to distinguish among the various forms of gain in foreign trade. Here one series of statements served as a model, being quoted well into the eighteenth century. If the collection of opinions known as mercantilism had any authoritative statement of doctrine, this surely was it. Mun warned that

'. . . we must not forget to distinguish between the gain of the kingdom and the profit of the merchant.'[1]

His emphasis, though, was hardly unflattering to the merchant. He noted first how the nation might easily gain from transactions when the merchant lost, since much of his overhead in wages and insurance went into the national coffers. Mun recorded the bewilderment with which many merchants greeted this situation,

[1] *The Petition and Remonstrance of the Governour and Company of London, Trading to the East Indies* (1628), p. 9 (B: A 9.10 Linc.). A slightly altered version of the same appeared in 1641 and parts of the argument were reproduced verbatim in Mun's posthumously published work *England's Treasure by Foreign Trade* (1664).

'. . . for (say they) how can the kingdom gain by this trade when we who are members thereof, have lost so grievously ?'[1]

Grudgingly he conceded that the reverse might also happen, with the merchant gaining at the expense of the public,

'. . . which he doth sometimes justly and worthily effect even though the commonwealth be a loser.'[2]

This was so because the nation might consume more foreign goods than it could pay for. He mentioned no instance of the merchant making an unjust gain at the expense of the public; if fault there was, it was for the authorities to correct it, not the merchant. Naturally the ideal situation was for the merchant to gain as well. In Mun's words:

'. . . consider how much more the realm is enriched by this trade when all things pass so happily that the merchant is a gainer also, together with the king and kingdom.'[3]

Perhaps his fellow merchants might be forgiven their confusion, for he was saying that profit to the merchant contributed to the national gain, though not always sufficiently to offset a damaging trade. This position was further refined by his reluctance to admit that merchants were at all blameworthy in profiting at the national expense. This made it quite easy for later writers to say that the nation gained when the merchant did, without adding the qualification that his efforts only produced a net gain under certain circumstances.

In fact one well-known writer had already claimed as much, though in confused and inconsistent fashion. The earliest surviving debate about the merchant and the public good was that between Gerard de Malynes and Edward Misselden.[4] Misselden complained of monopoly, which

'. . . causeth the body of the commonwealth to be wounded sore through the sides of many particular members thereof.'[5]

Malynes defended government in trade, alleging that,

[1] *Petition . . .*, p. 14.   [2] *Ibid.*, p. 16.   [3] *Ibid.*, p. 15.
[4] The background of the argument is presented in E. A. J. Johnson, *Predecessors of Adam Smith* (London, 1937), pp. 45–69.
[5] Misselden, *Free Trade: or, the Meanes to Make Trade Florish*, 2nd edn. (1622), p. 3.

'. . . albeit that the general is composed of the particular, yet it may fall out that the general shall receive an intolerable prejudice and loss by the particular and private benefit of some.'[1]

Malynes was not greatly restrictive here, though he was clearly the conservative protagonist. He added that in such cases regard should not be had for private interests,

'. . . especially if they may make the like benefit (in some measure) without hurt or detriment to the general.'[2]

This provoked Misselden to write his most explicitly individualistic work in which he asked:

'. . . is it not lawful for merchants to seek their privatum commodum in the exercise of their calling? . . . Is not the public involved in the private, and the private in the public? What else makes a commonwealth but private wealth . . . of the members in the exercise of commerce amongst themselves and with foreign nations?'[3]

Seen in its context, both temporal and textual, the opinion was hardly unique. Malynes had already conceded as much in replying to a less strongly worded plea for private profit. Nor did Misselden intend to rule out all concern for the common interest, for he often mentioned his own zeal for the public and he allowed that some measure of regulation was needed. His general orientation was certainly on the side of freedom, though, and he saw in trade a 'natural course' that made it most profitable when it was not artificially forced.[4]

No significance may be drawn from the fact that both disputants favoured 'freedom of trade'. Few were willing to call their favourite policies anything else, so that the most ardent monopolists might embrace the cause of a trade that was free and regulated. The slogan 'freedom of trade', then, had almost as many meanings as there were writers. It could be the rallying cry for an assault on monopoly or, after the Restoration, on all government interference. It could even cover the merchant's desire to trade across the lines during the Civil War.[5] Freedom

---

[1] Malynes, *The Maintenance of Free Trade* . . . (1622), p. 3.
[2] *Ibid.*, p. 3.   [3] *The Circle of Commerce* (1623), p. 17.
[4] *Free Trade*, p. 56, and *Circle*, p. 112.
[5] See *The Moderate*, No. 6 (15–22 August 1648), p. 42, misnumbered 34.

meant particular freedoms, though often a writer might be led by the momentum of his own eloquence to prove more than his own interests required. *Laissez-faire* could hardly be consistently advocated by merchants, because they so often called upon state power to restrain their competitors and make their freedom effective.

In foreign trade most men must have taken it for granted that a degree of regulation was, at worst, a necessary evil. The general bent of government policy favoured regulation. The Navigation Acts were only strengthened with the Restoration, however unpopular they may have been in some quarters.[1] One of the great battles between free-traders and protectionists was a triumph for the latter when, early in the eighteenth century, the French treaty of commerce was defeated. Hence it would be a mistake to perceive any inexorable trend away from stultifying restraints on trade. While old restrictions lost their force, they were replaced with new ones. It remains true, though, that with all the official concern for regulation, theory and argument was becoming increasingly liberal. Students of nineteenth-century social policy have noted the same discontinuity between theory and practice. At that time collectivism advanced, unheralded by any noticeable shifts in opinion.[2] In the seventeenth century a marked increase in the frequency and strength of liberal arguments left policy largely untouched. These arguments appeared in the works of some of the most prominent of the early economic thinkers, men, one might add, who were well known in their own time, and were not just resurrected centuries later as notable for their anachronistic liberalism. Most of these writers were merchants who were vitally

---

[1] See Anon., *Inconveniences to the English Nation Which Have Ensued the Act of Navigation in Reference to the Growths of Norway, as was Proved before the Honourable Committee of Parliament . . . April 4, 1668* (n.d.) (B: G.P. 2208), and Anon., *A Short View of the Act of Navigation* (1691) (BM: 8246 bbb. 6). Impatience with regulation of trade in general sometimes appears in unexpected places. Thus the dispensing power came to be justified by citing the great need of nullifying some of the numerous acts governing trade. See Sir Peter Pett, *The Obligation Resulting from the Oath of Supremacy* (1687), p. 127.

[2] See A. V. Dicey, *Lectures on the Relation Between Law and Public Opinion in England during the Nineteenth Century*, 2nd edn. (London, 1914), p. 68. The point is put more strongly in Karl Polanyi, *The Great Transformation* (New York, 1944), pp. 146-7.

concerned in the outcome of the issues they dealt with. This undoubtedly lent a flexibility, even an inconsistency, to their doctrines, which makes them difficult to classify in the liberal–mercantilist spectrum.

Following the Malynes–Misselden debate in the reign of James I, the next spate of literature came with the assault on monopolies during the Long Parliament. It is not easy to say whether the private traders seeking an open trade or the companies defending a closed one resorted more frequently to liberal arguments. Completely different policies could be supported by arguments that sounded very much alike in so far as the relationship between private and public profit was concerned. A liberal cause was one thing, a liberal argument another.

The private traders were quite clear about one thing. The aggregate riches of the nation could not be a sufficient measure of economic well-being. The maxim *'bonum quo communis, eo melius'* meant that

'. . . to bar any freeborn subject from the exercise of his invention and industry, to convert this universal native commodity to his best advantage at home or abroad, is to deprive him of part of his birthright.'[1]

The would-be interlopers pleaded on the grounds of natural right and on the obvious evils of monopoly. Many traders automatically meant a great trade, so the national interest was supposedly taken care of.[2] They also alleged that the kingdom's strength consisted 'in the riches of many subjects, not of a few'.[3] If conventional mercantilist thought had actually been as power-oriented as it was pictured, this would have constituted rank heresy. Actually, this was a fairly common theme.

[1] Anon., *A Discourse Consisting of Motives for the Enlargement and Freedome of Trade Especially that of Cloth, and other Woollen Manufactures* (1645), p. 3 (BM: E 260).
[2] See Anon., *The Reasons Humbly Offered to Consideration, Why the Incorporating the Whole Trade of Woollen Manufactures of this Kingdom to the Company called the Merchant-Adventurers of England is . . . Detrimental to the Country in General . . .* (n.d.), p. 2 (BM: 712 g. 16). This tract probably dates from shortly after the Restoration. The British Museum suggests 1662, the Kress Library, Harvard, some time in the 1670s.
[3] *Discourse Consisting of Motives . . .*, p. 22.

On regulation their views varied. Some unambiguously consented to the current policy, saying, 'we desire still a government, but not a monopoly'.[1] Occasionally one gets the impression that private traders were generalizing their dislike of government by patent to include all forms of regulation even by the ordinary organs of government. This is implied in one of the more sophisticated tracts, where the writer departed from the unsatisfactory claims of natural right to follow purely economic reason. The cloth-making industry was being ruined, he claimed, and the workers were beginning to seek a more favourable situation in Holland. The answer was simple,

'. . . it will not be so well looked into, by any law or provision, as by the dispersing of the trade into every place (which freedom will occasion) where every trader for his own profit and livelihood, will be necessitated to look to it, and by all means to restrain it.'[2]

By restraining it, he meant keeping it for England.

The brunt of the attack was borne by the Merchants Adventurers. They replied with more finesse and through better-known agents. The company's spokesmen were Henry Robinson and Henry Parker, both known for their writings on a number of subjects. They were undoubtedly, as their joint biographer calls them, 'men of substance'. As defenders of the *status quo*, they were in no position to advocate unregulated trade, but they sought regulation on terms that suited the incorporated merchants.

Government was most necessary in English trade, because of the number of tyros involved and consequently the great danger of failures. The state should be limited to the function of an incorporating body and the companies themselves would receive extended powers so that

'. . . such several societies understanding their own mysteries best may have full authority to order and govern them accordingly.'[3]

To the charge that merchants like him sought only their own profit, Robinson countered that

---

[1] *Discourse Consisting of Motives . . .*, p. 25.
[2] Anon., *The Golden Fleece Defended; or Reasons Against the Company of Merchant Adventurers* (1647), p. 4 (BM: E 381).
[3] Robinson, *England's Safety in Trades Increase . . .* (1641), p. 46.

'. . . all encouragement is little enough, because the more the better for the state in general, and many hundreds of men are employed and maintained by one merchant.'[1]

Robinson has been called one of the earliest free-traders.[2] He does seem to have held extreme opinions,[3] but one must look elsewhere for consideration of the public interest as it was affected by the company.

Since Parker was a noted political thinker, it was natural that he should conceive the issue in more theoretical terms. He too posited a harmony of interests between the merchant and the state, while closing the way to profit to thousands of small men. His main concern was to describe a system of trade consistent with the 'general interest' or 'public reason of state'. In all respects merchants organized in a company were seen as preferable to single men. The argument that the more traders the better was specious; everything depended on their organization. Significantly, he contemplated no loss to the public if private traders gained. His fears were for an ill-organized trade which

'. . . undoes many private men, and in their undoing proves injurious to the state.'

This was not a difficulty that could arise with the Merchants Adventurers, for the

'. . . whole company by common advice and consent sets its stint for its own good; and as the whole company best understands its interests, so neither has it, or can it have any interest but such as is consistent with the interest of the state.'[4]

This harmony of interests apparently rested upon the great social benefit provided by the successful merchant, and companies were nothing if not successful.

This particular form of harmony was set in a larger scheme embracing foreign nations. Unlike the more nationalistic mercantilists, Parker had no animus against foreigners, seeing their

[1] *Robinson*, p. 47.
[2] W. K. Jordan, *Men of Substance, A Study of the Thought of Two English Revolutionaries, Henry Parker and Henry Robinson* (Chicago, 1942), p. 231.
[3] See Robinson, *Certain Proposals in Order to the People's Freedom and Accommodation* (1652), pp. 11–12.
[4] H. Parker, *Of a Free Trade* (1648), p. 20.

profit as quite compatible with that of England. In one statement he contrived to draw together the interests of the foreigner, the companies and the English nation. Of these he said:

'. . . all these interests are so interweaved that the benefit of the stranger is requited with the benefit of the English merchant, and the benefit of the English merchant to be regarded as the benefit of the English nation. For in some things that are immediately advantageous the English merchant advantages mediately the English nation, even as in other things, that which immediately brings prosperity to the English nation mediately brings prosperity to the English merchant.'[1]

The merchant's ultimate profit was not merely dependent on his being a member of the nation. Parker was clearly thinking of the position of a company with enough capital to sustain initial losses in order to ensure greater long-term returns. This was a standard argument against interlopers, who, it was claimed, could not afford to sustain the losses involved in getting a trade established.

Parker's identification of the merchant and the state was conditioned by immediate circumstances. He thought that a free state was most conducive to trade, owing to the fact that

'. . . the merchant usually has more share in the administration of public affairs.'[2]

Most merchants who wrote of public affairs pressed for a larger dignity and responsibility for the merchant. But not all of them defended their claims on his behalf so carefully.

Occasionally Parker made a gesture towards separating merchant and state. 'The state,' he said,

'. . . is not to consider what is most beneficial to the merchant, what to the clothier separatim, or whether the benefit of the one alone, or the other may be more favoured but how they may both be favoured conjunctim, and how the state may most be benefitted by twisting their interests together.'[3]

This sounded very much like the 'fusion of interests' read into Robinson's economic outlook by his biographer.[4] Parker recognized how important it was that

---

[1] *Of a Free Trade*, p. 13.   [2] *Ibid.*, p. 3.   [3] *Ibid.*, p. 30.
[4] Jordan, *op. cit.*, p. 214.

'. . . as many persons and professions in England as may be, may come to be sharers in the general interest.'[1]

It was not only the private traders who saw that the distribution of national wealth was important, though doubtless they were more whole-hearted in their professions than was Parker. The latter immediately amended his noble sentiment with the complacent comment that if a choice ever had to be made between the merchant's interest and other ones, the government should remember how conducive trade was to the national welfare.[2] Parker's statement remains important, however, because he went beyond the opportunistic argument that private profit added to the national stock. He also described a national interest consisting in the enrichment of as many people as possible.

Monopolists and private traders might draw upon the same arsenal of arguments and both could contribute to the process of bringing the public interest closer to particular interests. Already a separate commercial interest was recognized and the first attempts were being made to reconcile it with the landed interest. These tracts illustrate the needs of any convincing harmony of interests. If the selfish endeavours of private men were to benefit the public, in most cases this involved showing how one set of particular interests harmonized with others. Perhaps this form of argument was easier to sustain during the Commonwealth, when the problem of the king's profit had been eliminated. Some pamphleteers also thought that calling the state a 'commonwealth' should make some difference in the way it treated its citizens. If the Commonwealth really justified its name and embodied a common good, then more attention ought to be paid to trade and traders.[3] The chief obstacle here was the landed interest. For most purposes the two interests could be reconciled. However, when attacks on the landed men by merchants first became common, it was for purposes of securing tax reform, and here was a *prima facie* conflict of interest.[4]

[1] Parker, *Of a Free Trade*, pp. 30–1.   [2] *Ibid.*, p. 31.
[3] See W. C., *Trades Destruction is England's Ruine* (1659), p. 5 (BM: 518 h. 1).
[4] *Ibid.*, pp. 6–8, and Z. G., *Excise Anatomized and Trade Epitomized* (1659), p. 11 (BM: E 999). Both of these writers contrasted the concerns of the 'landed men' with those of the merchants. Neither specifically wrote of a 'landed interest', although the expression 'the interest of land' seems to date from this period, probably reflecting the influence of Harrington. See W.C., *A Discourse for a King and Parliament* (1660), pp. 3–4 (B: Wood 608).

One defender of the trading interest made a very illuminating distinction between the common good and interest of state. He seems to have used state interest to cover the usual considerations regarding national strength and defence, while reserving the 'common good' for satisfaction to particular interests.[1] Thus he observed that governmental manipulation of the value of money in order to increase revenue was a 'great oppression, when no excuse can be pleaded other than state interest'.[2] Here, as in the constitutional struggle, it is easier to discover charges of unjust pleas of reason of state than explicit use of such a rationale by those in authority.

There was not a great deal of writing on foreign trade in the years immediately following the Restoration. Petty was active in this period, but his work tended to be largely statistical. Only in treating Ireland did he discuss political or economic interests and then he was silent about how their competing claims might be reconciled. He undoubtedly made allusions to a natural economic order that was best left alone, just as he expressed hostility to territorial expansion, but he did little to amplify these observations.

Josiah Child was quite another matter, though any consideration of his opinions encounters many difficulties. He wrote over a considerable period of time on a variety of issues, and without doubt he expressed himself strongly on both sides of some questions. Nor is it easy to distinguish his views from those of the East India Company, thus the authorship of some works attributed to him is conjectural.

Child exemplifies more clearly than any other seventeenth-century figure the precarious nature of generalizations about thought in the age of mercantilism. It is almost fair to say that he had one understanding of the public interest for his general statesmanlike pronouncements and another for his role as spokesman for the East India Company. Sometimes his two roles clashed within the same document. Statements of a forbiddingly conservative nature came easily to him. Indeed, as we shall see, scholars have assumed some opinions to be far more common than they actually were, just because Child made use

[1] S. E., *The Touchstone of Money and Commerce* (1659), p. 10 (BM: 8245 a. 13).
[2] *Ibid.*, p. 9.

of them. When playing the statesman, Child warned solemnly that one must

'. . . warily distinguish between the profit of the merchant and the gain of the kingdom, which are so far from being always parallels, that frequently they run counter one to the other.'[1]

He was perfectly faithful to Mun's position, even adding, now perhaps with more reason, that most men none the less confounded the two. All proposals for public good would cross the interests and opinions of some people.

When convenient, he might alter the emphasis. While advocating low interest rates, he contrasted the condition of England with that of Holland, where credit was much cheaper and

'. . . consequently the same trade being with them and us equally good for the public, is to the private adventurers lossful with us, with them very gainful and where the good of public and private men's go not together, the public is seldom greatly advanced.'[2]

This last phrase comes as an apparent contradiction to the first part of the sentence. If the public were unlikely to benefit from trade unless private men did so, how could a trade really benefit the nation in the manner first suggested? Did he mean that should private men not gain, the public would not gain for long, because the trade would stop? This seems to be the most sensible interpretation, but, then, why did he stress the limits on the quantitity of the public gain, why not its limited temporal dimension? Perhaps he meant that the public was composed of private men and unless they gained there was no gaining public left. Both these opinions were current by the end of the century. The first looked to the means of obtaining the public good, the second looked to the nature of the good itself.

Whatever he intended to say, Child gave an original twist to Mun's tired old dictum. Most writers had bewailed the injustice of private gain existing beside public loss. Child's worry was that the public might be seen as really flourishing while private men failed. In rejecting such profit as specious, he was not excusing all private profit. While, for some reason, it was a necessary condition, it was not a sufficient one.

Child was one of the most prominent merchant princes of the

---

[1] [Child], *A Discourse About Trade* (1690), sig. [C 6].   [2] *Ibid.*, p. 206.

age, so it is not surprising that he should have been credited with tracts that he never wrote. Letwin has effectively disposed of a number of these false attributions.[1] One of the tracts which Letwin lists simply as doubtful was a fairly extreme defence of free trade. A contemporary of Child's was subject to no doubts at all and assumed it to be his work.[2] It was a defence of the merchant's right to do as he pleased and, like all of the other tracts attributed to Child, had specific reference to the needs of the East India Company. Briefly, the writer felt that the company ought to be free to make its own decisions. In support of this plea, he made the most sweeping assertions about the need for unrestricted trade:

'. . . trade is a free agent, and must not be limited or bounded; if it be so in any nation, it will never prosper.'[3]

'. . . trade must be free for the public good, otherwise it will die or fly away.'[4]

Restraining the merchant's self-interest also offended against natural right, for it was clearly

'. . . against natural right that any men should be barred from doing what they think fit with their own estates.'[5]

Even were this written by someone else, with Child's blessing, it suggests that he is not adequately described as a perfectly conventional mercantilist, unless mercantilism is to be re-evaluated.

Charles Davenant presents problems of the same sort. He shows the same pattern of vacillation as did Child, but here his reputation as a free-trader seems merited by his writings. A measure of Davenant's reputation among his contemporaries is that a number of them specifically dissented from his views, while treating his opinions with great deference.[6] Henry Pollexfen

---

[1] William Letwin, *Sir Josiah Child, Merchant Economist* (Cambridge, Mass., 1959), Appendix I.
[2] Anon., 'A Discourse Concerning the East India Trade' (*c.* 1693), in *Somers' Tracts*, 2nd edn. (London, 1813), Vol. X, p. 639.
[3] 'The Humble Answer of the Governour and Court of Committees of the East-India Company to a Paper of Propositions for the Regulation of the East-India Company', in *Somers' Tracts*, Vol. X, p. 622.
[4] *Ibid.*, p. 624.   [5] *Ibid.*, p. 625.
[6] A. N., *England's Advocate, Europe's Monitor* (1699), p. 21 (BM: 8245 a. 39), and William Wood, *A Survey of Trade* (1718), p. 97.

probably did more than anyone else to brand Davenant as a free-trader. He noted the gross contradictions between the un-trammelled individualism of his most quotable statements and the large reservations made elsewhere. Still, he concluded that the dominant theme was that the merchant's profit was an ade-quate indication that the public interest was being served.[1]

Davenant was a free-trader in the sense that he considered that regulation was impossible to apply, for the course of trade was so complex and the interconnections so numerous that any intervention would have harmful consequences that were im-possible to anticipate.[2] He was not a merchant, though, but had served for some time as Excise Commissioner. This probably explains the quality of *étatism* in all of his work. He proclaimed the administrative difficulties in governing trade, not the right of traders to govern themselves. He queried the perverse opin-ion that any public good by which private men gained was somehow disreputable. But his answer was quite mild. It was really all that one could hope for

'. . . if the prospect of some honest gain invites people to do the public faithful service.'[3]

Davenant wrote much of the public interest, but never defined it. In one passage, though, he combined two of the most com-mon ideas about the public good in relation to trade:

'. . . trade is the general concern of this nation, but every distinct trade has a distinct interest. The wisdom of the legislative power con-sists in keeping an even hand to promote all and chiefly to encourage such trades as . . . add to the kingdom's wealth, considered as a collective body.'[4]

A certain balance among the prevailing particular interests was part of the public good. However, he was still not free of the old-

---

[1] [Pollexfen], *England and East-India Inconsistent in their Manufactures* (1697), p. 45.
[2] 'That Foreign Trade is Beneficial to England' (1698), in *The Political and Commercial Works of that Celebrated Writer Charles D'Avenant*, ed. Sir C. Whit-worth (London, 1771), Vol. I, p. 387.
[3] 'An Essay Upon the Probable Methods of Making a People Gainers in the Balance of Trade' (1699), in *Works*, Vol. II, p. 214.
[4] 'An Essay on the East-India Trade' (1697), in *Works*, Vol. I, p. 98.

fashioned concern for a single heap constituting the national stock.

One of Davenant's most frequently quoted maxims serves to illustrate a theme that was now very common:

'... trade is in its nature free, finds its own channel, and best directeth its own course, and all laws to give it rules and directions and to limit and circumscribe it, may serve particular ends of private men, but are seldom advantageous to the public.'[1]

The emphasis is most interesting for it suggests free trade without the explicit concern for private interests usually associated with individualism. Some of the most prominent writers of the time felt that private and public interest might conflict and certainly they neglected to labour the beauties of a natural harmony. Nevertheless, when they sought examples of potential conflict they turned to those private men who sheltered behind government regulations to enjoy privileges not freely won in the market. Roger Coke might be better known as a free-trader were it not for his hard mercantilist vocabulary. He insisted that 'many particular persons may be interested to the public detriment'.[2] However, all such observations were directed against those who benefited by monopolies, the Navigation Acts and other forms of regulation.

William Paterson, one of Scotland's foremost merchants and the founder of the Bank of England, took precisely the same position. One would not expect to find a plea for free trade in a writer who said:

'... in matters of trade, the interest of particular men and that of the country's is so far from being always the same, that they are oftimes directly opposite to one another.'[3]

Who were these men whose interests harmed the public? None other than those who begat prohibitions, monopolies or exclusions, or resorted to

'... this old threadbare shift of prohibiting the export of wool.'[4]

---

[1] 'An Essay on the East-India Trade' (1697), in *Works*, Vol. I, p. 98.
[2] Coke, *England's Improvement in Two Parts* (1675), Treatise III, pp. 4–5.
[3] [Paterson], *Proposals and Reasons for Constituting a Council of Trade* (Edinburgh, 1701), pp. 41–2.
[4] Paterson, p. 113.

He looked forward to a Council of Trade, one of whose chief functions would be to dispense with restraints and prohibitions.[1] While Coke does not seem to have visualized the public good in liberal terms, but in terms of total national wealth, Paterson said that the true national interest consisted in diffusing the profits of trade as widely as possible among the populace.[2] Both were liberals, of course, in the means whereby the national interest was to be secured. If restraints on trade aided only some private men, then free scope for private initiative necessarily produced the national good. The best explanation for their making a liberal case in illiberal language is that it must have been the least jarring way. Thus they might, as much as possible, maintain the traditional framework of ideas, while neutralizing their effect on policy.

The old warnings against private interest still figured in the neglected writings of Peter Paxton. Like some other pronounced individualists, Paxton may have been overlooked by economic historians because he was not a particularly able economist, preferring a few simple slogans to close causal analysis. However, for those interested in individualism and the public good, rather than in the technicalities of economic theory, Paxton is an important thinker. He seems to have been one of the most consistent free-traders of the period. Monopolies, bounties and duties all stood condemned as hindering the 'natural course of things'. They were no more than 'a violence upon nature'.[3] The distinction between the merchant's gain and that of the nation served only to discredit all monopolies, for the nation's profit was measured by the number of people profitably involved in trade.[4] The heart of his doctrine lay in one slogan with which he

[1] *Paterson*, p. 119.
[2] *Ibid.*, pp. 41–2. See too Anon., *Essay Upon Industry and Trade* (Edinburgh, 1706), p. 27 (BM: 8228 ccc. 16). Scotland produced other free-trade writings in this period, some of which consisted in arguments for unregulated free enterprise without any particular concern for maximizing the number of beneficiaries. See C. K., *Some Seasonable and Modest Thoughts Partly Occasioned by, and Partly Concerning the Scots East India Co.* (Edinburgh, 1696), pp. 7–8 (BM: 114 g. 15). This writer defended monopolies but otherwise sought complete freedom for the merchant.
[3] Paxton, *A Discourse Concerning the Nature, Advantage and Improvement of Trade* (1704), p. 16.
[4] Paxton, *A Scheme for Union Between England and Scotland* (1705), p. 12. See too *A Discourse . . .*, p. 10.

was obviously pleased, considering the number of times he used it. The cure for all cares about commercial policy lay in that

'. . . greatest secret in trade consisting in the uniting of these two differing interests, viz private and public; for without a regard for the first there can be no trade; and without a regard for the second, it is better to have none.'[1]

Only by freedom for self-interest was the merchant's interest united with that of the nation.

Evidence of concern for a public good that both arose from private interests and consisted in their greatest possible satisfaction was not just a curious aberration. Economic historians, primarily interested in theories of trade, have detected in late seventeenth-century writings various shifts in emphasis towards more liberal patterns of thought. Thus the task of promoting employment gained priority over the accumulation of a national stock of money and consumption ceased merely to be the handmaid of production and gained a certain importance in its own right.[2] For present purposes this might best be seen as an increased concern for promoting individual satisfactions and a tendency, in some quarters, to consider the usefulness of most forms of private profit. Employment had always been a concern of the government, but now it assumed new importance as the East India merchants made every effort to show that their apparently adverse trade balance disguised their major contribution in creating employment in other trades. While some of the more extreme individualists were rather vague about what principles guided their thought, the high priority of full employment was a better basis for a harmony of interests than any rigorous insistence on a favourable balance in each national trade.

There was surely some such thought behind the sentence upon which the fame of Sir Dudley North rests. The body of the tract dealt largely with the harmful effects of government restraint in domestic trade, but one statement in the preface seems to refer either to foreign trade alone or to all trade:

[1] *A Discourse . . .*, p. 19.
[2] See B. Suviranta, *The Theory of the Balance of Trade* (Helsingfors, 1923), pp. 142–3 and 162.

'. . . there can be no trade unprofitable to the public; for if any prove so, men leave it off; and whereever traders thrive, the public, of which they are a part, thrives also.'[1]

The author was familiar with the idea that in some domestic trades benefit to one person was loss to another and the public gained nothing. But his work was largely concerned with defending unregulated domestic trade, even the vending of luxuries being a stimulant to employment. It is conceivable, then, that the writer of the preface meant to include domestic trade in his far-reaching claim. Few, even after Mandeville, would have joined him in his defence of all profitable trades. However, applied to foreign ventures, the argument seemed more convincing. People who saw the retailers' profit as unrelated to the public good, because he enriched no one but himself, might see great virtue in the profits of an overseas merchant.

Dalby Thomas, a trader to Africa and America, argued in exactly this way. He had the common prejudice against those in home employments who merely shifted money from one hand to another. With an obvious eye to his own occupation, he said:

'. . . that man who by industry and labour not only maintains himself and family but makes himself rich, is to the proportion of his wealth just so much addition to the intrinsic value of the kingdom.'[2]

He equated this intrinsic value with the public good.[3] His method was to extol all in domestic or foreign trade who might add to this intrinsic wealth, and then by sweeping exceptions, to eliminate most merchants not trading abroad.

An argument, like North's, based upon the necessary relations between parts and the whole might seem artificial and *a priori*, and in his case it was. Still, it could be based upon coherent economic reasoning, at least as coherent as the similar case for enclosures. None but fairly strong individualists were

---

[1] *Discourses Upon Trade* (1691), sig. B^v (B: C 6.12 Linc.). The preface may have been by Dudley North's brother, Roger. See W. Letwin, 'The Authorship of Sir Dudley North's Discourses Upon Trade', *Economica*, n.s., Vol. 18, No. 69 (1951), pp. 35–56.
[2] Dalby Thomas, *An Historical Account of the Rise and Growth of the West India Colonies and of the Great Advantages they are to England in Respect to Trade* (1690), p. 3.
[3] *Ibid.*, p. 6.

likely to use the argument in foreign trade, but it was not entirely limited to complete and consistent free-traders. John Law explained it in two different ways. One approach was Davenant's appeal to the complexity of social causation. The enemies of private interests should examine the whole sweep of trade with all of its hidden connections, before they condemned any practice. Law insisted that an apparently adverse balance of trade might only mean that the excess of imports from a given trade could release for export goods originally intended for the home market. He also depended upon the extent to which a trade created jobs:

'. . . a nation may gain where the merchant loses, but wherever the merchant gains the nation gains equal, and so much more, as the maintenance and wages of the people employed, and the duty on the goods amount to.'[1]

Nicholas Barbon offered a sophisticated version of the argument in the course of exploding current fallacies about money. Underestimated as an intelligent liberal, Barbon was an enemy of all prohibitions on trade, but tolerated low duties. He was very dubious about the practice of measuring national interest by the rate of foreign exchange and suggested an alternative means of determining whether the nation profited from a trade. In essence, he held that an unfavourable exchange rate caused by any trade would not persist, since the merchants would then lose and consequently would direct their efforts elsewhere.[2] It followed that

'. . . all merchants get by their trade: and if they grow rich the nation thrives. . . . For a nation grows rich by its inhabitants growing rich.'[3]

Barbon shows how this very liberal formula might be compatible with some measure of restraint. He was certain that if the merchant made a profit the nation could gain without restricting his activities. No trade wasted resources if it provided income for the inhabitants. He entered one small caveat when he said:

[1] Law, *Money and Trade Considered* (1720) (1st edn. 1705), p. 16.
[2] Barbon, *A Discourse Concerning Coining the New Money Lighter* (1696), p. 39.
[3] *Ibid.*, p. 41.

'. . . there is no foreign trade but is profitable to a nation, or at least may be made so.'[1]

By his own criteria all trades were necessarily profitable, since they were still being carried on. It might be useful, though, to levy duties to protect some local industries. The duty was never to be so high as to constitute a prohibition, so the English merchant was not really inhibited in his hunt for profit. He might import whatever he wanted, but some items would obviously sell better than others. One finds the clue to Barbon's understanding of the public good in his treatment of the impossibility of calculating trade balances. Others had referred to some entity called the nation, but this was not a useful concept,

'. . . for a nation, as a nation, never trades, 'tis only the inhabitants and subjects of each nation that trade: and there are no set days or times for making up a general accompt, every merchant making up his own private accompt.'[2]

While not strictly accurate, this was an essential position for the consistent economic liberal in his treatment of the common good. A public was just so many individuals and groups. It was deemed a statistical impossibility to calculate its gain from a mass of unco-ordinated transactions. Thus the seventeenth-century individualist deduced the public good from the fact of private gain; he inferred it from visual evidence of prosperity, ignoring the jeremiads of those who sought a controlled trade. However, he refused to admit that it might be subject to accurate calculating, since, apart from the welfare of the discrete economic units, there was no basis for measurement.

The most sophisticated tract preaching individualism was written in defence of the vulnerable East India trade. It is disappointed to record that the supposed author was probably functioning only as a literary hack, for he argued the other way a few years later.[3] Martin's argument was no more liberal in emphasis than Paxton's, but it was more elaborate. In compari-

[1] Barbon, p. 45.   [2] *Ibid.*, pp. 36–7.
[3] The case for Henry Martin as author is made by P. J. Thomas in *Mercantilism and the East India Trade* (London, 1926), Appendix B. This Martin was not, of course, the regicide of the same name, but a sometime revenue collector who is thought to have been one of the leading contributors to the protectionist paper *The British Merchant.*

son with most of the writers of the previous decade, he dignified
the merchant's defence of profit-seeking to the level of economic
science. He frankly displayed the basis for his opinions, and
while Child or Davenant grasped at straws to justify an *ad hoc*
case, he expounded a coherent doctrine that unambiguously
dictated a general policy. There was only one concession to the
pressures of the moment, though this undoubtedly was important and probably was the reason for writing the tract. Eventually he hoped to see all trades opened. This would doubtless
mean that emulation between traders might reduce profit margins. He did not think that the trader's maximum profit was
necessarily the optimum for the public, but all such profit was
advantageous.

Despite an apparent distaste for corporations, he defended
the East India Company. Far from denying that weavers in
England might suffer from its activities, he accepted this as a
virtue in the direction of efficiency. He refuted traditional complaints about the export of bullion by the company and its importation of harmful goods:

'. . . it is objected that though the exchange is profitable to private
persons, yet the kingdom is not the richer for it. But if one man pro-
cures as much value by his labour from India as three procured
before in England, he produces as much as all the three before; and
the riches of the other three are not reduced to nothing; their labour
. . . is still worth something and whatever it is worth is so much gain
to the nation.'[1]

Here was one of the radical new uses to which one might put the
old idea of the national stock:

'. . . of £100. the value is the same, whether collected into the hands
of few, or distributed into the hands of many.'[2]

This was not quite so heartless as might appear, for his concern
for economic rationality meant that Martin placed unusual
reliance upon the mobility of resources. If men were inefficient
in one role, they might prove more profitable to themselves and
to the nation by moving to another job.

The argument culminated with that shibboleth of the extreme
individualist:

[1] *Considerations Upon the East-India Trade* (1701), p. 33 (BM: 1139 c. 9).
[2] *Ibid.*, p. 34.

'. . . the riches of every man is part of the riches of the whole community. Wherefore, if to erect a freeport is to increase the riches of the merchant, it must increase the riches of the kingdom.'[1]

Even when explained in terms of social processes, the argument might be no more than an unconvincing disguise for social irresponsibility. Everything depended on how carefully one explained the impact of a policy upon all of the affected interests. The same general point of view was expressed by people who had no obvious and sinister interest in a free market. Thus when Robert Molesworth wrote his much admired statement of Whig principles in the preface to Hotman's *Franco-Gallia*, he included the observation that

'. . . the thriving of any one single person by honest means is the thriving of the commonwealth wherein he resides. And in what place soever of the world such encouragement is given, as that in it one may securely and peaceably enjoy property and liberty . . . 'tis impossible but that place must flourish in riches and in people, which are the truest riches of any commonwealth.'[2]

At least some of these individualists considered themselves highly original. Certainly attempts to associate them as a school have not proved successful. Faced with these claims of creativity, it is refreshing to encounter an obscure man who just accepted such opinions as the new orthodoxy. Thomas Tryon was a merchant and a dispenser of advice on a wide range of subjects. He disliked prohibitions on trade, but many conventional mercantilists did as well. His real concern was to reduce duties, thus increasing welfare:

'. . . the promotion of navigation and a free trade, gives life to the trading people, more especially if the customs and imports be made easy . . . besides, merchants are . . . the engines of the whole nation, and if encouraged, have an innate power to set all hands at work and to advance all the manufactures and production of the nation and render the whole capable not only to live well and spend money liberally, but to pay taxes as freely.'[3]

[1] *Considerations* . . ., p. 125.
[2] *Franco-Gallia*, 2nd edn. (1721), p. XV. The preface did not appear in Molesworth's first edition, but apparently it was written as early as 1705. See Bookseller's Preface, sig. A 3.
[3] T. T., merchant, *Some General Considerations Offered Relating to Our Present Trade and Intended for its Help and Improvement* (1698), p. 18.

Tryon avoided abstract concepts and thus made no direct assertions about the public good. His nearest approach to the subject was a scorn for 'policy and grandeur, reason of state, empire and gold',[1] the substance of the statesmen's common good. Tryon also made very plain the need for new attitudes towards economic life, for

'. . . all the circumstances, management and methods that were formerly proper before we had so many rivals, cannot be supposed to be serviceable at present.'[2]

There seems to be every reason to believe that most of the chief economic writers of the day were personally interested in the causes they defended, and that exposition and advocacy were inextricably mingled.[3] Even more obvious were the interests of the anonymous authors in the literary underworld of the broadside. Here the protagonists were usually known only by their trades, and while Davenant or Child opposed Pollexfen or John Cary in a war of bulky treatises, their arguments were expressed often with more pungency, by little men identified only as 'linen-draper' or 'weaver'.

Nor were these ephemeral sheets mere vulgarizations of a more profound dialogue. The linen-drapers were more consistent free-traders than the East India magnates, for they were not so concerned to protect the monopoly of the trading companies.[4] The drapers made the strongest claims for the benefits of unfettered self-interest. It was true, they said, that in domestic trade

'. . . particular persons may improve their estates by buying and selling and the nation be never the richer.'

But this was an impossibility in foreign trade in general and in the East Indies trade in particular, for such trades provided employment and gave a stimulus to other trades.[5] Perhaps significantly, their reservation respecting inland trade never

---

[1] *The Way to Make All People Rich* (1685), p. 80.
[2] *Some General Considerations . . .*, p. 26.
[3] The point is developed in William Letwin, *The Origin of Scientific Economics: English Economic Thought 1660–1776* (London, 1963), pp. 79–98.
[4] The literature is surveyed in Thomas, *op. cit.*, pp. 82–8.
[5] *The Linnen-Drapers Answer to that Part of Mr. Cary his Essay on Trade that Concerns the East-India Trade* (1697), p. 1 (BM: 816 m. 13).

suggested that it might be harmful to the commonwealth, but simply a matter of indifference. Such claims for private profit did not always absolutely exclude the state from all concern in trade. The writers noted, with more sophistication than some later exponents of *laissez-faire*, that trade might have to be actively protected against attempts to restrain it. This is the explanation of their remark, when discussing how the interest of England might be provided for, that

'. . . we conclude from daily experience that it can be done by no law so effectively, as by leaving trade free and sheltering it against all prohibitions.'[1]

The rhetoric of individualism was also current in broadside attacks against the trading companies. Private traders opposing monopoly in a page or two lacked the opportunity to express their theoretical presuppositions. However, they followed the main lines of the first great wave of anti-monopoly literature fifty years before. The most common claim for an open trade was that it would increase the volume of trade in that

'. . . ingenuity and virtuous industry will be encouraged and new places of trade discovered.'[2]

The writers made much of the virtues of emulation and of the diffusion of benefit that would result.[3]

It would be tedious to delve further into this sort of literature. The essential point is that the linen-drapers and others had brought individualism into the market-place, where it passed as the ordinary coin of debate. Such ideas were not limited to the lucubrations of essayists; they had an important role in public affairs. The publications noted here did not constitute important literary events. They were quite a good index, though, of the sort of argument that might reasonably be expected to convince members of the public whose own interests were not immediately involved. Thus the claim by Viner

[1] *Ibid.*, p. 3.
[2] *Reasons Humbly Offered Against Establishing by Act of Parliament the East India Trade in a Company with a Joint Stock* (*c.* 1711) p. 3.
[3] For two examples illustrative of such literature see *Reasons Against Establishing an Africa Company at London* (*c.* 1711), p. 2 (BM: 816 m. 11), and *A Letter to an Member of Parliament Concerning the Africa Trade* (*c.* 1711), p. 3 (BM: 8223 e. 4).

that free-trade sentiments were obscure and not even deemed worthy of refutation in their own day seems odd. It all depends, of course, on what one means by free trade. But by the end of the century writers used it in its modern sense of trade unrestrained by prohibitions or high duties, and it was an expression much in use. Opponents of Child and Davenant had no possible motive for magnifying the incidence of opinions that they abhorred, yet several of them lamented the 'present vogue of free trade'.[1]

While not all notions about foreign trade are helpful in discussing the public good, most of the arguments about trade may be reduced to claims that a certain policy was in the national interest. This is not just an abstract category imposed upon the technicalities of economic discourse; few writers on trade neglected to introduce the concept at some stage in the argument. The free-trade argument that bears the most immediate relevance to the public interest was the one in terms of profit to a part redounding to the whole. Tudor moralists would generally have considered such an idea just impertinent, not a serious moral claim. Their community was more a unity than a collectivity. Nevertheless, many writers in the seventeenth century offered this idea quite seriously. It was nothing but the obverse of the traditional teaching that benefit to the whole must enrich every part. Now, no one had to wait for Pareto to tell him that the ancient doctrine was psychologically unsatisfactory and often plainly incorrect, since the diffused, long-term general benefit might well be outweighed by an immediate, concrete and obvious personal benefit. The public good was insubstantial and wraith-like compared to a personally sensed individual good. On purely objective grounds, the individual might stand to gain more from pursuing his own interests, especially if other people were sufficiently patriotic to maintain the commonwealth strong. However, it is difficult to discover any individualist who advocated letting community institutions decay, while each man enriched himself. *'Sauve qui peut'* might be a fair

---

[1] Anon., *The Interest of England Considered in an Essay Upon Wooll* (1694), sig. A 4 (B: Art. 8° T 118). See too Anon., *A Discourse of the Duties on Merchandize* (1695), p. 21 (BM: 1471 h. 4); H. Pollexfen, 'England and East India', *op. cit.*, p. 46; and Francis Brewster, *Essays on Trade and Navigation* (1695), p. 29.

description of actual behaviour; short of a few nineteenth-century anarchists like Stirner, it was not the material from which social theory was made. Nor would it serve any better in winning arguments in public life. Thus all the individualists claimed that men might, in varying degrees, pursue their profit, while the commonwealth also prospered. Some chose to show how the total wealth and power of the nation would be augmented if private men were left to their own devices. This might be the view of men who were quite illiberal in some respects, since they defended monopolies. Others, including some of the enemies of monopoly, transcended this position. Self-interest not only produced the public good, however defined; the substance of that good was the greatest possible satisfaction of particular interests. We have already seen how the first argument easily led to the second.

One might also ask how the conventional mercantilist defined the public good. Commentators have long been in disagreement about the aims of the system and probably they always will be. In fact, trying to suggest any one end for these policies is a fool's errand. Obviously there were different aspects of national good relevant to different areas of life and the good might be described at a number of levels of generality. From the early days of crude misconceptions about the prevalence of a Midas fallacy, scholars have been unsure of what were ends for the mercantilists and what just means. The most common misconception here was that the mercantilists subordinated every other consideration to the pursuit of national power. This could certainly have provided a fairly objective index of the public good and in sixteenth-century England it was indeed common to justify a favourable trade balance by the need for a reserve of bullion to sustain foreign wars.[1] While the idea may have remained powerful on the Continent, in seventeenth-century England few apart from Mun may be said to have come close to it. Even scholars such as Heckscher, who accept this fact, have adhered to the myth of the power mania at the centre of mercantilist thought.[2]

[1] See W. D. Grampp, 'The Liberal Elements in English Mercantilism', *Quarterly Journal of Economics*, Vol. LXVI, No. 4 (1952), pp. 465–501, at p. 474.
[2] Heckscher, *op. cit.*, Vol. II, p. 212. Chapter I and Addendum I contain some qualification of the position taken in the 1935 edition. Heckscher has at

In support of the contention that welfare was important only as a basis for power, Heckscher quotes various writers in the Hobbesian tradition of the 'public ego'. However, the examples of Filmer and John Hall, defenders of the ruler's self-interest, who were also economic liberals, should make us wary of reading economic policies into such dicta.

Without doubt, some people introduced considerations of national power as a rein to private ambitions. Power might at times be preferable to wealth as the content of the public interest, because in the former case, it might be more difficult for the interest of a few private persons to masquerade as a genuine public good. An appeal to national honour sounds more plausible than one to national wealth, no matter how distributed. However, the evidence just does not sustain the opinion that power was usually, or even frequently, the prime concern in trade. To be sure, the opinion that trade was the interest of England linked the subject to reason of state. One of Heckscher's examples is a letter written in reply to a book by Slingsby Bethel, the best-known Restoration writer on the interest of England.[1] He might better have quoted Bethel himself, who came as close as anyone to treating trade as an adjunct to power.[2] One effective answer to Heckscher has been that, far from being alternatives, power and plenty were the essential conditions of each other.[3]

least been aware that English mercantilist thought differed in some respects from that of Europe. By contrast Edmund Silberner associates all mercantilists equally with the opinion that economic activity was directed towards national power and independence rather than welfare. See *La Guerre dans la Pensée Economique du XVIe au XVIIIe Siècle* (Paris, 1939), p. 111 and *passim*. Silberner's own study of mercantilism and war mentions many English writers who opposed the policy of power and expansion. Englishmen wrote 'Saint George for England', but no known equivalent of *Osterreich über Alles*.
[1] Heckscher, Vol. II, p. 29.
[2] Bethel, *The Present Interest of England Stated* (1671), p. 2.
[3] See J. Viner, 'Power and Plenty as Objectives of Foreign Policy in the Seventeenth and Eighteenth Centuries', *World Politics*, Vol. I (1948), pp. 1–29. Of course, relatively few tracts were aimed at clarifying the ends of trade, but those that were seem to support Viner's position. One such work only introduced considerations of national strength and honour after the writer had insisted that as many Englishmen as possible might share in the wealth of the nation. See *A Discourse of the Nature, Use and Advantages of Trade* (1694), pp. 8 and 30 (BM: 1139 g. 19). John Evelyn had a different perspective. He

This qualifying of the 'power' interpretation has important implications for a study of the public interest. Those who accepted the old theory used it as a means of explaining the subordination of private interests to the public. The mercantilist becomes a cold, ascetic nation-builder possessed by the odd opinion that one could enrich the nation without enriching its inhabitants.[1] Little wonder, then, that one such author has said that, for the mercantilist,

'. . . national aims are apart from, and superior to, individual self-interest.'[2]

One author was so influenced by the idea of mercantilism as the theory of a garrison state that he actually drew cautious parallels between its doctrine and that of the totalitarian dictatorships of the twentieth century.[3] This must surely be based on the assumption that a hard idealism of sacrificing personal interests to an abstraction prevailed in the seventeenth century. Occasional suggestions of it appear in efforts to justify special privileges for merchants, but after the middle of the century it was definitely rare.[4] Monopolists undoubtedly used such arguments when it suited them, just as they adopted the most extreme individualism when it served their turn. This is not sufficient reason to transform a monopolist's opportunism into

emphasized trade's contribution to peace and its civilizing influence, while relegating power to a secondary position. See 'Navigation and Commerce, Their Original and Progress', in *Miscellaneous Writings*, ed. W. Upcott (London, 1825), pp. 625–86. Davenant once remarked on how difficult it was to say what the riches of a people were. See *Works, op. cit.*, Vol. I, p. 381. Barbon repeated the conventional wisdom about trade providing the 'magazine of war'. This was incidental, though, to his plea against a policy of foreign conquest. He saw 'peace' and 'plenty' as the benefits that normally followed from trade. See N. B. M. D., *A Discourse of Trade* (1690), pp. 34–61.
[1] See Heckscher, *op. cit.*, Vol. II, p. 166, and E. S. Furniss, *The Position of the Labourer in a System of Nationalism* (New York, 1920), p. 8.
[2] Furniss, p. 7.
[3] See P. W. Buck, *The Politics of Mercantilism* (New York, 1942), p. 185 *et seq.*
[4] Thus Samuel Fortrey's defence of monopolies included the harsh sentiment that 'the prejudice that may happen by them to the workmen or home-chapmen, is fully recompensed by the clear profit they return to the public; of which they are members as well as others'. See 'England's Interest and Improvement' (1673), in J. R. McCulloch (ed.), *Early English Tracts on Commerce* (Cambridge, 1952), p. 245. One similar statement may also be gleaned from Child. See Heckscher, *op. cit.*, Vol. II, p. 29.

the ethos of the century. An anonymous writer, whose economic views seem at least as conventional as Child's, attacked his East India monopoly as well as his alleged sympathy for free trade. At the same time he criticized Child's reliance upon calculating the nation's profit or loss from trade on an arithmetical basis, adding:

'. . . the true balance of trade . . . I understand to be in the first place to make trade equal to all their majesties subjects in their stations, that some by private ingrossing . . . may not oppress others.'[1]

The main doctrine of this tract appears to be the quintessence of mercantilist distrust for self-seeking, yet the author refused to contemplate either national power or wealth as the standard of public good, but looked to the extent to which riches were dispersed among the people. Why may not this equally well be seen as the authentic voice of mercantilism?[2]

A modern author, adhering to the conventional interpretation of mercantilism, has observed that writers believed in a 'harmony of interests' whereby the various professions and classes all shared in the nation's wealth and power. According to him, it was taken for granted that a happy dispensation made the strength of the state coincide with the welfare of the citizens.[3] This theory of harmony certainly existed, and in some cases it took this form. However, a great many works assumed another sort of harmony, not primarily between the state and private welfare but between the various particular interests in the state. Perfectly orthodox men with a horror of economic liberalism took account of private interests to a much greater extent than has been realized. They did not first calculate the best way of strengthening the nation and then force all particular interests into the pattern. In many cases they deemed it impossible to know where the national benefit lay unless the profit of the chief interests were first assured.

Since Child sometimes stressed strategic considerations, it

---

[1] *Interest of England Considered . . . upon Wooll* (1694), p. 97.
[2] According to one militant eighteenth-century imperialist, the mistaken habit of reckoning national gain by wealth rather than by territorial expanion dated from the time of Petty! See Anon., *Reflections on the Domestic Policy Proper to be Observed on the Conclusion of a Peace* (1763), p. 75 (BM: E 2054).
[3] Buck, *op. cit.*, pp. 87 and 107.

257

might be best to start with him. On certain important issues he gave great attention to the welfare of the various interests in England. In answering the question as to how one knew how a trade was 'nationally profitable', he listed all of the professions which were certain to gain from a heavy volume of trade.[1] In admitting the necessity of sacrificing the interests of one segment of the people, he argued that they

'. . . are not one to twenty of the whole people; and its the wisdom of the law-makers to provide for the good of the majority of people, though a minor part should a little suffer.'[2]

It is understandable that if a merchant were writing about a trade such as the importation of Baltic timber for the fleet, he might use other criteria of benefit. Both indicators of the national good were equally valid in their respective contexts.

Child was being quite orthodox when he tried to calculate what proportion of the people would benefit from some policy. Thomas Papillon, a much more conservative East India trader, treated the question of importing Irish cattle in this way. In reaching a decision, Parliament must not be guided 'by any particular interest, but to mind the general concern of the Kingdom'. He justified free importation because it was in the interests of nine-tenths of the people, and nothing that benefited such a proportion could be a common nuisance, but had to be a common good.[3]

Surely there can be no better example of this sort of argument than its appearance in a controversy about the exportation of unwrought wool. The participants were William Carter and an anonymous advocate of the unpopular practice of wool export. The exporter claimed to speak for the landed interest, and, of course, for the public interest as well. His emphasis was most interesting in its reversal of a traditional form of reasoning. It was common for the defenders of any group to claim that it was not only patriotic, but also bound to the public by its interests. He said:

[1] *Discourse About Trade*, pp. 150–1.
[2] *Ibid.*, sig. Cᵛ.
[3] A. F. W. Papillon, *Memoirs of Thomas Papillon* (Reading, 1887), p. 144. For a similar approach see 'The East India Trade and Manufactures Beneficiall to England Proved', Bodleian MSS: Rawl. A 400. fol. 16.

'. . . it is the greatest concern and interest of the nation, to preserve the nobility, gentry and those to whom the land of the country belongs, at least much greater than a few artificers . . .'[1]

As far as he was concerned, the landed interest was the national interest, for out of the ground which was theirs all national profit arose. The landed man also bore the brunt of taxes and of public employments. Still, he did his best to minimize the degree of conflict, asserting, for a variety of specious reasons, that the poor would benefit from the export, as would the manufacturers. The only people who might perhaps be prejudiced by a change were a few unproductive middlemen, the 'caterpillars of trade'.[2]

In a rebuttal, completely at variance on policy, Carter used the same sort of argument. He claimed, incorrectly, that his opponent had assumed that

'. . . the interests of the merchant, mariner and artificer, were not only opposite to, but wholly inconsistent with the interest of the nobility, gentry and farmers.'[3]

Carter's advice to the landed men was that if they really wished well to the nation, they should do all in their power to uphold shipping, the national life-line. This involved upholding the merchant. Then he proceeded to duplicate the opposition case with the priorities reversed. In his opinion, the moneyed interest was the national one. Nevertheless, he strove to dissolve apparently irreconcilable interests by a piece of logical legerdemain.

The landed interests were bound by economic ties to the fortunes of trade. By taking the immediate interest of the traders and the long-term interest of the landed men, he tried to show that the necessary harmony already existed. Of course rents were related to the state of trade, but it was ludicrous to expect the landed interest to sacrifice its current profit in prospect of that gain that might fall from the merchant's table. Having perpetrated this offence against logic, he plunged into a second

---

[1] Anon., *Reasons for a Limited Exportation of Wooll* (1677), p. 5 (BM: 712 g. 16).
[2] Anon., *Reasons for a Limited Exportation of Wooll* (1677), p. 17.
[3] 'The Reply of W.C.', in A Summary of Certain Papers, *op. cit.*, p. 9.

attempt. This time he tried to deduce the harmony of interests from a complicated system of interlocking interests. He began with the components of the landed interest. The interests of the nobility and gentry were identical with that of the farmer. In the opposite camp the mariner and manufacturer had interests similar to that of the poor worker. This is more difficult to swallow, but he argued that all of them gained when trade and industry flourished. The farmers, on one side, and the worker and manufacturer, on the other, were deemed mutually useful. Since he had already indicated that both great interests were homogeneous, it followed that a community of interests might be uncovered. The farmer stood as a bridge between the camps, a common term. If the commercial interests were serviceable to the farmer, they were also serviceable to the other parts of the landed interest.[1] Harmony reigned. While he did not say so explicitly, he tacitly assumed the worse-than-dubious formula that interests convergent with the same interest were convergent with each other. Since Carter was a great believer in the maxim that interest would not lie, he also expected the various interests to appreciate his theorem. Since interests are not the same sort of entities as are dealt with in geometry, it is not surprising that his deduction was unconvincing.

Such deficiencies were not very important. The vital point is that a very explicit examination of the competing claims of the two great economic interests should take this form. Neither combatant felt able to begin discussion from any set of policies deemed in the national interest. Both started from the general interests of the group deemed central to the economy and then tried to demonstrate that all other interests were linked to it. This approach was inherent in the sort of problem being treated and was independent of one's preconceptions about the proper scope of individual initiative. Carter adopted the same tactics as his more liberal opponent. In both cases, defining the public interest became a matter of discovering that point where all the relevant interests converged. Naturally, each in his own way managed to build an economic bias into the picture. This was not the same thing as saying that a free rein to all interests would promote optimum results. However, for purposes of describing the public interest, what they did say was even more

[1] *Reply* . . ., pp. 10–11.

important. On both sides the debate was constructed from false premises badly combined. But a national interest qualitatively different from the particular interests had no part in it.

Even Roger Coke, a writer with very little appreciation of the human element in economics, wrote in this way. For all his free-trade views, he often assumed a most forbidding aspect in treating employment as a fillip to trade, as if men traded for some purpose other than making a living. He also subscribed to the uncharitable opinion that the great merit of full employment was that it prevented the poor becoming a charge on the rates. Still, he clearly relegated national strength to a secondary position when he said, with no hint of criticism, 'after men's interest, they consult their security'.[1] He also justified certain policies by their favourable effect on all of the interests in the nation.[2]

If any mercantilist had visualized individual interests swallowed by the national interest, it should have been John Cary of Bristol. He was a man of quite exceptional public spirit, an inflexible enemy of uncontrolled private interest and a widely respected figure.[3] He serves as a promising subject because he made a good deal of the need of strengthening sea power. However, when confronted with the great controversy over the East India trade, he revealed surprising new resources. Instead of elevating a remote national interest over all partial ones, he analysed the particular components of the nation's interest. He opposed free trade upon the Dutch pattern because it leaned too far towards the merchant's interest. This was a suitable policy for Holland, he said, because

---

[1] Coke, England's Improvement, *op. cit.*, p. 18.
[2] *Ibid.*, pp. 26–7.
[3] Locke was among his admirers. See Thomas, *op. cit.*, p. 69. Cary seems to have been fond of lecturing his acquaintances on the need of protecting the public good from private interests. See his friendly admonitions to the arch-Tory Edmund Bohun on the score of the latter's liberal views on trade in *Diary and Autobiography of Edmund Bohun* (Beccles, 1853), pp. 131–6. These letters show that Cary, the traditionalist in respect to economic morality, was more favourable to popular government than was Bohun. The possibility of a connection between Tory principles and free trade is suggested by W. J. Ashley. See 'The Tory Origins of Free Trade Policy', in *Surveys Historic and Economic* (London, 1900), pp. 268–303. It seems that Davenant, North, Child and Barbon were all Tories.

'. . . the interest of Holland in trade is but one single interest; they live by buying and selling. . . . In England, we have two interests, that of the freeholder and that of the trader, and these are in themselves of different natures.'[1]

He further explained that, while different, these interests were not antithetical. Indeed, they had to be reconciled, and in the normal course of events they were. The government's job was 'uniting these two interests', thus making them serviceable to each other.[2]

When Buck wrote that under mercantilism the dominance of the national interest reconciled all conflicts, he may have been thinking of such passages, but his interpretation is all wrong. There is a sense in which the national interest did this in all social theories, for, at the risk of being repetitious, it must be said that no social thinker has ever said that the public interest was indistinguishable from all of the personal interests of all citizens. However, he has neglected to point out that before one appealed to patriotism, it was often first necessary to say what was good for the community. Here the particular interests of major groups were always relevant and often they were all that was relevant.

A good deal of the mystery about the mercantilist's common good is dissolved if one fact is kept in mind. A great many writers assumed that there was an enduring harmony between the main economic interests. If the merchants and the landlords differed on a particular policy they were advised to remember that in general their fortunes waxed and waned together. Some few statements suggest permanent sources of tension, as when a crusader against usury wrote that

'. . . land and money are ever in balance one against the other, and when money is dear, land is cheap, and where land is cheap money is dear.'[3]

---

[1] John Cary, A Reply to . . . the Linen Drapers Answer . . . (1697), p. 3 (BM: 816 m. 13).

[2] Cary, A Reply, p. 3. See too Anon., The Interest of the Nation as it Respects all the Sugar-Plantations Abroad and Refining of Sugar (1691) (BM: T 361 d. 4). Here the writer discovered the 'interest of the nation in all its parts' by describing the 'union of interests' behind his own policy (pp. 4 and 7).

[3] Quoted by R. H. Tawney in the introduction to Thomas Wilson, A Discourse Upon Usury (London, 1925), p. 42.

Even here, if one took the perspective of the trader, and not the money-lender, the main interests were again the same, for traders needed that cheap credit that also raised rents. William Petyt spoke for most public men when he referred to the

'. . . concatenation and sympathy between the interest of land and trade, and between these and that of the government.'[1]

Here was a harmony of interests embracing the main social units and cohering as well with the demands of national policy. Perhaps this theme was more frequently used by writers favourable to the landed interest or at least those who were eager to maintain regulations on trade. There appears to have been a feeling in these quarters of being the more vulnerable of the two partners, having always to restrain the exuberant independence of the merchant. However, writers of all persuasions recorded their thoughts on the harmony between land and trade.[2]

Obviously the division of the commonwealth into these two interests was a gross simplification. It is impossible to argue that the labourer was given equal consideration in his role as one sub-division of one of these interests. The poor were exploited, it is true, but this must be carefully distinguished from theoretical defences of the system. Everyone wanted to see the poor employed, and there is good reason to believe that not all mercantilists were as coldly oblivious to their needs as human beings, as is sometimes claimed.[3] After all, if a general complacency about low wages is to figure in the indictment, this provided no distinction between the era of mercantilism and that of *laissez-faire*. All those tracts that listed as a benefit of some policy that it put the poor to work need not have been limited in intent to removing burdens from the community. It would be reasonable to assume that the poor generally desired work, especially in view of the alternative.

A modern scholar has observed of the economic doctrine of this period that seventeenth-century writers were superficial owing to a failure to realize that the contrary interests of various

[1] William Petyt, 'Britannia Languens' (1680), in McCulloch, *op. cit.*, p. 277.
[2] See [Pollexfen], *A Discourse of Trade and Coyn* . . . (1697), pp. 2 and 59; Davenant, *Works*, Vol. II, p. 81; Carew Reynel, *The True English Interest* (1674), sig. a.; and J. Puckle, 'England's Path', *op. cit.*, p. 30.
[3] See Charles Wilson, 'The Other Face of Mercantilism', *Transactions of the Royal Historical Society*, 5th ser., Vol. 9 (1959), pp. 81–101, at p. 97.

classes made it difficult to speak of the national welfare or interest.[1] The charge has substance, but is not entirely just. For one thing, there was a perfectly comprehensible understanding of the national interest in old-fashioned thinkers who adhered to Tudor social morality and in those who wrote of trade in terms of reason of state. The sources quoted by Schlatter to document his remark are scholars belonging to the discredited 'power' interpretation of mercantilism,[2] so it becomes relevant to consider this approach in so far as it appeared in the seventeenth century. It was quite easy for some such people to refer to the national interest, since they were concerned with defending the national territory or protecting and augmenting the king's revenue and not with maximizing private utilities.

However, it has already been established that such writers were few and that most did set themselves the task of promoting the main particular interests. Their analysis was not entirely adequate, but one cannot properly accuse them of assuming *a priori* that all interests were identical. They frequently spelled it out in economic terms. Of course they did not identify classes as the significant units and the omission of economic classes in the modern form may, in some measure, be excused.[3] Some tried to relate issues to the interests of the king, nobility or clergy, but the nature of their concerns led them to write more often of shipwrights, rope-makers, graziers or drapers.

If this view of the national interest suffered from some defects, they were peculiarly modern ones. They were the same defects that were present in the public interest found by Heckscher in the theorists of *laissez-faire*. This he described as 'the sum of the interests of all individuals'.[4] Applied to early thought, it is misleading, failing to explain those factors that make the idea intel-

---

[1] See R. B. Schlatter, *The Social Ideas of Religious Leaders 1660–1688* (Oxford, 1940), p. 81. Schlatter considers the attempt to unite self-interest and public good a 'vicious philosophy' (p. 129). For a further comment by this scholar see *Private Property* (New Brunswick, N.J., 1951), p. 171.

[2] He quotes Heckscher and Furniss.

[3] Werner Stark's insistence that doctrines be construed in their social context is relevant here. For his justification of the mercantilist's tendency to overlook class conflict see *The History of Economics in its Relation to Social Development* (London, 1945), p. 25. For another perspective on this problem see Peter Laslett, *The World We Have Lost* (London, 1965), Chapter 2.

[4] Heckscher, *op. cit.*, Vol. II, p. 328.

ligible. The sum did not include all interests of all individuals, just those relating to the use of property. All individuals could not even gain equal satisfaction for their economic interests, for people wanted different things. But few writers made an attempt to consider individuals in isolation. Whatever was true of a later era, early mercantilists, and many individualists, shared an appreciation of the social role of groups. They grouped interests into large categories and assumed that the individual member of the group subscribed to its interest. While unsatisfactory, it was an improvement over using the commonwealth as a single irreducible unit. Thus understood, the definition becomes less bizarre.

As men came increasingly to view 'plenty' as the substance of the public good, it was tempting to describe this good as an aggregate. Naturally there were obstacles to adding interests as if they were only sums of money. Those who merely recounted how instances of self-seeking augmented total national wealth did not generally think of an aggregate of interests. The others, who insisted that the common weal was best served by maximizing welfare, could more readily visualize a collection of particular interests.

When Heckscher described the national interest in liberal theory, he exaggerated the difference between mercantilism and liberalism. A perceptive scholar has observed that both schools were equally concerned with realizing the public good, while contemplating different ways of attaining or preserving it.[1] He might have added that for both the content of the concept might be the same. The claims of national power were rarely ignored entirely by any school of thought; but often it was more relevant to consult particular interests.

[1] Grampp, *op. cit.*, p. 468.

VI
PHILOSOPHY, POLITICS AND
THE PUBLIC INTEREST,
1660–1720

THE NEW SOPHISTICATION—WILLAN, CUMBERLAND,
LOCKE

THE DYNAMIC QUALITY in most discussions of the public interest derived from the relevance of this concept to the most important public controversies of the century. Few writers paused in their pursuit of certain concrete policies to ponder the nature of a public interest; the great majority implicitly assumed a certain relation between private interests and the public, and at most devoted a few sentences to demolishing any perspective inconsistent with their own. Prior to the Restoration there had been few works of a reflective nature that had anything of importance to say about the subject. Most clergymen with any literary pretensions and many laymen seem to have published at least one slim volume of moral and divine meditations, which often included the warning that one must seek the common good in which one's own was included. White and Hall had gone further, to examine the concept rather more carefully within a political context. But they were almost unique.

They would not have been unique had they written after 1660. Philosophical consideration of the public interest became very fashionable at this time. The reason is not far to seek. The new emphasis on interest as the governing force in human affairs necessitated a more sophisticated treatment of one's duty to the public. Perhaps the message remained the same in many cases. Men were still expected to have some regard for the good of the community, and unvarnished egoism as a social philosophy had virtually no defenders. The Restoration was the great age of Epicureanism in England; and this ranged from the refined appreciation of Abraham Cowley to the crude self-indulgence of the Earl of Rochester.[1] This particular theme, however, suggested no social philosophy at all, being basically concerned with the private pleasures available to those who withdrew from public life.

More revealing than Epicurean doctrine itself was the response that it provoked from moralists of the day. Edward Stillingfleet dismissed the Philosophy of the Garden, not because of its ingrained self-regard but because it attempted to inculcate virtue independently of divine sanctions. As far as he was concerned, there could be no obligation to a supreme being who took no interest in mundane affairs, for the vital prick of divine rewards and punishments would be absent. Surely, he exclaimed,

". . . that philosopher could not be ignorant, that it is not worth, but power, not speculation but interest that rules the world.'[2]

For all their apparent scorn for Hobbes, the men of the Restoration had fully absorbed his teaching on human nature. Sometimes he was called an Epicurean, presumably because of his alleged atheism and his emphasis upon self-interest. Actually the Epicurean ideal of a purely secular virtue, followed for its own sake, would have made as little sense to Hobbes as it did to Stillingfleet. Increasingly, respectable men joined Hobbes in asserting that intelligent self-interest was an adequate guide to the citizen and to the Christian.

Not everyone embraced the idea of 'interest' with the same enthusiasm, or even the tolerance, of Stillingfleet. There were dissenters, but they too were aware that traditional dicta regarding social duties had been undermined. Robert South seems to have demanded old-fashioned self-sacrifice as the essence of his moral teaching. His defence of it shows something more than the normal belief of the self-righteous that they are a small and

[1] The subject is treated in T. Mayo, *Epicurus in England* (Dallas, 1934).
[2] Stillingfleet, *Origines Sacrae . . .* (1662), p. 471.

dwindling band. In one of his sermons he reviewed the various kinds of social 'policy' constituting the 'wisdom of the world'. He passed briefly over common dishonesty and irreligion, ancient and familiar complaints. He was more concerned about the emergence of a new sort of man, one who said quite frankly that the

'. . . general interest of the nation is nothing to him, but only that portion of it, that he either does, or would possess.'[1]

Here was the man who saw himself enriched not by the common but by the enclosure, who would rejoice at the wrecking of the ship of state, could he but salvage the debris.[2] What shocked South so much was not the currency of such attitudes as reflected in practice but the candid way in which they were now admitted:

'. . . for though there have not been wanting such heretofore, as have practised these unworthy acts (for as much as there have been villains in all places and all ages) yet now adayes they are owned above board; and whereas men formerly had them in design, amongst us they are openly vouched and argued, and asserted in common discourse.'[3]

This underlines the fact that to at least one perceptive thinker the problem of the public interest had ceased to be the old one founded upon human imperfection. Men no longer just fell short of acknowledged standards of behaviour; now they challenged the very standards themselves. They did not attack traditional doctrine in quite the manner claimed by South. His remarks seem to have been directed largely at Hobbes and, typically, exaggerated the anti-social elements in the Malmesbury philosophy.

There were various ways of weakening the tyranny of the common good over private interests. Some writers treated the issue within a specifically political context, building upon the tradition of the Commonwealth democrats. Others, sometimes of a more conservative cast, amplified the insights of the Commonwealth writers in an apolitical context. These were the

[1] Sermon preached in Westminster Abbey on 30 April 1676 in *Twelve Sermons Preached upon Several Occasions*, Vol. II (1692), p. 440.
[2] *Ibid.*, p. 414.   [3] *Ibid.*, p. 442.

moral philosophers, who doubled as theologians. One very curious character fits into neither category. While most other things about him remain obscure, it is safe to say that Leonard Willan was *sui generis*.

Were he remembered at all, and apparently he is not, it would be as the author of some rather mediocre pastoral plays. He will never be numbered among the giants of political thought. The fact remains that he had something important to say, though he was clearly the wrong instrument for saying it. On the face of it, the task that Willan had set himself seems rather old-fashioned. He set out to describe the requisite qualities of the statesman, that combination of politician and functionary who controlled most of the business of monarchies before elected legislatures played much of a part. In many ways his efforts find a parallel in French books of the first half of the century. Béthune and Silhon serve as archetypes here.[1] The impression is only heightened in that he discussed political life in terms of the content of official policy rather than of the machinery by which policy was to be formed. The most vital questions of the century, those dealing with the relative power of king and people and the disposition of the various parts of the constitution, seem to have had no interest for him.

For all this, he was not entirely like a cameralistic expert advising the ruler of some petty German principality. From somewhere Willan had gained certain important ideas about the conditions necessary for the health of a political system. Like most political cook-books of the day, his lacked organization, and in starting from the qualifications of the councillor, he was unavoidably some time in arriving at his prescription for the whole polity. His remarks on this theme are instructive. What he sought was nothing less than a 'perfect harmony in the civil frame'.[2] The means of securing it was best expressed in his statement that the dignity and credit of the civil power must be secured 'by the mutual interest of her parts'.[3]

[1] See P. de Béthune, *The Counsellor of Estate*, trans. E. Grimston (1634), and J. de Silhon, *The Minister of State*, trans. H. Herbert, Part I (1658), Part II (1663).
[2] L. Willan, *The Exact Politician* . . . (1670), p. 128. The first edition, published in 1668, was called *The Perfect Statesman*. The later edition has been used because it was more accessible.
[3] *Ibid.*, p. 170.

There was not any clear structure in his ramblings, but there was one idea that recurred again and again in different contexts. His prime insight, from his point of view, and certainly from ours, was that any totality, such as a community, was reducible into constituent parts, in this case individuals and their interests. He experienced some difficulty in putting his case into words, though not, one thinks, as much difficulty as his readers must have had. The prime difficulty rests on the nature of his intentions. He quoted no sources and so could not be seen as arguing with anyone. He addressed himself to no burning issue. He simply chose his own ground, and so his arguments have no context other than that provided by him. One cannot say whether he chiefly saw himself as a spokesman for the state, insisting upon its welfare, or as a champion of individual rights. Most previous writers since the outbreak of the war had taken one side or the other and the distinction was to become more pronounced after the Restoration. It is curiously appropriate for a writer with no obvious party ties that he should seem equally to embrace both causes.

Sometimes one gains the impression that he was writing as the cold administrator advising a certain indulgence to private interests for the good of the state. But when dealing with the state, he consistently analysed it into its individual components. Nothing could more vividly depict the sort of quandary implicit in his subject. He described his efforts as aimed at

'. . . the peculiar welfare of those simple parts whose joint composure forms one common good.'[1]

At the same time he obviously felt that he had to justify his concern with individual welfare, suggesting that it might well seem 'an impropriety in civil use to take more care of us than we do of ourselves'. Such attention could only be justified on the grounds that 'the common good consisteth in the welfare of sundry parts'.[2]

Willan seems always to have been seeking some neat formula by which to capture the elusive ideas of part and whole, private and public. He never found it and had to be satisfied with repeating several key expressions. One of these was the dictum that

[1] Willan, p. 183.   [2] *Ibid.*, p. 172.

'. . . every part of the civil body should, in their several constitutions, hold the same analogy with the whole as the whole should with her parts.'[1]

Surely by this he was striving to suggest the mutual dependence of the two. Private ambition was restrained by the needs of the public, which was itself, from one point of view, no more than the title given to a mass of private ambitions. The interpretation seems all the more credible when the sentence was linked with another, to the effect that

'. . . what falleth under the distinction of our private usage is our property, what under the regulation of the public, hers. So that in the miscarriage of the meanest part, the damage is resented in the whole.'[2]

Private good benefited the public, private failure injured it. Neither observation was unfamiliar to readers of contemporary literature, but most writers favoured a different emphasis. It was normal to note that the parts prospered with the whole. If the parts really enjoyed the same relation with the whole that the whole enjoyed with the parts,[3] then more emphasis might be placed upon the good of the parts. The point that he was trying to make was a difficult one, if only because no one normally denied it except tacitly. What his case badly needed was some effective examples to show the practical effects of his perspective on individuals and the community.

Willan saw himself as a legal reformer and so his general position was reflected in proposed changes in the law. The connection between his concrete proposals and his principles was not always apparent, but in fairness to him, it should be added that he presented most of this material before he had explained the principles upon which his thought was based. Caring for the individuals of whom the state was composed could dictate several departures in policy. The prevailing laws of inheritance were an infringement upon the laws of nature which led all animals 'by secret and instinctive motives to the preservation of their kind.'[4]

---

[1] Willan, p. 172.   [2] *Ibid.*, p. 183.
[3] This was certainly what Willan was saying, although it may be argued that a whole and its parts are necessarily asymmetrical in their relations.
[4] *Ibid.*, p. 53.

In his opinion, primogeniture should be replaced by gavel-kind.

He was concerned with the whole basis of penal laws. They should be redrawn so that penalties might

'. . . hold a just proportion with the nature of the offence, in reference both to the public and the private interest.'[1]

Discussing the extra-legal rewards of virtue, he complained that the civil law provided insufficient incentives to obedience. This was probably owing to the fact that 'virtue in herself is held to be her own implicit recompense'.[2] He proposed that the legal system should be reconstituted to encourage men to 'pursue the public benefit included in their own'.[3] He did not say, be it noted, that they should be made to pursue the public benefit in which their own was included; the difference in construction represented an important difference in emphasis. The common problem of the law was that

'. . . virtue wants more material ornaments to plead for her reception.'[4]

Willan was much more concerned than most men of his time with procedural protection for the subject. In an age newly reconciled to the unpleasant aspects of state security, he even suggested that England might well emulate the supposed Roman practice of placing some private rights above considerations of reason of state. Thus he strongly approved of the solicitude shown by Roman courts for citizens accused of treason. Apparently the slaves of someone so accused were still legally obliged to assist him in every way.[5] Natural rights he considered as closely related to the public advantage.

His concern for private interests is only emphasized by his treatment of the statesman's responsibility. The vital point was

---

[1] Willan, p. 60.   [2] *Ibid.*, p. 107.   [3] *Ibid.*, p. 106.
[4] *Ibid.*, p. 114. The doctrine that material interests should be sacrificed to one's supposed spiritual interest had been rather overstated by clerics who defended the monarchy. After the Revolution, one clergyman complained that conscience and religion had been used to promote an unreasonable obedience to authority. This official rationale for absolutism neglected the fact that it was impossible for men to act contrary to their 'true interest, their natural principles of freedom and self-preservation'. Francis Carswell, *England's Restoration Parallel'd in Judah's* (1689), p. 13.
[5] Willan, pp. 21–2.

that he must not be in a position to consider himself in the execution of the laws. All such opportunities as could give 'some private motion to a public interest' were denied him.[1] In the new fashion, he thought that statesmen should be wealthy, since it was unreasonable to leave public affairs to those 'who had not a competent share of interests in the transaction'.[2] But this suggested no indulgence for his private interests. Indeed, Willan noted the apparent incongruity between his concern for the interests of private men and the rigorous dedication to public service expected from the rulers. He defended this difference in treatment, saying:

'. . . although the nature of our subject might properly be extended to public ministry; yet in respect the dignity of such a faculty can warrantably not pretend to the advantage of a private interest, whose regular improvement we pursue as a collateral to the public welfare, our present agitation only shall insist on such particulars as thereto have relation.'[3]

There must have been an easier way of making the point, but the careful reader can discern his meaning.

It is not necessary to infer all of Willan's attitudes towards the public good from his comments on related subjects. He specifically treated the matter, and in a most interesting way. Discussion of the statesman naturally led him to consider the general object of his office. In all systems, this was the public good. However, said Willan, this in itself was not very illuminating. All agreed that the public good was the aim of government,

'. . . but in what the nature of this good consisted; few have sufficiently enlarged upon, so consequently obscurely . . .'[4]

It would be interesting to know who the few were; Willan did not say.

He reduced the most frequent observations about the public good to three headings. Material for this generalization was drawn from discourses about imaginary commonwealths and from the practice of all 'essential states'. Prescriptive treatises, such as his own, fit into neither of these categories, but doubtless he meant to include them as well. Wherever one looked, the same alternatives presented themselves:

[1] Willan, p. 16.   [2] *Ibid.*, p. 15.   [3] *Ibid.*, p. 189.   [4] *Ibid.*, p. 46.

'. . . the means to attain the common good neither is, nor ever hath been really believed to have been raised on any other base than wealth, greatness or glory.'[1]

Therefore, he said, he would take each of these attributes separately and examine to what extent they contributed to a common good.

Riches within a state might be useful, of course, and to some extent they were necessary. To describe wealth as the means to the public good was unsatisfactory, however. It might be ill-distributed and contribute only to vice or sloth. The other two standard measures were very much alike and he made no great effort to distinguish between them. Both related to the strength of the state. Willan understood greatness to mean military or diplomatic successes that served to enlarge the national territory in a literal way. The danger here was that the vastness of a commonwealth might have no other effect than to produce an unhealthy disproportion. It is not entirely clear what sort of disproportion he was thinking about. Probably this was a reference to the then common notion that the great size of some of the eastern despotisms contributed to their despotic character, while small political units were more favourable to the establishment of popular government. Disproportion would then mean an incongruity between size and political institutions. Certainly size was no necessary means to the 'common welfare'.[2] He disposed of 'glory' in similar fashion.

All such means were defective through their failure to promote, first and foremost, the welfare of the individual citizens. No doubt wealth, greatness and glory might

'. . . consequent associates often be, but no essential materials to the composure of our civil structure.'[3]

Willan's own definition of the proper means to the public good was that it existed

'. . . where by an authentic, equal, known and insubvertible law, the lives and properties of the members of a civil government are timely and impenibly secured and improved both to the private and the public use.'[4]

Several things are worth noting here. When Willan's work

[1] Willan, p. 46.   [2] Ibid., p. 48.   [3] Ibid., p. 50.   [4] Ibid.

did not suffer from an infelicitous pedantry, it was imprecise. His reference to the members of a civil government was most misleading, for by this he undoubtedly meant the subjects, all of the citizens in the land, and not just the rulers. Another point is that Willan began by mentioning the 'nature' of the public good, but ended by discussing the means of attaining it. This was somewhat unfortunate for the structure of his argument because, in comparing different means to the public good, he introduced, as a criterion of judgment, that good itself. These references to the public good were in terms of 'the exact contexture of our edifice'[1] and 'the composure of our civil structure'.[2] These were not very enlightening expressions, suggesting nothing more than a general well-being on the part of everyone, and it would have been helpful had he said explicity that he saw the means to public good and the good itself as the same.

The two were naturally most difficult to separate for purposes of analysis and rarely did anyone try.[3] In political argument such a distinction was especially elusive since the public good was so often visualized as a continuing process of protecting private rights. In an economic context it was somewhat easier to isolate those actions of individuals that might contribute to the common good, which, as we have seen, still left open the question as to what the content of that good was. Thus, while the traditional dichotomy between a natural and an artificial harmony of interests may fail, owing to the difficulty of finding examples of the former, it remains true that the public interest assumed rather different forms in economic and political writings.[4] In choosing to analyse the public interest in a broad political context, Willan was then unlikely to make the desirable distinction and there is no need to give uncomplimentary form to the only attention he has ever had. He was breaking new ground in an area where the established conventions were already in flux. A writer as idiosyncratic as this one is not easily fitted into categories

---

[1] Willan, p. 46.   [2] *Ibid.*, p. 50.
[3] An unusually explicit attempt had appeared at outset of the Commonwealth. See Edward Gee, *A Vindication of the Oath of Allegiance in Answer to a Paper Dispersed by Mr. Samuel Eaton* (1650), p. 11.
[4] For other aspects of the contrast between political and economic interests see the literature cited in Hanna F. Pitkin, *The Concept of Representation* (Berkeley and Los Angeles, 1967), p. 199 n. 37.

made by other people. Willan thought that he was original, and, to a large extent, he was. He was not entirely novel in his outlook, but no other thinker up to that time seems to have contrasted the alternatives of private satisfaction and national strength in such a detailed and explicit way. Thomas White perhaps came closest to Willan's position, for he too was aware that his opinions on the subject were extremely unconventional. Willan seemed less comfortable in his heresy than that perpetual heretic White. He was concerned lest his emphasis upon private welfare might seem perverse. His critics would quote the maxim '*bonum communis eo melius*'. When this happened, he would answer that 'the mutual coherency of parts' resulting from his recommendations was of 'a far greater efficacy to the structure of a happy union'.[1] Time after time he returned to the theme that the health of the community had to depend upon the welfare of the individuals through whom it existed. Even when repeating the most banal of inducements to regard the common good, he returned to the theme:

'. . . the public welfare in general is but remisly pursued, nor the particular members thereof but faintly supported.'[2]

The parts had to be supported in order to achieve the ideal political structure, which he defined as an

'. . . agreement in the motion of the parts, whence issueth, as it were, a silent harmony.'[3]

Willan gave few clues as to the main influences behind his thought. He had acquired a good deal of the vocabulary of the Commonwealth republicans, speaking, like Harrington, of the regular motions of the body politic. He also called the polity a 'machine',[4] a metaphor more in keeping with his individualism than any organic analogies. One theme, normal in republican literature, was absent, for Willan was uninterested in the machinery for making policy, only in the policy itself. This meant that there was nothing democratic about this book. If he had any one source of inspiration it was more likely to have been one of the sophisticated champions of one-man government, such as White, Hall or Wren, than any republican.

The question as to where Willan's contribution led is easily

[1] Willan, p. 113.   [2] *Ibid.*, p. 107.   [3] *Ibid.*, p. 20.   [4] *Ibid.*, p. 10.

answered. In terms of any immediate influence the answer is, nowhere. His book, like his plays, seems to have lain unread. Even modern scholarly accounts of the Commonwealth and Restoration stage ignore him. One of the rare scholars who does mention Willan remarks upon his originality of mind and called the dedication to one of his plays 'turgidly unintelligible'.[1] That seems to cover the subject. Original ideas poorly expressed were not promising material for fame. *The Exact Politician* sank without a ripple, and now, in both its editions, is an extremely rare book. Perhaps it deserved no other fate. Still, if Willan were not an influence, he was certainly a symptom. In later years it would become increasingly difficult to claim originality for the opinion that the true common good lay in protecting particular interests. Support took various forms, and came sometimes from unexpected sources.

Restoration England saw a flowering of that theory of morality later called theological utilitarianism. The basic idea was nothing new, it consisted only in a sharpening of arguments that had always been used to promote social cohesion. From the age of Hobbes to that of Bishop Butler and beyond, ethical speculation was dominated by the nature and consequences of self-interest.[2] Thinkers redrew the cosmic harmony that a previous generation had found in Hooker and Grotius. This time they made almost no effort to coax men into an altruistic pattern belonging to the universe as a whole. They wrote directly of men's interests, secular and spiritual, and showed how they harmonized with that of society. As long as most people believed in some sort of heaven, much of the argument could be left to old-fashioned concern for one's soul. However, saying that self-love and social good were intertwined still left the question as to what was best for self and society an open one. This was unavoidable in moral theories framed to suit all occasions. But few thinkers were prepared to leave all harmonizing of interests to a heavenly sphere. Thus many were led to ask how self-interest and social good were joined in a purely secular context. This really involved asking what a public good was and how it was related to private interests.

[1] A. Harbage, *Cavalier Drama* (Oxford, 1936), p. 218.
[2] For contemporary testimony to this effect see W. A. Spooner, *Bishop Butler* (London, 1901), pp. 59–61.

The most important examination of this idea was by Richard Cumberland, ultimately Bishop of Peterborough. His major work appeared in Latin in 1672.[1] It is somewhat disorganized, characterized by a certain obscurity of purpose and a good deal of weak reasoning. It is also an invaluable indication of how a liberal understanding of the public interest grew in importance in English thought. His aim in this vast book was a dual one. He set out to describe a system of ethics in accord with the law of nature, and to refute the system constructed by Hobbes. Central to these tasks was the idea of a public good; for the chief law of nature was that

'. . . the fullest, most vigourous endeavour of each and all rational agents, in promoting the common good of the whole rational system, contributes effectively to the good of each single part in such a system.'[2]

Cumberland's whole argument turned upon this point. Because the good of private and public converged, he was quite uncritical about the means whereby the two should meet. Sometimes one finds in him echoes of those moralists who had endlessly pleaded with citizens to look to the ship of state, while neglecting their private cabins. That had been the ethic so conveniently suited to a king's view of the common interest, one conceived primarily in terms of national strength. Cumberland never managed to decide just how altruistic men could, or should, be. He recognized, though, that almost everyone would seek the common good with an *arrière-pensée*, saying:

'. . . we are endued and prompted to a studious concern for the common good; which prospect or expectation is not merely of itself the only, no, not even a principal motive with us; any farther than as such an hope or expectation conspires and joins with those rewards . . . which are in their own nature inseparably joined to such a hope or expectation.'[3]

Since he was so hostile to Hobbes, he had to demonstrate the presence of a degree of benevolence in human affairs, but his claims were quite modest. Ulterior motives abounded, but al-

---

[1] The edition used was *A Philosophical Enquiry into the Laws of Nature*, trans. J. Towers (Dublin, 1750).
[2] Cumberland, p. XXVI.   [3] *Ibid.*, p. LIV.

truism was not impossible.[1] Like Harrington, Cumberland mentioned the behaviour of beasts, but he was more guarded in his statement, saying only that all animals saw the connection between self-preservation and community-preservation. This led to actions that might be called benevolent, based on instinct, or whatever else one wished to call it.[2] Cumberland worried very little about isolating so-called 'benevolence' from all taint of calculation, just as he frankly admitted his ignorance about what determined animal behaviour. The vital thing for him was that, for one reason or another, men treated each other in a civilized fashion that was not entirely Hobbesian. As well as mentioning animals he appealed to the findings of Newtonian physics for evidences of a divine order. However, he never tried to leap, as had Hooker and Harrington, from the traces of order in the universe to a social harmony among human beings. Cumberland was not sure why men could be depended upon to advance the common good, but his various answers explored the problem much more thoroughly than had either of the last-mentioned writers.

The most general explanation of how the common good came to be realized was that it was providential. Cumberland's language sometimes suggested God's imprint on human nature, but his most explicit passage looked more at the providential direction of relations between men than to any quality innate in individuals. This was expressed in his statement that God and nature

'. . . occasion that we in some respect necessarily, whether we will or no, actually promote this general good. Nay, even at the very time we are gratifying our brutal appetites, and acting, even as much as we can against such a good.'[3]

Here was a new note; God not only encouraged altruism, but he also so arranged matters that those who neglected the common good, even those who were its declared enemies, had eventually to realize it, in the course of seeking their own good.

Cumberland was too good a philosopher to write continually of the public good without defining it. Actually, he defined it in various ways, all more or less compatible with each other. His

[1] Cumberland, pp. 187–8.   [2] Ibid., p. 198.
[3] Ibid., p. 171.

first attempt came in demonstrating how all labours for the public would benefit the individual agent. In that connection he wrote:

'. . . the whole concern about the common good carries no other meaning than the public worship of a deity, the security of public trade, a right discipline both in civil and family concerns, and the obligations or ties of friendship, as the several constituent parts of one universal whole in essential conjunction.'[1]

Of course, it was not enough to list these conditions; they had to be related to individual interests. In his words, it had to be established that

'. . . several advantages of mutual peace and social assistance, may be, and are, conferred . . . upon individuals.'[2]

Some of his demonstrations are rather odd. He defended the public worship of a deity, not in terms of the advantages of personal salvation but because of its quality,

'. . . by virtue of which public, religious sanction, all . . . are restrained and deterred from perjury.'[3]

Possibly he was thinking of the advantages to commerce of the sanctity which established religion gave to oaths.

His remarks on the benefits derived from preserving government made the now-familiar connection between government and property. The virtue of government was that it was the system under which 'the several distinctions of power and property are considered'.[4] The last comment suggests a view of the role of government faith fully reproduced in the rest of the book. Cumberland chose to emphasize the negative contributions of government, its beneficial restraint, rather than any services of a positive nature. Thus he phrased the chief functions of government and the limits placed on it in very much the same way. The first duty of all government was the protection of

'. . . the distinct, separate rights, privileges and properties of each and all.'[5]

The second reason for its existence was to allow for the improve-

[1] Cumberland, p. LIV.   [2] *Ibid.*, p. LV.   [3] *Ibid.*, p. LIV.
[4] *Ibid.*, p. LIV.   [5] *Ibid.*, p. 72.

ment of such properties for the good of all. While not saying specifically that these conditions were the common good, he said that

'. . . the right of establishing this distinct division or property can easily and only, be derived from the common good of the whole.'[1]

The first prohibition laid upon governors was that

. . . they don't confound and destroy the separate right of distinct dominion and property.'[2]

In the second place they were prohibited from abolishing any of those other laws of nature necessary for the common good.

Since Cumberland applied the notion of a common good in all spheres of experience, it is understandable that he recognized other aspects of the good, beyond the protection of property. It would have been helpful had Cumberland used a separate term, such as 'public interest', to cover the idea of a common good applied in a political context. As it was, he sometimes used the expression 'public good', which had fewer traditional moral associations than had the scholastic notion of a common good.[3] The reason why he did not separate ethical and political vocabulary is obvious. He reduced all common goods to those enjoyed by particular people. This served to fuse all kinds of good, political, moral or economic. All common goods, as we shall see, were put together in the same way, beginning with the realization by individuals of a personal good.

Cumberland described the relation between public and private good in two different ways. The first way was the more conventional:

'. . . the happiness of each single person, e.g. of Plato, of Socrates, and of each other individual respectively, cannot particularly, and specifically be distinguished and separated from the happiness of the whole. . . . For the efficient cause of each single happiness . . . necessarily

---

[1] Cumberland, p. 72.   [2] *Ibid.*, p. 551.

[3] A modern author suggests that the concept 'public good' is a broader one than public interest. See Brian Barry, *Political Argument* (London, 1965), pp. 202–3. The distinction was not recognized by people in Cumberland's time and it is even questionable whether modern usage conforms to it. A distinction helpful for Cumberland's approach may have been intended by Hume. See Silvana Castignone, *Giustizia E Bene Commune in David Hume* (Milan, 1964), pp. 87–8.

inheres in the whole, as the subject of the said general proposition: and which truth is established upon this maxim, "That the whole differs nothing from all its parts taken together".'[1]

This was perhaps not a very novel opinion; it all depended on the emphasis. He could have meant nothing more than that the particulars profited with the general, and that looking to the good of the community would, in some undefined way, realize the good of all particulars. However, he also claimed that the process might be reversed. Far from knowing private goods only as inferences from a public one, he said the opposite:

'. . . the several kinds of public good are no other than (but exactly the same with) the good of individuals: and, from the true happiness of every one man, there may, by an easy analogy, be deduced the happiness which is to be sought for and expected, as it either regards one particular society: or, even all mankind collectively taken and considered. For every particular civil polity or society (as being necessarily constituted, compounded and made up of individuals) is arrived at its fully complete happiness, when all single individual members of it, but more especially the governing parts or heads, enjoy minds endowed with the natural perfection of understanding and will: and sound, healthy bodies, vigourous and strong.'[2]

It seems unlikely that his qualification referred to any Hobbesian notions of kingship. More likely, he just recognized that the happiness being sought for individuals was unevenly distributed, especially since he saw the chief political good as the defence of property.

Cumberland showed the same concern, previously seen in Willan, for charges that his position on the public good was unorthodox. A common good built of individual goods might attract the criticism that it was 'postponed and made subordinate to the private happiness of each individual'.[3] This statement lay open to the same ambiguity already noted in the case of Harrington. It might mean either that the public good was subordinated to all private goods collected, or it might mean that it was subordinated to the interest of one individual. Clearly Cumberland was chiefly concerned in refuting the latter criticism, though some of his remarks suggest that he was also defending the first interpretation, which was, of course, his own position.

[1] Cumberland, p. 16.   [2] Cumberland, p. 310.   [3] *Ibid.*, p. 387.

One defence against the charge of advocating egoism was that he had claimed throughout that no man had any right to satisfaction that did not contribute to the common good, or at the very least, was compatible with it.[1] He pointed to the presumption of anyone who might expect the whole universe to

'. . . conspire as united causes acting only for our own good, in preference to the good of all other beings, nay, even in preference to the good, each respectively of himself.'[2]

Here he was perfectly correct. Individualism in social theory could be entirely different from egoism, although many seventeenth-century moralists confused the two.

His other argument was in defence of his own position rather than a repudiation of misunderstandings of it. He explained how it was natural to approach the common good through its components, more natural than to reverse the process by first discovering the common good and then the good of particulars. It was simply a matter of treating the most obvious matters first, and the goods of particular persons had to be the starting-point for ordinary men. This was an important point. He seemed to be saying that apart from God, there was no mind capable of grasping the common good in isolation from its own. He allowed that eventually some people could learn to value the common good for its own sake, but this came at the end of the process, not at the beginning. At the outset, they would have to attain it while seeking primarily their own good.

Since he is known primarily as a theological utilitarian, it is not surprising that Cumberland should have made some use of pains and pleasures of the hereafter to moderate conduct. Most surprisingly, he made very little use of them. Instead, he relied heavily upon the universal nature of self-love to limit the damage done by any particular manifestation of it. If all citizens were equally concerned about their own interests, they would control each other. This idea is reflected in his discussion of domestic politics in terms of a balance of power. The essence of the international balance of power, as he understood it, was that the rights or claims of all nations might be so balanced

'. . . as to render it extremely difficult and hazardous for any one to crush and destroy another; but on the contrary that all be allowed

[1] Cumberland, p. 421. [2] *Ibid.*, p. 425.

the sufficient means of self-preservation, as also the means, in some degree or other, of bettering and enriching themselves . . .'¹

Applied to the domestic scene, it meant that

'. . . the powers and abilities of individuals be so poised and balanced, that each, by preserving himself against outward force and violence, must not destroy any other being, to the danger, detriment and loss of the whole.'²

This was obviously an important consideration for Cumberland, although the *concordia discors* was never the *idée fixe* that it was with Penn. Cumberland even showed how, before the formation of society, irrational or excessive self-interest was subject to such checks in the state of nature.

In judging Cumberland's efforts one should not lay too much emphasis upon his hesitations and inconsistencies in treating a difficult subject. He deserves great credit for his attempt to pour some social content into the abstract notion of a common good, and one should commend him for his concern for individual welfare. He neglected to place his contribution in the history of thought on the common good, nor, apart from his distaste for Hobbes, did he mention his contemporaries. One sentence serves quite well as a commentary upon his aims, though it was not intended to sum it up. He regretted that 'public or common good, carries a pompous sound'³ He thought it unfortunate, because promoting the common good was not really such an onerous task; certainly it was well within ordinary capacities.

Apparently he felt that most writers had been too harsh in drawing the distinction between public and private good. Thus he made the point now first becoming prominent in economic argument:

'. . . whatsoever gives an additional strength or force, even to one single individual part of this whole, (all the other parts continuing, without loss or damage, exactly in the same state) this same whole, I say, (composed of this one, single part, and of all the other parts) receives an additional, an increase, an advantage.'⁴

Characteristically, he first observed that this justified charity

¹ Cumberland, p. 173.   ² *Ibid.*, p. 172.   ³ *Ibid.*, p. 312.
⁴ *Ibid.*, p. 254.

even to a single person and then he added that it also made a measure of self-regard legitimate.

Cumberland displays, as clearly as anyone in the century, the liberal understanding of the public interest. This is the purport of his most succinct explanation of the concept. By 'common good or public good', he meant

'... the whole aggregate or sum total of all those various and several kinds of good, from which all individual, rational beings, collectively considered, can be benefited.'[1]

This formula seems to express the essence of the Benthamite idea of a sum of interests. Without denying the reality of a community that could have a common good, Cumberland preferred to see the good of the community as the goods of all the discrete members compounded to form an aggregate. He went so far as to write of the 'constituent parts' of the common good, in a sense that clearly meant the welfare of individual citizens.[2]

There is one problem, of course; Cumberland always wrote of goods, public and private, not of interests. This may be explained by the fact that he wrote in Latin. The word interest existed in that language, indeed, it had its origin there, as a verb meaning 'it concerns'. But the way in which Restoration England used the word seems to have had no equivalent in Latin. It is, then, quite likely that Cumberland would have written of interests had he used English. This cannot be certain, but in the period when most people seemed to be agreed that interest would not lie, a man's good and his interest came to very much the same thing. The best source of support for this hypothesis comes from those people who presented Cumberland in a more popular and accessible form. James Tyrrell wrote of the 'interest of mankind' where Cumberland had written of their good.[3] Tyrrell's work was actually a translation and abridgment of the original, differing in a number of respects from it, but done with the approval of the author. James Lowde saw no incongruity in summarizing Cumberland's teaching in terms of interests. He commended him for showing how virtue was no more than one's 'interest'. In founding obedience to the laws of nature on the 'principle of real advantage to our selves' he had proposed a

[1] Cumberland, p. 307.   [2] Ibid., pp. 539 and 432.
[3] Tyrrell, A Brief Disquisition of the Laws of Nature (1692), p. 122.

design that was 'very agreeable to the genius of the present age'.[1]
The most paradoxical aspect of Cumberland's thought was that he offered an individualistic rendering of the common good while advocating a philosophy of benevolence. This should not be very surprising, unless one identifies individualism and egoism. It just shows that profound thinkers went beyond the shallow cleverness of the Restoration pamphleteers, who were so intrigued by the selfishness of all social relations. Of course all men were self-interested, Cumberland was saying, but they were selfish to some socially useful purpose. This was the transition from cynicism to social theory.[2]

Samuel Parker, Archdeacon of Canterbury, illustrates the new tendency very well. Like Tyrrell, he admired Cumberland and sought only to make his message less obscure for the general reader. Parker's whole theme was embodied in the observation that a wise providence had so ordered affairs that 'interest' was usually compatible with honesty.[3] True to Cumberland's theory though more crudely, he added that because the two did not always coincide, a heaven was indispensable. Without it, self-interested mortals had no obligation to self-sacrifice. This had been White's point, less than thirty years before. Then it had been the quintessence of jesuitical wickedness; now it was respectable.

[1] J. Lowde, *A Discourse Concerning the Nature of Man both in his Natural and Political Capacity . . . With an Examination of Mr. Hobbes' Opinions Relating Hereunto* (1692), pp. 69–70.
  Of course there were philosophers who did not share in the genius of the age. Chief Justice Matthew Hale (d. 1676) was extremely hostile to all self-interest and tried as well to dissociate the national good from that of particular persons. With this in mind, he insisted that 'the community considered as a community is a distinct thing from the particular persons that are integrals of that community'. See his essay on the law of nature, BM: Harl. MSS. 7159 fol. 19. For a similar dissenting opinion see Anon., *A Discourse of Present Importance*, subtitled 'Of Public and Private Interest' (1704) (BM: 114 g. 22). One would expect a few such counter-offensives in a period when traditional precepts were being explicitly challenged.
[2] This point is well made in Albert Schatz, *L'Individualisme économique et social* (Paris, 1907), p. 558. Although he deals almost entirely with ideas in later centuries, his work is indispensable for an understanding of early individualism. Its main defect seems to be an exaggeration of the difference between a natural and an artificial harmony of interests.
[3] Parker, *A Demonstration of the Divine Authority of the Law of Nature and of Christian Religion* (1681), p. XX.

Parker had much to say about purely temporal self-interest and a wholly secular common good. Men could be moved to benevolence and co-operation only if they saw some profit in it. This could be found in

'. . . the necessity of a public concern in order to the preservation of every man's private interest.'[1]

Parker had some notions about one's social functions, but they were expressed in the new idiom, not that of the Tudor moralists. Like Cumberland, he emphasized that serving the public was not nearly so difficult as was sometimes supposed, for providential reason

'. . . promoted the interest of the community by engaging every single member of it to do his own work and mind his own business.'[2]

This meant that

'. . . whoever performs the duty of his station and employment, serves both himself and the commonwealth; in that the prosperity of the whole arises from the industry of the several parts.'[3]

Men of the previous century might have said this, thinking in terms of the estates and their duties, but they would not have extended their analysis to insist in the same way that the prosperity of the whole was dependent on the welfare of the parts. However, Parker claimed that

'. . . those causes that preserve the whole, preserve its parts also; and those that preserve the parts; preserve the whole.'[4]

A follower of Cumberland was automatically a critic of Hobbes. Parker was concerned that Hobbes might have convinced some people that there really was no common good. Thus he strove to display it:

'. . . Now if there be a common interest, in which every man is concerned, as he is concerned in his own, that is it that makes society: and if no man from the natural condition of his faculties be able to carry on either the one or the other without having a peculiar share divided and appropriated to himself for the exercise and employment of his industry: it is that that assigns and settles propriety.'[5]

---

[1] Parker, p. 28.　　[2] Parker, p. 39.　　[3] *Ibid.*　　[4] *Ibid.*, p. 26.
[5] *Ibid.* Cf. Cumberland, *op. cit.*, p. 257, and Tyrrell, *op. cit.*, pp. 214–15.

The common good was apparently not just the existence of government but the existence of those forms of satisfaction that were dependent upon it. The only way of preventing strife about property was

'. . . by dividing the common interest into particular shares, and setting out every man his own propriety, so plainly does there follow from the fundamental principle of seeking the public good an obligation upon every man to accept his own lot and to leave all others undisturbed in theirs.'[1]

This was the full extent of one's social duty, whether in a public or a private capacity.

This is surely one of the clearest examples of how one now went about gaining support for the common good. The idea was to parcel out this good to those individuals who could control property and might then exercise those other rights dependent upon it. If the only way in which to gain support for the common interest was to divide it into shares, then that interest consisted of all the shares collected. This had been the gist of Cumberland's treatise; Parker just made the claim more explicit.

Tyrrell's version of Cumberland was written some time after Parker's, and was both less lucid and less explicitly individualistic. His excuse for providing another version of Cumberland was that his was more faithful to the original text,[2] but he offered no criticism of Parker's book. Inevitably, since he followed the general course of Cumberland's argument, Tyrrell made substantially the same points. He was particularly concerned lest the Hobbesian blend of contract and nominalism might appear to have destroyed all trace of a common good. In his opinion, Hobbes had turned the concept into

'. . . a meer platonic idea, or turn of art, without any reality in nature to support it.'[3]

Tyrrell was defending a common good, not alternatives to nominalism. With the help of Locke's metaphysics, he undertook to explain how this common good might be discovered, without recourse to any innate ideas or Platonic fictions. It was one of the recognised traits of human beings that they could abstract universal ideas from particular things and then give gen-

[1] Parker, p. 40.   [2] Tyrrell, *op. cit.*, sig. A 4.   [3] *Ibid.*, p. 213.

eral names to those ideas. Each man sought his own happiness and by a knowledge of his own nature might understand it. Owing to a basic similarity of human nature, one might then tell

'. . . what things or actions will conduce not only to our own happiness and preservation but to all others of the same kind.'[1]

This position did not really depend upon any great sympathy with the aims of mankind; he was primarily concerned with vindicating an understanding of the common good. An understanding of one's own good would suffice, because, as Penn had affirmed in another context, the same general conditions would serve for all. This makes sense, once it is put in its context. He was not of the opinion that surrendering to every irrational impulse was in one's interest. His case rested on the assumption that in complying with the common good there was no reason to believe that

'. . . a man either could, or ought to neglect his own preservation and true happiness.'[2]

The concrete policy behind the statement was that

'. . . the constitution of a distinct property in things, in the labours of persons . . . [was] . . . the chief and necessary medium to the common good.'[3]

Tyrrell's writings are important to the present theme in a number of respects. One other was his statement of the current understanding of duties. It has been suggested that the dominant theme in the political philosophy of the late seventeenth century was an attitude rather than a formal doctrine, an attitude called the 'freeholder view of society'.[4] Its most striking characteristic, as explained by Kennedy, was that it did away with the duties and functions that had been the foundations of Tudor social theory. They were replaced by a concern for rights, without corresponding duties to any community, though there

[1] Tyrrell, p. 215.   [2] *Ibid.*, p. 214.   [3] *Ibid.*, sig. E 4.
[4] See the admirable discussion in W. Kennedy, *English Taxation 1640–1799, An Essay on Policy and Opinion* (London, 1913), Chapter V. The same point was suggested in S. N. Patten, *The Development of English Thought* (New York, 1899), p. 163.

was a duty to respect the rights of other single members. Kennedy expressed the distinction between the old and the new by saying that the state ceased to be thought of as an

'. . . instrument for the general regulation and defence of the whole community.'

It was now considered as 'an instrument for protecting the rights of the members'.[1] Unfortunately, the state was seen as a more useful instrument for some citizens than for others. Defoe provides a remarkable illustration of this attitude. He stated that *salus populi* meant the protection of the 'people's property'. More importantly, however, he said that the 'people' meant the freeholders. They alone had 'a right to the possession of England'; all others existed on suffrance.[2] The distinction between the defence of the realm and the protection of private rights thus had two implications. The defence of property came closer to the particular interests of private men, but with an unavoidable cost; some people's interests had to be overlooked. National defence had entailed the protection of private rights in an indirect way; the new emphasis did not entirely neglect national honour. However, these perspectives afforded different views of the public interest. This had been the case early in the Civil War. It was more obviously true in the second half of the century.

Cumberland had provided some sort of philosophical foundation for the new attitude when he demoted the idea of a common good to human, rather than angelic proportions, just at the time when natural rights were becoming important. Tyrrell went farther towards clarifying the implications of Cumberland's doctrine for one's social duties. Thus he suggested that men adequately served the common good of mankind when they cared properly for their children.[3] Later he discussed the 'public good' by which he seems to have meant the common good applied to one society. Here again, he saw any real sacrifice of one's interest as very much a work of supererogation. A man was to be

[1] Kennedy, pp. 64–5.
[2] 'The Original Right of the People of England, Examined and Asserted', in *A True Collection of the Writings of the Author of the True Born Englishman* (1703), Vol. I, pp. 138, 139 and 160. The work also contains an attack on 'reason of state' as one of the pretexts for the acts of statesmen (p. 145).
[3] Tyrrell, *Patriarcha Non Monarcha* (1681), p. 17.

considered 'righteous' when he had done his duty in private relationships. He was even more virtuous if he worked for the public good in the sense of the welfare of those beyond his immediate
family, but this was not strictly necessary.[1] It had not been unusual for earlier thinkers to damn a failure to work for the public
with almost the same fervour applied to condemning those who
wilfully worked against it. Now, a position of benevolent neu-
trality was becoming more acceptable.

The social relevance of Tyrrell's doctrine may again best be
seen against the background of his idea of property. His defence
of the current distribution of property was based upon man's
obligations to the common good of mankind and the good of the
commonwealth. Once he allowed that some people might feel
that leaving property inviolate was

'. . . contrary to their interests, as having perhaps little share either
in lands or goods.'[2]

The context suggests that he also meant that, objectively considered, it might not be in their interests. However, he found it
easy to put aside such objections. Raising the subject again, he
affirmed that no one had a right to interfere with a man's possessions, even though the latter might have accumulated more
than he could use. He now claimed quite without qualification
that

'. . . such an agreement is but a rational assent of every particular
man's understanding that the abstaining from the doing of such a
thing is every private man's interest, and likewise for the good of
humane society.'[3]

It was then both the true interest of every man and also recognized as such.

John Locke fits rather easily into this tradition. For some
reason scholars have long been interested in Locke's opinions on
the common good. This is unfortunate, for here he was reticent,
as always. His position in relation to his time is strikingly similar to that of Hobbes. He is clearly the most powerful of a number of thinkers sharing a general orientation, but he expressed
this position less effectively than did some minor figures.

[1] *Patriarcha Non Monarcha*, pp. 116–17.   [2] *Ibid.*, p. 147, misnumbered 107.
[3] *Ibid.*, pp. 109–10.

Almost all aspects of his political thought have been analysed at one time or another in order to understand what he meant by such expressions as public good. However, there does not appear to be any great problem. His opinions were really quite conventional; conventional, that is, within the new individualism.

One writer ended an exhaustive examination of Locke's position, by claiming that Locke meant by the common good

'. . . a condition where the government protects the rights of its citizens and the citizens can recognize their moral obligations to others.'[1]

Certainly Locke's well-known concern for rights made the first part of the statement incontestable and the second part may well be inferred from the text. The passages in which Locke introduced the idea of the public good generally dealt with the duties of the government. While it is true to say that it might serve both as the end of the government's grant of power and as a means of defining its limits,[2] he seemed to be saying the second more than the first. Thus Locke wrote in relation to government power that it was

'. . . limited to the public good of the society. It is a power that hath no other end but preservation and therefor can never have a right to destroy, enslave, or designedly to impoverish the subjects.'[3]

This suggests that government was expected to protect already existing goods more than to provide any positive contribution.

The most important problem in Locke's theory is, of course, the connection between public and private interests. Several writers have observed that Locke identified the two in the sense that he seemed unaware of the difference between aggregate goods of a number of individuals and a common good belonging to a community.[4] It can hardly be denied that he made this identification, as when he wrote that laws were made for the

[1] C. H. Monson Jr., *Common Good in the Political Philosophy of Locke, Green and Perry*, unpublished Ph.D. dissertation (Cornell, 1952), p.65.
[2] See W. Kendall, *John Locke and the Doctrine of Majority Rule* (Urbana, 1941), p. 92.
[3] *Two Treatises of Government*, ed. P. Laslett (Cambridge, 1960), p. 375.
[4] See J. W. Gough, *John Locke's Political Philosophy, Eight Studies* (Oxford, 1950), p. 31; S. P. Lamprecht, *The Moral and Political Philosophy of John Locke* (New York, 1918), p. 135 n.; and Kendall, *op. cit.*, pp. 92–3.

'public good, i.e. the good of every particular member of that society'.[1]

Though Locke wrote normally of 'goods', rather than of interests, it seems quite reasonable, then, to say that he tended to identify private and public interests. Some versions of this interpretation go too far, however. Kendall accuses Locke of a lack of circumspection in stating his case. Instead of postulating a perfect harmony between private and public interests, he might better have said, with Rousseau, that

'. . . in a certain kind of society, promoting one's own interest is the same thing as promoting the public good.'[2]

Now any commentator who accuses Locke of incaution deserves a hearing if only for his originality. However, the comment is somewhat misleading. Were anyone to claim that seeking one's own interest was the same thing as seeking that of the public, he would have to provide some means of reconciling conflicting private interests. A perfect harmony among them would not be necessary; a balance of conflicting interests, such as that offered by Penn, would do just as well. But Locke offered neither answer.

He was perfectly aware that no uniform law was possible if it had to be adapted to suit all particular interests

'. . . because it is impossible to have regard for the interests of all at one and the same time.'[3]

In treating economic life, Locke recognized the apparently conflicting interests of land and trade. Actually, he thought that each was wrong in seeing the other interest as a hindrance to its prosperity,[4] but he saw too that it might sometimes be necessary to choose between the two. In that event, he favoured all possible consideration for the landed interest, since it was 'a settled, unmoveable concernment in the commonwealth'.[5] Like most sophisticated economic thinkers, he realized that the fortunes of land and trade waxed and waned together, but land, in his

[1] *Two Treatises* . . ., p. 228.   [2] Kendall, *op. cit.*, p. 93.
[3] *Essays on the Law of Nature*, ed. W. von Leyden (Oxford, 1954), p. 211. The word here translated as 'interest' was 'utilitas' in the original.
[4] *Some Considerations of the Consequences of the Lowering of Interest and Raising the Value of Money* (1692), p. 115.
[5] *Some Considerations of the Consequences* . . ., p. 41.

opinion, felt any national reverse first, and so deserved consideration. A criticism like Kendall's seems to be founded upon an undue reliance upon the theory of economic individualism. In some respects political individualism was different. Here the sort of claim attributed by Kendall to Locke was quite extraordinary. One may well say that Locke believed in a common good consisting wholly in the satisfaction of individual interests, each individual's concern for protecting his property being one of them. It is quite another thing to attribute to him the idea of a common good consisting in the free and harmonious exercise of all particular interests.[1] Such an opinion banishes government and so, by definition, excludes normal political processes. Locke was not writing about the process of promoting one's interests in any active way. He was concerned with vindicating the quiet possession of certain rights. His model was passive; he described conditions rather than activities.

It might have been less misleading had Kendall thought in terms of Locke's own language. He wrote of one's good, not of one's interest. There is no objection to using the word 'interest', which might mean no more than a good that was or might be recognized. But one must then be careful to avoid too much emphasis upon self-interested activity. Locke was concerned only with some interests; and the right of property required less promotion than preservation. Locke was individualist enough. There is no need to read impossible claims into his theory. Merely saying that men joined society in order to protect their property was individualism of a sort. An even more pronounced form was the opinion that the common good consisted in a mass of particular goods. He might have gone further in noting how men best knew their own interests. As it was, others remedied that omission.

TOWARDS ORTHODOXY

It is impossible to say whether Locke was aware that there might be a basic difference between one public good and many par-

[1] Others who have assumed that Locke's position logically required an invisible hand are L. C. McDonald, *Political Theory: The Modern Age* (New York, 1962), p. 149; G. Niemeyer, in C. J. Friedrich (ed.), *The Public Interest* (New York, 1962), pp. 6–7; and T. P. Neill, *The Rise and Decline of Liberalism* (Milwaukee, 1953), pp. 59 and 63.

ticular ones. However, the distinction had been present in political literature for some time. It is also true that some writers with a liberal tendency had challenged the distinction in the course of opposing that view of the public good centred upon power and national honour. The same distinction was present in contexts farther removed from the current conflicts in political theory. Most practical men, writing to advance certain policies, had nothing to gain from discussing such a question. However, some thinkers had not been so vitally concerned with using the concept of the public good in a way favourable to themselves. They had the opportunity to indulge in dispassionate analysis, although politics invaded even the dignity of the courts.

One area where the distinction cannot have been unfamiliar was the law. Perhaps the major issue of constitutional law in this period was the matter of the dispensing power. The particular relevance of the public good to this issue was the doctrine that the king might not dispense with an offence if this prevented any citizen from bringing an otherwise legitimate action in the courts. The issue then turned on what constituted adequate grounds for a private action. The definitive statement on the dispensing power was made by Sir John Vaughan in *Thomas* v. *Sorrell*. His judgment was not universally accepted, but it did provide the basis for future discussion.[1]

Vaughan contended that there were instances where individuals might be prejudiced by some act, but were barred from seeking redress because they could not demonstrate any damage peculiar to themselves that was not shared by all of their fellow citizens. He cited infringement of the law forbidding the export of unwrought wool as an example. Sir John added:

'. . . and though such laws are pro bono publico in some sense, they are not laws *pro bono singulorum populi*, but *pro bono populi complicati*, as the king in his discretion shall think fit to order them for the whole.'

The king's position in caring for the community as a single, irreducible unit was analogous to the legal status of the *pater familias* whose estate

'. . . may be said to be *pro bono communi* of his family, which yet is but

[1] This case was one of the more important constitutional decisions of the period. See W. S. Holdsworth, *A History of English Law* (London, 1937), Vol. VI, pp. 223–4 and 501.

at his discretion and management of it; and they have no interest in it, but have benefit by it.'[1]

In some cases, then, the king could dispense with offences, for he alone would suffer damage. As a later commentator noted, quoting the relevant parts of Vaughan's judgment, the decisive fact was not that the public good was involved, for all offences against penal laws affected the public good in some sense. The point was that this public good might take two different forms in relation to private persons.[2]

Unfortunately, Vaughan had neglected to give any example of a law that was *pro bono singulorum populi*. This left an opening for a Whiggish attack upon prerogative. One ardent Whig interpreted Vaughan to mean that

'. . . when the law extended in interest not only to individual persons, but to a considerable part of the nation, much more when to all, in either of which cases the statute is *pro bono singulorum populi*, in neither of these can the king dispense.'[3]

Atwood was correct in assuming that laws *pro bono singulorum populi* might involve the interests of a large section of the populace. Apart from that, he seems deliberately to have misrepresented the learned Vaughan. The latter had been distinguishing between that sort of a public interest belonging to the nation as a unit, and that which afforded some connection with identifiable particular interests. Atwood's attempt at a numerical criterion for determining the sort of public good involved in any situation, did scant justice to the original distinction; the point was the way in which they were affected.

Atwood's disregard for Vaughan's distinction was matched by James Tyrrell, a writer whose chief merit was that he faithfully reflected all prevailing ideas. His immense *Bibliotheca Politica* was constructed in the form of a dialogue between a moderate Tory and a Whig, the latter obviously speaking for Tyrrell. When discussing the dispensing power he put the argu-

[1] *The Reports and Arguments of that Learned Judge Sir John Vaughan Kt., Late Chief Justice of H.M.'s Court of Common Pleas* (1677), p. 342.
[2] Sir Edward Herbert, *A Short Account of the Authorities in Law Upon Which Judgement was Given in Sir Edward Hales his Case* (1688), p. 21. Herbert was merely supporting a point already made by Vaughan in less emphatic fashion.
[3] W. Atwood, *The Lord Chief Justice Herbert's Account Examined* (1689), p. 46.

ment of Vaughan and Sir Edward Herbert into the mouth of his Tory, while the Whig, to some extent, followed Atwood. While the Tory patiently expounded the theory of the two types of public good, the Whig interjected sceptical criticism. The outcome of the Whig's position was the same as with Atwood; it involved a fairly crude impatience with such 'little distinctions' as that between laws made *pro bono publico complicati* and those 'of more private regard'.[1]

While Atwood had assumed that the category of laws '*pro bono singulorum populi*' was very large, Tyrrell tried to reduce it to insignificant proportions. As far as he was concerned

'. . . whatsoever is prejudicial to the public safety of the commonwealth, must be also prejudicial to the safety of every private person.'[2]

If there were any priority in the king's duties, he thought that he should be bound in the first place to enforce laws for the whole community

'. . . above the private good or interest of particular men which you call *bonum singulorum populi*.'

He referred sarcastically to the distinction as a 'subtle piece of learning', then added:

'. . . but pray let us take a little out of these Latin terms, and then the meaning of it is no more than this, that the King can do nothing to the prejudice of the people in their private capacities, but he can do what he will with the public.'

He would have thought that this reversed the proper priorities. Then he remarked ironically that clearly private interests could only be protected if the laws were dispensed with and Popish judges came to deal with the 'lives and estates of Protestants'. Such horrors might follow the introduction of those dispensations

'. . . grounded upon the distinction of the public good of the whole taken together, as different from that of the public good of each particular person.'[3]

By the 'public good' of a person he presumably meant that good

---

[1] Tyrrell, *Bibliotheca Politica* . . . (1718), p. 592. The first edition was in 1694.
[2] *Ibid.*, p. 596.   [3] *Ibid.*, p. 597.

or interest, such as protecting property, that might normally be advanced by political means.

This dialogue makes clear that one might reject Vaughan's distinction for more than one reason. It was possible to reject it from quite conservative premises. Tyrrell sometimes sounds very much like the Tudor divines who thought that the profit of the whole necessarily benefited the parts. The only real difference was that the rest of Tyrrell's work shows that he saw the public good primarily in terms of the protection of private rights, while the divines had usually been thinking of other matters. There can be doubt that the fusion of particular interests and the public interest was a characteristic of liberal thought. However, one might reach the desired conclusion by alternative routes. Tyrrell moved easily between these approaches. At one point he might imply that Vaughan's distinction involved the sacrifice of the public good to private interests. In the same paragraph he suggested that the pernicious theory might lay the basis for an invasion of private rights, or in his terms, the 'public' rights of private men. Tyrrell's position was not anachronistic, because few earlier thinkers had dealt carefully with the public good. It had just not been an issue. The fact remains that his rendering of the controversy in a legal context depended upon certain notions that had no necessary connection with individualism.

One cannot readily refer to early literature to discover which of the protagonists was breaking with tradition. Traditional doctrine supported a certain antithesis between private interest and public good, so probably the Whig's argument, however crude, was the more modern. Tyrrell's discussion leaves one entirely dissatisfied, because he obviously understood the Tory distinction better than is indicated by his Whig spokesman. His summary of arguments by Vaughan and Herbert was accurate and fair, indicating careful study of the texts involved. The writer of a dialogue may gain a certain expository force by being able to argue with himself, but in this instance it was at the cost of clarity regarding his own position.

Vaughan had cited no precedents for his comments in the case of *Thomas* v. *Sorrell*, hence we cannot know where he got his distinction. One possible source that would be familiar to most educated Englishmen was the legal writings of Suarez. It was quoted by Tyrrell in his discussion of Vaughan's distinction.[1] When Bishop Stillingfleet wished to discuss the public good he took the unusual precaution of noting the ambiguities in the concept. Quoting Suarez, interspersed with his own commentary, he wrote:

'. . . there are two sorts of laws . . . which respect the public good; some which concern *ipsum statum reipub. et utilitatem communitatis*; the general state of the commonwealth, and benefit of the community: Others which concern *bonum commune mediante privato*; that common good which results from every man's good.'[2]

As a defender of established institutions, Stillingfleet gave primacy to the first definition, but he recognized the validity of both.

This affords a new insight into Locke's position. The failure to distinguish between a common good of a community and the aggregate goods of a number of individuals was not an inevitable part of his age. Some people had appreciated that the public good could be conceived in various ways. This was not too helpful for purposes of political argument, hence most writers used that definition appropriate to their circumstances as though it were the only proper one. Perhaps Locke was careless in not saying exactly what good the members of the community had in common. On the other hand, he may purposely have chosen the liberal view, while recognizing that there was an alternative. Instead of a mere philosophical muddle, one would then have a piece of propaganda. The argument might still be confused, of course, but it then becomes confusion with a purpose.

---

[1] *Bibliotheca*, p. 592.
[2] Anon., *A Discourse Concerning the Unreasonableness of a New Separation* (1689), p. 11. Authorship has always been attributed to Stillingfleet. Suarez made this distinction in his *De Legibus, Ac Deo Legislatore*. See *Selections from the Works of Francisco Suarez, S.J.*, ed. G. L. Williams *et al.*, (Oxford, 1944), p. 94. Some medieval glossators had previously made the same point. See Gaines Post, *Studies in Medieval Legal Thought* (Princeton, 1964), pp. 378–9. Such subtlety of analysis seems to have been exceptional, although the great number of Roman Catholic treatises on law and morals makes any generalization hazardous. A summary of orthodox Roman Catholic doctrine makes no mention of it. See T. Eschmann, 'A Thomistic Glossary on the Principle of the Preeminence of a Common Good', *Mediaeval Studies*, Vol. 5 (1943), pp. 123–65.

In fact the liberal concern for a public good consisting of the good every particular citizen makes sense, but the content of this good fell short of the mark. Individualists often overlooked those particular interests unrelated to preserving estates. Less defensibly, they were then led to ignore the fact that people with no property had rights that they could not use. The virtue of protecting rights was that it fused particular and general interests very well. The very nature of a right to enjoy property and other freedoms entailed a diversity of interests consistent with the known selfishness of mankind. People obtained thereby a greater opportunity for personal and unique satisfaction than in the case of a common good consisting in national strength. At the same time such rights had to be general if they were to be effectively maintained.[1] Hence men could be seen as uniting to achieve a set of conditions that ensured to each the means of individuality. One could justify concern for the strength of the state on the same grounds, but calling this the common good made for an attenuation of particular goods. These two formulas might not differ in the least in the sort of policies visualized by their respective proponents. There was more difference in the general perspectives on society, how it had been established and why. Not all of the people who gave an individualistic interpretation of the public good were believers in a social contract, but this sort of notion tended to be related to it.

Liberal or republican thought in this era was largely based upon the premise that the public good was most obviously and immediately related to the preservation of private rights. In this respect it stemmed from very much the same assumptions as those of the Commonwealth republicans. Much the best-known representative of latter-day republicanism, both in his own age and subsequently, was the martyr Algernon Sydney. He was not an unusually original thinker; his strength of feeling for noble causes was perhaps his greatest merit.

His theme was a fairly limited one. In opposition to Filmer, he maintained that government had not originated in patriarchial rule and it functioned only according to the will of the people. His remarks about 'public good', 'public interest' and '*salus populi*' fill most of the book. All such terms seem to have meant the same thing, though in one passage listing the ends of

[1] See below, Appendix B.

government, he included provision both for the public safety and for the 'true interest' of the nation.[1] If these referred to different aspects of policy, he neglected to say what they were.

The same paragraph gave the content of the public good, for he said that government had not been established for the king's interest

'. . . but for the preservation of the whole people, and the defence of the liberty, life and estate of every private man.'

As always, in such a construction, the word 'and' might, or might not, be used in an exclusive sense. Presumably, in this case, he was not trying to draw any distinction between these two tasks, for elsewhere he said that

'. . . if the safety of the people be the supreme law and this safety extend to, and consist in the preservation of their liberties, goods, lands and lives, that law must necessarily be the root and beginning, as well as the end and limit of all magesterial power.'[2]

The discussion of democratic thought in the commonwealth has brought out the importance of the idea that the people themselves were competent to discern what was in the public interest and this Sydney asserted at great length. He made much of the fact that all men properly followed their own good, or at least, that which appeared to them to be good. Like his republican predecessors, he was fond of treating public affairs as analogous to private business. In a number of ways he implied that competence in handling one's own affairs was closely connected with capacity to judge the needs of the public. Certainly, incompetence in the first should incapacitate anyone to attempt the second. This was what disqualified so many hereditary rulers. A ruler might be a child, a woman, senile or an idiot. Even in the case of a ruler not disqualified by age or madness there were great dangers, for he admitted that someone capable of going about the ordinary business of life might not be a good judge of affairs of state.[3] Like Aristotle, he felt that while many citizens

---

[1] Sydney, *Discourses Concerning Government*, 2nd edn. (1704), p. 320. The spelling of Sydney's name adopted here might be questioned. An edition of his writings quoted in Chapter I used this spelling, and it has been employed throughout.
[2] *Ibid.*, p. 290.   [3] *Ibid.*, p. 387.

might be similarly limited, all together could provide the necessary skills. It need not be emphasized that Sydney obviously felt that the 'people' would be led by their betters. Radicals of the seventeenth century were not champions of the mob.

The remarks about judging affairs of state weakened the connection between the ability to judge one's own interest and the right of judging the public's. However, there was a great difference between an actual capacity to govern and the ability to know when things were going well. Sydney's confidence in the people related mainly to this latter. Only those who had set up a government could decide 'whether it be employed to their welfare'.[1] The people who

'. . . smart of the vices and follies of their princes, knew what remedies were most fit to be applied, as well as the best time of applying them.'[2]

He was not claiming that the people could frame the public good as a day-to-day policy, but that they were the final court of appeal when disputes arose. It was surely with this in mind that he defended their competence to discern their own good. No great skill was required, for such knowledge consisted

'. . . not in formalities and niceties, but in evident and substantial truths, there is no need of any other tribunal than of common sense, and the light of nature to determine the matter.'[3]

Sydney never said categorically that no one man could ever judge effectively of the public good. He preferred to criticize the endowments of those people who actually functioned as kings. He remained dubious about the prospects, for

'. . . the public interests and the concernments of private men in their lands, goods, liberties and lives . . . cannot be preserved by one who is transported by his own passions or follies.'[4]

This serves both as an effective statement of the people's right to determine their own good and of what this good, in general terms, consisted.

He never seems to have appreciated that his discussion of the

---

[1] Sydney, p. 399.   [2] *Ibid.*, p. 399.   [3] *Ibid.*, p. 333.
[4] *Ibid.*, p. 336. For a discussion of 'public interests' of this sort see above, p. 33.

relative qualifications of king and people was unnecessary. Throughout he had insisted upon the subjective nature of any concrete formulation of the public good. The people did not have to be correct in determining the policies favourable to themselves; calculations of public benefit were subject to the same errors as any estimate of private interest. However, he had already claimed that this was immaterial. The people could never be tied to any set of policies other than those 'consistent with the common good according to their judgement'.[1] Private men sought their good according to their understanding, so, with equal justification, did communities.

The culmination of his argument was his rebuttal of Filmer's complaint about the people being judge in their own case. This objection had been well met about the time Filmer had been writing. Now, when his work was published, it had to be dealt with again. In dismissing Filmer's inappropriate legal analogy, Sydney went furthest in asserting that the people's will, right or wrong, was the strongest indication of the public good. If Filmer's maxim had application to anyone, surely it was to kings, who were less capable of determining the people's good than were the people themselves.[2] This left the general principle unscathed, and he returned to the attack, assuring that:

'I am not afraid to say, that naturally and properly a man is the judge of his own concernments. No-one is or can be deprived of this privilege, unless by his own consent, and for the good of the society into which he enters. This right therefore must necessarily belong to every man in all cases, except only such as relate to the good of the community, for whose sake he has divested himself of it. If I find myself afflicted with hunger, thirst, weariness, cold, heat or sickness, 'tis a folly to tell me I ought not to seek meat, drink, rest, shelter, refreshment or physic, because I must not be judge in my own case. The like may be said in relation to my house, land or estate; I may do what I please with them, if I bring no damage upon others.'[3]

The statement is more interesting for what it implies than for

[1] Sydney, p. 376.   [2] Ibid., p. 397.
[3] Ibid. My attention was drawn to this passage by a quotation from it in Élie Halévy, The Growth of Philosophic Radicalism (London, 1928), p. 129. The debt to Halévy would have been even greater had he cited the correct section of the Discourses. Some of Sydney's other writings also dealt with this point. See the passages quoted in The Arraignment, Tryal and Condemnation of Algernon Sidney Esq. for High Treason (1684), p. 23 (B: Wood 428).

any overt assertion. His aim was to prove the right of a community to determine its own public good. This right was not so much derived from the right of each man to regulate his own affairs as it was suggested from it, by analogy. His argument took the form that if this right belonged to each single man, it must surely belong to whole nations. His statement provided the single limit on each man's capacity to satisfy his needs, that he must not act contrary to the common good. In an argument purporting to move from rational self-interest in personal affairs to the same in public life, this sounds paradoxical. However, there was really no contradiction. He had not been saying that each citizen had a perfect understanding of the public good, though he felt that broad moral questions concerning the rights of property were obvious enough. Still less had he been saying that each man could be allowed in all cases to follow his interest. His position allowed for the fact that caring for one's physical needs might sometimes conflict with social needs. His own example was that, for all the rights of property, no man could erect a fort on his land. The example was a curious one, because the case was atypical; but it does avoid contradiction. In his private capacity, a man might not challenge the public good. However, when united with others and dealing with matters such as the protection of rights, Sydney saw no alternative but to let him determine the public interest. The areas in which Sydney visualized this power being used were those where private citizens might readily be expected to be of one mind. He feared a general assault upon those 'public interests' of men in their estates.

It is extraordinary that Sydney never closely considered the lacuna in his argument. The gap between acting for one's own physical needs and providing for the public good might be bridged, but the bridge had to be constructed by the reader from materials left scattered by Sydney. This argument was not an isolated and casual remark; it was the basic premise of his system. Earlier he had said:

"'Tis ordinarily said in France, Il faut que chacun soit servi à sa mode; every man's business must be done according to his own mind: and if this be true in particular persons, 'tis more plainly so in nations.'[1]

[1] Sydney, p. 290.

No doubt the connection between spheres, public and private, may best be explained by the common subject matter—private property. The long list of affairs in which a man might be his own judge ended with the right to dispose of his own estate. Another favourite theme was the right to instruct rulers, based on the analogous right to control servants. Man's rationality in his private capacity culminated in his control over his estate. The essence of the public good also consisted in protecting this estate and associated rights. Thus a skill was made transferable from the private to the public domain.

Sydney may have felt that his assumptions were made all the more plausible by the fact that he expressly excluded foreign affairs.[1] When he asserted the people's right to do as they wished, he was thinking of the means of protecting their freedoms against their rulers; foreign disputes were not to be dealt with in the same way, presumably because here the people lacked both the knowledge and the power to have their own way. Sydney did not wholly neglect foreign policy; indeed, his admiration for the ancient commonwealths made him unusually bellicose, but this area was excluded from his claims for a popularly determined common good. Here again, the parallel is with the earlier republicans, who tacitly ignored this area of policy.

Halévy suggests that Sydney's understanding of an identity of interests anticipated that of Adam Smith.[2] There was the same faith in a spontaneous order based upon rational self-interest. It is perfectly true that a new harmony between public and private interests was emerging in a variety of ways. However, the difficulties involved in equating economic and political ideas has already been noted. There were similar processes at work in different areas of social thought, but the results were not identical. Sydney's similarity to economic liberals might better be expressed by saying that both altered the traditional relationship between private and public interests. But they did not do it in quite the same way. Political thinkers could never conceive of a spontaneous harmony in quite the manner of economists. One must also add that if Sydney anticipated Smith, so did a great many other writers, at least as early as 1646.

Sydney's general outlook was quite frequently expressed in

---

[1] *Ibid.*, p. 398.   [2] Halévy, *op. cit.*, p. 129.

political literature at the time of the Glorious Revolution. Such writings were not usually avowedly republican, though the writers had a more than average concern for popular government. This usually took them some distance beyond the uninspiring Whiggish orthodoxy of a balanced constitution. Some writers just asserted the people's right to determine the public good, without examining their credentials or giving any content to such a good. As one put it, in examining forms of government, efficiency was not the prime consideration. Citing examples from economic life, he observed that resources in agriculture and commerce might often be used most efficiently if the supposed interests of the participants were ignored. This was impossible, however, for people would fiercely resent any interference with their affairs,

'. . . they will as soon part with their eyes; it being clearly against their interest.'[1]

Critics of popular government still had to learn that, in his metaphor, one had to please the dancers, not the spectators. The same outlook was displayed by another writer who emphasized the moral obligation to seek the common good. When faced with the need of saying what it was, he said:

'. . . and what is for the public good, they that feel are best able to judge.'[2]

Democrats continued to appeal to private life to find the basis of this political right. An anonymous writer justifying popular government said:

'. . . as every man is the best judge of his own health . . . so in the body politic, the people must be judge how this or that governor or law agrees with their constitution, and contributes to their health, peace and welfare.'[3]

---

[1] Anon., *A Plain and Familiar Discourse Concerning Government* (1688), p. 1 (BM: E 1964). This writer did, in fact, have republican leanings.
[2] *The Thoughts of a Private Person, About the Justice of the Gentlemen's Undertaking at York, Nov. 1688* (1689), p. 19 (B: C 11.13 Linc.). Wing credits this to Thomas Newsam; other sources offer different candidates.
[3] A. B., N. T., *Some Remarks Upon Government and Particularly Upon the Establishment of the English Monarchy . . . in Two Letters Written by and To a Member of the Great Convocation Holden at Westminster the 22nd of Jan., 1688–89* (1689), p. 9 (BM: T 1675).

After the Revolution, such ideas became more the current coin of political discussion, appearing in works that showed no alienation from the prevailing order or any reforming zeal. One self-styled 'country-gentleman' discussed prevailing notions of what was called the 'common good' or 'good of the whole'. His slight tract captured perfectly the new ethic. Civil society had been established for the good of mankind. This was not a very manageable concept, so he did his best to reduce it to terms that suggested institutional arrangements. Thus he argued that the good of mankind

'. . . is intended in respect of the greater number: and consequently, that as the good of individuals, so the opinion of 'em too, is involved in that of the majority.'[1]

He then found himself with three units to manipulate, the good of the whole, that of single individuals and that of the majority. He cannot be said to have mastered the insuperable problems posed for the individualist by majority rule. Like Harrington, a pioneer in the process of deriving a public interest from private ones, he found difficulty in including all such private interests. His answer serves, however, to underline the basic relationship:

'. . . as every man is presumed most fond of his own interest, so the greater number must be supposed to be equally careful of theirs and by consequence, that what is done by the majority is best for the whole.'[2]

While this may have raised more problems than it answered, it was symptomatic of the new bent of political thought. The public good had to be discussed within the context of private interests, not, as in the past, solely in terms of community institutions.

These were tracts by obscure or anonymous men. However, very much the same doctrine was upheld by Matthew Tindal, of All Souls, Oxford, surely one of the ablest of the pamphleteers who ushered in the reign of William and Mary. The political theory of these years is quite interesting, for the new government had to be supported with reduced reliance on the discredited

[1] Anon., *The Country Gentleman's Notions Concerning Government in a Letter to his Friend at Leeds* (Nottingham, 1696), p. 2 (B: Pamph. 221).
[2] *Ibid.*, p. 3.

Jacobite doctrines of non-resistance and passive obedience.[1] Service, not divine right, had to be the monarch's chief rationale. The sacrosanct character of oaths was a Jacobite argument; when people were pressed to take the new Oath of Allegiance it was impossible to plead any previous obligation. Thus even the more old-fashioned writers were forced on to grounds of present utility. Tindal, in defending the Revolution, was not one of the old-fashioned writers.

There could be no doubt that the people had acted for their own good in overthrowing the Stuarts, for

'. . . there can be no greater argument than the universal consent of the nation, that what they so unanimously concurred in, was not against their common good.'[2]

Nor was there much likelihood that the 'common interest' could be successfully opposed, for James II could never hope to influence a sufficient number of the nobility and gentry to reverse the process. The lands and riches of the nation were in too many hands to make that possible.

For present purposes, the most important stage of his argument came in the third chapter, entitled 'Of the Public Good'. For some reason, perhaps because of a feeling for the dramatic, he kept his most compelling and original arguments until the end of the chapter. He spent the first few pages establishing the importance of the concept. Subjects were obliged to support a ruler, if, on the whole, he promoted the public good. He included some very conventional phrases about the lustrous character of this common good. Many men had pressed such considerations upon recalcitrant subjects; Tindal turned each argument against the deposed king. Thus he noted how no one

---

[1] Such ideas did not, however, suffer a complete eclipse. See Gerald M. Straka, *Anglican Reaction to the Revolution of 1688* (Madison, 1962), *passim*. He notes too the tendency after 1688 for defenders of the *status quo* to resort to the maxim '*salus populi*' (pp. 107–8). This may help to explain why much later, in the age of Wilkes, the expression had ceased to be a rallying cry for radical opinion and had become a ministerial justification for necessity of state.

[2] Tindal, *An Essay Concerning Obedience to the Supreme Powers, and the Duty of Subjects in All Revolutions* (1694), p. 14 (B: C 2.25 Linc.). Both of Tindal's works cited here were anonymous, but he is generally credited with writing them.

might enjoy a right inconsistent with the common good, 'because the more universal a good is, the more it ought to be embraced'.[1] Then, surprisingly, he added:

... societies could not subsist, but must necessarily fall [in] a state of war and confusion, *if every man should prefer the advantage of any particular person before the good of the whole.*'[2]

This was unusual, because at this point it was normal to say that society could not survive if each man preferred his own advantage before the common good. Since he put the last part of the sentence in italics, he obviously wanted the reader to notice his unusual emphasis.

Similarly, he said in the approved manner, that as particular interests must yield to the public, so must the interest of a particular society be subordinate to the good of all societies. Here his target was the Jacobite theory of legal right which they opposed to *de facto* possession. Adherence to this doctrine would overthrow most of the governments then in existence and produce universal anarchy.[3] All the while he avoided any direct consideration of the relationship between the interests of private men and the public good.

Coming to consider the state of England, he observed that obedience to the *de facto* government was in the interest of the members of that society. Such obedience would promote the 'general interest' of all the particular members. Allegiance to the Stuarts was antithetical to the ends of the community, for it was impossible that unsettling the people's estates, liberties, lives and religion could be for the public good.[4] Then came the remark that altered the whole quality of the chapter:

'... and that common objection, or rather reflection, that it is interest makes these tenets, which require obedience to the present government, so universally embraced, which (howsoever it be uncharitably designed) is so far from destroying the credit of them, that it is a demonstration of their truth; because they are for the good of particulars of which the public is made up.'[5]

This is the argument which in the work of William Ball had sounded so revolutionary. It was no longer unfamiliar, but rarely can it have been put so clearly, certainly not by Ball.

[1] Tindal, p. 19.   [2] *Ibid.*, p. 19.   [3] *Ibid.*   [4] *Ibid.*, p. 21.
[5] *Ibid.*, pp. 21–2.

Tindal was saying that the people had to judge their own interest. He insisted that the interest of the community had to be
construed in a manner which would give adequate protection
to the interests of private men. Doubtless he appreciated that
the public interest implied other conditions as well. Thus Jaco-
bites were wholly off the mark when they complained of men
being their own judges. This was to confuse two different forms
of oppression, that proceeding from private persons and that for
which the government was responsible. In the event of the first
sort, there was an adequate means of redress; in the case of the
second, there was none but self-help. He reaffirmed his earlier
comment about the public interest, saying:

'. . . if anyone by fraud or violence possesseth himself of another's
right, the law is open and redress may be had without any danger to
the public; nay the public safety consists in having private men's
wrongs redressed.'[1]

In the case of Tindal, this definition of the public good in
terms of the rights of private men is especially significant, for he
also wrote of foreign policy and national defence. Discussing this
area, an obvious one in which to use an old-fashioned common
good, he adhered to his original position. Again, he met the
strongest conservative arguments on their own ground and refuted them. As before, he ventured a seemingly vulnerable
argument and then anticipated the objection. For instance, he
claimed that the magistrate acted against the common good if
he failed to protect 'the property, quiet and life of every individual person' as much as was possible, consistent with any
greater good of society. No doubt the High Tory would have
agreed to this formula, but he would have insisted that there
was frequently a greater good in the form of state security. Tindal must surely have been thinking of this retort, for he quickly
added that there was no possible conflict between the two, for
the

'. . . safety or good of the civil society . . . either against foreign or
domestic enemies, is best provided for by the people's union, which
arises from the mutual enjoyments of their liberty, whereby the
source and foundation of domestic enmitys is taken away, and their
strength against foreign enemies increased, which union, and with it

[1] Tindal, pp. 30–1.

the general welfare of the people can only be secured by such a conduct in the governors as gives impartial encouragement to all . . . and perfect security to everyone in the fruits of their labours.'[1]

In the same work Tindal subscribed to a number of ideas that had been previously defended by William Penn. Securing the rights of all citizens was the best defence of the Protestant interest. He also subscribed to Penn's characteristic idea of the merits of a balance of religious parties.[2] Some writers, especially in the Commonwealth, had thought only of a common interest in domestic policy because of their limited range of experience. This could never be said of Tindal, the author of a learned treatise on the laws of nations and the rules of war. Thus he had to defend his formulation of the public interest from critics based in the lore of *raison d'état*, and he had done so most effectively.

Tindal was not an extreme individualist in any sense connoting irresponsibility. He recognized certain duties to the community, though he was individualist enough to wonder whether a man were obliged to give his life for the public.[3] It is difficult to see how he could have fused public and private interests any more than he did. Henry Parker and all early champions of *salus populi* would have rejoiced in Tindal's proclamation that 'the good and interest of the people is the supreme law'.[4]

Other versions of these ideas appeared, but they introduced nothing new. Tyrrell summed up all the thinking on the subject in his *Bibliotheca*. He used the same argument to counter the doctrine of state security. While defence was a legitimate concern of government, no particular emphasis had to be given to it, and certainly no standing army was needed. If the people were left undisturbed in the enjoyment of their rights, they would be their own best defence against all enemies both domestic and foreign.[5] Now that the status of the army had become a burning political issue, this weakness in the liberal case had finally been remedied. The point was made by various writers who were hostile to a standing army. An anonymous writer, probably Walter Moyle, emphasized the threat that such an army posed to private estates. He noted that the unity that

[1] Tindal, *An Essay Concerning the Power of the Magistrate and the Rights of Mankind in Matters of Religion* (1697), pp. 11–12 (B: Vet. A 3 e. 1140).
[2] *Ibid.*, p. 149.   [3] *Essay Concerning Obedience*, p. 24.
[4] *Ibid.*, p. 33.   [5] *Bibliotheca Politica*, p. 83.

would follow the satisfaction of the citizens would be a better defence than any army. Rohan might serve the liberal cause here, for Moyle insisted that

'. . . the Duke of Rohan is our guarantee that we cannot be conquered from abroad.'[1]

The new understanding of the public interest appears to have been accepted by the most prominent political thinkers of the age. Non-Jurors might prate about divine right or the legal niceties of an ancient constitution, but the political ideas of Sydney, Locke, Tyrrell and Tindal all pointed in the same direction, From similar notions about the origin and purpose of governments, they reached a common understanding of the public interest. The theory of the public interest also had some standing in its own right and was not merely a reflection of other ideas regarding the origin of government. Thinkers like the apolitical Cumberland or the eccentric Willan differed from Locke in their general political ideas but offered much the same view of the public interest. Tyrrell's *Bibliotheca* serves as a repository of these opinions, the ideas for which the gallant Sydney died. While the argument of state necessity would reappear, its opponents were now well armed.

There remained one major omission in the liberal case as it had been constructed. Private citizens had been justified in consulting their own property interests in deciding on a common good, but only in narrowly restricted circumstances. It was a power to be exercised when all the normal channels of communication had failed. In a sense, of course, this was all it could be were government not to become a perpetual plebiscite. However, there was one other way of consulting particular interests without encouraging direct action by the masses. There appears to be no clear illustration of this mode of thinking in the seventeenth century. But it did appear at the very beginning of the next century.

Like so many other figures introduced here, Peter Paxton remains completely unknown. In this case it is unfortunate, for he was a powerful and original thinker. He was a doctor, like Locke, and like him, he wrote on both politics and trade as well

[1] Anon., *The Second Part of an Argument Shewing that a Standing Army is Inconsistent with a Free Government* (1697), p. 17 (B: Pamph. 226).

as on scientific subjects. While lacking the master's subtlety, nevertheless in most respects he presented a clearer version of the liberal case. All Paxton's contributions to political theory were set in an elaborate historical framework, at least it is historical as moderns understand the term. Paxton's interests ranged far beyond the constitutional narrative that served as seventeenth-century history. He asked the large, important questions and asked them in a way that must have had few, if any, counterparts up to that time.

Human diversity was Paxton's main interest. He wanted to know why societies differed from each other. The material within his purview ranged from theories about the origin of language to the political factors that determined the content of the Restoration stage. Throughout he kept asking what aspects of society were responsible for changing others. The question that most occupied him was, strangely enough, the one for which he already had the answer. Why was it that in some systems of government the good of the whole people was pursued, in others, that of only a part?

The answer relied heavily on the balance of property as a determining factor. However, he lacked Harrington's confused outlook on human nature. He borrowed nothing but the idea of the balance, which was by then common property. Paxton described the nature of man free from what he called all 'chimerical whimsies, or speculative hypotheses'.[1] Man was always moved by some good for himself, though it might be

'. . . so remote, or may be so intermixed with the good of others, or of the public, as thereby not to be clearly distinguished or regarded.'[2]

Any person not moved by his own pleasure or gain was quite simply '*non compos*'.[3] Still, he insisted, in a manner becoming increasingly common, that this doctrine need shatter none of the current ideas of virtue. There was ample room for piety and benevolence, for

'. . . by man's acting for some end, or his someways regarding his own interest, or himself; I do not only intend his aiming at only some private gain, profit or advantage, as it is applied to riches or worldly

[1] [P. Paxton], *Civil Polity, A Treatise Concerning the Nature of Government* (1703), p. 5.
[2] Paxton, p. 7.   [3] *Ibid.*, p. 14.

wealth; but in general to any other thing that he is pleased with; for it is certain men's minds are as different as their palates.'[1]

He insisted in the strongest way that personal interest was irremediably subjective. Rest and food were necessary to everyone, but apart from such simple needs, 'relative' or 'imaginary' goods were as various as the circumstances of people.[2] One had to appreciate that 'man alone can judge of his own happiness'.[3] He returned several times to this idea.[4] No one else could judge a man's interests and every man judged all things by the standard of his own interests and opinions. He could have no other basis for judgment. Later he was to integrate this portrait of human nature to his theory of history.

The answer to his query about differentials in the standard of consideration was simple. Wealth and civil power could not for long remain separate. In this case property was not just land, but wealth in any form. Thus, in one respect, he brought Harrington up to date. Paxton denied any intention to trace the early relationship between government and property, for there were no records. Instead, he treated the question in the manner of the 'conjectural history' of the mid-eighteenth century. Government must have been set up to protect property, for without property, there were no differences in 'dignity' and hence no great need for strong institutions of government.[5]

While all governments were established to protect private property in a complex society, all did not perform equally well. Some, as in France, served only to distinguish the rights of *meum* and *tuum*, the rights and goods of private men. There was no property over which the ruler might not exercise arbitrary control.[6] There was a tendency, though, for citizens to demand security against the interference with property by the government. This he illustrated from the course of English history, where the Norman conqueror had distributed estates to his followers who were banded together against the erstwhile owners. It was inevitable, he thought, that

'. . . these people, in time, would naturally run into a common or national interest, by reason they now having the estates or land

[1] Paxton, p. 21.　[2] *Ibid.*, p. 47.　[3] *Ibid.*, p. 17.　[4] *Ibid.*, pp. 78 and 180.
[5] *Ibid.*, p. 223.　[6] *Ibid.*, p. 625.

would now be as jealous to preserve what they had against the encroachments of the prince, as the former natives.'[1]

He made the same point without recourse to history. There was a sense in which all political systems were for the common good, because

'. . . laws are what secure men's persons and good, and so are befitted for the common benefit of the community, every man having protection by them.'[2]

Yet while laws served the whole (i.e. all men) in all systems, 'they principally intend the advantage of that authority that made them'.[3] Measured by the protection of property from the government, only popular governments, such as those of England and Holland, provided for the 'general good of the whole community'.[4]

How did popular governments preserve this common good? The answer came as part of a description of the social effects of trade. There was a tendency for trade to increase as society became more complex and its social distinctions more pronounced. Absolute monarchies were exceptions to the rule, for their foreign trade was inhibited owing to the weakness of property rights. This led to the general principle that

'. . . a legal and lasting property can never be ascertained in any community unless each particular member, or at least each class of men, have either by themselves or proxy some share in the legislature; because whosoever is not somehow concerned in that, can have no sure defence against the oppression of those that are.'[5]

This followed directly from nature, for all men regarded themselves

'. . . and only collaterally others, as their interests, or concerns, are intermixed and interwoven with his own. Such persons then, that are not immediately in person or mediately by their representatives, someways concerned in the making, altering or giving laws, their private interests being often separated from those that are, will be most assuredly oppressed, by reason there is [sic] no persons that regard their proper good.'[6]

Thus the Benthamite form of liberalism had finally emerged.

[1] Paxton, p. 410. [2] Ibid., p. 63. [3] Ibid., p. 64. [4] Ibid., p. 64.
[5] Ibid., p. 226. [6] Ibid., p. 227.

To attain the public good, in this case the protection of property and other rights, it was not necessary to suppress one's self-interest in its political form. It was necessary only to maximize opportunities to articulate interests. Every writer who had said, with Harrington, that a genuinely common interest could only exist in a popular government had approached this position. Many had been diverted, though, by concern for limiting the interest of the king. Harrington had been concerned about the self-interest of all rulers, of course, but relied excessively upon his constitutional inventions.

Paxton did not call himself a reformer and may have been fairly satisfied with the existing system, although occasionally more than a hint of republicanism does emerge. In discussing the probable origins of government, he observed that it had involved collecting privately owned parcels of land into one integrated territory. He explained the role of monarchy in early government in the following terms. The government was

'. . . a subordination of tenures, which tenures being branched out into different persons, each of which had an entire property in that part he possessed, and all being collected or united into one polity, it is plain there was required one principal head or common point wherein they all centre.'[1]

Only in this way was it possible to ensure that it was 'the interest of their members to preserve the public peace'.[2] This description of a monarch who acted as a focus for property owners would appear to be valid for all time. Perhaps because of the greater reality of a common good in a popular government, perhaps because of the emergence of non-feudal property, Paxton did not think so. Speaking of his own time, he observed that with the dispersal of power and property in so many hands

'. . . the very nature of our present polity does not so essentially require a king or head, as the ancient did.'[3]

He hastily added that this implied no ill will to the present ruler, though it can hardly have appeared reassuring. It would have been interesting had he said exactly what he meant in his comments about the current state of affairs. One can visualize how giving a large number of citizens the property to justify their political power, and the power to secure their property,

[1] Paxton, p. 381.   [2] *Ibid.*   [3] *Ibid.*, p. 421.

might solve all problems. Closer examination of the means of representing all interests would have been useful, however. It is never clear to what extent he was commending the British system for its realization of these conditions or suggesting some further improvement.

Certainly he considered most other governments as infinitely worse. At the same time, he recognized a problem from which England was not exempt; for 'in all governments' most people were very poor and so took less interest in 'civil rights' than in religious ones. The first he considered vital, the second interested him far less. He offered no solution, but his analysis implied that nothing less than a widening of the propertied classes would be in order. It was eloquent testimony of the content of his 'civil rights' that he could claim that those

'. . . having but little or no property, wealth, or estates, have no advantage by them.'[1]

One could go beyond Paxton's form of liberalism, but surely only in terms of desire and not of understanding. On a purely intellectual level he had reached the essence of the later liberalism.

One of the problems of saying, with Halévy, that some liberals applied an economic view of harmony to politics was that so few political liberals in this period were also liberal in their economic thought. One of the few was Paxton. As we have seen, he was completely lacking in the curious economic conservatism that was quite common among anti-monarchical writers. Self-interest made the economy function, just as it protected political liberties. In both cases, it was best if private interest were allowed freedom to do its work. It is important, then, that a new synthesis between economic and political liberalism appeared at the turn of the century. The alliance would flourish as the century progressed.

For the immediate future, however, the individualist pattern of argument lost some of its urgency. The Revolution had been carried out and soon required little defence. The echoes of old causes did appear occasionally early in the new century, especially in the interminable controversies indulged in by Benjamin Hoadly. Much of his writing on political topics was

[1] Paxton, p. 616.

317

nourished by the now-familiar claim that private citizens, not rulers, should have the ultimate say as to public good. Meanwhile, his non-juring opponents propounded variants of the argument for passive obedience and prerogative. While Hoadly frequently recorded his concern for discovering the 'true common interest', neither he nor his adversaries clashed directly on the meaning of the expression. More than many earlier champions of Whiggism, Hoadly emphasized that he was unconcerned with interests peculiar to individuals; his case rested upon the 'united interest of the whole'.[1] Indeed, so moderate was his position that one wonders how it could sustain this early Bangorian Controversy. Once all concessions had been made, the Bishop's political theory was reduced to a suspicion of those governments that would arbitrarily restrict 'civil rights' because of some supposed danger to the state. As Hoadly drily observed, any government could always see such dangers if it looked hard enough, but this did not warrant taking away all rights 'for the safety of the governed'.[2]

More succinct and useful was the modest treatise by a Wiltshire clergyman. Here conventional praise for securing individual rights was supported by the argument that

'. . . as the whole is made up of parts, so each person, as a member and part of the whole, has a claim to be secured in his rights and properties.'[3]

Burnett was especially concerned lest people be deprived of their rights 'under any pretence of the publick good'.[4] With this in mind, he insisted that

[1] Hoadly, *The Original and Institution of Civil Government . . .* (1710), p. 139.

[2] Hoadly, *The Common Rights of Subjects Defended . . .* (1719), p. 156.

[3] Thomas Burnett, *An Essay Upon Government: or, the Natural Notions of Government, Demonstrated from the Fundamental Principles of Society* (1716), p. 43. For the similar idea that the right of society was a 'sum' of the rights of private persons, see R. W. (i.e. Richard West), *A Discourse Concerning Treasons and Bills of Attainder* (1716), p. 98.

[4] Burnett, *op. cit.*, p. 47. The same message apparently appeared in a sermon of the day of which no copy seems to have survived, although there were two editions. See Rev. Dr. R. S., *Particular Men not to be Injured for the Public Good*, as recorded in *The Monthly Catalogue 1714–17*, ed. D. F. Foxon (London, 1964), Vol. II, No. X, p. 54 and Vol. III, No. IX, p. 43. The catalogue describes the sermon as 'proper to bind up with Mr. Burnett's Essay Upon Government'.

'. . . the welfare of the society does not consist in the largeness and extent of their dominions, much less in the grandeur and flutter of their princes, but in the enjoyment of their rights and properties.'[1]

His individualism was nowhere better displayed than in his constant use of 'society' as a plural noun.

Equally important was the very able presentation of rights as a social and not just a selfish claim. The same emphasis has been present in the Levellers, in Penn and in others, but these people had not been very explicit. Of the individual citizen, Burnett wrote:

'. . . Yet if he be considered relatively, as a member of society, so far as the rights of others depend upon his defending and maintaining his own, they are not then entirely his own, and he has no such right to give 'em up, but on the contrary, is under an obligation to defend 'em, it being the duty of every member of the society, to do what is necessary to the welfare of the society.'[2]

In the history of ideas there is almost no way of demonstrating a consensus of opinion. Attitudes change slowly, and at the time of their greatest strength, all social theories have had their detractors. Thus one cannot say in any precise sense how great the hold of these ideas was. The individualistic interpretation of the public interest attracted little opposition and hence generated little discussion. An age when Tories mistrusted standing armies and foreign adventures may fairly be said to signal a shift in the priorities of policy. The dynastic element, so prominent before, seems to have found little support in current opinion, whatever William III may have thought to the contrary.[3] Apart from the occasional Jacobite, anachronistic now, with his outdated vocabulary, there were few people who disagreed, even by implication, with the writers discussed here.[4] Of course, most writers

---

[1] Burnett, p. 121.   [2] *Ibid.*, p. 85.
[3] For much supporting evidence see G. B. Hertz (Hurst), *English Public Opinion After the Restoration* (London, 1902), pp. 140–1 and 150.
[4] Out of power, even men of Jacobite sympathies became more critical of rhetoric about the common good. One said that 'the public good is generally made a delicate fine thing in the abstract; a separate invisible being, distinguished from all personal interest and benefit'. This he dismissed as an 'airy notion'. See Anon., *A Brief Answer to a Late Discourse Concerning the Unreasonableness of a New Separation* (1691), pp. 9–10. The author was Samuel Grascome.

gave support to neither side, since they did not treat the subject of the public good. When current ideas about the public interest were criticized, the offending passages were quite likely to be those that linked the interest of England to a party. Such comments left individualism unscathed. One might then say with Thomas Wagstaffe that

'. . . the interest of England is an intire thing, and subsists of itself; it supports all parties, but is none of them . . .'[1]

The most effective way of showing that private rights had triumphed over national power is to record some instances where utilitarian ideas were expounded by men who were not conventional liberals. One would not expect to find individualism in the writings of Mandeville's critics, who were presumably defending the public good against his subtle paradoxes. In one passage of his *Fable*[2] Mandeville noted how the 'worldly greatness' of states had to be built not only on the vices but even on the unhappiness of particular persons. His opponents probably made too much of an assumed connection between vice and unhappiness, but several of them agreed in condemning his understanding of the public good. As one of them put it, Mandeville had assumed that

'. . . a wide extent of dominion is necessary to the wealth and happiness of a people. And as to that, it must be considered that the happiness of a community, is nothing but the happiness of the private individuals who compose it. To say that a community may be happy where the private individuals are unhappy, is to say, that an army may be well cloathed, though every single man in every regument were forced to go naked. 'Tis highly absurd to call a nation happy and flourishing, only because it makes a figure abroad. . . . For the greatest power and force that ever any nation has possessed . . . has been of no real use, but as they tended to make each indi-

---

[1] *A Letter to a Gentleman Elected a Knight of the Shire to Serve in the Present Parliament* (n.d.), p. 1. This tract dates from the reign of Anne at the latest, since Wagstaffe died in 1713.
[2] *The Fable of the Bees*, ed. F. B. Kaye (Oxford, 1924), Vol. 1, p. 365. His remarks on the public benefit of private misfortune are not so well known as other of his paradoxes, but this is plainly what he was saying. He said unequivocally that an 'uninterrupted series of successes that every private person could be blessed with' might be inimical to national strength, and hence not in the public interest.

vidual happy in his private life, by securing to him the free and quiet enjoyment of his own.'[1]

The law, scarcely the vanguard of new ideas, took the same position. Later in the century Blackstone produced his version of the public good in the *Commentaries*. To illustrate it, he chose the expropriation power of the state, the procedure most frequently cited by lawyers of the previous century as a case where public good overrode all considerations of private right.[2] Blackstone restricted this power to very narrow limits, saying:

'... in vain may it be urged, that the good of the individual ought to yield to that of the community; for it would be dangerous to allow any private man, or even any public tribunal, to be the judge of this common good, and to decide whether it be expedient or no. Besides the public good is in nothing more essentially interested, than in the protection of every individual's private rights, as modelled by the municipal law.'[3]

Perhaps Blackstone was unenlightened in comparison to Bentham, but on the question of the public good, the two sound surprisingly alike.

In the eighteenth century 'interest' became the moving force in the great game of places, pensions and personalities.[4] The minor forays of party warfare replaced the ideological struggles of the seventeenth century. However, the very battles of principle that marked the seventeeth-century revolutions served to legitimize the particular material interests that came to the fore in the age of Walpole and the Pelhams. Concern for the interests of the subject became itself a principle and informed the practice of quieter and more cynical times.

---

[1] George Blewitt, *An Inquiry Whether a General Practice of Virtue tends to the Wealth or Poverty, Benefit or Disadvantage of a People* (1725), p. 19. The point seems more justified than some brought against Mandeville. See too Anon., *The True Meaning of the Fable of the Bees* (1726), p. 46 (B: G.P. 9), and A. Campbell, *An Enquiry into the Original of Moral Virtue* (Edinburgh, 1733), p. 470.

[2] Standard sources for the first half of the seventeenth century are cited in John Clayton, *Topicks in the Laws of England* (1646), p. 14.

[3] *Commentaries on the Laws of England in Four Books*, 2nd edn. (1766), Vol. I, p. 139.

[4] A good discussion of the later history of 'interest' is to be found in John Carswell, *The Old Cause* (London, 1954), pp. 342-4.

CONCLUSION

ALL VARIANTS OF the idea of a common good involve the assumption that there is a connection between the welfare of the community and that of its members. Thus the arguments examined here differed only in emphasis—but that emphasis was all-important in the growth of English political culture.

Having an interest could mean only that one derived advantage from a state of affairs and enjoyment of his advantage might be perfectly passive. People often appealed to the interests of others without suggesting that anything be done to preserve or advance these interests except to remain peaceful. Many writers who contrived to reconcile private and public interest were thinking only of each man's interest in the general protection of property and related rights. The capacity of having such an interest might imply doing something about promoting it, but some commentators have exaggerated the amount of positive activity contemplated by individualists. The very fact that Mandeville's defence of self-seeking and vice clashed with the new understanding of the public interest is enough to distinguish individualism from ordinary licence. It remains true that individualists usually wrote of public interest of which the members of the public might be aware; their opponents were more conscious of what was good for the public, whether it knew it or not.

The most important difference in emphasis between the two positions lay in the way in which the content of the public interest was described. Having demonstrated the alternatives in so many contexts, the pattern should now be clear. The conventional position was that the unquestioned common interest was that the state remain secure from all disorder, whether from internal dissension or foreign invasion. An interest of this sort was no doubt a shared one, but it was not as dear to the defenders of liberty and property as their rulers must have wished. It seems doubtful whether many thinkers before the rise of socialism entirely discounted such matters of order and national power. If one did not dismiss them, it was still possible to honour the responsibility of defence while expressing it in terms of private satisfaction. This was the theme that ran through most liberal interpretations of the public good. Often it took the form, following Rohan, that there would be no danger from abroad if domestic interests were placated, for a united England had nothing to fear. The debates over ship-money, liberty of conscience and the standing army all fit into this pattern. The government that prejudiced the rights of property, using the pretext of national security, did not have to look abroad for trouble.

This does not mean that the two positions came to the same thing. They entailed different social priorities and a different relationship between private interests and the public interest. Interest always involves choice. In the case of a private person the realization of an interest, or even the understanding of it, necessitates ranking one's concerns, since they are not all equally and simultaneously attainable. The same applies with equal force to a community and its interest. National power might very well be compatible with private rights in most cases, but the critical decisions had to be made at the margins where one of the two conditions had first to be established in order to secure the other.

The difference in content between these definitions of the public interest also affected the degree to which particular interests were allowed free play. The virtue of a public interest conceived in terms of maintaining private rights was that it reduced the lustrous and distant goal of a public good to proportions that were comprehensible to private persons. They might both understand it and do something about maintaining it without prejudicing their legitimate private interests. Indeed, while bent only on securing these interests, they might often serve the public. The nature of these legitimate private interests is very important. Not all interests were included, only those relevant to public policy. Such interests were also usually described at a high level of generality. It is this factor which saves the individualist from the twin imbecilities of advocating either anarchy or a dead uniformity.

The interests, the protection of which constituted the public interest, were considered as the chief social concerns that most men had at most times. Generally these writers did not stoop to consider what one might normally deem typical conflicts of interest. It was not only Harrington who dismissed disputes between tanners and clothiers; even a number of writers on economic subjects thought more in terms of broad groups within the population and their long-term relations. The rights claimed in opposition to reason of state tended to be general conditions that could be shared by all men, and indeed would be ineffective unless all shared them. This applies both to political claims, such as equality before the law and preservation of estate, and to the more narrow demands of religious sects. This explains how such people might think that there was something common in the common interest. This interest was not merely a collection of entirely different and incompatible demands brought to bear on a single narrow question of policy. The common interest was not just $(X + Y + Z \ldots + N)$, for the claims being considered were not competing tenders or sectional interests in the modern sense.

Private interests as defended by political writers related mainly to the erecting of barriers against the state's incursions on private property largely in the form of unconstitutional or excessive taxation. Commercial argument obviously had to be concerned with private transactions, but even here a surprising number of the claims of individualism might be reduced to demands for equality before the law. The great trouble with regulations in an infant administrative structure was that they were liable to inconsistent application. Thus the common interest might be described by a single general rubric, while this interest consisted in the satisfaction of private interests. If men could have a common interest in the fate of their country they could also have one in the conditions that allowed them to preserve and extend their estates. Of course, some people had no estates to protect, thus making the common good a mockery for them. Few joined Paxton in concern at this problem, but one could suggest that the freeholder's common interest was at least more immediately and concretely tied to the welfare of some of the people than the earlier dynastic interest.

The same condition that gave some shared interest to the common good also explains why the individualist's position was not dependent upon all people wanting exactly the same things. Harmony was severely limited in its scope and there is no reason to assume that a *Harmonielehre* assumed any idyllic state of brotherhood. Not only were most individualists realistic about the limitations of human nature, they also added to the understanding of the function of social conflict. The sophisticated defenders of absolute monarchy had doubtless always known that self-interest made conflict inevitable, but official doctrine followed the church in assuming that citizens should just prefer the common good without inquiring too closely about what became of their own interests. The contribution of Hobbes and those influenced by him was to make very plain that 'interest' inevitably moved all men. As with Hobbes, their main concern may have been to remove all of the earlier confusion about the extent of royal self-interest, but they justified self-interest on the part of private men as well. In *Leviathan* the appreciation of how self-interest made conflict inevitable led Hobbes to emphasize the restraining function of authority. White and Hall adhered to the same basic pattern, but made more provision within the temple of the common good for legitimate private interests.

Certainly there was a temptation for commonwealthsmen to overlook self-interest and to say that all men should lay aside their selfish designs and love one another. It was difficult to apply Hobbes's insight to a popular government, for unleashing, self-interested multitudes seemed to invite anarchy. Few of the defenders of quasi-popular government examined the machinery with any care. Those who did, like Harrington, accepted the fact that it was necessary to balance private interests against each other. The numerous writers, both before and after the Restoration, who claimed that the 'people' knew their interest were concerned with the basic need of protecting general private rights, and with day-to-day policy. The more sophisticated early commonwealthsmen thought almost solely of institutional checks to channel self-interest into the stream of the common good. After the Restoration, other perspectives appeared. Penn, his antecedents and his imitators applauded the *concordia discors* that allowed people with contrary interests of one sort to join together for a common interest of a different sort. Even a philosopher such as Cumberland, who had no liking for popular government, showed how the common good might be preserved as one selfish interest checked the extravagancies of another. Paxton showed the way into the next century by explaining that the maintenance of the public interest was dependent upon maximizing the opportunity to articulate particular interests.

Again it must be said that the interests of individuals might be very broadly conceived ones or highly specific. The harmony of interests in liberal writings included only one level of particular interests. An apparent exception was Cumberland, who conceived of a general good consisting of all the goods of particular men. However, he had made this comment in relation to ethics in general, and in the passages treating specifically political values he was correspondingly more concerned with the right of property rather than all of an individual's interests. Seventeenth-century concern for the right of private property suggested no uniformity of interest as to the routine of social life. There was ample scope for diversity and even contrariety of interests in areas that did not impinge on the general rights of citizens. Of course people wanted different, and perhaps incompatible, things. The protection of private rights merely guaranteed the means of unique individual development. It was a matter on which most private citizens might unite against any rapacious government without having to be in complete agreement among themselves.

If the liberal notions about the public interest were inadequate as tools of understanding and sometimes produced unfortunate social results, this is reason enough to criticize them. But first it should be understood what the individualist was saying. His argument was a response to another version of the national good couched in the language of reason of state. While the former school seemed negligent in considering the welfare of some persons, the latter too frequently ignored private satisfaction entirely. The seventeenth-century insight that a community was, in one sense, a collection of individuals served a number of good causes. It aided the establishment of constitutional government and religious liberty. Often it was useful in reducing unjust monopolies of power, either economic or political. Such an idea

326

might be turned to ill use, as may most social ideas, but those who used it appear to have been men of goodwill. They doubtless had quite as much compassion as their more paternalistic opponents, but their social circumstances were different. It was the private citizen with a grievance, not the courtier, who was likely to diminish the pretensions of the public good.

The public interest may be analysed in different ways, but all of them seem to require some data drawn from what people have actually said about it. For these purposes the language of argument is much more useful than that of formal utterances by government officials. British railway dining cars carry notices to the effect that it is not in the public interest to bring dogs into the carriage. One could analyse this piece of intelligence for ever without learning any more about what people mean by a public interest. An attempt has been made here to break the circuit of that academic discussion which feeds upon itself, without getting back to the content of political argument. While it may be perfectly sensible to ask what 'we' mean by the public interest, the normal lines of inquiry appear self-defeating. Official sources will not answer such questions in other than narrow, substantive terms, while scholars have been unduly restricted by a net composed of each other's language. There may be other periods of history richer in materials for this sort of analysis, but the natural advantages of the seventeenth century have already been explained.

The literary formula of describing the public interest as a 'sum' of particular interests was not common until the late eighteenth century, although the same message was often expressed much earlier in different language. The aggregative imagery was most plausible in instances where it was apparent that the particular interests being 'added' were all of the same sort. This condition obtained in the great majority of the cases treated here, for the writers in question were concerned with protecting the general rights of private men. A figure such as Harrington, who carried his analysis to the extent of examining the clash of various interests in a legislature, had less reason to describe the process of balancing these interests in terms of producing a sum. But even here the formula was something more than just an extended exercise in the fallacy of composition.

There was widespread realization on the part of individualists that while it might sometimes be sensible to describe the public good as a collection of private utilities, this description would not always be meaningful. To say with Filmer and Houghton that there might be occasions when the common good was the good of every particular man was unexceptional, unless it was being claimed that the common good must always be so described. Both of the writers in question were perfectly explicit in limiting the application of the formula. Many others would no doubt have agreed, although they were less explicit.

The purpose of this study had been accomplished if an historical dimension has been added to current discussions about the public interest. The treatment here has not followed those sets of antitheses so often employed. The distinction between a natural and an artificial harmony of interests seems inappropriate either for describing stages in economic thought or for contrasting economic and political ideas. The differences between the opposed traditions recorded here may seem very much like that between domestic and foreign contexts of the national interest, but the two sets of categories do not really coincide. The debates forming the material for the thesis dealt, for the most part, with the impact of domestic policies on private citizens. There were other disagreements about the national interest in foreign affairs that are not relevant here.

One distinction that has proved rewarding is that between the process of preserving the public interest and the manner in which that interest might be described. This allows one to distinguish various forms of individualism. When merchants argued that liberated self-interest would promote the public good they were not always led to describe that good. It might be maximum national wealth or maximum private satisfaction. A large number of writers, including most early 'democrats', and not a few concerned with economic life, took another approach. They claimed that the public interest consisted in the satisfaction of private interests, while not denying that a measure of active self-interest might be required to realize this condition. The first view has frequently been taken to represent the liberal position on the public interest. However, the second seems the more plausible and responsible doctrine, since often it consisted only in the plea that government make an effort to preserve legitimate and universal rights.

The question 'is there a public interest?' dominates modern academic discussion of the topic. The problem of location and definition of this interest is vastly complicated by the fact that scholars remain unsure about what they are looking for. The public interest is now variously identified as some concern consciously shared by all members of the public, the product of certain procedures, an ineffable absolute value or as a useful myth. Without doubt the analysis of this century far surpasses in sophistication any earlier consideration of the concept. However, for all this wealth of analysis, contemporary discussion is not free from a pursuit of essences that seems curiously inappropriate to the modern temper. A number of scholars purport to offer a single valid definition in terms of the preservation of community institutions. Others, failing to discover such an essence, boldly declare that the public interest is a fiction. Both the believers and the sceptics often suggest that if there is a public interest it must be capable of description by a single set of predicates; it is one, not many. Of course a number of scholars have indeed suggested various levels of meaning, and many have withheld judgment. But the terms of the question 'is there a public interest?' appear to call for an answer consisting of one formal definition.

Unlike modern scholarly disagreements, those of the seventeenth century often involved evasions and suppressed premises. This was no doubt unscholarly, but these men were not, for the most part, scholars. It is significant, however, that whatever they said for purposes of argument, many seventeenth-century thinkers were aware that there was more than one way of saying what the public interest meant. When they listed the components of the public good they often included both general unassignable goods, like national defence, and matters such as the protection of private rights. Of course, formal definitions of the public interest were rare and most active polemicists used the notion in a number of ways. Nevertheless, the distinction made by Suarez was undoubtedly more familiar than a survey of polemical writings would suggest.

The most difficult problems in the use of the concept of the public interest have arisen in the relationship between private concerns and those supposedly shared by a whole community. Controversy in the seventeenth century gave at least two coherent meanings to the concept, one of them accommodating particular interests, the other paying them little regard. Perhaps ideas derived from early individualism and its critics need adaptation to a century when 'interests' refer more frequently than before to groups rather than to individuals. However, evidence drawn from early political argument is relevant to the assessment of ideas about the public interest. It indicates that disagreement on the point is no new thing, but can be traced back to the origins of the expression. Interests, public and otherwise, are not concrete entities; they exist in the minds of men and are appealed to by argument. It is difficult to contemplate any empirical investigation that could conclusively affirm or deny the presence of a public interest. Evidence of various sorts drawn from sources in the seventeenth century attests to the stubborn diversity of ideas about this indispensable political concept. The greater sophistication of the twentieth century is matched by a more complex play of social forces; thus it seems unlikely that a *single* meaning of the concept will emerge. The seventeenth century still produced alchemists, but it would be a repudiation of the *best* teaching of that age to pursue this particular philosopher's stone.

APPENDIX A

A SUM OF INTERESTS
IN PHYSIOCRATIC WRITINGS

SOME OF THE most important documents for an understanding of eighteenth-century notions about the public interest were the writings of the Physiocrats in France. Without trying to prove any direct connection between their ideas and English social thought, it is still safe to say that the work of the Physiocrats was well known in Britain. Adam Smith, for instance, had almost all of their books in his library, including a complete set of their journal.[1] It seems probable that the practice of describing the public interest as a sum of particular interests owed something to physiocratic vocabulary.

Several aspects of physiocratic thought on the common interest correspond with English attitudes of the seventeenth century. Claims for a natural order in which self-interest harmonized with the public good were made in response to illiberal official emphasis upon national power. However much some Physiocrats may have supported absolute monarchy, they had no sympathy with a public interest conceived in terms of reason of state. With great regularity the Physiocrats complained of the unsatisfactory character of a public interest that consisted only in military aggrandizement and national honour. Dupont de Nemours was indignant that the interests of private men should

[1] See T. Yanaihara, *A Full and Detailed Catalogue of Books which Belonged to Adam Smith now in possession of the Faculty of Economics, University of Tokyo* (Tokyo, 1951), pp. 97–8.

be contrasted with a public interest. It was a scandal that some statesmen should visualize a national interest that was opposed to 'la conservation des droits des particuliers', which was the end of society.[1] Once such a principle was granted, the way lay open to any 'pretext', such as foreign wars or colossal building, matters that had no connection with the legitimate satisfactions of private men. In the same manner, Mirabeau attacked

'. . . les idées vagues de gloire, de politique, d'intérêt des princes . . . de raison d'état et autres grands mots vuides de sens.'[2]

National strength was but 'la force intérieure d'un état',[3] and this followed from protecting private rights. Other texts noted both the normal function of the expression 'public good' to rationalize all arbitrary interference with private men, and specific objectionable policies, such as unnecessary expenditure on the navy.[4] Certainly the hostility of the Physiocrats was directed at targets familar to English liberals.

The content of the public interest was also in keeping with earlier English notions. The harmony between national and particular interests depended upon the government's respecting private rights, especially that of property. For the Physiocrats, 'property' chiefly meant the right of disposing of capital and physical possessions, but they also linked all other rights to this one. Without security for property in the narrow sense, no other right was safe. This was what made the general interest 'le résultat des intérêts particuliers'[5] and 'la chose publique', 'un tissu des choses particulières réunies de façon qu'elles forment un tout'.[6] Their journal contained an explanation of how these property interests might unite to form a common interest. Each

[1] 'Physiocratie' (1768), introduction in E. Daire, *Physiocrates* (Paris, 1846), p. 31. The work was by Quesnay, the introduction by Dupont.
[2] *Theorie de l'Impot* (Paris, 1760), p. 86.
[3] *Ibid.*, p. 504.
[4] See Louis-Paul Abeille, *Lettre d'un Négociant sur la Nature du Commerce des Grains* (1763), ed. E. Depitre (Paris, 1911), p. 101, and *Ephémérides du Citoyen*, Vol. I (1768), pp. 218–20.
[5] Accarias de Serionne, *Les Intérêts des Nations de L'Europe, Devélopés Relativement au Commerce* (Leyden, 1766), Vol. II, p. 36. While not strictly speaking a Physiocrat, this writer adhered to part of their programme.
[6] Victor Mirabeau, Marquis de Riquetti, *L'Ami Des Hommes, ou Traité de la Population* (Avignon, 1758), Vol. IV, p. 47.

APPENDIX A

man found it impossible to ensure security of his own property
unless all others were equally well protected:

'. . . l'intérêt de mon voisin qui est l'immunité de sa proprieté
fonciére, crée donc une multitude des propriétés et de nouveaux
intérêsts, qui se trouvent tous indivisiblement unis à un seul et même
intérêt, qui ne nous paroissent tout à l'heure qu' individuel.'[1]

An opponent of the school may have been one of the first to
observe that their view of society assumed that the public good
was 'nothing but the collection of all particular goods'.[2] It may
have been Mercier de la Rivière who later coined the slogan of a
sum of interests; if so, he was probably only repaying a debt to
Cumberland, who was a major influence on the Physiocrats.
The interest of property, presumably common to all individuals,
was the one with which Rivière was concerned. It was with reference to such a right of property that he wrote of

'. . . cette somme d'intérêts particuliers, dont la réunion forme ce
qu'on peut appeler l'intérêt général du corps social.'[3]

This entailed no assumption that all interests could be reconciled. The Physiocrats were certain that the most serious conflicts of interest would disappear in a free market; but they were
equally aware that market conditions necessarily involved a
'débat d'intérêts'.[4] Mirabeau used the metaphor of the recipro-
cal pressure of bricks constituting a wall.[5] This provided the pattern for particular interests which by crossing and containing
each other would sustain the social edifice. The physiocratic
sum of interests was dependent only on one common interest,
that of the free use of one's property in certain areas previously
subject to regulation. By its very nature the exercising of this
right involved clashes of interest, the interests in this case being
of a less general, more immediate sort.

[1] *Ephémérides du Citoyen*, Vol. III (1768), p. 79.
[2] J.-J. Louis Graslin, *Essai Analytique Sur la Richesse et Sur L'Impot* (1767), ed.
A. Dubois (Paris, 1911), pp. 126–7.
[3] *L'Ordre Naturel et Essential des Sociétés Politiques* (Paris, 1767), pp. 56–7.
[4] *Ephémérides du Citoyen*, Vol. X (1767), p. 211. See too a passage translated
from Quesnay in R. L. Meek, *The Economics of Physiocracy* (London, 1962),
p. 212.
[5] *L'Ami des Hommes*, p. 34.

333

The Physiocrats strove to demonstrate and to create a genuine common interest out of particular ones. While they insisted that any other economic system would function in the interests of one class, their own system went unheeded largely because of popular pressure from those who felt that it would cause suffering to some interests.[1] However, the practicability of their schemes is not the issue here. The important factor is that they rebelled against reason of state in much the same way as had earlier English individualists.[2] Physiocratic doctrine established the two factors present in other liberal versions of the public interest. Property was the basis of any public interest, without protecting the rights of property, no public interest existed. In this case property involved not only the peaceful enjoyment of one's own possessions but also the right to trade without restraint. The Physiocrats said both that the public interest was a condition where private rights were protected and that freely functioning private interest would preserve the common interest. Many of the English enemies of *raison d'état* had emphasized the first proposition rather than the second.

Even when the slogan of a sum of interests was assimilated into English vocabulary, probably through the influence of the Physiocrats, there was no necessary connection between it and a policy of *laissez-faire*. When Sir James Steuart said that it was 'the combination of every private interest that forms the public good',[3] he was not justifying an invisible hand but asserting the rights of private men against the grandiose policies of the statesman.[4] Paley also employed an aggregative notion of the public good, writing of 'the sum of public prosperity'.[5] Here, too, the point of the argument was to discredit 'stately imposing terms' such as national honour, which were used to support a policy of

[1] See Georges Weulersse, *Les Physiocrates* (Paris, 1931), pp. 290–2.
[2] Indeed, in the late seventeenth century this theme had already been prominent in French thought; for the policies of Louis XIV raised the problem of private rights versus national honour in a more pronounced way than did English statecraft of the period. See Henri Sée, *Les Idées Politiques en France au XVII Siècle* (Paris, 1923), pp. 192, 195, 200 and 276.
[3] Steuart, *An Inquiry into the Principles of Political Economy* (1767), Vol. I, p. 164, and again p. 471.
[4] *Ibid.*, p. XII.
[5] William Paley, *The Principles of Moral and Political Philosophy* (Dublin, 1785), Vol. II, p. 158.

conquest at whatever cost to the welfare of individual citizens.[1]
The doctrine of a sum of interests may have led in turn to other
defective policies, but placed in its context, it becomes intelligible.

[1] *Ibid.*, pp. 444–8.

THOMAS PAINE AND THE PUBLIC GOOD

PAINE PROVIDES SOME guidance as to status of the public good in later English liberalism. Although Bentham's thoughts on the subject are better known, Paine's remarks appeared earlier and were more detailed. The critical passage exemplifies both individualism and a concern for some good that was genuinely common to all citizens:

'... Public good is not a term opposed to the good of individuals; on the contrary, it is the good of every individual collected. It is the good of all, because it is the good of every one: for as the public body is every individual collected, so the public good is the collected good of those individuals.

The foundation principle of the public good is justice, and wherever justice is impartially administered the public good is promoted; for as it is to the good of every man that no injustice be done to him, so likewise it is to his good that the principle which secures him should not be violated in the person of another, because such a violation weakens his security, and leaves to chance what ought to be to him a rock to stand on.'[1]

This has been called 'verbiage', since his definition of the public good gives no clear guides to policy.[2] As usual, political

[1] 'Dissertations on Government' (1786), in *Political and Miscellaneous Works* (London, 1819), Vol. I, p. 9. Cf. Bentham, *An Introduction to the Principles of Morals and Legislation* (1789), pp. 2–3.
[2] C. M. Kenyon, 'Where Paine Went Wrong', *American Political Science Review*, Vol. 45 (1951), pp. 1086–99, at p. 1098.

scientists have expected a controversialist to provide some understanding of the public interest that accounts for the entire political process. However, one might better ask what Paine was trying to accomplish. He was an internationalist and thus an enemy of most claims for national power. In seeking security for individual rights he had to discredit claims by kings to have their good taken for that of the nation. The passage quoted here was part of an argument contrasting the good of ordinary citizens with that of the sovereign. Statements of this sort were frequently encountered in earlier literature and are quite comprehensible. But they were not intended as a prescription for all government policy.

The quotation from Paine expresses perfectly the point of liberal political argument as early as 1642. Each man's concern for preserving his own rights necessitated certain general conditions to be shared by all citizens. This was individualism, but it was a form of individualism that served to connect private interests to form a common good. There could be no better illustration of the fact that it mattered a great deal what sorts of interests were seen as together composing the public interest.

BIBLIOGRAPHY

IN PREPARING THIS bibliography no attempt has been made to record all of the works mentioned in the footnotes. More than five hundred early books, tracts, broadsides, newspapers and manuscripts have been cited in the footnotes with sufficient information to allow for their identification and location. The nature of the topic precludes any selective bibliography based upon these materials, since the whole intent of the argument has been to indicate how general was the concern for the problem under discussion. Nor would a selection of works other than those in the footnotes have proved useful; each document has required analysis in order to explain its relevance, and sources were cited for various purposes.

The bibliography then is limited to modern publications, i.e. those of the nineteenth and twentieth centuries, cited in the text. The repetition of these sources seems justified in that it affords an opportunity to record information, such as the name of publishers, not contained in the footnotes. There would be no comparable advantage in listing seventeenth-century works, where information about the publisher is irrelevant and difficult to obtain.

The first section of the bibliography is devoted to modern editions of works written during the period under examination. The other section treats secondary sources. Some unpublished theses have not been recorded, since the original acknowledgments gave all of the necessary information.

COLLECTIONS AND MODERN EDITIONS OF WORKS FIRST
PUBLISHED PRIOR TO 1800

ANON., *A Discourse of the Common Weal of this Realm of England.* ed. E. Lamond, Cambridge: Cambridge U. Press, 1929.

AUBREY, John, *Brief Lives*. 2 vols. ed. A. Clark, Oxford: Clarendon Press, 1898.

BACON, Francis, *Works*, 10 vols. London: F. C. & J. Rivington, 1819.

BOHUN, E., *Diary and Autobiography of Edmund Bohun*. ed. S. W. Rix, Beccles: privately printed, 1853.

BOURNE, H. R. FOX, *The Life of John Locke*. 2 vols. London: H. S. King & Co., 1876.

CROMWELL, Oliver, *The Writings and Speeches of Oliver Cromwell*. 4 vols. ed. W. C. Abbott, Cambridge, Mass.: Harvard U. Press, 1945.

CUNNINGHAM, W., *The Growth of English Industry and Commerce in Modern Times*. 2 vols. Cambridge: Cambridge U. Press, 1917.

DUNHAM, W. H., and PARGELLIS, S. (eds.), *Complaint and Reform in England 1436–1714*. New York: Oxford U. Press, 1938.

ELIOT, Sir John, *De Jure Majestatis or Political Treatise of Government*. ed. A. B. Grosart, London: privately printed, 1882.

ELYOT, Thomas, *The Boke Named the Governour*. 2 vols. ed. H. H. S. Croft, London: C. Kegan Paul, 1880.

EVELYN, John, *The Miscellaneous Writings of John Evelyn*. ed. W. Upcott, London: 1825.

FILMER, Sir Robert, *Patriarcha and Other Political Writings*. ed. P. Laslett, Oxford: Basil Blackwell, 1949.

FIRTH, C. H., and RAIT, R. S., *Acts and Ordinances of the Interregnum, 1642–1660*. London: Wyman and Sons, 1911.

HALIFAX, *The Complete Works of George Savile, First Marquis of Halifax*. ed. Sir W. Raleigh, Oxford: Clarendon Press, 1912.

HILL, J. E. C., and DELL, E. (eds.), *The Good Old Cause*. London: Lawrence and Wishart, 1949.

HOBBES, Thomas, *De Cive*. ed. S. Lamprecht, New York: Appleton-Century-Crofts, 1949.
The English Works of Thomas Hobbes. 11 vols. ed. Sir Wm. Molesworth, London: J. Bohn, 1839–45.
Leviathan. ed. M. Oakeshott, Oxford: Basil Blackwell, 1955.

HOOKER, Richard, *The Works of that Learned and Judicious Divine Mr. Richard Hooker*. 3 vols. ed. John Keble, Oxford: Clarendon Press, 1888.

JAMES I, *The Political Works of James I*. ed. C. H. McIlwain, Cambridge, Mass.: Harvard U. Press, 1918.

LILJEGREN, S. B., 'James Harrington's Oceana edited with Notes', *Skrifter Vetenskaps-Socienteten I*. Heidelberg: 1924.

LOCKE, John, *Essays on the Law of Nature*. ed. W. von Leyden, Oxford: Clarendon Press, 1954.

Second Treatise of Civil Government and a Letter Concerning Toleration. ed. J. W. Gough, Oxford: Basil Blackwell, 1948.

Two Treatises of Government. ed. P. Laslett, Cambridge: Cambridge. U. Press, 1960.

LUDLOW, E., *The Memoirs of Edmund Ludlow.* 2 vols. ed. C. H. Firth, Oxford: Clarendon Press, 1894.

MACHIAVELLI, N., *The Discourses of Machiavelli.* 2 vols. ed. C. J. Walker, London: Routledge and Kegan Paul, 1950.

MANDEVILLE, B. de, *The Fable of the Bees.* 2 vols. ed. F. B. Kaye, Oxford: Clarendon Press, 1924.

MARVELL, A., *Complete Works.* 4 vols. ed. A. B. Grosart, London: Robson and Sons, 1872–5.

McCULLOCH, J. R. (ed.), *Early English Tracts on Commerce.* Cambridge: Economic History Society, 1952.

PAPILLON, A. F. W., *Memoirs of Thomas Papillon.* Reading: J. J. Beecroft, 1887.

PAULI, R., 'Drei Volkswirthschaftliche Denkschriften aus der Zeit Heinrichs VIII', *Konigliche Gesellschaft der Wissenschaften.* Bd. 23 Gottingen: 1878.

SMITH, Adam, *Inquiry into the Nature and Causes of the Wealth of Nations.* 2 vols. ed. E. Cannan, London: Methuen, 1930.

SPINOZA, B. de, *The Political Works.* ed. A. G. Wernham, Oxford: Clarendon Press, 1958.

STARKEY, Thomas, 'A Dialogue Between Cardinal Pole and Thomas Lupset', in *England in the Reign of King Henry VIII.* ed. S. J. Herrtage, London: Early English Text Society, 1878.

SUAREZ, F., *Selections from Three Works of Francisco Suarez, S.J.* ed. G. L. Williams *et al.*, Oxford: Clarendon Press, 1944.

TAWNEY, R. H., and POWER, E. (eds.), *Tudor Economic Documents.* 3 vols. London: Longmans, 1924.

UNDERHILL, E. B. (ed.), *Tracts on Liberty of Conscience and Persecution 1614–1661.* London: Hanserd Knollys Society, 1846.

WILSON, Thomas, *A Discourse Upon Usury.* ed. R. H. Tawney, London: G. Bell & Sons, 1925.

WOODHOUSE, A. S. P. (ed.), *Puritanism and Liberty, being the Army Debates.* (1647–9.) London: J. M. Dent, 1951.

SECONDARY SOURCES

ALBEE, E., *A History of English Utilitarianism.* London: Swan Sonnenschein, 1902.

ALLEN, J. W., *English Political Thought 1603–1660.* Vol. I. London: Methuen, 1938.

ASHLEY, W. J., 'The Tory Origins of Free Trade Policy', in *Surveys Historic and Economic*. London: Longmans, 1900.

BARBU, Z., *Problems of Historical Psychology*. London: Routledge and Kegan Paul, 1960.

BARRY, Brian M., *Political Argument*. London: Routledge and Kegan Paul, 1965.

'Public Interest', *Supplement to the Proceedings of The Aristotelian Society* (1964), pp. 1–18.

'The Use and Abuse of "The Public Interest" ', in C. J. Friedrich (ed.), *The Public Interest*. Nomos V. New York: Atherton Press, 1962.

BAUMGARDT, David, *Bentham and the Ethics of Today*. Princeton: Princeton U. Press, 1942.

BEARD, Charles A., *The Idea of the National Interest*. New York: Macmillan, 1934.

BEATTY, E. C. O., *William Penn as Social Philosopher*. New York: Columbia U. Press, 1939.

BAUMER, F. LeVan, *The Early Tudor Theory of Kingship*. New Haven: Yale U. Press, 1940.

BENTLEY, A. F., *The Process of Government*. Bloomington, Indiana: Principia Press, 1949.

BERESFORD, M., 'Habitation vs. Improvement: the Debate on Enclosure by Agreement', in F. J. Fisher (ed.), *Essays in the Economic and Social History of Tudor and Stuart England*. Cambridge: Cambridge U. Press, 1961.

BETHELL, S. L., *The Cultural Revolution of the Seventeenth Century*. London: Dennis Dobson, 1951.

BLITZER, Charles, *An Immortal Commonwealth: The Political Thought of James Harrington*. New Haven: Yale U. Press, 1960.

BLUHM, William T., *Theories of the Political System*. Englewood Cliffs, N.J.: Prentice-Hall, 1965.

BOWLE, John, *Hobbes and his Critics*. London: J. Cape, 1952.

BUCK, P. W., *The Politics of Mercantilism*. New York: H. Holt, 1942.

BURANELLI, Vincent, *The King and the Quaker, A Study of William Penn and James II*. Philadelphia: U. of Pennsylvania Press, 1962.

CARSWELL, John, *The Old Cause*. London: The Cresset Press, 1954.

CASSINELLI, C. W., 'The Concept of the Public Interest', *Ethics*, Vol. 69 (1958–9), pp. 48–61.

CASTIGNONE, Silvana, *Giustizia E Bene Commune in David Hume*. Milan: Giuffrè Editore, 1964.

CHALK, A. F., 'Natural Law and the Rise of Economic Individualism in England', *Journal of Political Economy*, Vol. 59 (1951), pp. 332–47.

CHRIMES, S. B., *English Constitutional Ideas in the Fifteenth Century*. Cambridge: Cambridge U. Press, 1936.

COLTMAN, Irene, *Private Men and Public Causes*. London: Faber and Faber, 1962.

CLEVELAND, Harwell, and LASSWELL, H. D. (eds.), *Ethics and Bigness*. New York: Harper, 1962.

CUNNINGHAM, W., *The Common Weal, Six Lectures in Political Philosophy*. Cambridge: Cambridge U. Press, 1917.

DAIRE, Eugène, *Physiocrates*. Paris: Librairie de Guillaumin, 1846.

DEWAR, M., *Sir Thomas Smith, A Tudor Intellectual in Office*. London: Athlone Press, 1964.

DICEY, A. V., *Lectures on the Relation Between Law and Public Opinion in England during the Nineteenth Century*. 2nd edn. London: Macmillan, 1914.

DOVE, P. E., *Account of Andrew Yarranton, The Founder of British Political Economy*. Edinburgh: Johnstone & Hunter, 1854.

EINSTEIN, Lewis, *Tudor Ideals*. London: G. Bell, 1921.

ESCHMANN, T., 'A Thomistic Glossary on the Principle of the Pre-eminence of a Common Good', *Mediaeval Studies*, Vol. 5 (1943), pp. 123–65.

FINK, Zera S., *The Classical Republicans*. Evanston: Northwestern U. Press, 1945.

FRANK, Joseph, *The Levellers*. Cambridge, Mass.: Harvard U. Press, 1955.

FRIEDRICH, Carl J., *Constitutional Reason of State*. Providence: Brown U. Press, 1957.

FURNISS, E. S., *The Position of the Labourer in a System of Nationalism*. New York: Houghton Mifflin, 1920.

GERMINO, D. L., 'The Crisis in Community', in C. J. Friedrich (ed.), *Community*. Nomos II, New York: Atherton Press, 1959.

GOOCH, G. P., *English Democratic Ideas in the Seventeenth Century*. ed. H. J. Laski, New York: Harper, 1959.

GOUGH, J. W., *Fundamental Law in English Constitutional History*. Oxford: Clarendon Press, 1955.

John Locke's Political Philosophy, Eight Studies. Oxford: Clarendon Press, 1950.

GRAMPP, W. D., 'The Liberal Elements in English Mercantilism', *Quarterly Journal of Economics*, Vol. LXVI, No. 4 (1952), pp. 465–501.

GREENLEAF, W. H., *Order, Empiricism and Politics, Two Traditions of English Political Thought, 1500–1700*. London: Oxford U. Press, 1964.

GRUNDSTEIN, Nathan D., 'Bentham's Introduction to the Principles of Morals and Legislation', *Journal of Public Law*, Vol. 2 (1953), pp. 344–69.

HALÉVY, Élie, *The Growth of Philosophic Radicalism*. London: Faber & Gwyer, 1928.

HARBAGE, A., *Cavalier Drama*. Oxford: Oxford U. Press, 1936.

HAUPTMANN, Jerzy, 'The Concept of Public Interest', in Ralph M. Miwa *et al.*, *Problems in Political Theory*. Columbia, Missouri: Bureau of Government Research, University of Missouri, 1961.

HAYDEN, H., *The Counter-Renaissance*. New York: Scribners, 1950.

HECKSCHER, Eli, *Mercantilism*. 2 vols. 2nd edn. London: Allen & Unwin, 1955.

HERTZ, Gerald B., *English Public Opinion After the Restoration*. London: T. F. Unwin, 1902.

HILL, J. E. C., 'The English Revolution and the Brotherhood of Man', *Science and Society*, Vol. XVIII, No. 4 (1954), pp. 289–309.
   Society and Puritanism in Pre-Revolutionary England. London: Secker and Warburg, 1964.

HOLDSWORTH, W. S., *A History of English Law*. Vol. VI. London: Methuen, 1937.

JOHNSON, E. A. J., *Predecessors of Adam Smith*. London: P. S. King & Son, 1937.

JORDON, W. K., *Men of Substance, A Study of the Thought of Two English Revolutionaries, Henry Parker and Henry Robinson*. Chicago: U. of Chicago Press, 1942.
   The Development of Religious Toleration in England. Vol. IV. London: Allen & Unwin, 1940.

JOUVENEL, B. de, *Sovereignty*. trans. J. F. Huntington, Cambridge: Cambridge U. Press, 1957.

JUDSON, M. A., 'Henry Parker and the Theory of Parliamentary Sovereignty', in C. Wittke (ed.), *Essays in History and Political Theory in Honour of C. H. McIlwain*. Cambridge, Mass.: Harvard U. Press, 1936.

KAYSER, E. L., *The Grand Social Enterprise. A Study of Jeremy Bentham in his Relation to Liberal Nationalism*. New York: Columbia U. Press, 1932.

KENDALL, W., *John Locke and the Doctrine of Majority Rule*. Urbana: U. of Illinois Press, 1941.

KENNEDY, W., *English Taxation 1640–1799. An Essay on Policy and Opinion*. London: G. Bell & Sons, 1913.

343

KENYON, C. M., 'Where Paine Went Wrong', *American Political Science Review*, Vol. 45 (1951), pp. 1086–99.

KING, J. E., *Science and Rationalism in the Government of Louis XIV*. Baltimore: Johns Hopkins U. Press, 1949.

KLIGER, S., *The Goths in England*. Cambridge, Mass.: Harvard U. Press, 1952.

KNIGHTS, L. C., *Drama and Society in the Age of Jonson*. London: Chatto & Windus, 1957.

KOEBNER, R., *Die Geschichtslehre James Harringtons*. Breslau: M. & H. Marcus, 1928.

KRAILSHEIMER, A. J., *Studies in Self-Interest from Descartes to LaBruyère*. Oxford: Clarendon Press, 1962.

LAMPRECHT, Sterling P., *The Moral and Political Philosophy of John Locke*. New York: Columbia U. Press, 1918.

LASLETT, Peter, *The World We Have Lost*. London: Methuen, 1965.

LETWIN, Shirley R., *The Pursuit of Certainty*. Cambridge: Cambridge U. Press, 1965.

LETWIN, William, 'The Authorship of Sir Dudley North's Discourses Upon Trade', *Economica*, new series, Vol. 18, No. 69 (1951), pp. 35–56.
The Origins of Scientific Economics. London: Methuen, 1963.
Sir Josiah Child, Merchant Economist. Cambridge, Mass.: Harvard U. Press, 1959.

LEVETT, A. E., 'James Harrington', in F. J. C. Hearnshaw, *The Social and Political Ideas of Some Great Thinkers of the Sixteenth and Seventeenth Centuries*. New York: Barnes & Noble, 1949.

LEVI, A., S.J., *French Moralists, The Theory of the Passions, 1585 to 1649*. Oxford: Clarendon Press, 1964.

LEVY, H., *Economic Liberalism*. London: Macmillan, 1913.

MACKLEM, M., *The Anatomy of the World, Relations Between Natural and Moral Law from Donne to Pope*. Minneapolis: U. of Minnesota Press, 1958.

MACPHERSON, C. B., *The Political Theory of Possessive Individualism*. Oxford: Clarendon Press, 1962.

MAN, J., *History and Antiquities of the Borough of Reading*. Reading: Man & Snare, 1816.

MATTINGLY, Garrett, *Renaissance Diplomacy*. London: J. Cape, 1955.

MAYO, T., *Epicurus in England*. Dallas: Southwest Press, 1934.

McDONALD, L. C., *Political Theory: The Modern Age*. New York: Harcourt Brace, 1962.

MEEK, R. L., *The Economics of Physiocracy.* London: Allen & Unwin, 1962.

MEINECKE, F., *Machiavellism,* trans. D. Scott, London: Routledge and Kegan Paul, 1957.

MINTZ, S. L., *The Hunting of Leviathan.* Cambridge: Cambridge U. Press, 1962.

MOHL, Ruth, *The Three Estates in Medieval and Renaissance Literature.* New York: Columbia U. Press, 1933.

MOSSE, G. L., *The Holy Pretense.* Oxford: Basil Blackwell, 1957.

MYRDAL, Gunnar, *The Political Element in the Development of Economic Theory.* London: Routledge and Kegan Paul, 1953.

NEILL, T. P., *The Rise and Decline of Liberalism.* Milwaukee: Bruce Publishing Co., 1953.

NIEMEYER, G., 'Public and Private Utility', in C. J. Friedrich (ed.), *The Public Interest.* Nomos V, New York: Atherton Press, 1962.

OAKESHOTT, M., 'The Masses in Representative Democracy', in A. Hunold (ed.), *Freedom and Serfdom,* Dordrecht: Reidel, 1961.

PATTEN, S. N., *The Development of English Thought: A Study in the Economic Interpretation of History.* New York: Macmillan, 1899.

PERRY, Ralph Barton, *Puritanism and Democracy.* New York: Vanguard Press, 1944.

POCOCK, J. A., *The Ancient Constitution and the Feudal Law.* Cambridge: Cambridge U. Press, 1957.

POLANYI, K., *The Great Transformation.* New York: Farrar & Rinehart, 1944.

POLE, J. R., *Political Representation in England and the Origins of the American Republic.* London: Macmillan, 1966.

POLIN, Raymond, 'Economique et Politique au XVIIe Siècle: L'Oceana de James Harrington', *Revue Française de Science Politique,* Vol. 2, No. 1 (1952), pp. 24–41.
  Politique et Philosophie Chez Thomas Hobbes. Paris: Presses Universitaires de France, 1953.

POST, Gaines, *Studies in Medieval Legal Thought.* Princeton: Princeton U. Press, 1964.

PRIBRAM, Karl, *Die Enstehung der Individualistischen Sozialphilosophie.* Leipzig: Verlag von C. L. Hirschfield, 1912.

RAAB, Felix, *The English Face of Machiavelli.* London: Routledge & Kegan Paul, 1964.

RAMSEY, R. W., *Henry Ireton.* London: Longmans, 1949.

REARDON, J. J., *Selfishness and the Social Order.* Washington: Catholic U. Press, 1943.

345

ROBBINS, Caroline, *The Eighteenth-Century Commonwealthman.* Cambridge, Mass.: Harvard U. Press, 1959.

ROBBINS, Lionel, *The Theory of Economic Policy in English Classical Political Economy.* London: Macmillan, 1952.

ROBERTSON, H. M., *The Rise of Economic Individualism.* Cambridge: Cambridge U. Press, 1933.

SALMON, J. H. M., *The French Wars of Religion in English Political Thought.* Oxford: Clarendon Press, 1959.

SCHATZ, Albert, *L'Individualisme économique et social.* Paris: Armand Colin, 1907.

SCHLATTER, Rudolph B., *Private Property, The History of an Idea.* New Brunswick, N.J.: Rutgers U. Press, 1951.
  The Social Ideas of Religious Leaders, 1660–1688. Oxford: Oxford U. Press, 1940.

SCHUBERT, Glendon, *The Public Interest, A Critique of the Theory of a Political Concept.* Glencoe, Ill.: Free Press, 1959.

SEATON, A. A., *The Theory of Toleration Under the Stuarts.* Cambridge: Cambridge U. Press, 1911.

SÉE, Henri, *Les Idées Politiques en France au XVIIe Siécle.* Paris: Marcel Giard, 1923.

SHKLAR, Judith N., 'Ideology-Hunting: The Case of James Harrington', *American Political Science Review,* Vol. 53 (1959), pp. 662–92.

SILBERNER, Edmond, *La Guerre dans La Pensée Économique du XVIe au XVIIIe siècle.* Paris: Lib. du Recueil Sirey, 1939.

SMITH, H. F. Russell, *Harrington and his Oceana.* Cambridge: Cambridge U. Press, 1914.
  The Theory of Religious Liberty in the Reigns of Charles II and James II. Cambridge: Cambridge U. Press, 1911.

SMITH, H. R., *Democracy and the Public Interest.* Athens, Ga.: U. of Georgia Press, 1960.

SPOONER, W. A., *Bishop Butler.* London: Methuen, 1901.

STARK, Werner, *The History of Economics in Its Relation to Social Development.* London: Routledge and Kegan Paul, 1945.

STEARNS, R. P., *The Strenuous Puritan: Hugh Peter 1598–1660.* Urbana: U. of Illinois Press, 1954.

STRAKA, G. M., *The Anglican Reaction to the Revolution of 1688.* Madison: U. of Wisconsin Press, 1962.

SUTCLIFFE, F. E., *Guez de Balzac et son Temps, Litterature et Politique.* Paris: A. G. Nizet, 1959.

SUVIRANTA, B., *The Theory of the Balance of Trade in England. A Study of Mercantilism.* Helsingfors: 1923.

346

TAWNEY, R. H., *Religion and the Rise of Capitalism*. London: Murray, 1926.

THOMAS, P. J., *Mercantilism and the East India Trade*. London: M. S. King and Son, 1926.

THUAU, E., *Raison D'État et Pensée Politique a l'Epoque de Richelieu*. Paris: A. Colin, n.d.

TOENNIES, F., 'Contributions a L'Histoire de la Pensee de Hobbes', *Archives de Philosophie*, Vol. XII, Cahier II (1936), pp. 73–106.

TREVOR-ROPER, H. R., *Historical Essays*. London: Macmillan, 1958.

TUCKER, G. S. L., *Progress and Profits in British Economic Thought 1650–1850*. New York: Cambridge U. Press, 1960.

VINER, Jacob, 'Power and Plenty as Objectives of Foreign Policy in the Seventeenth and Eighteenth Centuries', *World Politics*, Vol. I (1948), pp. 465–501.

Studies in the Theory of International Trade. New York: Harper, 1937.

WALCOTT, R., *English Politics in the Early Eighteenth Century*. Oxford: Clarendon Press, 1956.

WARRENDER, H., *The Political Philosophy of Hobbes, His Theory of Obligation*. Oxford: Clarendon Press, 1957.

WESTON, C. C., 'The Theory of Mixed Monarchy under Charles I and After', *English Historical Review*, Vol. 75 (1960), pp. 426–43.

WEULERSSE, Georges, *Les Physiocrates*. Paris: G. Dion, 1931.

WHITE, Helen C., *Social Criticism in Popular Religious Literature of the Sixteenth Century*. New York: Macmillan, 1944.

WILSON, Charles, 'The Other Face of Mercantilism', *Transactions of the Royal Historical Society*, 5th series, Vol. 9 (1959), pp. 81–101.

WITMER, H. E., *The Property Qualifications of Members of Parliament*. New York: Columbia U. Press, 1943.

WOLIN, S. S., *Politics and Vision*. London: Allen & Unwin, 1961.

YANAIHARU, T., *A Full and Detailed Catalogue of Books which Belonged to Adam Smith now in Possession of the Faculty of Economics, University of Tokyo*. Tokyo: Iwanami Shoten, 1951.

ZAGORIN, Perez, *Political Thought in the English Revolution*. London: Routledge and Kegan Paul, 1954.

ZEEVELD, W. G., *The Foundations of Tudor Policy*. Cambridge, Mass.: Harvard U. Press, 1948.

INDEX